RACE

TWENTIETH CENTURY DILEMMAS— TWENTY-FIRST CENTURY PROGNOSES

* * * * *

VOLUME VIII

ETHNICITY AND PUBLIC POLICY
SERIES

iii

ETHNICITY AND PUBLIC POLICY
SERIES

*   *   *   *   *

RACE

TWENTIETH CENTURY
DILEMMAS—
TWENTY-FIRST CENTURY
PROGNOSES

WINSTON A. VAN HORNE
EDITOR

THOMAS V. TONNESEN
MANAGING EDITOR

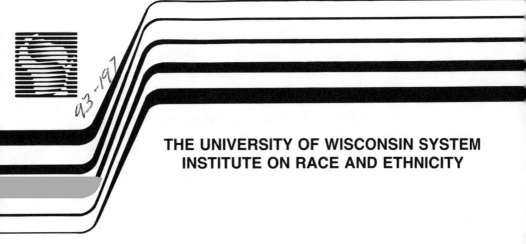

**THE UNIVERSITY OF WISCONSIN SYSTEM
INSTITUTE ON RACE AND ETHNICITY**

v

The University of Wisconsin System
Institute on Race and Ethnicity
P. O. Box 413, Milwaukee, WI 53201

International Standard Book Number ISBN 0-942672-14-3 (cloth)
International Standard Book Number ISBN 0-942672-15-1 (paper)
Library of Congress Catalog Card Number: 89-51910

Run ye faithful ones, run;
For the light giveth way to darkness,
The night draweth nigh, and the time
        Is short.
Tarry not, children of the light,
Tarry not, blessed ones;
For the day is gone, the night
        Is upon us,
And the work is not yet done.

Winston A. Van Horne

PREFACE

Thomas V. Tonnesen

University of Wisconsin-Milwaukee

As the reader can see, the words "dilemma" and "race" appear in the title of this book. The version of *Webster's* at my elbow informs me that one of the definitions of dilemma is "a problem seemingly incapable of a satisfactory solution." Defined as such, the word dilemma no doubt has our heads nodding in agreement as we apply its definition to the status of race in the United States as the end of the twentieth century approaches.

But perhaps our agreement should not be so forthcoming. Without attempting to split semantical hairs here, it is not race, but *racism*, that should be labeled as a dilemma. After all, race is really a social construct based on purported biological traits and distinctions. If race were merely a genetic characteristic, it would neither create intractable social problems for those of a particular racial type nor help alleviate them. As Leith Mullings reminds us in her chapter in this volume on health, it is not the biological significance but the *social context* in which race is placed that becomes the all-important, determining factor. Race does not inherently bring with it any certain debilities or advantages, but the way a particular racial type is defined and viewed in a society, especially American society, does. Wherever a type of hierarchial order is applied to racial status, racism exists and is at its heart. And just as all hierarchies are "seemingly incapable" of being overturned, so racism and not race is our dilemma according to *Webster's* definition.

The issue then becomes one of whether, and when, racism can be overturned. The chapters in this volume both explicitly and implicitly address this central question. Their contents serve to chronicle and analyze the impact of racism, private and public, in specific areas: civil rights and the law, education, the family, housing, health, the military, employment and politics. The various authors do make some recommendations regarding new tacks in public policy for these assorted arenas, but they do not attempt to lay out surefire schemes to eliminate racism and its effects. To endeavor to do so, unfortunately, would be sheer folly given how far we still have to go. What they do, though, is provide both historical insight and sharp sociological analysis to the dilemmas that racism poses, not just to racial minorities but to us all, thus allowing us to reconsider the issues from an informed and fresh perspective.

As I explore the message these chapters convey, I cannot help but think of the saying seen on a fairly prevalent bumper sticker: "If You Want Peace, Work For Justice." Although this statement most likely was not intended to be an axiom concerning race relations, to my mind the phrase is more applicable to this subject than to any other. If we substitute the word "harmony" for the word "peace," the former being one that is used more often in connection with race, we have a perfect fit. It seems to me that all segments of a society, regardless of race or class, desire harmony. But can harmony exist in the absence of justice? Some might argue yes, but they are incorrect. Those that do so confuse harmony with order, and the two are very different. Order can be imposed from the top, but the very fact that it must be imposed implies disharmony. True harmony emanates from within, and needs no external force to keep it in place. And how can harmony grow?—only on a seedbed of justice. To the extent that justice prevails, harmony will flourish, and the need for order as defined here will correspondingly diminish. It is this we must keep in mind as we stand on the eve of a new century in our struggle with racism.

The whole idea of a new century leads to another point. The editors of this volume realize that its title is a rather ambitious one. As the 1990s unfurl, we will no doubt be bombarded increasingly with reflective analyses of the past and prognostications, both cautious and bold, regarding the future. This tendency reveals itself at the change of every decade, and will no doubt gain momentum throughout the 1990s as the coinciding change in the century and the millennium looms ahead. But the fact of the matter is that such exercises of contemplative thought and projection based on periods of time can be the fountain of change. Few individuals take the time to reflect on their lives and make "resolutions" to themselves that will take effect on, say, July 18, but many do so for start-up on January 1. Given the significance that our society places on time, its passage and its measurement, the upcoming new century could well serve as the opportunity for us as a society to begin our quest for justice and harmony, racial and otherwise, with a new resolve. Granted, many resolutions are not kept—but in the absence of their formation we are left with little hope for self- or societal improvement.

And what will be necessary to realize such changes for the better? The list here could be a long one, encompassing everything from highly idealistic requirements like goodwill to more pragmatic ones like an expanding economy. The two that come immediately to this writer's mind, though, are leadership and education, ingredients which themselves could use some upgrading. A close friend who teaches at the junior high level, whenever he is asked about what he does for a living, answers that he "stamps out ignorance." In some ways this summarizes the purpose of education, and it is surely what is necessary to overcome racism. But a task as formidable as this one cannot be left to the schools alone, for much of our education occurs outside its walls and classrooms. This is where leadership must step in—leadership at all levels of government, in our churches and our schools, in our business relationships and our places of employment, and perhaps most importantly, on a personal level among our family members, friends, peers and associates. Racism must not only be addressed at the level of the institution, but also at the level of the individual. It is reflection and action on these larger questions and challenges that we hope this book spurs.

Here in the eighth volume of the *Ethnicity and Public Policy* series, it is difficult to be original when expressing gratitude to the many individuals that helped make this book a reality. I must admit that before becoming associated with the production of this series, I seldom read similar sections of prefaces where the author or editor recited the names of those who made contributions. I do, though, now, for although the actual names may hold little or no meaning for me, I have extreme empathy and appreciation for their work.

For this book we must begin with mention of Joanne Brown, whose knack for allowing sophisticated thoughts to be stated more simply, and her dogged work in the library, are indispensable. Although Claire Parker left us some months ago for greener pastures, her loyalty and determination to see this project through to its end had her coming in on nights and weekends to complete the laborious task of word processing and interpreting editors' changes. Two individuals whose job duties normally do not encompass the above, Thelma Conway and Judy Treskow, also contributed mightily in this area, and their willingness to pitch in when needed does not go unnoticed. Despite the size of this university, Linda Jallings has the ability to make one feel like one is her only client, and her guidance through the production and printing processes has become a given, though not taken for granted. For ten consecutive years now, Sharon Gutowski has been the key individual in organizing the colloquia that are the geneses of each book, and we look forward to her continued assistance.

Neither the *Ethnicity and Public Policy* series, nor any of the other varied activities of the University of Wisconsin System Institute on Race and Ethnicity, could be accomplished without the leadership and support of Clifford Smith, Jr., John Schroeder and George Keulks at the institutional level, and Eugene Trani and Manuel Lopez at the system level. The efforts of the members of the Institute's advisory committee are a key element in whatever successes we enjoy, and the leadership displayed in the area of race and ethnicity by the president of the University of Wisconsin System, Kenneth Shaw, cannot go unmentioned. We trust that they will all be in our corner again as we reach for new heights.

CONTENTS

INTRODUCTION

Bernard R. Boxill

University of North Carolina at Chapel Hill

The evolution of race relations in twentieth-century America reflects the cumulative effects of the interdependence of race and class in multiracial societies. In these societies, the effects of racial conflict mix with those of class conflict either to consolidate the old configuration of race and class or to produce a new one. The question of the causal priority of these conflicts is not at issue. Whether class conflict was the original cause of racial conflict, or vice versa, or whether both sorts of conflict are produced by more fundamental factors, race and class conflicts are now powerful and functionally autonomous forces in modern multiracial societies. Their importance cannot be reduced, one to the other, if one desires to understand the history of race relations in the twentieth century, as well as to articulate sound opinions about what they are likely to be and how their evolution in the twenty-first century might/ can be affected.

In the first half of the twentieth century, racial conflict in the United States was more obvious than class conflict. While class conflict was repudiated — the national ideology proclaimed America the land of opportunity, where everyone could aspire to wealth and status — there was no comparable attempt to conceal racial conflict. It was published in the very law of the land, most notably in the infamous "separate but equal" statutes. White people clearly were bent on excluding the other races, especially blacks, from their fair share of the advantages of society. For example, schooling, public accommodations and other public services were usually separate, but they were rarely ever equal. Indeed, those who drew the battle lines sought to make them clear and eternal. They defined race in terms of gross, easily recognizable and strongly inherited features like skin color, or in doubtful cases, in terms of one having an ancestor who possessed these features. While this conception of race is almost certainly not useful scientifically, it well served its ideological and political purpose, which was to enable one group of people to efficiently and effectively identify others as outsiders who would not be allowed to enjoy their fair share of the benefits of society.

Racial conflict in early twentieth-century America was not only more obvious than class conflict; together with the ideology of equal opportunity, it also tended to conceal and distort class conflict. This emanated from the empirical fact that blacks filled disproportionately the ranks of the poorest classes in the society, while the better-positioned classes were predominantly white. Black skin, intensified by the pseudo-science of racist ideologies, became an instrument in the service of whites in what C. Wright Mills termed "the ruling class." Countenanced by their kith and kin who were better-off than themselves, and encouraged as well as reinforced by racist ideologies, whites in the poorest classes found blacks to be convenient and easy objects of the animosities, which, for the most part, impelled them to overlook the fact that they had other more important and intractable class foes. Thus were natural class allies divided by a hard line of racial demarcation. And so, for example, when white workers formed labor unions to protect their class interests, not only did they exclude blacks but they also evinced the most raw and bilious racist sentiments and behaviors. One observes here a point of singular importance. Racial conflict changed the appearance, and to a considerable degree the nature, of class conflict. Racial conflict masked class conflict so convincingly that, in significant measure, the latter became the former.

Fortunately, the unhappy conflation of race and class that produced this corrosive and regressive state of affairs was gradually superseded. Despite strenuous efforts to keep blacks confined to the poorest classes, by mid-century a sizable black working class and a small black middle class had emerged. Once formed, these new classes began to seek their class interests, and their quest eventually led to civil rights reforms. The civil rights movement, which was the efficient cause of the civil rights reforms, was a notable example of the interplay of race and class conflicts. It appeared to be, and in one sense it was, a product of long-standing racial conflict. Blacks from all classes joined hands to overturn the "separate but equal" statutes which denied their human rights and civil rights. But, less obviously, and perhaps in a more important sense that only became clear much later, the civil rights movement was also a class struggle since the reforms it sought would mainly serve the interests of middle- and working-class blacks. These reforms were designed to guarantee blacks rights denied them by the "separate but equal" statutes. Many of these rights were negative liberty rights, that is, they outlawed legal restrictions *against doing* certain things, but did not actually enable anyone *to do* these things. Since such enabling took money, in securing these rights for all blacks, the civil rights movement and reforms ended up serving the interests of the black working and middle classes far more than those of the black poor, who lacked/continue to lack the resources necessary to take advantage of them. Once again, the particular configuration of race and class contrived to conceal the complex interplay of race and class conflicts, making it appear simply a racial conflict.

The black middle and working classes won their first major battle in 1954, when the Supreme Court struck down the "separate but equal" doctrine in public schools as unconstitutional. They won their second, and perhaps more decisive, battle in 1964, when Congress passed the Civil Rights Act. These victories changed dramatically the relative prominence of race and class issues, making racial conflict less and class conflict more prominent. Indeed, some optimists maintain that they mark the obsolescence of racial conflict, and the emergence of class conflict, as the fundamental source of contention in contemporary American society. This claim may well seem outrageous given the fact that blacks comprise only 12.2 percent of the total population, yet constitute an overwhelming majority of the underclass — the most deprived and needy class in society. Although this coincidence of race and class does not duplicate the earlier one, for there is now a substantial black working class and a growing black middle class, it does strongly suggest that whites continue to exclude blacks from their rightful share of the benefits of society. Hence, racial conflict persists, though less conspicuously than in its heyday. Still, the optimists have a plausible argument which depends on yet another instance of the interdependence of race and class. They admit that past racial conflict helped to confine blacks disproportionately to the worst positions in society, and consequently that it helped decisively to create the black underclass. But they deny that the black underclass persists because of racial conflict, maintaining that it persists because its members suffer from class-related disabilities, such as a dearth of marketable skills. And they attempt to clinch their argument by pointing to the successes of the black middle class. These successes would be impossible or much attenuated, they imply, if racial battle lines were still drawn firmly.

The heralding of the declining significance of race implicit in this analysis is premature, however. It is misled by the results of the interplay of race and class conflicts. Earlier, it was called out how racial conflict can, in certain circumstances, distract, distort and conceal class conflict. Now attention will be focused on how class conflict manages to conceal racial conflict.

The optimists are right that the underclass suffers from a range of class-related disabilities; in particular, that its members lack the skills necessary for profitable employment in a modern economy. They are also right that this provides a largely sufficient explanation of unemployment in the underclass, and accordingly, that appeals to racial conflict to explain that unemployment are probably superfluous. Yet, they are mistaken when they infer that the persistence of the underclass can be understood simply in terms of a class conflict. Although a class conflict is certainly involved, it is not the whole story.

It is important to begin by observing that while the class-related disabilities of the underclass may be enough to explain its members' high rate of unemployment, they may still fail to gain employment even if they were to shed these disabilities. Put differently, the unemployment of the black underclass may be overdetermined because the members of this class have more than one characteristic, each of which is by itself sufficient to assure their unemployment. In particular, while they may be unemployed because they are unskilled, it is possible that even if they acquired skills they would remain unemployed because they are black. At least this is plausible if they have to compete against white workers of equal skills in the context of the culture's reproduction of a range of dispositions towards race transgenerationally.

It will be objected that these are speculations which imply at most that racial conflict could reemerge in certain circumstances, not that it actually has anything to do with the persistence of the black underclass in present circumstances. But this implication is in fact strongly suggested by broader considerations of the reasons for the persistence of the underclass. If the underclass is to be assimilated into the mainstream, it must have massive financial aid for education and training. The society, however, has taken steps to reduce the various subsidies and welfare measures it extends to the poor. Now, this may seem like a straightforward class conflict over scarce resources; but it is also a racial conflict which the poverty and disabilities of the underclass contrive to mask as a simple class conflict.

One is led inexorably to this conclusion if one reflects on the fact that the society would almost certainly not be as slow to help the underclass if it were disproportionately white. It is surely not much of an objection for one to observe that the society tolerates poverty, and that most poor people are white. Those who wish to downplay the salience of racism in accounting for slavery offer a similar lame argument when they observe that when whites enslaved blacks, whites were also very brutal to each other. The answer to that argument is that enslavement was qualitatively different, and much worse, than the brutality whites inflicted on one another; and the similar answer to the present argument is that the condition of the underclass is qualitatively different from, and worse than, that of the poor in general. Moreover, the society has shown that it is prepared, if somewhat reluctantly, to bankroll various white groups when this is necessary to keep them in the economic and social mainstream. That a similar reluctant generosity is absent when it comes to the regeneration of the black underclass betrays the persistence and efficacy of racial conflict. It is critical to note that racial conflict is typically exemplified by active efforts to exclude the unwanted race from the benefits of society. However, when such efforts succeed so well that they are no longer necessary because a considerable number of the unwanted race are prostrated by then, racial conflict reveals itself by a refusal to take the steps necessary to help the unwanted race get back on its feet and enjoy the benefits of society.

The emerging struggle of the black underclass bears a striking similarity to the earlier struggle of the black middle and working classes. It entails both racial conflict as well as class conflict, and should it succeed, its main beneficiary will be a particular class — the underclass. This struggle should be the main item on the black agenda as the twenty-first century begins. Unless it succeeds, not only will the underclass continue to be in dire straits, but the negative images of all black people that it engenders also will compel the black middle class to engage in a racial conflict against its natural allies in the white middle class. Unfortunately, however, the struggle of the underclass has two great obstacles to overcome.

The first is a strategic difficulty. To increase its chances of success, every class seeking political guarantees of its interests tends to present these interests to society as universal. The black middle class followed precisely this strategy when it fought for its class interests. Although it would be the main beneficiary of the reforms it sought, it couched its demands that "separate but equal" be struck down as equally in the interest of all blacks. This strategy is likely to be more difficult to implement in the present case due to the nature of the interests at issue. These depend on reforms to provide such benefits as compensatory education and training, funds for day-care centers and improved health services for the underclass. Since the black middle class will have to share the financial burden of supporting these reforms, it could be lukewarm towards them. But this would be shortsighted. As noted earlier, as long as the black underclass persists, the black middle class is likely to be compelled to waste its energies in a racial conflict against its natural class allies in the white middle class.

The second and more formidable difficulty facing the underclass' struggle is ideological. Ideology was on the side of the black middle and working classes when they fought the major battles in their class struggle. Philosophers had long defended the idea that every human being has certain inalienable natural rights which governments were bound to protect. Consequently, when the black middle class pursued its struggle, on its ideological front it had only to prove that blacks were human beings. There were, of course, racist arguments that blacks were not fully human and thus did not have these rights, but these arguments were strained, implausible and never of high currency intellectually. Few could have been really persuaded by them, although many pretended to be because the arguments supported arrangements they found immensely profitable. Though many major philosophers were certainly racists, none ever dared to seriously examine his/her own prejudice, and then to argue that blacks were not fully human and without the same natural rights as whites. The strong philosophic grounding of its ideology thus enabled the black middle class to undercut effectively the little intellectual opposition it met when it argued that blacks were fully human, and deserved the same rights as whites. The task facing those presenting the intellectual case for the underclass' struggle is made of sterner stuff, and far more daunting. This emanates from the nature of the rights for which they must argue.

The natural rights of the philosophers, and by extension the civil rights demanded by the black middle class in its struggle, were mainly negative rights, which forbade interference in an individual's sphere of liberty. The rights which the underclass needs to have recognized and protected are positive rights, which require that economic and other benefits be *assured* to all human beings. But these rights historically have not been defended by philosophers as natural rights. Some contemporary philosophers have argued that economic and social rights are fundamentally different from civil rights, and are not genuine natural rights at all.

The distinction between civil, economic and social rights has been influential internationally where it is acknowledged, for example, in the Universal Declaration of Human Rights proclaimed by the General Assembly of the United Nations in 1948. Its first twenty articles provide a list of civil rights. These are the rights found in classical statements of the rights of man, for example, the right to equality before the law, to a fair trial, to freedom of movement and to privacy. The next ten articles of the Universal Declaration of Human Rights list rights of an apparently different kind, not usually found in the various classical statements of the rights of man. They are economic and social rights, including the right to work, to form trade unions, to medical care, to a decent education and to unemployment compensation. Further, when the United Nations Commission on Human Rights turned to the task of drafting a "more legally binding" covenant on human rights, disputes about the relative importance of civil, economic and social rights compelled it to write two covenants, one pertaining to civil rights and the other concerning economic and social rights.

These disputes have their domestic counterparts, although these counterparts do not replicate in toto the international ones. For example, civil rights laws since 1960 have tended to institutionalize rights to various social and economic goods such as education, employment, housing and public accommodations. However, it is this extension of civil rights laws into the social and economic spheres that has been most controversial and has engendered some of the most intense, and often acrimonious, debates, for example, between those favoring "equality of opportunity" over "equality of results," as well as between those having liberal or conservative interpretations of what counts as legally unjustifiable discrimination. More generally, it was the idea that the classical negative rights are the only genuine rights which slowed and ultimately brought the civil rights movement to a premature end, and it is now being skillfully exploited to urge the abolition of welfare measures and a return to a real laissez-faire.

Arguments that traditional civil rights enjoy an absolute moral priority over economic and social rights may be more intellectually respectable than the racist arguments that blacks are not fully human, but they must still be challenged for the sake of the underclass' well-being. Already, inroads have been made in the practical argument that traditional civil rights have priority over newer economic and social rights because the former can be cheaply and efficiently secured by legislation to restrain government. But the main battle is to show that there are no morally significant distinctions between traditional civil rights and some of the newer social and economic rights. Such an argument could well be grounded in Aristotle's claim that to be fully human is to be a member of a polis, that is, to be a citizen. If this is so, natural and human rights necessarily include all of those rights that persons must have in order to function as citizens. These rights include traditional civil rights, but they also include social and economic rights, without which the former cannot be exercised properly. For example, even if those in a certain segment of society have the legal right to vote, they cannot properly exercise this fundamental right of citizenship if they are so poor that they are easily induced to sell their votes, or if they are so ignorant that they cannot understand the issues on which they vote.

The chapters in this volume reflect the salience of race/class problems and issues, as well as the importance of reviving civil rights activities that continue into the twenty-first century until social and economic rights are acknowledged to have the same moral standing as traditional civil rights and liberties. As is to be expected, the various contributors to this volume do not agree on all the details, but are one in their belief that race and class are powerful and, apparently, autonomous, though interacting, forces, and that much work remains to be done to consummate the ends of the civil rights struggle. In the first chapter, "Is Further Civil Rights Legislation Irrelevant to Black Progress?", the argument is advanced that further civil rights legislation is not irrelevant to black progress, and a case is made for the claim that social and economic rights have the same moral standing as traditional civil rights and liberties. In the succeeding chapters the importance of this argument becomes evident as the authors take up the issues of education, health, economics, housing, politics, the military and the family.

In "Universal Education, Blacks and Democracy: The Expansion and Contraction of Educational Opportunities," Kenneth Tollett considers one of the most important of those social and economic rights which, as noted earlier, must be realized and institutionalized if the full substance of citizenship is to be truly open to all — the right to an education. As he argues, education is not only necessary for the material progress of blacks, it is also essential if people are to function as citizens in a democracy. His analysis bears out the claim that the right to an education is as much of a civil right as the right to vote, for both are necessary if persons are to function as citizens.

In "Inequality and African-American Health Status: Policies and Prospects," Leith Mullings examines the role of race and class in the health and health care of African-Americans. One school of thought tends to focus on genetic factors in explaining excess deaths among African-Americans, clearly emphasizing the role of race over class in explaining health differences between blacks and whites. But, as Mullings observes, although some diseases do have a definite genetic component, these have a relatively small impact on the overall health status of the African-American population. Of the eighty thousand excess deaths among African-Americans in 1977, she points out that "only 277 or 0.3 percent of the total excess could be attributed to hemoglobinopathies," and the rest must be attributed to class-related factors such as low income and poor education. This impels her to argue for closing the socioeconomic gap between blacks and whites, and for a national health service plan. Objections to such a plan rest ultimately on the traditionalists' view that health care is not a civil right which government is bound to implement. In the sphere of health, then, the unfinished struggle for civil rights must be continued.

The chapter on "Blacks in the U.S. Military: Trends in Participation" by Richard Hope, and the one entitled "Public Policy and the African-American Family" by Wade Nobles, continue the examination of the evolution of race relations in the United States through the themes of race and class. Hope's essay opens with an analysis of the class structure of armies, and how this structure has affected the sociological organization of the United States military. Still, in his historical survey, he notes the pervasive and independent role that race has played in the United States military. Up to and including World War II, blacks were allowed to enlist only when manpower pressures dictated it, and then they were usually consigned to unskilled jobs such as road building, stevedoring, laundry and fumigating. These restrictions eventually were discontinued, and during the Vietnam conflict, black enlistment soared. Although fears of black overrepresentation in the military have abated in consequence of the stabilization of black participation at about 20 percent, it is nonetheless the case that the racial atmosphere both of the military and the society at large, as well as a range of other factors, could occasion a noticeable reduction in the accession of blacks to the armed forces in the twenty-first century. This is again fundamentally an issue of civil rights, as one of the functions of the citizen is to participate in the defense of the state. In his essay on the African-American family, Nobles calls attention to the variety of cultures, and thus of family structures, which exist in the United States. He points out how exploitive and careless public policy has had detrimental consequences for the African-American family. This raises one of the most important of all civil rights issues, namely, the right to pursue and express one's culture.

The chapters by Ronald Walters on "Black Politics: Mobilization for Empowerment," Karl Taeuber on "Residence and Race: 1619 to 2019," and David Swinton on "Racial Parity under Laissez-Faire: An Impossible Dream," round out the discussion of race and class in terms of the categories by which eight of this volume's chapters are organized. Walters emphasizes the effects of racial cleavages and warns that if present trends were to continue, there could be a deepening of race and class cleavages, and the precipitation of a "new class war" based on differences in wealth and racial status, which would have disproportionately negative effects on blacks given their concentration in the nation's lower classes. In his discussion of residential segregation, Taeuber seeks to analyze and predict the consequences of statutes aimed at racial segregation in housing. The effects of race and class reinforce each other in black urban ghettos. Yet, as Taeuber notes, class may not completely dominate over race in determining residential location. As the increasing black middle class comes to comprise entire neighborhoods, either by choice or due to continued racial discrimination, race no doubt supersedes class as a key determinant of this state of affairs. Finally, in his review of black economic progress in the twentieth century, Swinton clearly reveals the necessity of continuing the struggle for civil rights if blacks are to achieve economic parity, and thus is impelled to call for more effective affirmative action, where the emphasis is placed on results. His last sentence is a firm rebuttal of the view of those traditionalists who, acknowledging only civil rights and civil liberties, reject the idea that social and economic rights are coterminous with these, and call for a return to laissez-faire. The "dream of black economic development under laissez-faire," Swinton concludes, "will turn out to be an impossible dream."

There is no doubt that the history of race relations in the twentieth century is marked by dilemmas that have perplexed and divided the black community in its search for a solution to its state of inequality in the United States. The two great and apparently mutually exclusive solutions laid down by Frederick Douglass and Martin Delany in the nineteenth century dominated the discussion and the strategies proposed in the twentieth century. Periods when the ideology of separatism, stoicism and hard work was in ascendancy alternated with ones in which most seemed to favor integration, protest and civil rights. In each period, the debate concerning which solution would be politically effective as well as morally sound and acceptable continued unabated. Thus, W.E.B. DuBois debated Booker T. Washington at the turn of the century; the NAACP excoriated Marcus Garvey in the early 1920s; the black power movement of the 1960s sought to confute persuasive integrationists of the period; and the persistent sway of the integrationists is now being challenged by separatists who argue that the former's strategy of affirmative action has been a significant contributory factor in the emergence and expansion of the black underclass.

The source of these twentieth-century dilemmas lies in the interplay of race and class conflicts, which often mimic one another and occasion effects that give varying degrees of credibility to both major solutions. A pessimistic prognosis for the twenty-first century is that the unsuccessful cycle of separatist and integrationist strategies will continue, though, perhaps, at a more sophisticated level. But black people have continued to learn from their mistakes, and so a more optimistic prognosis inclines one to believe that in the twenty-first century blacks will construct a new philosophic foundation on which to build strategies designed to achieve the equality in the United States that they have sought so long and so courageously.

The final chapter, entitled "Integration or Separation: Beyond the Philosophic Wilderness Thereof," by Winston Van Horne takes up the challenge of constructing "a new philosophic foundation." With compelling lucidity, vision and persuasiveness it calls out fundamental philosophic problems that inhere in integration and separation which trap each as a means for the transgenerational and transcenturial advancement of peoples of primary African origin and their descent. Focusing on what may be called the trap of the autonomous will in relation to both integration and separation, as well as on the effect of the corruption of the communal will into the heteronomous will on the well-being of black people in the United States, Van Horne reconstitutes the original communal will in the form of the conjunctive will. It is his conviction that this reconstituted will provides "an archetypal anchor" for a body of doctrine and behavior "designed to occasion fundamental transformations of culture and political economy in the societies of the Afroworld," to the end of the long-term good of peoples of primary African origin and their descent. The conjunctive will could well be the archetypal anchor that Van Horne envisions. If it is, let us build on it; if it is not, let us find another. But let none who has the means fail to work upon the philosophic foundation and edifice without which peoples of primary African origin and their descent will keep wandering in their philosophic wilderness.

IS FURTHER CIVIL RIGHTS LEGISLATION IRRELEVANT TO BLACK PROGRESS?

Bernard R. Boxill

University of North Carolina at Chapel Hill

As the twentieth century comes to an end, and the twenty-first century approaches, what role can we expect the law to play in helping to secure justice, freedom and equality for black people? The law has traditionally played a pivotal role, first in denying these goods to black people, and later in helping to assure them. Since the process of institutionalizing justice, freedom and equality for blacks is far from complete, the question naturally arises whether the law has a further part to play. Some believe that it does, and that new and innovative legislation will be necessary. Others contend that the law has gone as far as it can in helping to grant to black people what it helped to take away from them. They maintain that from now on, and increasingly into the next century, "self-help" measures must replace reliance on legislation in order to further black progress.

The latter view has affected public policy increasingly since the late 1970s. The nation seems to be taking a turn to the right as its power declines in relation to that of other nations, and presidents respond by shifting emphasis from domestic justice to national defense. The Supreme Court is likely to become an increasingly conservative body as the twenty-first century approaches. Nor must the influence of the black conservatives be underestimated. These articulate individuals urge the end of civil rights legislation. Moreover, they are often well-placed in prestigious universities and "think tanks," enabling them to control much of the research done on racial issues, and, through their access to respected journals and the media, to influence public opinion. Such influence has been enhanced by the important governmental posts which some have occupied. Since I am convinced that the views in question are wrong, and if implemented could have unhappy consequences, they should be rebutted firmly.

It is well to begin with a review of the evolution of the law in the twentieth century, how it began as an instrument of oppression and gradually became an instrument of liberation. On that basis, an assessment of the law's future role is presented. The first sections outline changes in the law, from *Plessy*, to *Brown*, to *Bakke*,[1] and their coincidence and possible causal interaction with economic and social changes. The later sections take up the question of the law's future role. This chapter will not try to predict what the law will be, or will do, though. Prediction is hazardous, and too often only disguised pessimism or optimism. It will limit itself to the question of what, given where we have arrived, the law ought to be if it can be expected to aid in the struggle for freedom, justice and equality for black people. It will examine critically the two main self-help views and argue that the positive role of the law which began with *Brown* has not yet been exhausted.

I

The legal status of black people has improved dramatically in the second half of this century. At the turn of the century it was very hazardous indeed. *Plessy* v. *Ferguson* in 1896 was the low point of a long downward trend. In *Plessy* the U.S. Supreme Court held that segregation of the races was permissible, as long as equal facilities were provided for each race. Writing for the majority, Justice Henry Billings produced a tortuous and implausible defense of the notorious "separate but equal" principle. Only one Justice dissented, John Marshall Harlan, affirming on this occasion his famous maxim, "Our Constitution is colorblind. . . ."[2]

Plessy v. *Ferguson* cast a long shadow. Strictly, it only affirmed the legality of racial segregation of passenger accommodations on railroads, but the principle of "separate but equal" on which it depended was used to justify racial segregation in practically all spheres of social life in states with substantial black populations. Thus it was that black people entered the twentieth century with only the most uncertain protection of the law. Facilities were separate, but they were, of course, not equal, and racist policies and practices flourished without fear of legal penalty. The legal principle of "separate *but* equal" had been transmuted into the societal norm of "separate *and* unequal." The Court made limited attempts to change this state of affairs prior to the 1950s; but on May 17, 1954, the tide was definitely turned in *Brown* v. *Board of Education* .[3]

Relying on the *Plessy* doctrine of "separate but equal," school boards had long been operating racially segregated schools. In accordance with this practice, Linda Brown had been prevented from enrolling in an all-white school in Topeka, Kansas. Her father filed suit against the Topeka Board of Education, charging that the equal protection clause of the Fourteenth Amendment prohibited racial segregation in public schools. By the time it reached the Supreme Court, *Brown* was consolidated with three other cases from South Carolina, Virginia and Delaware. The plaintiffs all argued that segregated public schools were not, and could not be made, equal, and thus denied their students equal protection of the laws. The Court already had been confronted with similar cases at the university graduate level in the so-called "graduate school desegregation cases." The most important of these were *Missouri ex rel. Gaines* v. *Canada* in 1938, as well as *Sweatt* v. *Painter*[4] and *McLaurin* v. *Oklahoma State Regents*,[5] both in 1950. But while granting the plaintiffs relief in these cases, the Court had avoided resolving the issue of the constitutionality of separate but equal educational facilities. The move was finally made in *Brown*. In a brief, unanimous opinion, Chief Justice Earl Warren concluded that ". . . in the field of public education the doctrine of 'separate but equal' has no place. Separate educational facilities are inherently unequal."[6]

Brown, however, had little immediate effect on segregated schools. After several years, only 2.3 percent of southern black students attended white schools. Part of the problem was that Congress and the executive branch did not throw their full weight behind the Court; without their support the Court's effectiveness was limited.[7] Many school boards were able to defy the *Brown* ruling. Frustrated by this display of white lawlessness, blacks began to lose faith in seeking relief through the legal process, and turned to more direct measures. Thus began a decade of civil rights protests, of sit-ins and, eventually, civil disobedience. Finally, ten years after *Brown*, and after dramatic events like the 1963 bombings in Birmingham and the March on Washington galvanized much of the nation, Congress was moved to enact the Civil Rights Act of 1964.[8]

This was a wide-ranging piece of civil rights legislation. It banned racial discrimination in public accommodations, public facilities, and in federally assisted programs and employment; promised federal assistance to states in desegregating their public schools; required a survey of voting statistics, and that registration standards, practices and procedures for federal elections be applied uniformly to blacks and whites; and created the Equal Employment Opportunity Commission. With the help of the Civil Rights Act, the Court began to make headway in compelling local school boards to comply with *Brown*. Success was not, of course, immediate, for school boards resorted to all kinds of artifices to keep schools segregated.

Brown itself was perhaps partly to blame. The segregated school systems it outlawed had two key attributes. On the one hand, school boards had explicitly stated policies of segregating black students and white students into different schools on the basis of their race; on the other hand, schools were all-black and all-white. Unfortunately, *Brown* did not say clearly which of these attributes it outlawed, or whether it outlawed both of them. Recalcitrant school boards exploited this ambiguity. Noticing that a pattern of all-black and all-white schools could exist even in the absence of policies segregating students into different schools on the basis of their race—that segregation could be de facto without also being de jure—they argued that the Court had outlawed only de jure segregative policies, finding it relatively easy to disclaim such policies while using other expedients to keep the pattern of all-black and all-white schools intact. This subterfuge was progressively outlawed beginning in the late 1960s.

In a series of important cases, beginning with *Green* v. *New Kent County*[9] in 1968 and continuing with *Swann* v. *Charlotte-Mecklenburg Board of Education* [10] in 1971 and *Keyes* v. *District No. One*[11] in 1973, the Court made it increasingly clear that, even if a school board did not admit to using explicitly segregative policies, a pattern of all-black and all-white schools might be in violation of the law if the school district had a history of de jure segregation, or if the policies the school board did admit to using showed "segregative intent." Indeed, some Justices were ready to dispense with even this last condition, arguing that wherever a pattern of all-black and all-white schools existed to a substantial degree, there was a *prima facie* case that the relevant school board was sufficiently responsible to warrant imposing on it the burden of demonstrating that it was not practicing segregation.[12] The *Green*, *Swann* and *Keyes* decisions eventually became the legal basis for widespread busing orders to end patterns of all-black and all-white schools.

Further, the comprehensive nature of the Civil Rights Act of 1964, coupled with the Voting Rights of 1965, ensured that desegregative outcomes would not be limited to the areas of primary and secondary education. These outcomes were also observed in employment, higher and professional education, and voting and housing, though, of course, considerable resistance had to be overcome in these areas as well.

Advances came most readily in higher and professional education. It is not difficult to see why. Desegregation at the primary and secondary levels was a means for broad-based racial uplift, with all the disruptive, unforeseen and unforeseeable possibilities which this raised. Affirmative action at the college and professional levels was a remedy limited to a small, upwardly mobile black elite, already within reach of college or professional education. Thus, while busing was usually court-compelled and court-controlled, affirmative action in higher education was for the most part neither compelled nor controlled by the courts, though even here change was certainly broadened and hastened by the demands of student militants.

Progress was slower in striking down racist barriers to employment. To avoid hiring or promoting blacks, employers used chicanery similar to what school boards used to avoid admitting blacks to all-white schools. In this case, too, the opening was provided by an ambiguity in the law. Congress had prohibited racial discrimination, but it had not defined unambiguously what racial discrimination was. Taking it to mean policies explicitly denying employment or promotion to blacks on the basis of their race, many employers simply replaced these policies by special qualifications involving education, training, experience, seniority and/or test scores, which alone or combined had the same effect as the ostensibly discarded policies.

Blacks challenged this ruse, and in 1971 in *Griggs* v. *Duke Power Company*[13] the Supreme Court agreed. It ruled that Title VII of the Civil Rights Act of 1964 prohibited not only discriminatory policies which were explicitly racist, but also those that had the effect, whether intended or not, of excluding or hindering blacks where these policies could not be shown to be related to job performance. Writing for the Court, Chief Justice Warren Burger noted that the Civil Rights Act "proscribes not only overt discrimination but also practices that are fair in form, but discriminatory in operation. . . . If an employment practice which operates to exclude Negroes cannot be shown to be related to job performance, the practice is prohibited."[14]

As in employment, barriers to blacks exercising their voting rights and their rights to housing were breached with some measure of success. The voting rights provisions of the Civil Rights Act of 1964 had several inadequacies, which provided impetus for the Voting Rights Act of 1965[15] that black people used—not, of course, without great opposition—to increase dramatically the number of black voters and elected officials. Moreover, the 1964 act was followed by the 1968 amendments to the Civil Rights Act,[16] whose Title VIII banned discrimination on the grounds of race, color, religion or national origin in the sale or rental of housing, and prohibited owners or realtors from refusing to sell or rent housing to prospective customers on those grounds.

II

Coinciding with, and arguably caused or facilitated by these legal advances, was substantial progress in black income, education and employment. Overall, black family income almost doubled in the 1960s, and the ratio of black family income to white family income rose from 53 percent in 1961 to 63 percent in 1971. These advances seemed even more striking when allowance was made for the fact that the average age of the black population was about seven years less than the average age of the white population, and that half the black population lived in the South, where incomes were and are generally lower than in the North and West. In these regions, the median income of black husband-wife families, with the head of family under thirty-five years of age, went from 78 percent of white income in 1959 to 96 percent in 1970; and in families in which both husband and wife worked, the figure rose from 85 percent in 1959 to 104 percent in 1970.[17]

In education, too, a breakthrough appeared to have been made. While only 36 percent of blacks finished four years of high school in 1960, the figure was 54 percent by 1970 and 68 percent by 1976; and while 10 percent of college-aged blacks were enrolled in college in 1965, 18 percent were enrolled in 1971. Indeed, by 1976, 33.5 percent of black high school graduates were enrolled in college.

The picture also seemed to be steadily improving in employment. In a comparison of two early years in the 1960s and 1970s, unemployment among black married men over age twenty dropped more sharply than in the population as a whole. Furthermore, blacks were holding better jobs. Especially after 1964, the penetration of black males into professional, technical and managerial jobs accelerated greatly.

In academia, progress seemed especially encouraging. By 1973, black male faculty earned about the same as comparable white male faculty; but black female faculty earned more than comparable white female faculty, and black male faculty with impressive publication records earned more than equally productive white scholars.[18] Finally, these general improvements in income and employment could not plausibly be attributed to the economic boom in the last years of the 1960s. The relative income and occupational position of black workers continued to rise in the early seventies, despite the largest labor market downturn since the depression,[19] which worsened during the catastrophic recession of 1981-83.

These advances in income, education and employment have been summarized in the claim that a "majority" of blacks are now "middle class," a claim that is hailed as "revolutionary."[20] They have also been attributed to the legal gains surveyed earlier. As one commentator put it, "The advances of the 1960's and 1970's represent a major social achievement and suggest that national anti-discriminatory policies have successfully altered the job market for black workers."[21]

III

Black gains in income, employment and education have not, however, been as broad-based as the previous paragraphs may have suggested. There certainly has been some improvement in their societal lot, but it seems to have been confined largely to better educated and skilled blacks, especially with college and university education, and to those from more advantaged family backgrounds. As these individuals have progressed, many of the others have retrogressed. Uneducated and unskilled, or with only the sort of labor-power that an increasingly technological society has rendered obsolete, other blacks have found it more and more difficult to find work. The data on welfare and crime tell a grim story. While in 1960, 7 percent of all black families were on welfare, by 1971 the figure had risen to 21 percent, and by 1983 it was 24 percent or nearly one-quarter of these families. Given this state of affairs, it is hardly surprising that blacks have constituted a disproportionate share of both the offenders and victims of violent crime. But it is the deterioration of the black family which seems to have the most somber implications.

In the 1960s, during the very period when advances in the law and in income, employment and education were being made, the number of single-parent, female-headed households rose precipitously and has now become a national scandal. William Julius Wilson observes that "[i]n 1965 . . . 25 percent of all black families were headed by women. The proportion surpassed 28 percent in 1970, reached 40 percent by 1979, and registered an alarming 43 percent in 1984."[22] Perhaps even more striking than these increases is a change in the major causes of single-parent, female-headed black families. At first it was death of the husband, divorce or desertion. By the 1970s it was more and more due to unterminated premarital pregnancies among black teenagers, a state of affairs that continued throughout the 1980s. Further, unlike typical welfare recipients, these black unmarried mothers seem to remain on welfare continuously.

General unemployment, crime and unmarried teenage mothers permanently on welfare have created a veritable "tangle of pathology."[23] Those who are entangled form what has come to be known as the "underclass."[24] The underclass is not simply the class of unemployed people. Observers describe it as a class of socially isolated and dislocated

persons demoralized by unemployment, dependency, poverty, ignorance and crime, who have created a culture, or set of values, appropriate to their condition. This culture, once commonly referred to as the
"culture of poverty,"[25] is apparently marked by an esteem for violence and a greater tolerance for irresponsibility and idleness than is
usual in cultures which have developed under more favorable conditions. It ultimately traps its members in the way of life to which at first
they had been forced by circumstance.

IV

The advent of the underclass is the most ominous domestic social development since the mid-twentieth century. Its members are, for the
most part, unemployed and unproductive, and therefore dependent on
the larger society. Yet, they are also a source of constant fear and ap-
prehension to that society because of violent crimes, with which they
are all too often associated, and their location in the heart of large urban areas. When one adds to these the fact that the underclass is potentially self-perpetuating, even perhaps inclined to grow, and, most important, is disproportionately black, the cause for alarm should be
obvious. Sooner or later, and probably sooner, the larger, predominantly white society will grow tired of being bitten. What it will do is
perhaps open to question, although the possibility, and even likelihood,
that it will try to eliminate the biters has been broached.

The economist William Darity, Jr., for example, reviews the "benign" policies which the ascendant "managerial class" has used to control the underclass—income transfer programs, spatial isolation, incar-
ceration and military participation—and finding that these have been
unsuccessful, cautions that the managers will "inexorably turn toward
exterminative policies."[26] These policies will include "a virtually unlimited application of methods to prevent and to terminate pregnancies" among the underclass, and because the black poor are overrepresented in that class, they will "take the brunt of the onslaught."[27]
Nor, Darity warns, will the black middle class be safe. The color which
its members share with the black underclass is likely to be used as an
easy prediction of undesirability, and since they function mainly to
"service" the black masses, they too will be endangered. As a consequence, Darity concludes grimly, it may well be that "blacks as a
group [will] become the victims of a cumulative process of planned
obsolescence."[28]

Optimists will no doubt view this scenario as farfetched. They are
likely to protest that blacks and their white allies would make use of

the legal instruments laboriously won since *Brown* to prevent such policies from ever being implemented—even if some groups do entertain
the idea of implementing them. Even though the scenario is certainly
not inevitable, and may even be unlikely, a slight acquaintance with
the history of the civil rights struggle fails to sustain the reassuring
faith that it is farfetched.

As legal theorist Derrick Bell observes, the legal headway made after *Brown* had an earlier parallel in the period after the Emancipation
Proclamation in 1863.[29] These earlier advances included the Civil
Rights Acts of 1866, 1870, 1871 and 1875, as well as the Thirteenth
(1865), Fourteenth (1868) and Fifteenth (1870) Amendments to the
Constitution. The first two acts gave blacks the right to be treated as
citizens in legal affairs, and the Fourteenth Amendment conferred citizenship on the former slaves. The Fifteenth Amendment declared it
illegal to deprive any citizen of the franchise because of race. The Civil
Rights Act of 1871 made it a crime to deny any citizen equal protection
under the law by means of "force, intimidation or threat"; and the act
of 1875 guaranteed blacks the right to use public accommodations.
Yet, by the time of the *Civil Rights Cases* of 1883,[30] which found key
portions of the act of 1875 (the last major piece of civil rights legislation passed by the Congress until the Civil Rights Act of 1964) to be
unconstitutional, these gains had been substantially liquidated. *Plessy*
in 1896 was only the low point of a downward trend which began in the
1870s. Is it impossible, Bell asks, that the present period of progress
"will end as did its nineteenth-century predecessor?"[31] Arguing that it
is not impossible, he notes that the "cycle of racial reform and repression in the nineteenth century has been duplicated with remarkable
similarity in the twentieth."[32]

The parallels in reform have been observed. Perhaps the most obvious parallel was the failure of the Reagan administration to adequately
enforce civil rights laws, but Bell finds an earlier parallel in the *Washington* v. *Davis*[33] decision of 1976. By refusing to extend the *Griggs*
standard to equal protection cases, and requiring instead that the "in-
vidious quality of a law claimed to be racially discriminatory" be
"traced to a racially discriminatory purpose,"[34] Bell maintains that
this decision handicapped minority groups trying to challenge discriminatory state action in housing and education. On these bases, Bell concludes that "it is not unreasonable to predict that in the absence of
intervening circumstances, the civil rights status of blacks in 2004 will
be an updated version of what they were in 1904, which is to say almost
nonexistent."[35]

The scenarios of Darity and Bell may not be very likely. Still, they
are likely enough, and dreadful enough, to be somber warnings that the

underclass represents not only an enormous waste of human life and talent, but also can serve as an excuse to undo the legal, social and economic advances made by the black middle class, plunge the country into a race war, and worst of all, be a pretext for genocide. Accordingly, it is of the utmost importance that ways be found to abolish the underclass, and that one inquire into what part, if any, the law, and in particular, civil rights legislation, can play in this process.

As this brief survey of civil rights legislation since *Brown* indicates, the black struggle for freedom, justice and equality in the second half of the twentieth century relied heavily on the law. But growing numbers appear to be skeptical that further progress depends on, or can be facilitated by, the law or additional civil rights legislation. Many, indeed, argue that future emphasis on such legislation would be counterproductive, and that in the past it has even helped to cause the problem. An inquiry into the part that the law and civil rights legislation have to play in enhancing black progress must begin with an assessment of the merits of these claims. These may be divided into two main classes: 1) those which affirm that additional civil rights legislation could facilitate future black advance, but deny that such legislation will be enacted or enforced; and 2) those which deny that further civil rights legislation could facilitate future black progress.

Both these claims agree that the black struggle for freedom, justice and equality in the twenty-first century should abandon the emphasis on the law which proved to be so successful in the second half of this century. They also agree that the struggle should increasingly take the form of "self help." Yet, the claims are very different. They raise different issues, rest on different premises, and suggest different self-help policies. Although both admit that there are limits to what the law can accomplish for black justice, equality and freedom, the sources of these limits are not the same. The first claim finds it in the racism and self-interest of whites. The second finds it in the nature of the law, and of progress itself. Consequently, the claims do not stand or fall together and must be considered separately.

Pessimism about the future enactment or enforcement of civil rights legislation favorable to black progress is widespread among black intellectuals. Derrick Bell is a prominent example. His thesis of the cyclical evolution of the law regarding racial matters, where the gains of one generation have often been neutralized, if not lost, in the next has been observed. On that basis he concludes bitterly that there is "little indication in this history to justify placing much faith in the law."[36] But there is nothing in the indictment which denies that suitable legislation would be an important factor in black progress could it be enacted and enforced. Thus, Bell's pessimism regarding reliance on more civil rights

legislation does not rest on any claim about what the law can justifia-
bly require in racial matters; rather, it rests on the claim that legal
reforms that are likely to further black advance will not, except in
rather special circumstances, be enacted, or if they are enacted, will not
be enforced.

This claim is based on the probable results of the interaction of two
powerful traits in the American character — economic self-interest and
racism—when they are confronted by the demands of justice. According to Bell, whenever, as is often the case, white self-interest can be
served by racism, justice goes to the wall: Racism gives way to justice
only when—and then often only after a struggle — it is opposed to
white self-interest. Thus, the special circumstances in which legal reform is likely to make an important contribution to black progress is
when it serves white self-interest. Where it does not serve white interests, as, for example, in the *Milliken* v. *Bradley*[37] setback when, in
Bell's terms, "the Court allayed middle-class fears that the school bus
would become the Trojan Horse of their suburban Troys,"[38] the reform is not likely to be introduced. Bell has reduced this theory to the
following formula, which he admits to being "simplistic and sardonic":

White Racism v. Justice = White Racism
White Racism v. White Self-Interest = Justice[39]

There is considerable truth in Bell's mordant formula. It shows that,
too often to be mere coincidence, significant legal gains in black rights
have served white interests.

This began with the abolition of slavery. A sense of justice long opposed slavery, but the balance was finally tipped in favor of abolition
by the perception that it served white interests. Thus it is widely, if not
universally, acknowledged that Lincoln's Emancipation Proclamation, in Bell's words, "served the best interests of the country and . . .
was issued primarily for that purpose."[40] De Tocqueville, for example,
whom Bell quotes, and who is conceded to be among the most acute
observers of the American scene, had come to a similar conclusion: "In
the United States," de Tocqueville wrote, "people abolish slavery for
the sake not of the Negroes but of the white men."[41]

The pattern thus started seems to have persisted throughout the
twentieth century. As Bell argues plausibly, for example, whites were
the main beneficiaries of: the *Brown* decision, which brought attention
to the poor condition of the public schools; the black challenge to the
discriminatory redistricting of Tuskegee, Alabama, which forced federal courts to interfere with gerrymandering; and the special admissions criteria which have been expanded to encompass disadvantaged
but promising white applicants.[42] And who can deny his prediction

that "white women will increasingly replace blacks as the group entitled to priority concerns in civil rights activities"?[43] Indeed, this prediction has already come true.

The evidence Bell gathers in support of his theory is strong, but it is not conclusive. It warrants the claim that *often* reforms allegedly intended as racial remedies actually serve white interests, but it does not warrant the stronger claim that the "most significant political advances for blacks resulted from policies which were intended to, and had the effect of, serving the interests and convenience of whites rather than remedying racial injustice against blacks."[44] The fact, if it is a fact, that reform ostensibly intended to remedy racial injustice usually, or even invariably, ends up serving white interests, is still consistent with the possibility that the reform was indeed intended to remedy racial injustice, not to serve white interests. Reform always has effects which are unforeseen or even unforeseeable, and therefore necessarily unintended.

Perhaps this possibility is unlikely when the reform is a piece of legislation. In a democracy, lawmakers are elected and usually tend not to pass legislation which they cannot justify to the majority of the electorate. The United States is a democracy, the majority of the electorate is white, and justifying legislation to them usually amounts to persuading them that it is in their own interest. It follows accordingly that civil rights legislation will not usually be passed unless lawmakers feel that they can show it serves white interests.

Now, this still does not entail that the lawmakers necessarily *intend* that the legislation serve white interests. They could still intend it to remedy racial injustice, while persuading the electorate that it serves white interests. It does suggest, though, that lawmakers normally foresee that the legislation serves white interests, whence, given their well-established disposition to aim at reelection, it is a fair, if falsifiable conjecture, that they also intend it to serve white interests. When, however, the reform allegedly intended to remedy racial injustice is a decision by the Supreme Court, it is very likely that the justices intend the decision to do just what they say—remedy racial injustice—even if it also turns out to serve white interests. They may, indeed, want to be just. Not concerned about reelection, they certainly are capable of making a decision intending it simply to be a remedy for racial injustice.

All this does not mean, of course, that the Court is insulated from popular and political pressures. This would be absurd. But it would be equally absurd to say that the Court is altogether political. It would be absurd to say even of the legislature that it is literally unable to intend justice. Further, even if hindsight allows one to see that a racial remedy

serves white interests, it is an illegitimate inference that the Court fore-
saw this. It is doubtful that Supreme Court justices are any more pre-
scient than social scientists, and notoriously, even the best of these,
with the most modern techniques at their disposal, often fail to anticipate key consequences of social policies. Also, even if the Court foresees
that racial remedies will ultimately serve white interests, it is again an
illegitimate inference that the Court first intends that these remedies
serve white interests, or that its foreseeing this consequence is a necessary condition for its decision. Bell unjustifiably suggests that this was
the case in the *Brown* decision, because the Court was aware that its
decision would improve America's image internationally.[45] Finally, no
matter what the Court intends to have, or foresees will, result from its
decisions, it is again an illegitimate inference that the white working
and lower classes share its prescience.

Looking at the matter in this way, rather than in the way Bell suggests, enables one to make better sense of white working-class opposition to racial remedies. If such remedies are introduced only when, as
Bell insists, they are "perceived by the white majority as a clear benefit
to whites,"[46] it is difficult to explain why, as Bell also insists, these
whites oppose the remedies so fiercely. The only explanation he can
muster is that they are in the grip of a "perverse form of racial para-
noia."[47] His view is apparently that working-class whites fiercely and
silently oppose racial remedies because, although they perceive that
these remedies benefit them "more than blacks,"[48] they fear that the
remedies "may threaten the traditional status relationship"[49] between
the working- and lower-class whites and blacks, with blacks clearly
subordinated and at the bottom.

This account of the matter is neither impossible nor altogether implausible. One should never underestimate the virulence of racist sentiments, nor forget that the disgruntled, and those who are themselves
subordinate and feel their humanity threatened, are comforted and
reassured by the perception that there are others below them. Still,
given the well-established human instinct for self-preservation, and the
human disposition to seek security and self-advancement, it seems a
useful rule of thumb not to resort to explanations which assume that
people are self-destructive unless other plausible explanations are unavailable. In the case at issue, another plausible explanation is available, namely, that when working-class whites oppose racial remedies,
they do not perceive that these remedies can be used to their own
advantage.

It may be objected that this account depends on an unduly narrow
sense of the security human beings seek. On Bell's account, working-
class whites may be seeking security when they oppose racial remedies,

i.e., the security of having a subordinate class, and it has just been admitted that people who are themselves subordinate tend to need, and to feel more secure, when they have others beneath them. But the argument articulated here does not depend on a denial of the white working-class desire for a subordinate black class. It in fact concedes the existence of this desire. In particular, it concedes that the white working-class opposes racial remedies because it fears black gains and the loss of a subordinate class. It differs from Bell's account only in denying that the white working class opposes racial remedies because it prefers to sacrifice its advance and keep a subordinate class, rather than to advance and risk losing a subordinate class. It suggests that the circumstances warrant a different, and simpler, view, to wit, that when the white working class opposes racial remedies it does not anticipate that these remedies can be used to its own advantage. It fears that the remedies benefit blacks only, or mainly, and worries that this threatens their superior position.

This, one must admit, is strongly suggested by the typical sequence of white working-class reactions to racial remedies: first, strong and sometimes violent opposition; second, if opposition fails, a frantic effort to find ways to use the remedies to benefit the white working class; third, when this inevitably succeeds, a gradual acceptance of the remedy.[50] If Bell's account were correct, the process would not get past the first stage. Unfortunately, the rejection of Bell's account of the implementation of racial remedies does not mean that his pessimism is unwarranted. On the contrary, the flaw in his account needs to be exposed because it may obscure reasons for a greater pessimism.

As Bell sees it, the ultimate cause of black subordination is the fierce and self-destructive racism of the white working and lower classes. So fierce and self-destructive is this racism that, as we have seen, Bell claims that these classes oppose policies, which will actually be to their own benefit, if they perceive that the policies will also benefit blacks. The logic of this view of the matter suggests that the solution to black subordination lies in revealing to working- and lower-class whites the self-destructive results of their racism. If this could only be accomplished, blacks and working- and lower-class whites would unite against those who, for their own selfish advantage, have for too long frustrated black and white working- and lower-class aspirations for a better life, i.e., upper-class whites.

This is a misleading and potentially dangerous way of understanding white opposition, and it suggests a solution to that opposition which is simplistic and, because of the vehemence of the racism, too optimistic. Consider its account of the white working class concerning racial remedies: The white working-class opposition to these remedies is

self-destructive. It opposes such remedies even while being fully aware
that it would benefit from them. Instead of challenging the favored-
status admissions policies given the well-to-do, it challenges the minuscule favors given blacks who have suffered discrimination. And all the
white working class hopes to get from this is the small comfort of having blacks subservient to them.

If this were true, white opposition to racial remedies could be easily
overcome. All that would be necessary would be to show whites where
their true advantage lie, and self-interest would do the rest. But the
result is a straightforward *reductio* of the self-destruction theory of racial antagonism. That racial antagonism is not overcome easily is clear
for everyone to see.

It is undeniable that some racists are insane and self-destructive,
and even that, in some cases, racism may lead to and become a kind of
insanity and self-destructiveness. The point is that most racists are
perfectly sane; indeed, many are rational, intelligent and well-educated, a fact which appears to surprise some naive people. Racism is
not commonly a "psychological" problem, nor a problem of ignorance
or confusion. *Racism is primarily a moral problem.* Most commonly, the
racist is someone who has beliefs of racial superiority and inferiority,
and attitudes and dispositions fed by these beliefs, which help the individual to get and keep the things he/she wants, usually economic and
social privilege. It is not intended to say that the racist always deliberately cultivates these beliefs, dispositions and attitudes because they
help him/her get what he/she wants, although this probably is often the
case. The point is that they do help him/her get what he/she wants, and
are therefore, from that point of view, functional.

These beliefs and dispositions *may* lead the racist to self-destructive
behavior; but this is no more necessary or typical than it is necessary or
typical that the disposition to tell the truth will lead a truthful person
to self-destructive behavior. Further, it is not claimed that people always easily desist from behavior they know to be self-destructive. Such
behavior may become a habit. One has only to think of smoking, drink-
ing and overeating. The typical pattern in these cases, however, is
quite different from that in cases of racial antagonism. The smoker who
admits the self-destructiveness of his behavior typically tries to stop
smoking, or if he gives this effort up, sees his behavior as simply imprudent. It is doubtful that the racist who tries unsuccessfully to desist
from racist behavior is likely to view his failure as simply imprudent. If
he thinks about it all, he is likely to think of it as immoral.

Finally, while one might deny that racism disadvantages the racist
in an ordinary sense, it is not to be denied that it disadvantages him in
a deeper sense. Racism is immoral; Plato may be right that justice

pays.[51] But even if he is right, and this may well be doubted,[52] the self-destruction theory of racism under discussion here is not made more attractive. In Plato's account, though justice does indeed pay, the advantage of justice to the just person is in the improvement it brings to his soul. In the theory under discussion, the advantage to working-class whites of giving up their racism is the mundane advantage of jobs and places in medical and law schools wrested from upper-class whites.

When Bell laments that upwardly striving whites like Marco DeFunis and Allan Bakke challenged neither "the exclusionary effect of the general admissions process nor the most-favored-status it provided well-to-do applicants," but rather "the relatively minuscule number of seats set aside for minorities to ameliorate the harmful effects of past discrimination,"[53] the implication is that, if upwardly striving whites can be made to see the advantages of an alliance with blacks, which in the form of admissions to professional schools and jobs are before their very noses, such an alliance will be forthcoming. This, in turn, encourages the belief that such an alliance is not unlikely, and a major and necessary step in the long march toward racial equality. Thus, despite the recent reverses, and his cyclical theory of black progress which augurs a repetition of the late nineteenth-century debacle in civil rights, Bell declares that "all is not lost" if, among other things, blacks can gain the alliance of "the millions of white working and nonworking poor who continue to resist black-led initiatives, including those that would benefit from them as much as blacks." [54]

Against this analysis and solution is set the following analysis, which, of course, suggests its own solutions. The first cause of racial antagonisms is not white working- and lower-class racism, but white working- and lower-class self-interest. Fundamentally, working- and lower-class whites do not oppose black gains because of racism, but due to self-interest. Specifically, they oppose black advance because they fear that the size of the economic pie is limited, so that if blacks get more, they will get less. Self-interest also impels them to oppose the advance of other whites as well; but while the more people they can exclude from a fair share, the greater will be their own share, this exclusion of others is both costly and in violation of what they acknowledge to be justice. Accordingly, they tend to choose for exclusion those whose differences from themselves are readily observable and relatively unalterable, for this reduces the social-psychological costs of exclusion. Generally, the differences between blacks and whites are less alterable and more readily observable than the differences between whites and other whites. Thus, whites tend to exclude blacks more than other whites.[55]

One has every reason to be wary of a black and white working- and lower-class alliance against upper-class whites. For one thing, this assumes a classless black community which, if it once existed, certainly does not exist now. Further, it is not unlikely that working- and lower-class whites perceive—and correctly too—that their self-interest is better served by an understanding with upper-class whites to exclude blacks, than by dispossessing upper-class whites and sharing the spoils equally with blacks. Finally, suppose that working- and lower-class whites did ally with blacks to dispossess upper-class whites; if self-interest is the object of this alliance, there is no good reason to believe that it would persist once its object were secured, and that the old, sordid strategy of excluding blacks for greater white shares, which in the past has proved so effective, would not reemerge. An alliance based on self-interest can last only as long as its basis.

This is a particular instance of a weakness which affects every theory that pins its hopes on a working- or lower-class revolution, not the least, that of Karl Marx. Marx constructed an elaborate theory to support his prediction that workers would unite to overthrow capitalism. But he had no comparable theory to support his further prediction—on the truth of which rests the moral attractiveness of his whole theory—that after the revolution the workers would remain united. There is simply the repeated and implausible insistence that capitalism is the cause of human divisiveness, bolstered by the assumption that the moral revolution to draw justice and inclination closer, which in Plato requires a revolution in child rearing and education, is effected by the process of capitalist production itself, or as some Marxist-influenced writers appear to believe, in the strong encounter of revolution.[56] This gap has not been lost on black students of Marxism. As Harold Cruse asks, "What guarantee do Negroes have that socialism means racial equality any more than does capitalist democracy?"[57]

It may be objected that racism will wither, and black workers and white workers will remain united if after dismantling capitalism they set up a classless, socialist society. But this begs the question. The victorious workers may set up a classless, socialist society. Still, it does not follow that the society they set up will be without racial antagonisms. In the first place, it is not so by definition. Class and race are distinct concepts. Even if the society established by the workers is classless, some further argument is needed to show that it will also be without racial antagonism. Such an argument is hazardous. It requires the premise that the existence of classes is a necessary condition for the existence of every social antagonism in society, and that premise is far from being clearly true. Marxists, of course, insist that it is clearly true—Marx himself sometimes spoke of it as obvious—but one should not be intimidated. Claims of obviousness are often bluff, a way of avoiding a careful and critical examination of crucial but potentially weak assumptions.

Consider the many domestic and international antagonisms. These are not, as it is sometimes suggested, only disguised class antagonisms. The antagonists may fight over economic advantage, but it does not follow that theirs is solely a class conflict, if by that is meant a conflict between classes. In religious or ethnic or national conflicts, the antagonists are often of the same class. The most that follows is that people are greedy or jealous or envious, and often use their religious, ethnic or national differences as a respectable cover for their lusts.

What must be demonstrated, then, is that although religious, ethnic and national conflicts are not at bottom disguised class conflicts, they are yet caused by class conflicts. A demonstration of this sort is not easy. It is not, for example, helped much by historical materialism's general and plausible theme that ideological differences have their roots in the different ways that human beings have had to make their living. This suggests that insofar as these differences are used to excuse conflict over economic advantage, a facilitating cause of social antagonisms is that human beings have had to make their living in different ways. From this it does not follow, however, that the efficient cause of social antagonism is class conflict. To show this it would be necessary to demonstrate that all desire for greater access to economic advantage which can create social antagonism stems from the existence of class conflict. It is unlikely that this is true, though. If a class controls the means of production, it will presumably appropriate more of the economic advantages than is good for the other classes, and class conflict causes the desire for greater access to economic advantage. All we can conclude is that class conflict is an expression of this desire.

It may be argued that this only shows at most that socialism is not sufficient for racial justice, not that it is not necessary. This claim should be rejected too. It has persuaded some theorists to hope for a shrinking economy, on the ground that this will hasten black and white working-class unity. Alas, it is far from certain that a shrinking economy would lead to working-class unity; on the contrary, it could lead to race war as black workers and white workers fight over scraps. More important, socialism is not a necessary condition for the economic abundance which it posits as essential for social harmony in general, and black economic advance in particular. This abundance is possible in an expanding economy, whether capitalist or socialist. As W. Arthur Lewis notes, economic growth is the "lubricant" which facilitates black gains in America.[58]

An expanding economy is not, of course, sufficient for black advance. It must also be accompanied by civil rights legislation, which ensures that blacks will share equally in the expansion. Now, if it were true that whites typically tried to frustrate black progress even at the expense of their own progress, such legislation would not be passed or enforced even in a period of economic expansion. On the contrary, though, the evidence does not support the view that most whites take such a self-defeating position. As has been argued, whites typically oppose black advance in zero-sum situations, when they believe that black advance means their reversal. If the latter is not the case, as when the economic pie gets bigger, the urgency to exclude blacks from an equal share in it will lessen, and legislation may well be passed and enforced which ensures that blacks will benefit from an economic expansion.

If this argument is sound, then, subject to the condition that the economy is expanding, pessimism that further civil rights legislation to aid black progress will not be passed or enforced may not be warranted. But the arguments presented here so far rebut only the first of the claims that the black struggle for freedom, equality and justice in the twenty-first century must abandon reliance on the law. The second, far more radical claim to that effect, namely, that civil rights legislation has exhausted its usefulness and can no longer contribute to black progress, must now be addressed.

V

To appreciate this claim, one must understand what its advocates mean by "progress." They mean more than just rising income. They also mean increasing employment at meaningful, worthwhile and important jobs, better health and education, increasingly significant contributions to the scientific, cultural, artistic and intellectual life of the nation, and most important, a flourishing of the virtues of self-reliance and self-respect. Their crucial claim is not that more generous welfare laws cannot raise black income. It is that such laws are not likely to lead to better education for blacks, nor to an improvement in their showing in the sciences and in the arts and letters, nor to an enhancement of black self-reliance and self-respect.

The opposition to further civil rights legislation, though, does not rest only on that claim. That people are poor is, ordinarily, sufficient reason to alleviate their poverty. Normally, it is not necessary to show that this also leads to progress in a broader sense. Thus, those who oppose further civil rights legislation as the way to raise black income must do more than merely insist that raising incomes in this manner is not progress. They must also affirm that raising incomes in this way undermines progress.

This theory comes in more or less extreme versions. The earliest and most extreme version appears to have been held by Booker T. Washington. Part of Washington's depreciation of the importance of civil rights legislation can be explained by his perception that such legislation would simply not be passed or respected in the South at the time that he wrote and lectured; but it also seems clear that he believed that much of this legislation, even such as would outlaw the blatant discrimination rampant at the time, was largely irrelevant to progress. Thrift, hard work and perseverance were, in his mind, certainly necessary to, and probably sufficient for, black advancement.[59] More recently, a very similar, if perhaps somewhat less extreme view, seems to have been urged by Thomas Sowell.[60]

The most recent and most plausible version of this theory is advanced by Glenn Loury, and the analysis which follows will focus mainly on his construction. Loury fully concedes the importance of past civil rights legislation in outlawing discriminatory behavior, even to the point of allowing that there is important work to be done in this area, although he suggests that this "consists mainly in defending past gains."[61] He insists, however, that the civil rights strategy has "reached the point of 'diminishing returns,' " and that "we now live in the 'post-civil rights' era."[62]

Civil rights legislation, he maintains, cannot help solve the problems blacks now face. These problems appear to be of two sorts: First, black underrepresentation in well-paying, responsible positions; second, with some outstanding exceptions, blacks' relatively slender contributions to the natural and social sciences and the world of arts and letters, and their diminished self-confidence, self-esteem and self-respect.

Loury's first argument is based on the nature of the law, i.e., the American "liberal political heritage" which, he maintains, provides legal protection to various freedoms and limits what civil rights legislation can do for future black economic advance. For example, the American liberal political heritage is such that housing laws cannot "prevent a disgruntled white resident from moving away if his neighborhood becomes predominantly or even partly black," and court-ordered busing "cannot prevent unhappy parents from sending their children to private schools." The point is that the freedoms this heritage protects have "important economic consequences" which can run counter to the achievement of equality since family and community backgrounds are crucially important "in determining a child's later success in life."[63]

Loury's second argument is based on the nature of the problem. This problem is grounded in the sorts of values, attitudes and dispositions that mark the black underclass. It is, he insists, beyond legal remedy of any kind. If this intractable problem is to be solved, black people must change their values and goals, and only they themselves can to that. Loury does not deny that the history of racial oppression has caused the problem. But, citing Orlando Patterson's essay, "The Moral Crisis of the Black American,"[64] he argues that "fault and responsibility must not be presumed to go hand-in-hand."[65] Even if a racist society is at fault, and a major contributing cause of the present condition of the black community, it does not follow that *responsibility* for relieving that condition falls on the racist society. For, declares Loury, "no people can be genuinely free so long as they look to others for their deliverance. The pride and self-respect valued by aspiring peoples throughout the world cannot be the gift of outsiders—they must derive from the thoughts and deeds of the peoples themselves."[66]

Loury sees the practice of blaming history and racism as "a self-defeating dynamic."[67] The idea that "individual men and women simply cannot fail on their own," he maintains, "militates against an emphasis on personal responsibility within the group," on the one hand inducing successful group members to attribute their accomplishments to fortuitous circumstances, and, on the other hand, encouraging those who fail to see their failure as inevitable.[68] Also, if blacks are not responsible for their failures, they are not responsible for their successes either, and Loury sees the acknowledgment of the personal success of individual blacks as crucial to further black advance. Again he draws on the work of Patterson. In his book entitled *Slavery and Social Death: A Comparative Study*,[69] Patterson argues that emancipation was not sufficient to convert former slaves or their descendants into genuinely equal citizens. There remained the problem of overcoming their "lack of honor."[70] Loury maintains that this problem is still with us. Blacks are legally free, but they lack the honor and respect of their peers. But this honor and respect cannot be conferred by legal fiat. They can be won, he maintains, only "through the unaided accomplishments of individual persons."[71]

According to Loury, these difficulties are compounded by the practice of preferential treatment, which, he argues, "undermines the ability of people confidently to assert, if only to themselves, that they are as good as their achievements would seem to suggest," and therefore, "undermines the extent to which the personal success of any one black can become the basis of guiding the behavior of other blacks."[72] Further, to continue the practice it becomes necessary, he argues, to say that almost no blacks can reach the highest rungs of success "without special favors." Thus, when black critics question the value of preferential treatment, they are attacked as criticizing the policy to which they owe their own prominence, on the clear presumption that *all* prominent blacks owe their success to policies of preference. This taints all black accomplishment.[73]

Finally, in Loury's account, the practice of seeking relief through civil rights legislation is "pathetic" because it seeks to evoke "the pity, and guilt, of whites." This makes it "inconsistent with the goal of freedom and equality for blacks. One cannot be the equal of those whose pity, or guilt, one actively seeks."[74]

This theory of the conditions for future black progress reduces to three distinct but interconnected propositions:

- Further civil rights legislation to promote black progress conflicts with basic principles of American law and morality.

- Such legislation is, in any case, likely to be ineffective and even counterproductive.

- It aims at evoking the pity and guilt of the white majority, and is consequently demeaning and pathetic.

These claims, which are conceptually distinct and independent, are the basis of a unified theory used to argue against further civil rights legislation.

VI

The argument which follows articulates why this theory is, from first to last, confused and mistaken. It presupposes a false idea of the ground of civil rights legislation and of American law and morality; misunderstands the justification of the demand for civil rights legislation; and, despite its brave championing of self-reliance and its evident confidence in the talents of black people, is based on a diminished conception of their moral status. Further civil rights legislation to aid black progress does not necessarily conflict with American law and morality and is not necessarily ineffectual and counterproductive; thus, the demand for it does not have to be either pathetic or demeaning.

According to Loury, the "civil rights approach" has two aspects: first, "the cause of a particular socioeconomic disparity is identified as racial discrimination; and second, advocates seek such remedies for the disparity as the courts and administrative agencies provide under the law."[75] Why does he think that while this approach was once useful and righteous, it must now be replaced by a "self-help" approach?

There seem to be two reasons: first, that "the historic cancer of racism has abated" and that, "despite a past history of racism and discrimination," white Americans are "now ready to welcome individuals of all races and creeds to make of their freedoms what they will";[76] and second, that while much of the disparity that exists between the black and white races may be due to "racial discrimination," this discrimination is of a sort which people have every right to practice.[77] These two claims will be examined in turn.

Consider first the assertion that racial discrimination of a wrongful kind has so abated that further legal action against it is no longer necessary. Events on the nation's campuses in the 1980s call out that this optimistic claim is premature, but this is a different point. Given the empirical fact that substantial disparities between the races continue to exist, and that these are in large measure due to past wrongful racial discrimination, why should it be outside the purview of civil rights legislation to try to remove these disparities?

One possible answer is that the proper role of the law is to protect people from interference, not to provide them with any positive good. On this account the law can be used against racial discrimination—which may be plausibly described as an interference—but not to promote black progress once racial discrimination has abated.

The view that the proper role of law is to protect people from interference, not to provide them with any positive good, is sometimes based on a dichotomy between negative rights and positive rights. Negative rights are ones not to be interfered with; positive rights are ones to be assured. For example, the right not to be assaulted is a negative right, while the right to receive food is a positive right. Similarly, the right not to be discriminated against on the basis of one's color is presumably a negative right, while the right to employment or education is presumably a positive right.

There is nothing necessarily wrong with classifying rights either as negative or positive. It may even be useful for certain analytical purposes. Unfortunately, it draws some people irresistibly to claim that, while government has an obligation to protect negative rights, it has no obligation to assure positive rights.[78] The arguments for this vary. Sometimes it seems to be that enforcing negative rights is cheap or even costless, while enforcing positive rights is expensive.[79] If this were true, perhaps negative rights should be protected before positive rights. At least this inference seems reasonable if negative rights and positive rights are of equal value, if resources are so limited that all rights cannot be protected, and if consequently we have to choose which rights to protect. But, it is false to state that enforcing negative rights is cheap or costless. Does not protecting people from assault and discrimination require a police force, courts, prisons and a whole legal apparatus, all at substantial cost?

A different sort of argument rests on an alleged difference in the goods secured by negative rights and positive rights. According to this argument, the good of noninterference, which is secured by negative rights, is the same for everyone, is equally valuable and desired, and consequently can be readily and impartially secured by law. But, the argument continues, the goods secured by positive rights vary enormously from one person to the next, since they depend on tastes and plans of life, and therefore cannot be readily and impartially secured by law. This argument is partially but not wholly persuasive. That some positive goods are not equally valuable to and valued by everyone does not imply that no positive goods are equally valuable to and valued by everyone. Food, basic education, housing, medical treatment and, arguably, employment, are positive goods which seem equally valuable to everyone. If they are, the present argument presents no good reason why they cannot, or should not, be assured by law.

Accordingly, the distinction between negative rights and positive rights provides no basis for the theory that government is obligated to protect negative rights, but is not equally obligated to protect positive rights. The most that can be said is that because resources are not unlimited, sometimes a decision must be made to protect some rights and not others. On that basis, it could be argued that, while it is feasible to protect blacks' negative rights against racial discrimination, it is not feasible to secure their positive rights to employment and other goods that would greatly aid their future progress.

Such an argument raises many questions. One could ask whether resources are, in fact, limited in the way suggested, or whether the resources employed to protect rights are fairly divided to assure the rights of blacks and whites equally. Loury's first argument was that wrongful racial discrimination had abated. As has been indicated, this suggests that he could be relying on the theory that government is obligated to protect only negative rights. This theory has now proved to be false. Attention must now be turned to his second argument for depreciating further civil rights legislation, that is, while much of the disparity between the races may be due to racial discrimination, this discrimination is of a sort which people have every right to practice.

The claim that white people have every right to practice the racial discrimination in question does not mean that they do not act wrongly in doing so. It means simply that even if they act wrongly, government cannot legitimately use the law to alter their behavior. White people may, for example, move out of a neighborhood because blacks move in, or they may take their children out of a school which becomes "too" integrated. They may act wrongly when they behave in this way, but, because they act within their rights when they do these things, government cannot pass laws to prevent them from doing so.

Loury places great reliance on this argument. He maintains that the racial discrimination involved has great economic consequences. Yet, because it appears to be protected from legal remedy by the right to freedom of association and other basic liberties, he insists that civil rights legislation can do nothing about it.[80] It is true that the liberties in question are given special protection in the Constitution, and that their protection enables some forms of racial discrimination to continue, even though they are rich sources of inequality. It is, however, not the case that civil rights legislation can do nothing to offset their deleterious effects.

First, as this author has argued elsewhere,[81] parents do not have a natural or prelegal right to place their children in any school they please. Children are not the parents' property to do with as they will. Children are human beings with rights to the kind of schooling which will enable them to grow up to be fair-minded adults. Normally, the state has overwhelmingly good reason not to interfere with how parents raise their children, and to accord them broad legal rights in choosing their children's schooling. The state is the ultimate protector of the rights of its citizens, including especially the rights of its vulnerable children-citizens. Nonetheless, it recognizes that in many circumstances it is well to delegate some of its responsibilities. For example, it recognizes that to protect the rights of its children-citizens, it normally does best to delegate this responsibility to their parents, and thus to accord to parents legal rights to determine their children's schooling. But if parents use these rights to give their children a schooling which ensures that they grow up to be narrow-minded bigots, the state may fairly withdraw these rights.

If this argument is sound, parents have no basic or inviolable liberty to withdraw their children from schools just because these schools become "too" integrated; and civil rights laws may, without contradicting any basic law or principle of morality, frustrate these ways of subverting busing strategies to improve the education of black children and white children. Even if this conclusion is justified, though, it leaves most of Loury's argument intact. It does not deny, for example, that people have a liberty, which ought not to be subverted by any civil rights legislation, to move out of neighborhoods when blacks move in; or that businesses have a legally protected right to move out of, or to avoid, ghettoes, even if this leaves many people without chance of employment. How can civil rights legislation avoid violating these and other liberties, and yet still prevent them from having their deleterious effects?

One possibility would be to offer white people economic incentives not to flee a neighborhood just because black people have purchased houses there. Generous tax breaks could be given to those who elect to stay, the neighborhood could be made more attractive, and schools could be improved and refurbished. Similarly, tax breaks and other incentives could be used to persuade businesses to locate in ghettoes and/ or not move out of them. If these strategies were successful in integrating schools, neighborhoods and businesses, and if a rich source of the economic disparity between the races is the absence of such integration, it seems that civil rights legislation to implement these strategies could play a considerable role in the black struggle for equality. Yet such legislation would not violate the various freedoms of association. It would be a violation of these freedoms to compel people not to move out of a neighborhood, or to compel businesses to locate in ghettoes. It is not a violation of these freedoms to make a neighborhood attractive enough so that people choose not to move out of it because some black family buys a house in it; nor is it a violation of these freedoms to offer a business economic incentives to stay or to locate in a ghetto.

It may be objected that taxing people to finance these strategies violates their property rights. Resort to this objection reveals the diminished moral status that the opponents of civil rights legislation accord black people. Taxation to improve the education, welfare and employment of white people is routine. It has been used successfully to help countless waves of immigrants climb out of their ghettoes. Ruling it out to help black people climb out of poverty can only be based on the idea that their poverty is less an abomination than the poverty of white people.

At this particular juncture in the struggle for black justice, freedom and equality, the great obstacle to overcome is the disproportionately large number of black people in the underclass. There are simply too many black people more or less permanently unemployed, and more or less permanently on welfare. Further progress requires the dissolution of the black underclass and getting black people gainfully employed and thus off welfare. If racism has abated, and black unemployment is no longer due to present discrimination but rather to blacks not having the skills and dispositions demanded by the workplace, reducing black unemployment seems to require that the members of the black underclass develop these skills and dispositions. How can this be accomplished? One necessary condition seems to be better schools, and in general, better education. It is in school that much of what is required by the marketplace is learned. But even if better schooling is a necessary condition for further black progress, it is not sufficient. Many of the skills and dispositions demanded by the workplace can only be acquired by work experience. Consequently, a further necessary condition for black progress is that there be skilled jobs, and that black people be employed in these jobs.

Securing these conditions for black progress will be costly. This is clear for the case of improving black education, but may be disputed for the case of increasing black employment. The objection can be summarized as follows: Welfare payments act as a disincentive to taking low-paying jobs; these jobs pay wages that are so little above welfare payments that it is more rational to go on welfare than to take them. Consequently, if the object is to get black people employed, the expedient is to eliminate or drastically lower welfare payments. This will increase efficiency: On the one hand, welfare costs will fall; on the other hand, work will be done which now remains undone. This argument assumes that those taken off welfare will find jobs, and that suitable jobs exist for them. This need not be true; if it is not, and if surely the proposal is not to deny welfare payments to those who cannot find work, the anticipated savings may not materialize. Further, even if the proposal is coupled with a repeal of minimum wage laws, and this generates a sufficient number of low-paying jobs, it is far from clear that these wages will be enough to sustain workers in minimum decency.

Eliminating welfare may thus require that government either train those taken off welfare so that they can acquire skills for the jobs that do exist, or create jobs suitable for those taken off welfare. Both schemes are likely to be more costly than current welfare programs. Other proposals are likely to have the same undesirable consequence. Consider, for example, raising minimum wages so that the difference between the wages paid for low-paying jobs and welfare payments is great enough to give people an economic incentive to get off welfare and take these jobs. Clearly, this could easily cost much more than current welfare programs. Or consider "workfare," requiring people to work for welfare payments. This too is likely to cost more than current welfare programs since, in addition to the welfare payments, there would be the cost of administering the job program. In any case, since the work required by workfare tends to be "make-work" or "busy-work," it is unlikely to foster development of the skills and dispositions demanded by the real workplace, and is therefore unlikely to be a positive factor in black progress.

If these considerations are sound, the dissolution of the black underclass, which is the next great step in the black struggle for freedom, justice and equality, will require a considerable outlay of capital, probably far in excess of the cost of present welfare programs. The increased taxation this may involve is likely to be more easily passed if the economy expands (this is one reason why it was noted earlier that an expanding economy is a condition for further black advance), though it is likely to be resisted even then. Loury is aware of this constraint, and gives it some weight.[82] But since it is not the reason he opposes further civil rights legislation requiring government expenditures of the kind suggested, the question of whether it is a morally weighty constraint will not be taken up; whether, that is, taxation to finance education and universal employment unjustly violates property rights. The focus instead is on the reasons he opposes such legislation; he thinks it will fail and thinks it is counterproductive. What are the facts at this particular juncture that justify such pessimism?

To answer this question, the principal reasons why gainful, productive employment is thought to be crucial to the overall flourishing and progress of a people will be reviewed briefly. These are four in number. First, work is the main way people provide for their security and well-being. Second, work supports self-reliance. If people cannot make their own living or provide for their own security, they have to depend on others, and if, as is not unlikely, this dependence develops into a trait of character, they become incapable of any bold and independent action. Third, work fosters dignity and self-respect. When one cannot find gainful, productive employment, the implication is that one's talents and abilities, skills and dispositions, are valueless, and this is liable to undermine one's dignity and self-respect. But dignity and self-respect are vitally important. Without these attributes, it may be difficult to think of one's projects as important enough to pursue with vigor. Finally, when work involves the development of talents and the mastery and exercise of complex skills, it is an important means to the blossoming of one's innate capacities and potentialities, and human beings tend to find this inherently enjoyable.

These reasons justify laws and governmental intervention in the economy to ensure, as far as is consistent with the realization of other equally valuable ideals, that everyone has an opportunity to get steady employment. It does not follow, however, that people will take work when it is offered to them. They may not take work if they have the wrong values. If people care so little about self-reliance that they are satisfied with being dependent on others, they will not be moved to take employment in order not to be so dependent, even if employment is offered them. If they have so little dignity and self-respect that they are not bothered by their lack of these, or by the implication that their talents and skills are valueless, they will not jump at the chance to make their talents and skills valuable. If they are so dehumanized that they do not enjoy the development of their talents and the mastery and exercise of complex skills, they will not be attracted to work because it offers the opportunity for this development or mastery. And finally, if they are lazy enough, they may be unable to apply themselves to any work which would assure them of material comforts, even if they are greedy and envious of those who are better off.

Loury's pessimism about the effectiveness of civil rights legislation requiring expenditures for education and job training stems from considerations of this sort. He believes that members of the black underclass lack the values which would lead them to take advantage of the education and job training that such legislation would make available. This is the point of his frequent references to black crime, promiscuity and illegitimacy.[83] He believes that these reveal that the values of the members of the black underclass do not foster their well-being, and consequently that until those in the black underclass change their values, they will fail no matter what laws are passed. He thus maintains that the focus should not be on more civil rights legislation, but rather on an honest criticism of the values of the black underclass. Its members must be made to see that they fail largely because of their values, and must be persuaded to change these values.[84]

The view that people are poor because of their values has, of course, a long history. Submerged by liberal reformism, it has recently acquired a new lease on life by the discovery of the underclass. It should still be regarded with distrust, though.

First, it is not altogether clear how much the values of the underclass differ from those of the wider society. That the behavior of its members is very different from the behavior of average citizens does not necessarily imply that the values of the two groups are also very different. The same values may prompt different behavior in different circumstances, and the circumstances of the underclass and of the wider society are certainly different. A black youth from the ghetto and a white youth from the suburbs may have similar values, but they often behave differently because their opportunities are so very different. Yet it is not simply a matter of opportunities. Equally important are *expectations*. Even if the black youth is bused to a white school in the suburbs, and in this way an attempt is made to give him opportunities more akin to those of his white counterpart, his behavior is likely to remain different from that of the white youth—and again, not necessarily because his values are different. He may continue to behave differently from the white youth because he expects, with considerable justification, that the law and his teachers will treat him differently.

Now, suppose that the values of the underclass actually do differ from those of the wider society. Its members may still not be poor because of their values. They may have the values they have because they are poor. One does not wish to deny that a person can be poor because of his values. The lazy scion of suburbia who ends up on skid row could well be there because of his values. But one cannot generalize from this case to that of the underclass. The cases are crucially different. Where the values of the suburbanite on skid row do not constitute a morality, the values of members of the underclass apparently do.

A morality is a response to given socioeconomic conditions. It is an interconnected system of values which interdependent people hold in common, enabling them to coordinate their behavior and to survive or flourish in the circumstances in which they find themselves. Thus morality has a necessary connection to natural human needs, wants and sentiments. As David Hume noted, the rationale for justice is its usefulness.[85] The very idea of justice would not exist, or if it already existed would soon be discarded, in circumstances in which it was useless as, for example, in cases of extreme abundance or extreme scarcity.

If this is so, then clearly the values of the lazy suburbanite are not a morality. They are not held in common by the members of his class, nor used by them to cope with their situation. In counterpoint, the values of the underclass do constitute a morality, being a response of the members to the social state which they share in common, enabling them to coordinate their activities to cope with their lot. If, then, one says that the values of the lazy suburbanite caused his poverty, one cannot also say the same thing for the members of the underclass; it would be more accurate to say that their poverty caused their values. While it may be reasonable to hope that moral criticism will help the suburbanite to do better, the same hope for the members of the underclass is less reasonable. In his/her situation, the suburbanite's values frustrate his/her human needs, wants and desires. In contrast, the values of the underclass help them in their situation to avoid frustration of their human needs, wants and desires.

If this is correct, one cannot hope to change the values of the black underclass unless such a change serves the overall well-being of its members. It is difficult to see how this can be accomplished if their socioeconomic conditions remain as they are. Given current conditions, to urge the black underclass to adopt new values, those associated with the "work ethic" for example, is to urge them to frustrate themselves. In conjunction with urging the work ethic, the socioeconomic conditions which make attempting to embody the work ethic a source of frustration and failure must be changed.

It may be objected that the process and change outlined so far appeal only to the self-interest of the underclass and can only be expected to lead them to cultivate a more enlightened self-interest, not the moral values to make them better citizens; for self-interest, no matter how enlightened, is not morality, since it may be in people's self-interest to cheat, lie, steal and murder. It is conceded that self-interest is not enough. If self-interest were unrestrained by morality, chaos or, at best, an enervating ceasefire, would be the best one could hope for. Morality sometimes requires the sacrifice of individual self-interest, as Aristotle calls out ever so compellingly in his discussion of equity. The question is how morality is acquired; in particular, how the members of the black underclass can be persuaded not to cheat and lie and steal when it is in their interests to do so? For this, they must have reason to feel a sense of belonging, of solidarity and loyalty with the larger community. As Hume admitted when he confessed himself unable to persuade the "sensible knave" not to act unjustly when it was to his advantage, no attempt at such persuasion can be successful if a person fails to appreciate the satisfactions of "society." [86] It is difficult to see how the black underclass can acquire a sense of belonging, solidarity or loyalty with the larger society if conditions remain as they are. Do we have a *society,* and can the black underclass appreciate the satisfactions of society when those who have reduced it to its present plight are prepared to make no further amends that stop discrimination?[87] This question is not asked rhetorically, but invites continued, tough-minded discussion.

To summarize, a brief review of the main points will have to suffice. By a survey of the evolution of the law since *Plessy,* it has been suggested that a good case can be made for saying that civil rights legislation has been an important factor in black progress. Next, the view that the usefulness of the law here has come to an end was addressed. There were two claims: 1) Further civil rights legislation would help, but it will not be forthcoming; and 2) Further civil rights legislation designed to help would conflict with the basic principles of American law, and would in any case be counterproductive. It is the belief of this author that both these claims are unwarranted. If correct, though non-legal, and in particular, self-help strategies, will certainly be useful—whenever were they not?—the right kind of laws will continue to be essential in the black struggle for justice, freedom and equality in the twenty-first century.

NOTES

[1] *Plessy* v. *Ferguson,* 163 U.S. 537 (1896); *Brown* v. *Board of Education,* 347 U.S. 483 (1954); *Regents of the University of California* v. *Bakke,* 438 U.S. 265 (1978).

[2] *Plessy,* 163 U.S. at 559 (J. Harlan dissenting).

[3]*Brown*, 347 U.S. 483.

[4]See *Missouri ex rel. Gaines* v. *Canada*, 305 U.S. 337 (1938) and *Sweatt* v. *Painter*, 339 U.S. 629 (1950), *reh. den.* 340 U.S. 846.

[5]*McLaurin* v. *Oklahoma State Regents for Higher Education*, 339 U.S. 637 (1950).

[6]*Brown*, 347 U.S. at 495.

[7]Earl Warren, *The Memoirs of Earl Warren* (Garden City, NJ: Doubleday, 1977), p. 291.

[8]Civil Rights Act of 1964, P.L. 88-352 (88th Congress, 2d Session).

[9]*Green* v. *County School Board of New Kent County*, 391 U.S. 430 (1968).

[10]*Swann* v. *Charlotte-Mecklenburg Board of Education*, 402 U.S. 1 (1971), *reh. den.* 403 U.S. 912.

[11]*Keyes* v. *School District No. One* , 413 U.S. 189 (1973), *reh. den.* 414 U.S. 883.

[12]Derrick A. Bell, Jr., ed., *Civil Rights: Leading Cases* (Boston: Little, Brown and Company, 1980), p. 322.

[13]*Griggs* v. *Duke Power Co.*, 401 U.S. 424 (1971).

[14]Bell, *Civil Rights: Leading Cases*, op. cit. note 12, p. 257.

[15]Voting Rights Act of 1965, P.L. 89-110 (89th Congress, 1st Session).

[16]1968 Amendments to the Civil Rights Act of 1964, P.L. 90-284 (90th Congress, 2d Session).

[17]These figures are cited in Ben J. Wattenberg and Richard M. Scammon, "Black Progress and Liberal Rhetoric," *Commentary* 55: 4 (April 1973): 35-44 at 36.

[18]Richard B. Freeman, "Discrimination in the Academic Marketplace," in Thomas Sowell, ed., *Essays and Data on American Ethnic Groups* (Washington, D.C.: The Urban Institute, 1978), pp. 167-201 at 174.

[19]Richard B. Freeman, "Black Economic Progress Since 1964," *The Public Interest* 52 (Summer 1978): 52-68 at 57.

[20]Wattenberg and Scammon, op. cit. note 17, p. 35.

[21]Freeman, "Black Economic Progress," op. cit. note 19, p. 52.

[22]William Julius Wilson, *The Truly Disadvantaged: The Inner City, the Underclass, and Public Policy* (Chicago and London: The University of Chicago Press, 1987), p. 26.

[23]The phrase is, of course, from Kenneth B. Clark, *Dark Ghetto: Dilemmas of Social Power* (New York: Harper & Row, 1965), ch. 5, pp. 81-110.

[24]See, for example, William Julius Wilson, *The Declining Significance of Race* (Chicago and London: The University of Chicago Press, 1978); Ken

Auletta, *The Underclass* (New York: Random House, 1982); and William Julius Wilson, *The Truly Disadvantaged*, op. cit. note 22.

[25]The term was coined by Oscar Lewis in a somewhat different context. See Oscar Lewis, "The Culture of Poverty," *Scientific American* 215: 4 (October 1966): 19-25.

[26]William A. Darity, Jr., "The Managerial Class and Surplus Population," *Society* 21: 1 (November/December 1983): 54-62 at 58.

[27]Ibid., p. 59.

[28]Ibid. This theme is quite consistent with Samuel F. Yette's observation that: "Black Americans have outlived their usefulness. Their *raison d'etre* to this society has ceased to be a compelling issue. Once an economic asset, they are now considered an economic drag. . . ." Samuel F. Yette, *The Choice: The Issue of Black Survival in America* (New York: Berkeley Publishing Corporation, 1972), p. 14.

[29]Bell, *Civil Rights: Leading Cases*, op. cit. note 12.

[30]*Civil Rights Cases*, 109 U.S. 3 (1883).

[31]Derrick A. Bell, Jr., "Civil Rights in 2004: Where Will We Be?" in Robert K. Fullinwider and Claudia Mills, eds., *The Moral Foundations of Civil Rights* (Totowa, NJ: Rowman and Littlefield, 1986), pp. 25-35 at 30.

[32]Ibid., p. 33. Over the course of his presidency, Ronald Reagan appointed Justices Sandra Day O'Connor, Antonin Scalia and Anthony Kennedy to the Supreme Court, and elevated Justice William Rehnquist to the Chief Justice's chair. By the Court's 1988-89 term, Reagan's desire for a solid conservative majority had clearly emerged (Justice Byron White provided the fifth vote) in relation to matters of civil rights and affirmative action. In a broadside, reminiscent of its assault on civil rights in the 1870s and 1880s, the Court curtailed sharply a range of protections that blacks and other minorities had come to take for granted—believing that they had been "settled" both legislatively and judicially. The following are some of the key decisions which the Court handed down in 1989:

- By a 6-3 vote in *Richmond* v. *J.A. Croson Company*, the Court struck down as constitutionally infirm a Richmond, Virginia ordinance that required contractors on city building projects to set aside at least 30 percent of the value of a given project for firms which were at least one-half minority owned. The Court did what many protagonists of affirmative action had long feared—it applied the judicial principle of "strict scrutiny," rather than the more elastic one of "rational basis," in declaring that the Richmond ordinance violated the equal protection of the laws clause of the Constitution's Fourteenth Amendment.

- The Court all but reversed *Griggs* v. *Duke Power Company* in its *Wards Cove Packing Company* v. *Antonio* decision. By a 5-4 vote, it ruled that plaintiffs who use statistical evidence to establish "disparate impact" in terms of patterns in a given work force pertaining to race must demonstrate that such patterns exist in consequence of the intentional discrimination of the employer. It ruled against Eskimos and Asians who had argued that they had been placed in low-paying and less-desirable jobs by the Wards Cove Packing Company due to their race, even though they used statistical evidence to establish that virtually all of the well-paying and more-desirable jobs were held by white males.

- In *Martin* v. *Wilks*, the Court, by a 5-4 vote, permitted the reopening of consent decrees pertaining to affirmative action years after they had taken effect. It allowed white male firefighters in Birmingham, Alabama, who had argued that they were not a party to the original consent decree which had been agreed upon by the city of Birmingham and its fire-fighters' union to facilitate the hiring and promotion of more blacks, to challenge it in court.

- The Court, by a 5-4 vote, limited sharply the use of the Civil Rights Act of 1866 to fight racial harassment on the job in *Patterson* v. *McClean Credit Union*. The majority declared that the act barred discrimination at the point where one was being considered to be hired, but it did not pro-hibit later discriminatory treatment on the job. (It did rule unanimously to permit the use of the Civil Rights Act of 1866 by persons who sought to sue private individuals for other forms of discrimination.) Writing for the Court's majority in *Patterson*, Justice Kennedy declared: "Neither our words nor our decisions should be interpreted as signaling one inch of re-treat from Congress's policy to forbid discrimination in the private, as well as the public, sphere." This cannot but stir one to recall Justice Brad-ley's sophistry in the *Civil Rights Cases* (1883) that "[w]hen a man has emerged from slavery, and by the aid of beneficent legislation has shaken off the inseparable concomitants of that state, there must be some stage in the progress of his elevation when he takes the rank of a mere citizen, and ceases to be the special favorite of the laws, and when his rights as a citi-zen, or a man, are to be protected in the ordinary modes by which other men's rights are protected. . . ." The Court's current conservative ma-jority appears to have heeded Justice Bradley's admonition that blacks should not "be the special favorite of the laws" as it restricted the scope of civil rights legislation and judicial decisions. But at what cost? Senators such as Edward Kennedy and Howard Metzenbaum are troubled by what they perceive to be the potential cost of the Court's recent decisions, and have promised to seek appropriate legislative redress.

[33] *Washington* v. *Davis*, 426 U.S. 229 (1976).

[34] Bell, *Civil Rights: Leading Cases*, op. cit. note 12, p. 360.

[35] Bell, "Civil Rights in 2004," op. cit. note 31, p. 33.

[36] Derrick A. Bell, Jr., *Race, Racism and American Law*, 2d ed. (Boston: Lit-tle, Brown and Company, 1980), p. 39.

[37] *Milliken* v. *Bradley*, 418 U.S. 717 (1974).

[38] Bell, *Race, Racism and American Law*, op. cit. note 36, p. 399.

[39] Ibid., p. 41.

[40] Ibid., p. 6.

[41] Ibid., p. 8, quoting Alexis de Tocqueville, *Democracy in America* (Garden City, NY: Anchor Books (Doubleday), 1969), p. 344.

[42] Ibid., pp. 455-456.

[43] Bell, "Civil Rights in 2004," op. cit. note 31, p. 32.

[44] Bell, *Race, Racism and American Law*, op. cit. note 36, pp. 7-8.

[45] Ibid., p. 437.

[46] Ibid., p. 457.

[47] Ibid., p. 455.

[48] Ibid., p. 456.

[49] Ibid., p. 454.

[50] This pattern is well exemplified in the reaction to affirmative action. First, there was fierce opposition; then practically every ethnic group tried to argue that it, too, had suffered discrimination, and so deserved preference; finally, there was a growing (if slow) acceptance as it became clearer that white women, of all groups, would after all be the major beneficiaries.

[51] Plato's greatest arguments are in *The Republic*.

[52] I have developed these doubts in "How Injustice Pays," *Philosophy and Public Affairs* 9: 4 (Summer 1980): 359-371.

[53] Bell, *Race, Racism and American Law*, op. cit. note 36, p. 455.

[54] Bell, "Civil Rights in 2004," op. cit. note 31, p. 35.

[55] This is essentially the analysis of racial discrimination by the first, and perhaps the most acute, of black nationalists, Martin Delany. According to Delany, those who proscribe others select as objects of proscription those who "differ as much as possible . . . from themselves," since this "ensure[s] the greater success" of their proscription as it "engenders the greater prejudice, or in other words, elicits less interest on the part of the oppressing class." Martin Delany, "The Condition, Elevation, Emigration, and Destiny of the Colored People of the United States," in Howard Brotz, ed., *Negro Social and Political Thought, 1850-1920; Representative Texts* (New York: Basic Books, 1966), pp. 37-101 at 41. I develop this analysis further in "How Injustice Pays," op. cit. note 52.

[56] I have in mind here chiefly Frantz Fanon, *The Wretched of the Earth*, trans. Constance Farrington (New York: Grove Press, 1968, © 1963).

[57] Harold Cruse, "Revolutionary Nationalism and the Afro-American," in Harold Cruse, *Rebellion or Revolution?* (New York: William Morrow, 1968), pp. 74-96 at 93. I have developed these points more fully in "Marxism, Justice and Black Progress," ch. 3 of my *Blacks and Social Justice* (Totowa, NJ: Rowman and Allanheld, 1984), pp. 52-72.

[58] W. Arthur Lewis, *Racial Conflict and Economic Development* (Cambridge, MA: Harvard University Press, 1985), p. 121.

[59]For a further discussion of Washington, see ch. 2, "Black Progress and the Free Market," in Boxill, *Blacks and Social Justice* , op. cit. note 57, pp. 19-51.

[60]Thomas Sowell has written a great number of books and articles. See especially *Ethnic America: A History* (New York: Basic Books, 1981), *Race and Economics* (New York: Longman, 1982, © 1975), and *The Economics and Politics of Race: An International Perspective* (New York: William Morrow and Co., Inc., 1983). I have criticized his theory in ch. 2 of *Blacks and Social Justice*, op. cit. note 57.

[61]Glenn C. Loury, "The Moral Quandary of the Black Community," *The Public Interest* 79 (Spring 1985): 9-22 at 14.

[62]Ibid., p. 13.

[63]Glenn C. Loury, "Beyond Civil Rights," *The New Republic* 3690 (October 7, 1985): 22-25 at 22.

[64]Orlando Patterson, "The Moral Crisis of the Black American," *The Public Interest* 32 (Summer 1973): 43-69.

[65]Loury, "Moral Quandary," op. cit. note 61, p. 11.

[66]Ibid.

[67]Glenn C. Loury, " 'Matters of Color'—Blacks and the Constitutional Order," *The Public Interest* 86 (Winter 1987): 109-123 at 120.

[68]Ibid.

[69]Orlando Patterson, *Slavery and Social Death: A Comparative Study* (Cambridge, MA: Harvard Univeristy Press, 1982).

[70]Patterson, ibid., chapter 3, discusses this problem.

[71]Loury, "Beyond Civil Rights," op. cit. note 63, p. 25.

[72]Ibid.

[73]Ibid.

[74]Loury, "Matters of Color," op. cit. note 67, p. 119.

[75]Loury, "Beyond Civil Rights," op. cit. note 63, p. 22.

[76]Glenn C. Loury, "Who Speaks for American Blacks?" *Commentary* 83: 1 (January 1987): 34-38 at 35.

[77]Loury, "Beyond Civil Rights," op. cit. note 63, p. 22.

[78]Perhaps the best known example is Maurice Cranston, *What Are Human Rights?* (London: Bodley Head, 1973), pp. 65-71.

[79]See, for example, Paul Streeten, "Basic Needs and Human Rights," *World Development* 8: 2 (February 1980): 107-111.

[80]See, for example, Loury's "Beyond Civil Rights," op. cit. note 63, p. 22, or his "Matters of Colors," op. cit. note 67, pp. 115-116.

[81]Boxill, *Blacks and Social Justice*, op. cit. note 57, pp. 106-108.

[82]Loury, "Who Speaks for American Blacks?," op. cit. note 76, p. 34.

[83]See, for example, ibid., p. 35.

[84]Loury, "The Moral Quandary," op. cit. note 61, p. 15.

[85]David Hume, with Charles W. Hendel, ed., *An Inquiry Concerning the Principles of Morals: With A Supplement, A Dialogue* (Indianapolis: Bobbs-Merrill, 1985), p. 19.

[86]Ibid., pp. 102-103.

[87]I reject without argument the incredible claim that, whatever may have been the sins of its fathers, the present white population is innocent of racial discrimination. *Brown* did not end discrimination, nor did it terminate the transgenerational reproduction of racism in the culture.

UNIVERSAL EDUCATION, BLACKS AND DEMOCRACY: THE EXPANSION AND CONTRACTION OF EDUCATIONAL OPPORTUNITIES

Kenneth S. Tollett

Howard University

Introduction

> And none of us should forget the observation of Epictetus who himself had once been a slave. In reflecting on the character of Greek society in his day, he observed that man has decided that only free men shall be educated, but God has decreed that only the educated shall be truly free.
>
> James E. Cheek

Universal education should contribute to the creation of common, democratic values which provide the foundation for a social compact and political covenant. Recognizing implicitly, if not always explicitly, the above, blacks have sought social, political and economic advancement primarily through education and secondarily through law.[1] Indeed, law has been the main instrument through which blacks have sought to expand their educational opportunities and, by attacking the "separate but equal" doctrine in graduate and professional educational arenas, laid the foundation for overturning the doctrine not only specifically in education, but also generally in the nation.[2] Thus, education has been the focus of many initiatives and accomplishments by blacks; but they have had to make an extraordinary effort during most of their history in the United States to obtain it.

Education cannot be overemphasized, particularly in the context of citizenship participation and socioeconomic empowerment. Blacks have understood well throughout their experience in America the profound insight of Epictetus, who himself had once been a slave. Whites have understood it, also. Mary Frances Berry and John W. Blassingame have written:

> Beginning in the colonial period, whites insisted on the compulsory ignorance of blacks to insure the continuation of slavery and caste distinctions. . . . Throughout the antebellum period state laws forbade the education of slaves and law and custom severely limited the education of free Negroes.[3]

After the Civil War, the southern white attitude towards educating blacks did not change significantly. Berry and Blassingame further observe:

> The blacks' passion for education in the 1860s was equaled by the whites' desire to deny or limit the education they received. During the early years of Reconstruction, southern whites burned schools (thirty-seven in Tennessee in 1869) and regularly insulted and whipped white teachers of blacks. In a typical case, white college students in Lexington, Virginia, regularly greeted one white woman as that "damned Yankee bitch of a nigger teacher." *What southern whites feared most was that the education of blacks would destroy white supremacy.*[4]

The desire of whites to impose "white supremacy" upon blacks is well-known historically; still, throughout most of the black experience in the United States, there have been whites who have sought to provide or expand educational opportunities for some blacks.

As one observes the state of blacks in the United States over historical time, it generally can be assessed in terms of how well the society has regarded and treated them educationally; likewise, their prospects for the future are no doubt contingent upon how well they fare educationally. The importance of education, which can empower some while simultaneously frightening or threatening others, requires that it be defined clearly and succinctly in this chapter. Education is an *intellectual, cultural* and *social* process, which creates and transmits *knowledge*, develops and nurtures *cognition*, patterns and structures *conduct*, and socializes as well as adapts individuals and/or groups, one to the other.[5] Education's great importance is further indicated by three key functions that it serves in most societies or communities: these pertain to production, consumption and citizenship.[6]

The production function of education provides activities and processes related to the production of goods and services such as discovering talent, giving instruction and engaging in research:

> To put this another way, higher educational institutions train people vocationally, they seek people with talent so that they can be educated and perform production functions for society, and they engage in research for the purpose of developing a technology and an economy which are continuously expanding.[7]

The consumption and citizenship functions of education are closely related to universal values and the creation of a social compact and a political community. The consumption function relates to those educational activities that develop tastes, sensitivities and values which in turn may lead to lifestyles of consumption of goods and services in a society. However, the consumption function is not a mere subspecies of the production function, although the development of values and tastes obviously may shape what goods and services in which citizens will have an interest, thus affecting what is produced. Family and community values may be developed and nourished by the consumption function, which is more closely related to public and civic concerns than it is to economic ones.

It is the citizenship function of education, though, that is the most important concerning the relationship between universal education and democratic values. It is central to universal education's role in creating the social compact and political covenant that ground a democracy. The citizenship function provides common information, knowledge and understanding that contribute to the growth, development and persistence of civic virtue and civil peace. Indeed, the Founding Fathers' effort to create what Forrest McDonald called a *novus ordo seclorum*, "a new order of the ages,"[8] had some of its roots in notions regarding dialogue and discourse in a republic grounded in a sense of civic responsibility. Such a republic should give high priority to the citizenship function of education.

Responsible dialogue and discourse can take place only in a community[9] of relatively well-educated persons. Such persons create or become a community by virtue of their shared experiences, knowledge, information, ideas and activities. Thus, this chapter will first deal with significant dialogic considerations of democracy and republicanism, touching obliquely upon the production and consumption functions of education while giving special attention to its citizenship function. The role of universal education in developing democratic values and in creating the social compact and political covenant that ground a democracy will then be disclosed, if not demonstrated.

Second, the history of the education of blacks from colonial days to the present will be chronicled. This chronicle will be divided into four parts: (1) From the beginning of blacks' entry into the New World up to the Civil War; (2) from the Civil War and Reconstruction to the late nineteenth century, or the enunciation of the "separate but equal" doctrine; (3) from the turn of the twentieth century until the *Brown* school desegregation decision; and (4) from *Brown* to the end of the 1980s. Special attention will be focused upon black colleges, including their beginning near the middle of the nineteenth century, and upon the "desegregation" of elementary and secondary education.

Finally, the educational opportunities of blacks in the twentieth century will be assessed and some prognoses will be made about what they may reasonably expect from education in the twenty-first century. Like many other groups, blacks' educational opportunites have ebbed and flowed, depending upon the generosity, humanity and enlightened self-interest of individuals, groups and institutions not only external, but also internal, to them. These prognoses will take into consideration the imperative need for blacks to continue their commitment to realizing full citizen participation, self-fulfillment and economic well-being through education—especially in the face of wavering or declining external support.

It is well to call out here that blacks cannot participate meaningfully in the social compact and political covenant which ground a democratic republic without the benefit(s) of universal or public elementary and secondary education, as well as higher or postsecondary education in representative, if not proportional, numbers. Moreover, given the demographic projections for blacks and other minority groups in the population into the twenty-first century, the welfare of the nation's future can be assured only by adequately educating them.[10] Education and well-being are so symbiotically related that if recent negative trends were to continue, the truly disadvantaged could well be more than the inner-city underclass about which William Julius Wilson has written so ably and perceptively.[11]

The New Order of the Ages: The Early and Ongoing Recognition of the Importance of Education

In the first place, [the compatriots of the American Revolution] insisted with Montesquieu that the laws of education be relative to the forms of government; hence, while monarchies needed an education to status that would fix each class of the citizenry to its proper place in the social order, republics needed an education to virtue ["some proper combination of piety, civility, and learning"] that would motivate all men to choose public over private interest. . . .

Second, they argued for a truly American education, purged of all vestiges of older monarchical forms and dedicated to the creation of a cohesive and independent citizenry. . . .

Third, they urged a genuinely useful education, pointedly addressed to the improvement of the human condition. . . .

> Finally, they called for an exemplary education, through which America would instruct the world in the glories of liberty and learning. . . .
> No theme was so universally articulated during the early decades of the Republic as the need of a self-governing people for universal education.
>   Lawrence A. Cremin

The importance of education in the United States was recognized early,[12] and a great emphasis was placed on what has been labeled herein as its citizenship function. Its consumption function was seen more as an outcome of religious education and inculcation than an outcome of education in private or common schools. Indeed, the motive for literacy and education in colonial times was for reading the Bible and otherwise receiving religious training and values.[13] Although the production function has been predominantly emphasized since shortly after the mid-nineteenth century, the primary focus of this chapter will be on the citizenship function.

The Early Recognition of the Importance of Education

The promotion of a dialogic community was probably the reason the first three presidents of the United States—George Washington, John Adams and Thomas Jefferson—were especially interested in education. George Washington wanted to establish "some system of American education." James Thomas Flexner reports that Washington regretted to see

> . . . American students sent to Europe before their minds were formed and they had "correct ideas of the blessing of the country they leave." Not that he objected to foreign learning. He visualized importing to the United States "the best European professors." But he feared that young Americans might acquire in Europe (where he himself had never been) "habits of dissipation and extravagance," and also "principles unfriendly to the rights of man."[14]

Flexner further stated that Washington thought educational opportunities would be invaluable to "young men from all parts of the United States"[15] because

> in addition to preparation for the professions they intended to pursue, they should "get fixed in the principles of the Constitution, [and] understand the laws and the true interests and policy of their country." Furthermore, the students from the various regions would "by forming acquaintances with each other early in life," be cured of "those local prejudices and habitual jealousies

which, when carried to excess, are a never failing source of disquietude."[16]

Thus, Washington fully understood the critical importance of education in nation building. To underscore his commitment to education, he not only provided for a national university in his will, but also expressed regret that his farewell address did not deal with the issue of education. (Alexander Hamilton, in assisting Washington with his farewell address, suggested that the matter of education could be better dealt with in his eighth annual address, given on December 7, 1796, specifying proposals for the future welfare of the United States, rather than in his farewell address.[17])

John Adams was as enthusiastic about the importance of education as Washington. He saw it as a positive response to the negative condition of "humankind as irredeemably quarrelsome, perverse and illogical."[18] Adams thought education was the solution to this state of humankind, as did many of his enlightened contemporaries.

In writing about the first decade of the nineteenth century, James MacGregor Burns states: "Two things were necessary to create the republic of virtue, one of them obvious at the time, the other less clear. The first was education,"[19] the second was leadership.[20] Moreover, Burns reports Thomas Jefferson felt even before the beginning of the nineteenth century that the solution to the social and political conflicts of 1786 and 1787 "lay in better education of the people and in the free exchange of ideas."[21] Further, in discussing "the emergence of a common, uniform, public school system," Burns observes that it was Jefferson's firm conviction that "[i]f a nation expects to be ignorant and free, in a state of civilization, it expects what never was and never will be."[22] The great biographer of Jefferson, Dumas Malone, reports that the third president of the United States had an "undying faith in private learning and public education" and "advocated for half a century" the establishment in Virginia of a "full-bodied system of public education."[23] Jefferson thought that "popular or universal education was vital" to the classical republican goals of liberty and equality.[24]

However, popular or universal education is not necessitated equally by popular sovereignty and popular democracy. Popular or universal education may be a necessary, if not sufficient, condition of a popular democracy, but it is less required of popular sovereignty than of popular democarcy. Popular sovereignty does not require that the people or populace rule, but only that they have ultimate power or sovereignty. Joshua Miller has elegantly and persuasively made good use of the distinction between popular sovereignty and popular democracy in discussing the views of the Federalists, Alexander Hamilton and James Madison. Popular sovereignty is consistent with a strong, centralized national government, but popular democracy is not. Popular democracy requires "ongoing and active political participation of the people [trying] to limit governmental power so that ordinary people can understand and wield it."[25] However, if a strong, centralized national government rules over a democracy, then it is critical that ordinary people, including, of course, blacks, have a sound education in order to understand, wield or control power.[26]

The Ongoing, Critical Importance of Education

Jefferson prefigured Frank Lentricchia's "Provocations" in *Criticism and Social Change*, where Lentricchia begins:

> I can tell you what my book is about, at its polemical core, by citing a distinction of John Dewey's that I first encountered in the amazing meditative labyrinth Kenneth Burke called *Attitudes Toward History*. The distinction is between "education as a function of society" and "society as a function of education." In the end, that is a way of dividing the world between those who like it and those who do not.[27]

In other words, if education is a function of society and thus probably in a normal or congenial relationship with it, then there will be

> . . . roughly the irony that Michel Foucault extracts from the term—education will involve itself in a process of "normalization," of *making normal*, or ensuring that its pedagogical subjects will be trained . . . so that they will be happy, useful, productive, and safe subjects, in the social and political sense of the term: they will be cunningly "subjected."[28]

This puts negatively the socialization function of education. Still, no society can exist without a measure of order, which itself cannot exist without some measure of consensus, tolerance, mutual respect and understanding which, in turn, are the products of adaptation and socialization. Obviously, adaptation and socialization are frequently the products, if not the processes, of education. Indeed, a commonality of knowledge and information may create and nurture the circumstances and conditions necessary for a community, including a social compact and a political covenant.[29]

Education, whether it is a function of society or society is a funtion of it, appears to parallel, if not coincide with, Robert Hutchins' view that a democracy is a learning society.[30] He argues that an "educational system is determined by the convictions of the community about what the community needs,"[31] further maintaining that, "[i]f all men are to be free, then all men should have . . . [a liberal] education." [32]

Therefore, a democracy, more so than a republic or popular sovereignty, implies universal education. Republicanism certainly means that select citizens should have an adequate education to enable them to contribute to the common good. Indeed, by definition, republicanism entails representative government, and it presupposes that the ones who should have the highest level of education are those who actually represent and govern the populace.

Cass Sunstein of the University of Chicago Law School, in an administrative law scholarship award-winning article, has posited that a central commitment "of the republican conception . . . is a deliberative democracy . . ."[33] He writes:

> To the republicans, the role of politics was above all deliberation. Dialogue and discussion among the citizenry were critical features in the governmental process. . . .
> The republican conception carries with it a particular view of human nature; it assumes that through discussion people can, in their capacities as citizens, escape private interests and engage in pursuit of the public good. In this respect, political ordering is distinct from market ordering.[34]

To the extent that Sunstein's analysis of what he terms Madisonian-deliberative democracy has validity, it implies a high level of intelligence, knowledge and education among a politically involved citizenry. But Charles Beard's construction of the formation of the nation is closer to the truth than the implied great deliberative-dialogue interpretation of Sunstein's analysis.[35]

Yet, much may be learned from Sunstein's and others' reflections upon republicanism. Frank Michelman of Harvard Law School, in the November 1986 foreword to the *Harvard Law Review*'s annual examination of the United States Supreme Court's term, writes of the law and alludes to Robert Cover's earlier foreword[36] to the corresponding 1983 issue in which he advances the idea of a "paideic" community. Michelman observes:

> Such a community is formed by strong interpersonal bonding through shared commitment to a specific moral tradition and its contemporary elucidation. The work of elucidation is the community's *paideia*, through which the members find personal integrity and moral freedom. By their joint engagement in that work—of clarifying the history and the current meanings of their shared precepts—they constantly create their *"nomos"* or "normative universe."[37]

As one reflects upon the ideas of Sunstein, Cover and Michelman, one discerns that they are projecting and unquestionably asserting the imperial importance of a reasoned decisionmaking process. Although it is vulnerable to "jurisgenesis" or judicial imperialism, if one takes one's tack from Epictetus and Hutchins, this dialogic, deliberative view of law implies and requires a high level of reasoning and discourse from a democratic citizenry, and the un- or undereducated will be virtual outcasts from the activity of governance.

Obviously, universal education did not exist at the founding of the republic. But surely education of a sort was as important, if not more so, than property in the development of the ideas and notions which gave rise to the Declaration of Independence, the Articles of Confederation and that most remarkable of all politically-produced documents, the Constitution. Thus, during the celebration of the bicentennial of the Constitution in 1987 it was especially appropriate to recognize, no, to insist, upon the indispensability of education and learning, not necessarily formal or bureaucratic, for meaningful participation in a democracy and, perhaps, for self-fulfillment. Blacks have intuited or known this from their earliest days in colonial America/the United States. And so, it is important to turn to the history of the education of blacks since their transatlantic passage.

A History of Black Education

In the beginning there was no thought of educating the Negroes; yet the necessity to do so was always present. During the early part of the seventeenth century, Europeans and Africans, caught in the tide of empire, were joined in a system of economic interdependency—a system which would inevitably require that Africans would have to be educated and would aspire to become a part of a society that would encompass the two races.

Henry Allen Bullock

For all the talk of refuge and asylum, American notions of citizenship managed to transcend the barriers of class, ethnicity, religion, and even—with persisting unclarities—gender, but not the barriers of race. Blacks and Indians were excluded from citizenship and hence from education for self-government. They were subjected instead to a demeaning education by the dominant white community that barred them from participating in public affairs. In the treatment they were accorded, the virtue of the Republic was sorely tested, and found wanting.

Lawrence A. Cremin

It is clear that racial issues tend to evolve in cyclical fashion. . . . [B]lack parents have struggled with the integrated-separate school dilemma in three periods: in 1795-1815; in the period before the Civil War; and, of course, in the post-*Brown* era.

Derrick A. Bell, Jr.

Before and especially after the Civil War, blacks were obsessed with education; indeed, they had a frenzy for book learning. This obsession and frenzy were so feared that they were thwarted by many southern states before the Civil War through severe laws which prohibited the education of slaves, and after the Civil War through violence, intimidation, arson and segregation or the "separate but equal" doctrine. Since the "separate but equal" doctrine was overturned in education in the *Brown* decision, the efforts of blacks to obtain an education have been impeded by white supremacist assaults upon their native intelligence as well as upon the predominantly black educational institutions which have sought to serve them. Thus, throughout the black experience in the United States, white supremacists have used the law, the courts and other social/political institutions to block or impair the educational opportunities of blacks.

Henry Allen Bullock, in his Bancroft Award-winning *A History of Negro Education in the South: From 1619 to the Present*, has documented how blacks effectively circumvented the legal obstacles to their education during slavery.[38] Confirming their humanity, blacks secretly obtained education before the Civil War. Indeed, Bullock observes that by "stealth" and "sentimental attachments between masters and selected slaves," the *"hidden passage* widened"[39] through which some slaves "acquire[d] some degree of literacy, develop[ed] an unplanned-for leadership structure and thereby experience[d] upward mobility within Southern society."[40] Bullock further maintains that "[a]ll the slaves could not be efficiently utilized, as the rational system required, unless they were trained in ways that the system prohibited."[41]

Reconfirming their humanity and commitment to education, blacks were very instrumental after the Civil War in establishing and spreading public education in the South. W.E.B. DuBois points out in *The Souls of Black Folk* that with significant assistance from missionaries, blacks established "schools to train Negro teachers" and "in a single generation they [historically black colleges] put thirty thousand black teachers in the South; they wiped out the illiteracy of the majority of the black people of the land, and they made Tuskegee possible."[42]

However, the post-Reconstruction betrayal of blacks through Jim Crowism and the fraudulent "separate but equal" doctrine in education as well as in other public services and accommodations not only forced blacks to seek education "under crippling limitations,"[43] but also resulted in the grossly inadequate education that many of them received.[44] The denial of equal educational opportunities to blacks was essential for maintaining them in second-class citizenship, excluding them from the social compact, and breaching their rights under the political covenant.[45]

A brief chronicle of the history of the education of blacks sheds much light upon how poorly blacks have fared in the social compact and political covenant of the United States. The report card on the nation's treatment of blacks ranges from fair to unsatisfactory to outrageous, reflecting the ebb and flow of the tides of racism, white supremacy and other social, economic, cultural and political forces which affect that treatment. The soundness of this observation has withstood the vicissitudes of time since colonial days.

From Colonial Days to the Civil War

In his *History of Negro Education*, Bullock observes that slavery was a "system of economic interdependence devoid of personal sentiment and emotion."[46] Southern plantations were organized along the same lines as business enterprises and attempted to use the same means to protect their "capital"—including slaves. Although the "rationality" of this economic system soon began to break down, it "structured master-class relations . . . almost solely along functional lines: the profitable purchase, production and utilization of slave labor." [47] The profitable utilization of slave labor required that slaves acquire a degree (even if very modest) of skills and training, which necessitated some measure of education.

The most common form of education for slaves pertained to crafts. Bullock notes:

> As the power of individual planters expanded, many plantations tended to become self-sustaining worlds, and the slaves trained for effective service to the rational order came to have higher value. The food consumed, clothing worn, tools used, and houses inhabited were all produced by slave labor. This type of development caused an increase in the complexity of slave duties, and rising slave prices very quickly reflected this fact.[48]

Bullock further observes:

> The informality and permissiveness inherent in these practices [craft education] reduced the rigors of plantation life and produced leadership within the Negro population. It fostered a higher self-concept among the slaves and, because of the many manumissions that resulted, led to the rise of an aggressive and mildly secure middle class within the free Negro population.[49]

Many slaves took upon themselves the forbidden task of learning to read and write. They employed various subterfuges to this end. Bullock points out that foreign missions formed "the nucleus of a movement for formal schooling among free Negroes and slaves."[50] Quakers and Presbyterians were particularly active in the education of slaves and free blacks. The basically positive and upbeat approach of Bullock towards this subject is evidenced by his further observation that "[as] early as 1620, when the slave trade began, English clergymen had expressed an interest in extending religious training to those 'in bondage beyond the seas' and had made some progress in this direction."[51] This seems to indicate that there were more than economic forces driving the education of blacks.

Two additional observations should be made before proceeding to the next subsection. First, blacks faced the separate/integrated school dilemma as early as the late 1780s. For example, although public schools in Boston "neither barred nor segregated" black children, "by 1790, racial insults and mistreatment had driven out all but three or four black children."[52] The black Revolutionary War veteran and community leader, Prince Hall, recognized the problem as integrated schools, as Bell reports: "In 1787, Hall petitioned the Massachusetts legislature seeking an 'African' school because, in his words, 'we . . . must fear for our rising offspring to see them in ignorance in a land of gospel light.' "[53] Hall's petition was rejected on the grounds of "the additional expense involved in maintaining special schools for blacks," and the School Committee insisted "that in the existing schools, ample provision [was] made for the education of all."[54] Although a separate school was established in 1806, dissatisfaction among blacks continued so that by mid-century "a suit to desegregate Boston's public schools was filed in state court."[55]

Bell reports the following about this prophetic situation:

> Using arguments in 1850 remarkably similar to those that the Supreme Court would hear and accept a century later, Charles Sumner, abolitionist lawyer and later United States senator, aided by Robert Morris, one of the nation's first black lawyers, maintained that the black schools were inferior in equipment and staffing; that they were inconvenient for those black children living closer to white schools; that neither state nor federal law supported segregated schools; and finally that: "The separation of the schools, so far from being for the benefit of both races, is an injury to both. It tends to create a feeling of degradation in the blacks and of prejudice and uncharitableness in the whites."[56]

The decision in *Roberts* v. *City of Boston*[57] rejected all of these arguments, maintaining that "prejudice, if it exists, is not created by law, and probably cannot be changed by law,"[58] thus in effect enunciating for the first time the "separate but equal" doctrine, prefiguring *Plessy* v. *Ferguson*. [59] Black leaders agitated against this decision and got school desegregation through the Massachusetts legislature, but state officials complied with the desegregation law by closing black schools and dismissing black teachers.[60]

Finally, an extensive quotation from this author's comment on *Between Two Worlds: A Profile of Negro Higher Education* by Frank Bowles and Frank DeCosta will end this section:

> The first contribution the Bowles-DeCosta study makes to the issue of black education is that it corrects, in the way much black history is preoccupied with correcting, mis- or noninformation about the education of blacks prior to the Civil War. It is important to know that there were 28 acknowledged black graduates of American colleges before the Civil War. This sounds like a small number, but it is not so small if one realizes that in 1820 only 234,000 blacks were free and in 1860 the number had grown to only 488,000. The figure becomes even more noteworthy if it is realized that in this early period very few schools would admit blacks, although two—Oberlin and Berea—were especially noted for their nondiscriminatory policies. A number of higher educational institutions were established especially for training blacks, three of which have survived—Cheyney State and Lincoln in Pennsylvania, and Wilberforce in Ohio.[61]

From Reconstruction to the "Separate but Equal" Doctrine

The effort to abolish slavery and its vestiges through the Thirteenth, Fourteenth and Fifteenth Amendments and their enforcing civil rights and other Reconstruction acts was accompanied by an expansion of public education in the South. This all helped project the principle of equality to the prominence that the Bill of Rights to the original Constitution had given freedom or liberty. The intense desire of blacks for book learning and their obsession with education were sources of not only self-help but also of inspiration for others, especially for missionaries from the North who lent a special helping hand to the education of blacks. This included the establishment of colleges and universities for blacks which, for the most part, operated well into the twentieth century as normal schools or advanced secondary institutions.[62] (These commendable efforts were, in part, undermined by the infamous "separate but equal" doctrine, which was applied to education at the end of the nineteenth century.[63])

Bullock gives much credit to northern missionary societies and associations for the development of educational institutions for southern blacks after the Civil War. Along with the Bureau of Refugees, Freedmen, and Abandoned Lands, popularly known as the Freedmen's Bureau, Bullock credits "the direct responsibility for establishing the freedmen's educational system in the South . . . [to] the strongly motivated people who composed the active teams of the benevolent and religious groups of the North."[64] Southern blacks, however, began to pressure the missionaries and agents for more schools. Although the bulk of the funds and teachers came from the northern missions and the Freedmen's Bureau, when these two institutions did not respond, black communities often organized their own schools. Bullock makes a most important observation about the source of educational funds when he reports:

> In all fairness to the freedmen, it must be said that they carried a significant share of their own burden. They contributed $672,989 in taxes and tuition through the Bureau and donated approximately $500,000 through their church organizations. In doing this, Negroes established a practice that was to be repeated less than a half century later: the tendency to match funds given in the interest of establishing schools for them.[65]

The "Republican-Negro regimes" of the early Reconstruction era drafted state constitutions that gave impetus to and strengthened publicly supported schools in the South.[66] However, as time passed and "Redemption" Democrats regained control of southern state legislatures, they did not reciprocate the earlier thoughtfulness and generosity. The funding and extension of educational opportunities to blacks were grossly unequal. Only three southern states made any of their Morrill Act (1862) monies available to blacks. The 1890 Morrill Act, however, specifically provided that such state funds should be "equitably divided." It also permitted separate funding, thus anticipating and sanctioning the "separate but equal" doctrine.

Although the North, especially through missionaries, other philanthropic leaders and organizations, and Republican leaders of the Reconstruction period, sought to do justice to blacks or freedmen, the consolidation of Jim Crowism in the 1880s and early 1890s culminated in the Supreme Court's 1896 decision in *Plessy* v. *Ferguson*.[67] The Court, alluding to the Boston school segregation decison, held that officially separating Americans on the basis of race did not violate the Equal Protection Clause of the Fourteenth Amendment. Justice Harlan was the lone dissenter, opining that "our Constitution is colorblind" and that "[t]he thin disguise of 'equal' accommodations for passengers in railroad coaches will not mislead any one, nor atone for the wrong this day done."[68]

Nonetheless, Justice Harlan's dissenting opinion in *Plessy* did not prevent him from writing the majority opinion in *Cumming* v. *Richmond County Board of Education*, holding that the "separate but equal" doctrine applied to education and, thus, upholding or condoning the closing of a black, publicly supported high school in Augusta,

Georgia, because public funds were inadequate to support both it and a high school for white students.[69] He further observed that white students should not have to suffer for this fiscal exigency. This "subtle and ingenious" analysis or "verbal criticism" not only "sacrificed the substance and spirit of the recent [Fourteenth] Amendment," including the supposititious "separate but equal" doctrine glossed upon it, but also symbolized and projected the betrayal of blacks well into the twentieth century.[70] Thus, in the very first decision applying the "separate but equal" doctrine to education, the Court condoned obviously unequal educational facilities for blacks, as well as no facilities at all for them at the high school level.

The "Separate but Equal" Doctrine until Brown

Indeed, much of Reconstruction policy was essentially educational, based on the generally held northern assumption that the best way ultimately to regenerate the South would be through the wide dissemination of the northern version of the American *paideia*. This was deemed particularly relevant to the freedmen, for whom the very act of emancipation had carried "the sacred promise *to educate*. . . ." And, in this century no phenomenon appeared more forcefully or universally than the eagerness of southern blacks to obtain an education. Booker T. Washington described it years later as a "veritable fever."

Lawrence A. Cremin

At the beginning of the twentieth century, the Conference for Education in the South (also known as the Southern Education Board) was the dominant educational force in the South. The conference led in the development and growth of industrial education for blacks. Manual training and industrial education became the standard—if not just about the only—kind of education available to blacks. Black schooling remaining inferior. Bullock writes:

In all the South as late as 1910, there was not a single eighth-grade rural Negro public school. No Negro public school, rural or urban, was approved for two years of high school work. The schools, such as they were, operated for an average of four months out of each year. They were run by teachers whose average training was that of an eighth-grade student and whose annual salary in many states was less than $150 on the average.[71]

Bullock completes his description of the first thirty years of blacks' educational experience by observing:

By the third decade of the twentieth century, a complete financial structure for educating Negroes along special lines had been laid. Adequate support for building those rural schools that aimed at training young Negroes for a better rural life had been assured. More uniform standards and closer supervision of these [elementary and secondary] schools had been provided, and the South's fears that these changes would lead to social equality between the races had been reduced by placing supervision of the work ultimately in the hands of the white school officials. The private Negro colleges that had received the blessings of the Southern Education Board, but whose future was still uncertain, had been given greater economic security and had even learned that this security increased in proportion to the emphasis they placed upon industrial education.[72]

As indicated above, until thirty years into the twentieth century, the educational opportunities for blacks were very limited. Few high schools in the South or elsewhere provided education for blacks through the twelfth grade. Of course, where blacks could attend high schools in the North, they usually could do so through the twelfth grade. The predominantly or historically black colleges, principally in the South, filled the gap in part by incorporating into their curricula many components of elementary and particularly secondary education.[73] These colleges expressed, and were responses to, the continued frenzy of blacks for book learning and education, although they had limited resources and means for its satisfaction.

However, early in the fourth decade of the twentieth century, lawyers and others associated with Howard University and its school of law began a concerted assault upon the "separate but equal" doctrine. Charles Hamilton Houston, former vice-dean at Howard University Law School, conceived the strategy for eliminating the "separate but equal" doctrine, or at least making sure its enforcement and operation complied more strictly with its theory. Indeed, in the early 1930s, as a result of discussions within the National Association for the Advancement of Colored People (hereinafter NAACP), Houston developed more fully his notion that black lawyers should engineer social changes beneficial to blacks. He thought early on that the assault upon the "separate but equal" doctrine should begin by seeking to get blacks into graduate and professional education, particularly law. His sound reasoning was that judges would more readily recognize that the educational opportunities of blacks in law school were not equal to those of whites than they might do so in other educational areas.

The first case in this arena, a 1936 decision, is *Pearson* v. *Murray*,[74] where the petitioner, Donald Murray, sought admission to the University of Maryland Law School. Maryland sought to defend its refusal to provide a legal education for blacks in Maryland on the grounds that it provided funds for black law students to attend law school outside the state. But the Maryland Court of Appeals decided that this did not constitute equal opportunity for blacks, and directed Murray's admission to the University of Maryland Law School. This was an important victory and precedent, and was a source for encouraging an attack on such provisions for professional education in other states. However, since it was the supreme court of Maryland that handed down the decision concerning the admission of Murray, it had precedential value only in Maryland. An opportunity to bring the issue into the federal court system, and ultimately to the United States Supreme Court, would be the most desirable development.

This opportunity arose when Lloyd Gaines sought admission to the University of Missouri Law School and the state court maintained that providing a state subvention for Gaines to attend law school outside Missouri satisfied the "separate but equal" requirement. Gaines found this position to be unacceptable, and appealed the decision to the United States Supreme Court, where the first important blow against a form of the "separate but equal" doctrine was struck in 1938 in *Missouri ex rel. Gaines* v. *Canada*.[75] The Supreme Court held that it was not sufficient for Missouri to provide subsidies or funds for Gaines to attend law school outside the state. The "separate but equal" doctrine required that the opportunity to attend law school be made available in Missouri. Gaines was admitted to the University of Missouri Law School, but mysteriously disappeared and has never been heard from or accounted for since.

This development was a vindication of Houston's "program of litigation" strategy. Taking one step at a time, he felt that courts would be more willing not only to recognize the denial of equal educational opportunity in professional and graduate schools, but also to demand black students' admission into them than into elementary and secondary schools. Houston also anticipated Gunnar Myrdal's rank order of discrimination, in which Myrdal hypothesized that elementary and secondary education, as well as marriage, would be two areas in which whites would most resist mixing racially with blacks.[76]

Houston began his assault on the "separate but equal" doctrine in graduate and professional education, but the great *Brown I*[77] decision, handed down in 1954, was in the arena of elementary and secondary education. (Paradoxically, from 1954 until 1978, when the Court decided the *Bakke* case,[78] hardly a single significant decision in the educational arena concerning postsecondary education was made by the Supreme Court. This complicates and compounds the tension between society's most resistant area to race mixing and the central importance of elementary and secondary education in a popular democracy.) Following some preliminary and encouraging successes in graduate and professional schools, the NAACP launched a full-scale assault upon the denial of professional and graduate educational opportunity for blacks. The case that laid the predicate for the success of *Brown I* was *Sweatt* v. *Painter*.[79] The latter involved the effort of the state of Texas to avoid integrating or desegregating the school of law at the University of Texas by establishing a physically separate law school for blacks almost overnight in the library of the supreme court of Texas in Austin. This abortive effort at blocking the desegregation of postsecondary education had the unintended effect of creating Texas Southern University in Houston, where the overnight law school established in Austin was later moved.[80]

However, the Court did not countenance Texas' effort to avoid desegregation. It maintained that there were many intangible factors, difficult to measure, that made legal education creditable, such as the reputation of a faculty, the experience of a school's administration, the position and prominence of its alumni, its standing in the community, and its traditions and prestige. This made it virtually impossible for Texas to provide substantial equality in the educational opportunities of blacks so long as they were denied admission to the school of law at the University of Texas.

This decision led almost inevitably to *Brown I*, particularly if it is noted that on the same day as the *Sweatt* v. *Painter* decision, the Court held that the graduate school at the University of Oklahoma could not meet its equal protection requirement by admitting George W. McLaurin while cordoning off and assigning him to a classroom seat in a row specified for black students.[81] Thus, Earl Warren, who was appointed by the Republican President Dwight D. Eisenhower, near the end of his first term as Chief Justice of the United States Supreme Court, stated that separate educational facilities were inherently unequal. This decision inaugurated what Philip Kurland calls the "egalitarian revolution."[82]

From _Brown_ to the Present

Brown I was a turning point in the civil rights struggle in the United States. The 1954 opinion of Chief Justice Warren for the Court galvanized the hopes and aspirations of black Americans. Indeed, the egalitarian revolution inaugurated by *Brown I* was initially concerned with doing justice to, and vindicating the rights of, blacks. But it later became a universal rights revolution, moving beyond the civil rights struggle that had been defined as principally identified or concerned with the rights of blacks. (The civil rights movement, having been transmogrified into a universal rights movement, displaced blacks from its core and ironically ended up attacking them and their institutions with the very precedents and rhetoric of the civil rights struggle.)

Although the Court adjudged in 1954 that separate educational facilities were inherently inferior, and thus in violation of the Equal Protection Clause, it nevertheless did not immediately decree the abolition of the separation of the races in the schools. The Court asked the lawyers involved in the case for briefs on how to implement the decision in the light of more than a half century of social customs and practices which conformed with the "separate but equal" doctrine. In 1955, the Court decided *Brown II* , enforcing the judgment of *Brown I* and decreeing admission to "public schools on a racially nondiscriminatory basis with all deliberate speed."[83] The formula of "all deliberate speed" sought to take into account the political and social realities of the South, [84] but this meant that blacks' rights were not enforced immediately, an example of what Richard Wasserstrom calls conceptual institutional racism.[85]

The decision was massively resisted. Governor Orval Faubus of Arkansas, for example, used the National Guard to prevent the implementation of a federal court order to desegregate the schools in Little Rock.[86] The pace of desegregation was slow from the mid-fifties through the late sixties. Many states across the South, in resisting desegregation, invoked the idea of "interposition" and others to avoid desegregation. Prince Edward County, Virginia, where one of the initial *Brown I* cases was filed in 1951, closed its public schools to avoid desegregation, which the Court held, nine years after *Brown II*, that it could not do constitutionally.[87]

In the late 1960s the Court finally began to tire of the various devices and subterfuges for avoiding the *Brown* decision, resulting in a series of opinions and judgments in which it struck down "freedom of choice," "free transfer," and other evasive strategies or question-begging "persuasive definitions," indicating that it wanted more results in bringing down the barriers separating the races in education.[88] The South made some significant progress while the North, as a result of the migration of blacks to metropolitan areas and white flight from the central city, became racially more separated than the South. A spate of decisions regarding intra-/interdistrict, de facto/de jure segregation in the North percolated through the Court, ventilating the ideas of busing, interdistrict or metropolitan remedies, and the proper racial mix of students.[89]

The controversy associated with intergration/separation has been so intense that it has caused scholars such as Derrick Bell and others [90] to question the desirability of the *Brown* decision itself. These critics of *Brown* have stated that it implicitly slanders blacks by maintaining that they can only get an equal education in the presence of, or in association with, whites.

In *And We Are Not Saved: The Elusive Quest for Racial Justice*, Bell criticizes school desegregation litigation as focusing more upon the litigators' perception or conception of the abstract interest of their clients than upon the the clients' concrete desires and needs. He calls out once more that civil rights lawyers got so enmeshed in the rhetoric and dynamics of desegregation/integration that the "intended beneficiaries [were] forgotten," if not lost, long ago.[91] In setting forth his interest-convergence thesis about civil rights laws and litigation in *Shades of Brown: New Perspectives on School Desegregation*, Bell observes that "remedies for racial discrimination . . . tend to secure or advance the interests of the society's upper classes."[92] He further writes:

> The interest of blacks in achieving racial equality will be accommodated only when it converges with the interests of whites: however, the fourteenth amendment, standing alone, will not authorize a judicial remedy providing effective racial equality for blacks where the remedy sought threatens the superior societal status of middle- and upper-class whites.[93]

Citing and quoting from Laurence Tribe's *American Constitutional Law*, Bell writes, " '[j]udicial rejection of the 'separate but equal' talisman seems to have been accompanied by a potentially troublesome lack of sympathy for racial separateness as a possible expression of group solidarity.' "[94]

While the "integrated-separate school dilemma" played itself out in both the North and South, a range of individuals and groups, unmindful of, or indifferent or hostile to, the needs, interests and rights of blacks, insidiously began to usurp or borrow the rhetoric of civil rights to advance their claims and later to oppose those of blacks. This has occasioned what this writer earlier termed "an ominous pincer movement." In May 1974, in a lecture at Harvard Law School celebrating the twentieth anniversary of *Brown I*, this author stated the following:

> Disingenuous rhetoric about equality and integration has placed the educational opportunities of Blacks in an ominous pincer movement. One force is converging upon Blacks in the name of equal protection and in the form of an assault against special minority admission programs in white higher educational institutions. The other force is converging upon Blacks in the name of integration and in the form of an assault against predominantly Black public higher educational institutions. . . . Thus, at the same time the survival of predominantly Black higher educa-

tional institutions is being threatened, the gateway for Blacks into white higher educational institutions may be closing.[95]

The Case for Black Colleges: Attacks and Defense

The case for and attacks on black colleges were set forth in *Black Institutions of Higher Learning: Inadvertent Victims or Necessary Sacrifices?* and *Black Colleges as Instruments of Affirmative Action.*[96] Ironically, the initial major legal threat to black colleges resulted from the NAACP Legal Defense Fund bringing a comprehensive class action suit against the Department of Health, Education and Welfare (HEW) to require the department to enforce Title VI of the Civil Rights Act of 1964. The litigation (styled *Adams* v. *Richardson* , 356 F.Supp. 92 (D.D.C. 1977)), was designed to disestablish the dual system of public higher education as well as elementary and secondary education by forcing HEW to cut off federal funds to those states which had not complied with guidelines it had issued in the 1966-67 school year.

In the early phases of the litigation, all of the parties apparently felt that any institution which was racially identifiable, that is, predominantly black, was separate and thus perpetuated the dual system which was to be eliminated "root and branch." This ominous situation was described as follows:

> Title VI of the 1964 Civil Rights Act posed the most serious threat to the institutions [black higher educational] through the *Adams* v. *Richardson* litigation. Because of the Friend of the Court brief of the National Association for Equal Opportunity in Higher Education (NAFEO) prepared by Professor Herbert O. Reid, Charles Hamilton Houston Distinguished Professor of Law at Howard University, the most damaging threat to the survival of Black colleges was averted.
>
> The *Adams* Court (United States Court of Appeals for the District of Columbia Circuit), in affirming the District Court's order regarding the commencement of compliance proceedings under Title VI . . . and in response to Professor Reid's NAFEO brief, decreed that, in the "desegregation or the integration process, the historically Black higher educational institutions should not bear the major burden and that their 'special problems,' as well as those of minority students, should be taken into account."[97]

As the case became increasingly entangled in the web of the judiciary and the bureaucracy, it did not just linger but became enlarged with the addition of the interests of the Women's Equity Action League and the intervention of the National Federation of the Blind. After observing that "[t]he most difficult problems in educational desegregation exist in the area of higher education" and the " 'defendants' basic argument that this court had 'lost sight of the specific goals of the initial suit,' " District Judge John H. Pratt on December 11, 1987, understandably dismissed the suit on the grounds that the plaintiffs and intervenors "lack[ed] standing to continue this litigation." This is another paradoxical development, since the suit had become sensitive about and supportive of black colleges, although, as has been the case with so much of the early civil rights struggle, it had been broadened substantially and unquestionably did lose sight of its initial purpose. Though "reverse discrimination" suits are still being brought against black colleges, the legal threat to their survival has been attenuated.[98]

The case for black colleges is based upon their functions and the fact that, with the adoption of the Reconstruction Amendments, the Constitution and fundamental or constitutional law and public policy were tilted in favor of blacks.[99] This author's *Black Institutions of Higher Learning* sets forth their functions as follows:

> Four functions peculiar and unique to predominantly Black colleges are that they continue to provide creditable models of success, psycho-socially congenial settings, special-group-oriented transitional educational enclaves, and insurances against a generally declining interest in the education of Blacks. However, I now posit three additional functions which are important, but are not necessarily unique and peculiar to these institutions. The three additional functions [are:] provide political-economic resources for their communities, express and contribute to educational pluralism by widening freedom of choice for both Black and white students, and discover, store, and preserve the Black cultural heritage.[100]

White supremacy and blacks' internalization of racism limit not only the scope of support and encouragement for black colleges, but also blacks as well as whites from understanding that the Reconstruction Amendments tilted the Constitution in favor of blacks, which Justice Miller understood ever so well when he wrote the following in the first decision of the United States Supreme Court interpreting the amendments:

> We repeat, then, in the light of this recapitulation of events, almost too recent to be called history, but which are familiar to us all; and on the most casual examination of the language of these amendments, no one can fail to be impressed with the one pervading purpose found in them all, lying at the foundation of each, and without which none of them would have been even suggested; we mean the freedom of the slave race, the security and firm establishment of that freedom, and the protection of the newly-made freeman and citizen from the oppressions of those who had for-

merly exercised unlimited dominion over him. It is true that only the fifteenth amendment, in terms, mentions the negro [sic] by speaking of his color and his slavery. But it it just as true that each of the other articles was addressed to the grievances of that race, and designed to remedy them as the fifteenth.[101]

The epigraph that follows explains succinctly why the above construction of the amendments has not controlled constitutional law jurisprudence and United States public policy, nor limited attacks upon affirmative action, which will now be discussed briefly. [102]

Attacks on Affirmative Action

[T]he problems [of affirmative action] do not seem to me to be really legal in anything but a rather narrow and technical sense. Rather, they are social, philosophical, and moral problems of our society, which, insofar as they can be resolved by governmental action—and I think governmental action is important—may well be better resolved by legislative action than by the courts. Congress has the power—certainly as to blacks—under section five of the fourteenth amendment and it may well be that the congressional power . . . under the commerce clause, extends to other racial minorities as well.

Erwin N. Griswold

A further paradox of the black experience in the emergence of desegregation law is that just as graduate and professional school cases laid the predicate for the *Brown I* school desegregation decision, elementary and secondary school cases such as *Green* v. *County School Board* and *Swann* v. *Charlotte-Mecklenburg Board of Education* laid the constitutional predicate and basis for affirmative action in general, and in higher education in particular. The cases, just as affirmative action itself, were driven by the goal of effectiveness and results in reversing discrimination.

Green implicitly and *Swann* explicitly decided that "benign" racial classifications could be a necessary and, thus, proper requirement for occasioning the affirmative obligation of a de jure segregated school system to desegregate.[103] Chief Justice Warren Burger persuasively argued that just as race had to be taken into account in determining a violation of the Equal Protection Clause, so too it may be required in shaping a remedy. This should be kept in mind when one reflects upon the *Bakke* decision. The Court held in *Bakke* that race might be taken into consideration in the admission process to obtain a diverse student body, but not through the mechanism of rigid quotas. The former dean of Harvard Law School and United States Solicitor General, Erwin N.

Griswold, wrote the following about the judgment: "Having come out in support of the *Bakke* judgment, basically on social and moral grounds, but with, I believe, an adequate legal foundation, I will now say that it leaves me with a feeling of profound unease."[104] Although taking race into account understandably caused Griswold's "profound unease," it is noteworthy that he thought that all should meet the responsibilities to address positively and deal effectively with the predicament of blacks because "we are all members of society." This is the short answer to those who oppose affirmative action.

Affirmative action today cannot be disassociated from the over 250 years of slavery and more than a century of second-class citizenship that blacks have experienced in this country. It is, at best, a rationalization and, at worst, a callous capitulation to racism and a selfish unconcern for the well-being of blacks to say that today's generation of whites has absolutely no responsibilities or obligations growing out of the past oppression of blacks.[105] This is akin to an heir today saying that he/she may inherit property free and clear of the debts and obligations of deceased benefactors. Children cannot take property free and clear of the debts their parents and forebears have incurred to obtain it, and for which it has been used to secure other obligations. Moreover, many of the benefits that white society enjoys today have been procured through unjust enrichment obtained not only at the expense of the labor and to the harm of blacks, but also in clear violation of the Thirteenth, Fourteenth and Fifteenth Amendments, and the civil rights acts of the Reconstruction era. Blacks have been unjustly excluded from employment in, and admission to, many white educational institutions, especially postsecondary, throughout their history in this country. It is most unreasonable and irresponsible to think that this exclusion or discrimination can be corrected without taking aggressive and affirmative action. Affirmative action is essential for the reversal of exclusion and discrimination, and the achievement of an integrated and just society.

The Expansion And Contraction of Educational Opportunities for Blacks

The Educational Opportunities of Blacks: Twentieth-Century Assessment

Blacks entered the twentieth century having wiped out illiteracy among a substantial portion of their numbers. This and the thirty thousand teachers trained principally in predominantly black postsecondary educational institutions were sources of pride for W.E.B. DuBois and many others. However, the forces which were solidifying the second-class citizenship of blacks stymied this progress.

The educational achievement of blacks improved steadily throughout most of the century, particularly with thousands of blacks taking advantage of the GI Bill of Rights, which was essentially an educational subsidy for returning World War II veterans. World War II enlightened the United States about the rest of the world and the important leadership role it must play in it, not the least of which was encouraging and expediting worldwide decolonization. The United States could hardly do this while treating its own black citizens as colonial subjects, many of whom had made the supreme sacrifice in the armed struggle against Nazism and the Axis powers.

The overturn of the "separate but equal" doctrine which took place within a decade after the end of the war, and the "egalitarian revolution" initiated by *Brown*, resulted in desegregation not only in education, but also in public places and accommodations as well as in the electoral/political process. Of course, all of these developments were reinforced and strengthened by the Civil Rights Acts of 1964, 1965 and 1968, which dealt respectively with desegregation/nondiscrimination in federally assisted programs, public accommodations, public schools and interstate commerce; voting rights; and housing. The quality of life and the participation of blacks in all sectors of the American economy, society and politics improved considerably as a result. But, paradoxically, the expanded opportunity and mobility emanating from the dismantling of many racial barriers have led to the development of the physical isolation of a significant sector of the black community, one now dubbed the "underclass."[106] It is concentrated principally in the inner cities and ghettoes of major urban communities throughout the country.

The isolation of the underclass and the increasing emergence of inadequately educated and trained blacks, particularly males, have brought to the forefront problems which appear to be intractable. The physical isolation can be corrected substantially only by reintroducing a critical mass of working- and middle-class blacks into these communities. The unemployment level for black males has reduced the number of marriageable men, increasing significantly the number of single female-headed households, and resulting in many impoverished families with inadequate resources, particularly a shortage of positive male role models for young black males. A vicious cycle or downward spiral has gained momentum, which can only be braked by massive efforts to improve the elementary and secondary education delivered to the young men and women of inner-city schools.

The situation just described has caused some to believe that desegregation or, more accurately, integration, has contributed substantially to the isolation of roughly one-third of the black community and the undermining of indigenous institutions, all with significant adverse effect. However, these unintended consequences should not undermine *Brown*, which is the capstone of the "egalitarian revolution." Indeed, were *Brown* to be undermined or eroded seriously, the entire structure of civil and equal rights could be weakened, if not collapsed. *Brown* should never have been construed or interpreted to mean that blacks could only get an equal education in the presence of whites. Yet, in many instances, because of white supremacy and racism, blacks could experience equal facilities and resources only where there was a significant white presence.

This assessment cannot be completed without a brief statistical sketch of the educational achievement problems of blacks. Virtually every index for measuring blacks' educational well-being, from literacy and school attendance to level of achievement and graduation rates, has improved steadily throughout most of the twentieth century. The first decade of the century did witness the tail end of a steep decline in most of these measures from about 1890 to 1910. The most disappointing period has been from 1976 to the present, though. Yet, except for the distressing difficulties of black males, educational improvement has slowed down or leveled off; not declined. Indeed, in the area of high school completion rates, even black males have shown a greater rate of increase, 62.3 percent to 72.1 percent between 1976 and 1986, than comparable figures for black females, 71.8 percent to 80.2 percent.

The postsecondary arena has been most discouraging since the mid-1970s. The percentage of black faculty declined from 4.4 percent in 1975 to 4.1 in 1985. Thirty-four thousand fewer black males participated in postsecondary education in 1986 than in 1976. The production of most postsecondary degrees, from the bachelor's degree through the doctorate, has seen a decline, especially since the mid-1980s. The percentage declines between 1977 and 1985 were 1.8 percent for the bachelor's degree, 33.7 percent for the master's, and 26.8 percent for the doctorate. Virtually all of the declines were linked to black males, for black females were slowly but steadily improving in most of these categories. Despite an increase in the young adult black population, blacks earned fewer degrees in 1985 than in 1977 at all degree levels, except for professional degrees, for example M.D. and J.D.

As one reflects upon the education of blacks in the United States, one cannot but be troubled by the empirical fact that the society either has refused to provide, or has given only grudgingly, assistance and resources to blacks to obtain an education. This has been true from colonial days to the Civil War, from Reconstruction to the application of the "separate but equal" doctrine to education in 1899, from the latter date to *Brown* in 1954, and from *Brown* to the present.

The Educational Opportunities of Blacks: Twenty-First Century Prognosis

As the United States moves toward the twenty-first century, demographics project a significantly higher percentage of the population and especially the work force being comprised of minorities than is the situation at the end of the 1980s. However, the mid-eighties saw thirty-four thousand fewer black males attending postsecondary education than the mid-seventies, and three hundred fewer black Ph.D.s graduating than at the beginning of the eighties. This deteriorating enrollment of blacks in postsecondary education, especially the decline in the number of blacks earning doctorates, is an ominous development. It threatens the national weal, because nearly one out of every three active workers who will have to support the social security system in the future may come from minority groups, with blacks constituting a majority of these.

Thus, if large numbers of blacks are not well-educated, productive workers, they will impair the economic competitiveness, political stability and national security of the United States. Higher education must recommit itself seriously to advancing equal educational opportunity by supporting affirmative action and other programs designed to maintain and increase minority group participation. The claim that affirmative action constitutes "reverse discrimination" and helps only the black middle class is a most destructive and racially insensitive stance. Affirmative action not only reverses or remedies past and present discrimination, but it also creates and expands the black middle class in the face of a wavering and, sometimes, erratic commitment to racial equality.

The lack of, or insufficient, self-esteem seems insidiously and intractably to thwart black progress in higher education as well as in many other areas of life in the United States. Self-esteem is indispensable for successful achievement in higher education and for productive lives in the political economy of the society. Unfortunately, too many blacks continue to define or esteem themselves according to how external forces, institutions, and individuals or groups view and treat them in the society. To the extent that the social, political and economic systems take blacks seriously and make special efforts to bring them into the mainstream, they inspire and reinforce self-esteem while overcoming or attenuating self-doubt. This is especially the case in elementary, secondary and postsecondary education.

The forces of neglect, indifference, and even hostility, which have done so much to undermine blacks' self-esteem generally, have had their greatest impact on black males, giving rise to a "new black male morbidity" of disproportionately high rates of school failure and drop-out, joblessness, unwed fatherhood, criminal and violent behavior, and premature death. Educational systems, including their kindergarten through twelfth grade and postsecondary components, can significantly counteract these forces by redoubling their support for compensatory programs, affirmative action, and other racially sensitive programs to help blacks and other minorities.

Just as the first section of this chapter opened with words from former President James E. Cheek of Howard University, this penultimate section will close with the concluding words of his opening convocation address of September 26, 1980, to the university. He observed:

> We make no apology for doing what our times and circumstances compel us to do. For the First Emancipation was the burden of the white man, and that is why it remained only a proclamation. But the Second Emancipation is the burden of the black man, and that is why it must be made a reality.
>
> And I ask you, if we do not assume this burden, then who will?[107]

Conclusion and Recommendations

> In closing, I think that the way one looks at *Brown*, or *Green*, or *Swann*, or *Bakke*, depends largely, I'm afraid, on the interests with which one is primarily concerned. This is not to say that those who disagree with me are all hostile to blacks or bigoted. It is to say that they identify with different interests and the interest of blacks is not very high on their agenda.

Kenneth S. Tollett

The health of the political and economic orders depends upon a well-educated populace. Likewise, the well-being of the citizens of a community depends upon how well they have been educated and trained for work, leisure and citizenship. This chapter has focused upon and emphasized the citizenship function of education because it is the one most relevant to the relationship between universal education and democratic values, and to the role of the former in creating the social compact and political covenant that ground a democracy.

However, current rhetoric surrounding the issue of competitiveness tends to overemphasize the production or economic function of education, and correspondingly not give the citizenship function its just due. This rhetoric indicates that the economic stability of the United States may be jeopardized by the inadequate education of blacks and other minorities. The matter of economic competitiveness, though, may compel adequate resources to be invested in the education of blacks. The 1986 $100 million set-aside —in the reauthorization of the 1965 Higher Education Act—for historically black colleges was a modest though encouraging development. But persistent attacks upon affirmative action will make the future of blacks less secure. Emigrants from Europe, Latin America and Asia could well be used to meet the nation's labor force and production needs, which would result in un- and undereducated blacks being further reduced to a dispensable helot class. This portentous possibility must be recognized and resisted firmly and forcefully. Now is most assuredly not the time for blacks to lose their obsession with education and frenzy for book learning.

Still, a revival of interest in republicanism and democratic and human values has projected the importance of not only the citizenship function, but also the consumption function of education. To the extent the United States has not invested adequately in the education of blacks and other minorities, it has not fully recognized them as citizens. The necessary investment must be made.

Yet, blacks must do much more for themselves, particularly the reconstitution of their underclass communities by reintroducing working-, middle- and professional-class persons into them. Understandably, individual blacks may not want to sacrifice themselves to salvage isolated, impoverished black communities. However, if the seriousness of the isolation and powerlessness of underclass communities is fully recognized, a critical mass of working-, middle- and professional-class blacks may be persuaded or induced to return to, or not further leave, these communities. Their presence is especially needed in the educational enterprise.

This is so because of four critical requirements of effective schooling, instruction and education for blacks. First, those who educate and instruct blacks, particularly the young, must have a genuine and virtually unconditional respect for the dignity and integrity of black youth. Second, they must have a strong and heartfelt conviction that all students are educable and have a capacity to learn. Third, they must be enthusiastic about, and committed to, learning and knowledge. Finally, they must have competence and learning themselves. Generally, middle- and professional-class blacks will be more likely to meet these requirements than others.

As one reflects upon the imperatives of the society's political economy and what the state of blacks is likely to be, say, over the first two generations of the twenty-first century, it is evident that greater co-operation and reciprocal reinforcement among blacks are critical to the life chances that they will have open to them. Given the three functions of education, especially the centrality of the citizenship function in a free society, blacks, now more than ever, must seek and maintain their freedom and nurture their well-being through the expansion of their educational opportunities. Commonality of knowledge, learning and understanding is one of the surest ways to achieve community. Universal education may be the only route and opportunity most blacks have for access to, and full participation in, the American political community, for if not God, surely fate "has decreed that only the educated shall be truly free."

NOTES

[1]Law as the authoritative matrix through which rights and duties, privileges and immunities, and powers and limitations are created, recognized, defined, articulated, allocated and enforced has been, for much of black history, a disappointment in practice. Only in the post-Civil War era, early Reconstruction period, and later during the mid-twentieth century, when the United States Supreme Court, saying that "education is perhaps the most important function of state and local governments," concluded "that in the field of public education the doctrine of 'separate but equal' has no place," have black children not been denied equal protection. *Brown* v. *Board of Education*, 347 U.S. 483, 493, 495 (1954). However, law has been a source of limited hope in theory for nearly two centuries. See Derrick A. Bell, Jr., *Race, Racism and American Law*, 2nd ed. (Boston: Little, Brown and Company, 1980), particularly chapter 1, "American Racism and the Uses of History," pp. 2-51.

[2]Ibid. See also Richard Kluger, *Simple Justice: The History of Brown v. Board of Education and Black America's Struggle for Equality* (New York: Alfred A. Knopf, 1975); Genna Rae McNeil, *Groundwork: Charles Hamilton Houston and the Struggle for Civil Rights* (Philadelphia: University of Pennsylvania Press, 1983); and Kenneth S. Tollett, "Blacks, Higher Education and Integration," *Notre Dame Lawyer* 48: 1 (October 1972): 189-207.

[3]Mary Frances Berry and John W. Blassingame, *Long Memory: The Black Experience in America* (New York: Oxford University Press, 1982), pp. 261-262.

[4]Ibid., p. 264. (Author's italics.)

[5]This is a variation of a definition given of higher education at the 1973 American Council on Education Annual Conference. It stated:

. . . education is essentially an intellectual process that creates and transmits knowledge, develops and structures critical cognitive powers, enhances and reinforces sensitivity and sensibility, and combines the dominant urges of self-conscious humankind to explain, control and revere or reunite with nature in a purposeful pursuit of understanding human relationships and the relationships between humans and nature.

Cited in Kenneth S. Tollett, "The Faculty and the Government," in John F. Hughes, ed., *Education and the State* (Washington, D.C.: American Council on Education, 1975), p. 212.

[6]A further indication of the fundamental perspective undergirding the above definition of education may be useful. A presentation to the World Congress on Philosophy of Law and Social Philosophy at Gardone Riviera, Italy, in 1967 provides that perspective. The presentation assessed the role of law in social ordering after reviewing the role of art, science and religion in such. This author stated:

> It may be improper to distinguish art, science and religion from each other in early historical times. Hawkes and Wooley [*History of Mankind: Prehistory and the Beginning of Civilization*, Vol. I, 1963] have said:
>
>> As man's consciousness drew him apart from the concourse of unselfconscious nature from which he was emerging, he was bound to turn to look at nature, and having contemplated it to seek to explain what he saw, to affect it for his own ends and finally to regard it with awe and reverence and a desire for reunion.
>
> Here we have three urges which have marked and dominated the history of man: *intellectual* (to explain), *practical* (to affect) and *mystical* (to awe, revere and reunite). These urges were and are the germs of *myth, magic* and *religion*, hardly distinguishable processes in very early times, but much more distinguishable in contemporary times, except in "primitive" societies. Thus the same may be said of *art, science* and *religion*. The precursors to the former two were myth and magic respectively. Religion and, especially mysticism, to the extent they exist today, hardly have changed significantly throughout history until most recently.

Cited in Kenneth S. Tollett, "The Legalization of Social Ordering," in Gary L. Dorsey and Samuel I. Shuman, eds., *Validation of New Forms of Social Organization* (Wiesbaden, W. Germany: Franz Steiner Verlag GmbH, 1968), p. 133.

[7]Kenneth S. Tollett, "Higher Education and the Public Sector," in Ben Lawrence, George Weathersby and Virginia W. Patterson, eds., *Outputs of Higher Education: Their Identification, Measurement, and Evaluation* (Boulder, CO: Colorado Western Interstate Commission on Higher Education, 1970), p. 63. This chapter discusses the three functions of education, showing the influence of economic thought models in a human development context.

In 1976, the author discussed several ideal models of educational concepts or functions in part III, entitled "The Relationship of Education to Employment and Work," of Thomas F. Powers, ed., *Educating for Careers: Policy Issues in a Time of Change* (University Park, PA: The Pennsylvania State University Press, 1977), pp. 62-79. The title of the contribution, "Certification, Articulation, and Caste," implicitly or explicitly recognizes the vocational function of education, although the author's personal bias or orientation to education follows emphatically a *liberal arts* model. In addition to criticizing adversarial professors and liberals for playing into the hands of reactionary

forces by hypercritically evaluating higher education and the Great Society
with its liberal reform efforts, the article elucidated diverse models, purposes
and functions of education, for example elite (autonomous university), manpower, open access and universal attendance models; and scholastic, vocational, action-oriented, utopian, consumer and experiential models. Before
enumerating and discussing the *functions* of education, I set forth and adopted
the purposes of the Carnegie Commission on Higher Education, *Purposes*
(New York: McGraw-Hill, 1975), p. 1:

1. The provision of opportunities for the intellectual, aesthetic, ethical and
   skill development of individual students and the provision of campus environments which can constructively assist students in their more general developmental growth;
2. The advancement of human capability in the society at large;
3. The enlargement of educational justice for the postsecondary group;
4. The transmission and advancement of learning and wisdom;
5. The critical evaluation of society—through individual thought and persuasion—for the sake of society's self-renewal. Cited in Tollett, "Certification, Articulation, and Caste," ibid., p. 69.

[8]Forrest McDonald, *Novus Ordo Seclorum: The Intellectual Origins of the
Constitution* (Lawrence, KS: University Press of Kansas, 1985), p. 262.

[9]See Stephen K. White, "The Trial of Postmodernism: Poststructuralism
and Political Reflection," *Political Theory* 16: 2 (May 1988): 186-208. In grap-
pling with deconstruction's endlessly unsettling and questioning analyses of
language, if not thought, White constructively observes:

The language distinction can be described as that between language use
that *coordinates action-in-the-world* and language use that *discloses
worlds*. And Jürgen Habermas, as a social and political theorist, finds it
best to give the former approach preeminence in his conceptual machin-
ery. As he puts it, he charts his way into language "in terms of its prob-
lem-solving capacity for interaction." With this assertion, one can see
how, ultimately, Habermas's research program affirms the responsibility
to act in the world. This means that he intends his research program to
generate interpretations that will enhance our capacity to act in contemporary circumstances.

   Habermas also argues that the deconstructionist's opposite emphasis on the uncoordinating, world-disclosing capacity of language
makes it unclear how one could ever account for the reproduction of social life in general and the occurrence of many learning processes that
take place within it. The focus on world-*disclosing* gives one no adequate
way of appreciating the fact that "linguistically mediated processes such
as the attainment of knowledge, identity formation, socialization, and
social integration master problems *within the world*." Linguistic interaction "makes learning processes [in these dimensions] possible thanks to
the idealizations" built into it. And it is within such learning processes
that the world-disclosing power of language "must be *confirmed*." (Ibid.,
pp. 194-195.) (Author's italics.)

Of course, the importance of this allusion to post-modernist thought is that dialogue and discourse create community as well as are nourished and made possible by community. White further observes:

> Fred Dallmayr has argued that a "conversational" model of interaction can cope with each of these problems. Conversation, understood in a hermeneutical sense, has the primary goal of achieving a mutual understanding among participants. Unlike Habermas's notion of communicative action, in conversation the relationship between actors is construed "not so much as a confrontation of subjective views as rather the endeavor to grasp a topic on subject matter 'common' to them." Conversation, in this sense, implies a "relative 'I-lessness' of communication" and a deep openness to all forms of otherness or "strangeness." As Gadamer says, in genuine conversation "I have let some things count against myself, even if there is no one there pressing the claim." Thus, in conversation the poetic, world-disclosing capacity of discourse is shifted into the foreground, and this shift is intended to instantiate the deconstruction moment. Ibid., pp. 200-201.

[10]Thirteen active workers supported each Social Security beneficiary in the late 1940s. In the late 1980s, less than four (3.4) workers are supporting each Social Security recipient. Early in the twenty-first century, barely three active workers may be around to support each retiree. Roughly one out of three workers then will be from minority groups, with blacks constituting a majority of these groups.

[11]See William Julius Wilson, *The Truly Disadvantaged: The Inner City, the Underclass, and Public Policy* (Chicago: The University of Chicago Press, 1987).

[12]George Washington and Thomas Jefferson both recognized that the United States of America would not long thrive as a "democratic" republic if education were not generally given and well received. Indeed, the Continental Congress during 1787, the year the United States Constitution was drafted, enacted the Northwest Ordinance, "which sought to encourage the establishment of schools and the means of education," and "supplied land, resources and other assistance for the advancement of education and related activities." (See Kenneth S. Tollett, "The Propriety of the Federal Role in Expanding Equal Educational Opportunity," *Harvard Educational Review* 52: 4 (November 1982): 431-443 at 431.) Although this provision was not carried over into the United States Constitution, it indicated and symbolized clearly education's preeminent significance at the founding of the Republic.

[13]The latest contribution to the debate regarding the influence of republicanism and liberalism among the Founding Fathers seems to transcend this dichotomy in *time* with a new emphasis upon religious and biblical notions of piety, sacredness and evangelism that includes "evangelicals [seeing] their ancestors as a chosen people dedicated to the cause of religious revival." Michael Lienesch, *New Order of the Ages: Time, the Constitution, and the Making of Modern American Political Thought* (Princeton, NJ: Princeton University Press, 1988), p. 36.

[14]James Thomas Flexner, *George Washington,* Vol. 4 of "Anguish and Farewell (1793-1799)" (Boston: Little, Brown and Company, 1969), p. 199. President Lyndon Baines Johnson, during his presidency in the middle 1960s, probably ascribed more importance to education than any other president in the history of the United States. Surely, there was an explosion of congressional legislation and executive initiatives in this arena. See Tollett, "The Propriety of the Federal Role in Expanding Equal Educational Opportunity," op. cit. note 12.

[15]Flexner, ibid., p. 199.

[16]Ibid.

[17]Ibid., p. 326.

[18]James MacGregor Burns, *The American Experiment: The Vineyard of Liberty* (New York: Alfred A. Knopf, 1981), p. 109.

[19]Ibid., p. 144.

[20]Ibid.

[21]Ibid., p. 19.

[22]Ibid., p. 501.

[23]Dumas Malone, *Jefferson and His Time,* Vol. 6 of "The Sage of Monticello" (Boston: Little, Brown and Company, 1981), p. xv.

[24]Burns, op. cit. note 18, p. 502.

[25]Joshua Miller, "Foundings of America: I. The Ghostly Body Politic: *The Federalist* Papers and Popular Sovereignty," *Political Theory:* 16 (February 1988): 99-119 at 99.

[26]Robert M. Hutchins, *The Learning Society* (New York: Frederick A. Praeger Publishers, 1969, © 1968).

[27]Frank Lentricchia, "Provocations," in his *Criticism and Social Change* (Chicago: The University of Chicago Press, 1983), p. 1.

[28]Ibid. [The citation to Michel Foucault is omitted in Lentricchia's work.] (Author's italics.)

[29]Kenneth S. Tollett, "Community and Higher Education," *Daedalus* 104: 1 (Winter 1975): 278, 283-286.

[30]Hutchins, op. cit. note 26.

[31]Ibid., p. ix.

[32]Ibid., p. 45.

[33]"Sunstein Receives First Award for Administrative Law Scholarship," *Administrative Law News* 12: 1 (Winter 1987): 1.

[34]Cass R. Sunstein, "Interest Groups in American Public Law," *Stanford Law Review* 38 (November 1985): 29-87, at 29 and 31.

[35]Charles Beard, *An Economic Interpretation of the Constitution of the United States* (New York: The MacMillan Company, 1936, orig. copyright 1913).

[36]Robert M. Cover, "The Supreme Court, 1982 Term—Foreword: *Nomos* and Narrative," *Harvard Law Review* 97: 1 (November 1983): 4-68.

[37]Frank I. Michelman, "The Supreme Court, 1985 Term—Foreword: Traces of Self-Government," *Harvard Law Review* 100: 1 (November 1986): 13-77.

[38]Henry Allen Bullock, *A History of Negro Education in the South: From 1619 to the Present* (Cambridge, MA: Harvard University Press, 1967). However, because the author of this chapter does not agree entirely with what he regards as Bullock's overly positive and sociological or functional interpretation of slavery and the black experience, the author also has consulted or used Blassingame and Berry, op. cit. note 3; Frank Bowles and Frank A. DeCosta *Between Two Worlds: A Profile of Negro Higher Education* (New York: McGraw-Hill Book Company, 1971); Robert L. Church and Michael W. Sedlak, *Education in the United States: An Interpretive History* (New York: The Free Press, 1976); Lawrence A. Cremin, *American Education: The Colonial Experience, 1607-1783* (New York: Harper and Row, 1970); Lawrence A. Cremin, *American Education: The National Experience, 1783-1876* (New York: Harper and Row, 1980); Lawrence A. Cremin, *American Education: The Metropolitan Experience, 1876-1980* (New York: Harper and Row, 1988); Harold Cruse, *Plural But Equal: A Critical Study of Blacks and Minorities and the American Society* (New York: William Morrow and Company, Inc., 1987); John E. Fleming, with the assistance of Julius Hobson, Jr., John McClendon and Herschelle Reed, *The Lengthening Shadow of Slavery: A Historical Justification for Affirmative Action for Blacks in Higher Education* (Washington, D.C.: published for ISEP by Howard University Press, 1976); John Hope Franklin and Alfred A. Moss, Jr., *From Slavery to Freedom: A History of Negro Americans*, 6th ed. (New York: Alfred A. Knopf, 1988); and Benjamin Quarles, *The Negro in the Making of America*, 2nd rev. ed. (New York: Collier Books; London: Collier Macmillan, 1987).

[39]Bullock, ibid., p. 5. (Author's italics.)

[40]Ibid., p. 4.

[41]Ibid., p. 5.

[42]W.E.B. DuBois, *The Souls of Black Folk: Essays and Sketches* (New York: Faucett Publications, 1961; orig. published Chicago: A.C. McClurg and Co., 1903), pp. 79-80.

[43]Bowles and DeCosta, op. cit. note 38, p. 2.

[44]Bowles and DeCosta have written the following about the above "crippling limitations" and inadequate education of blacks:

These limitations—that it was basically controlled by white society (even though, as DuBois and John Hope pointed out in the Atlanta papers, white society contributed little to the support of the system, and sometimes actually directed Negro tax funds to white schools); that it could not educate Negroes to compete for positions held by whites; that is was basically limited to the training of school teachers; that without intellectual encouragement and support from the white educational system it could not adjust itself to white educational standards, hence could

not prepare Negro students for those Northern graduate and professional schools which were prepared to admit them—had not emerged
into full view at the time DuBois was writing. (Ibid., pp. 2-3.)

[45]In writing about "Community and Higher Education," this author stated
that the overarching goal of higher education should be to create a universal
community. This universal community would be the product of a communality of thought, knowledge, images, ideas and, to some extent, values.

My hope for a national and universal community is instrumentally
placed in the teaching and curriculum of higher education. Without suc-
cumbing to cultural and educational chauvinism, I believe that the
United States is in a strategic position to foster world community and
that the best place to start is in its institutions of higher education.
. . . My ultimate or overarching goal for higher education is that
it should provide and create the intellectual and emotional conditions for
a universal community. It should nurture and sustain a universal community of thought and aspiration within the framework and context of
pluralistic societies. Tollett, "Community and Higher Education," op.
cit. note 29, pp. 278-279.

The above was an argument that higher education could contribute to an
international community of comity and understanding in a way analogous to
the way universal or public education in the United States has contributed to
the communalization of the ethnically diverse and nationally pluralistic states.
The abiding interracial and intergroup difficulties in the United States have
undercut the above argument some; however, its overall validity remains.
Concurring in one of the first United States Supreme Court decisions establishing the separation of church and state, Associate Justice Felix Frankfurter
wrote:

Designed to serve as perhaps the most powerful agency for promoting
cohesion among a heterogeneous democratic people . . . , [t]he public
school is at once the symbol of our democracy and the most pervasive
means for promoting our common destiny. In no activity of the State is it
more vital to keep out divisive forces than in its schools, to avoid confus-
ing, not to say fusing, what the Constitution sought to keep strictly
apart. *Illinois ex rel. McCollum* v. *Board of Education*, 333 U.S. 203, 216,
231 (1948).

[46]Bullock, op. cit. note 38, p. 2.

[47]Ibid.

[48]Ibid., p. 5.

[49]Ibid., pp. 6-7.

[50]Ibid., p. 11.

[51]Ibid., pp. 11-12.

[52]Bell, op. cit. note 1, p. 365.

[53]Ibid.

[54]Ibid.

[55]Ibid., p. 366.

[56]Ibid.

[57]*Roberts* v. *City of Boston*, 59 Mass. (5 Cush.) 198 (1850).

[58]*Roberts*, 59 Mass. at 209.

[59]*Plessy* v. *Ferguson*, 163 U.S. 537 (1896). It is another paradox of the black experience that *Plessy* relied significantly upon *Roberts* in making the "separate but equal" doctrine the law of the land. Indeed, segregation was probably most entrenched in state law concerning education when *Plessy* was decided. See, for example, *People ex rel. Dietz* v. *Easton*, 13 Abb. Pr. (New Series) 159 (1872), holding that the Albany, New York school board could separate black school children from whites without violating the Fourteenth Amendment, although the white school was nearer to the black student's residence; substantially the same holding occurred in California four years later in *Ward* v. *Flood*, 48 Cal. 36 (1874); *Cory* v. *Carter*, 48 Ind. 327 (1874) held that the Thirteenth and Fourteenth Amendments did not entitle black children who were citizens and residents of Indiana to attend common schools in an Indiana district with whites; separate schools were again upheld in New York against a Fourteenth Amendment challenge in *People ex rel. King* v. *Gallagher*, 93 N.Y. 438 (1883). One positive exception was Ohio whose general assembly passed a law in 1887 repealing "[t]he power to establish and maintain separate schools for colored children," thus abolishing separate schools for black children. *Board of Education of the Village of Oxford* v. *State ex rel. Gibson*, 45 Ohio St. 555, 556 (1888).

[60]Bell, op. cit. note 1, p. 368. Bell further reports:

White parents, [state officials] feared, would not send their children to the [black schools] nor allow them to receive instruction from [black teachers]. Textbook aid provided black children under segregation was also ended, and after a decade or so, state officials conceded that Boston's public schools had again become identified by race. (Ibid.)

[61]Kenneth S. Tollett, "Commentary" in Bowles and DeCosta, op. cit. note 38, p. 256.

[62]Recognizing the need for higher education, benevolent societies and the Freedmen's Bureau began establishing colleges and universities for blacks. These institutions soon became divided into one of two kinds: those that offered liberal arts and "classical" education and those offering a manual arts and industrial education. For an excellent history of these institutions, see Bowles and DeCosta, op. cit. note 38.

[63]*Cumming* v. *Richmond County Board of Education*, 175 U.S. 528 (1899).

[64]Bullock, op. cit. note 38, p. 24.

[65]Ibid., p. 27. Benjamin Quarles observes that the black church made an invaluable contribution here. He notes:

As a patron of schools, the organized Negro church performed one of its greatest services. Bent upon giving its young people a "Christian Education" and upon the better training of its future clergymen, Negro church groups markedly expanded school-founding efforts. Every major Negro denomination was represented in the movement. Negro Baptists were supporting eighty elementary and high schools by 1900. See Quarles, op. cit. note 38, p. 162.

Eighteen Baptist colleges or semicolleges designed for blacks—all in the South—were established by 1900; eleven such institutions were established by Black Methodists such as the A.M.E. (six); C.M.E. (four); and Zion Methodists (Livingston College). (Ibid.) Quarles further observes:

The typical church-related school or college was notable for the eagerness of its students, many of whom were adults responding to opportunity no matter how belated it had come. Having to meet the student where he was, most of these schools, even those designated as colleges or universities, spent most of their time on basic elements of knowledge. (Ibid., p. 163.)

[66]Quarles, ibid., p. 164.

[67]*Plessy* v. *Ferguson*, 163 U.S. 537 (1896).

[68]163 U.S. at 559, 562.

[69]Blacks were definitely sacrificed for the benefit of whites. See also the discussion in note 70 below of how the "spirit and substance" of the Fourteenth Amendment were sacrificed by a "subtle and ingenious verbal criticism." However, whites as well as blacks were sacrificed in holding blacks down. Harold Cruse has observed that from 1890 onward into the twentieth century, " 'educational lethargy' settled all over the South. Millions of illiterate whites were sacrificed by southern leaders whose main objective was to keep millions of illiterate blacks ignorant, impoverished, and politically impotent by denying them education." Cruse, op. cit. note 38, p. 14.

[70]Justice John Marshall Harlan dissented in the *Civil Rights Cases*, 109 U.S. 3 (1883), which held the 1875 Civil Rights (public accommodations) Act unconstitutional because Congress had proscribed private (nonstate) discrimination. Justice Joseph P. Bradley in his opinion for the Court stated that the Fourteenth Amendment "does not authorize Congress to create a code of municipal law for the regulation of private rights; but to provide modes of redress against the operation of State laws, and the action of State officers[,] executive or judicial, when these are subversive of the fundamental rights specified in the amendment." Justice Harlan complained that "the substance and spirit of the recent amendments of the Constitution have been sacrificed by a subtle and ingenious verbal criticism." 109 U.S. at 11 and 26.

"Subtle and ingenious verbal criticisms" are very important because they create the norms for communities as well as express or disclose those norms through dialogue and discourse in a community. James Boyd White, in *Heracles' Bow: Essays on the Rhetoric and Poetics of the Law* (Madison: The University of Wisconsin Press, 1985), persuasively continues Stephen White's argument or interpretation of law and rhetoric as instruments for creating as well as expressing "character, community, and culture in language." Ibid., p. x. Blacks have lost ground in recent years because they are losing the verbal and rhetorical civil rights battles as well as a sympathetic white populace and federal judiciary. Ongoing racism and white supremacy (Charles R. Lawrence III, "The Id, the Ego, and Equal Protection: Reckoning with Unconscious Racism," *Stanford Law Review* 39 (January 1987): 317-388) make it imperative for black intellectuals, scholars and pundits to counter consciously verbal and symbolic assaults upon blacks and their institutions, leaders and communities. Kenneth S, Tollett, "Solving the Problems of Developing Leadership and Power Through Communications: The Continuing Need for Black Consciousness, Power, and Sensitivity," paper presented at the Sixteenth Annual Howard University Communications Conference (Washington, D.C., 1987).

[71]Bullock, op. cit. note 38, p. 123.

[72]Ibid., p. 127.

[73]Related to the above issue, Quarles observes, "As late as 1916 none of the sixteen existing Negro land-grant institutions was offering college-level work." Quarles, op. cit. note 38, p. 164.

[74]*Pearson* v. *Murray*, 182 A. 590 (Md. Ct. App. 1936).

[75]*Missouri ex rel. Gaines* v. *Canada*, 305 U.S. 337 (1938).

[76]Gunnar Myrdal, *An American Dilemma: The Negro Problem and Modern Democracy*, 20th anniversary edition (New York: Harper and Row, 1962), pp. 60-61:

> When white Southerners are asked to rank in order of importance, various types of discrimination, they consistently present a list in which these types of discrimination are ranked according to the degree of closeness of their relation to the anti-amalgamation doctrine. This rank order—which will be referred to as *"the white man's rank order of discriminations"*—will serve as an organizing principle in this book. . . .

> The rank order was (1) "the bar against intermarriage and sexual intercourse involving white women"; (2) "barriers against dancing, bathing, eating, drinking together, and social intercourse generally"; (3) "segregations and discriminations in use of public facilities such as schools, churches and means of conveyance"; (4) "political disfranchisement"; (5) "discriminations in law courts, by the police, and by other public servants"; and (6) "[f]inally . . . the discriminations in securing land, credit, jobs, or other means of earning a living, and discriminations in public relief and other social welfare activities." Ibid.
> However, Myrdal went on to observe "that the *Negro's own rank order is just about parallel, but inverse, to that of the white man*. The Negro resists least the discrimination on the ranks placed highest in the white man's evaluation and resents most any discrimination on the lowest level." Ibid., p. 61. Of course, this is another paradox of the black experience.

[77]*Brown* v. *Board of Education*, 347 U.S. 483 (1954), (hereinafter *Brown I*).

[78]See the *Regents of the University of California* v. *Bakke*, 438 U.S. 265 (1978).

[79]*Sweatt* v. *Painter*, 339 U.S. 629 (1950).

[80]For a brief history of the Texas Southern University School of Law and the successful effort to resist its closing or merger with the University of Houston in the name of integration, see Kenneth S. Tollett, "Making it Together: Texas Southern University Law School," *Judicature* 53: 9 (April/May 1970): 366-372. The article also defends predominantly black higher education institutions and the desirability of whites experiencing a minority status and blacks experiencing the temptations of control and some power.

[81]*McLaurin* v. *Oklahoma State Regents for Higher Education*, 339 U.S. 637 (1950). Two years earlier, the Court had decided Oklahoma must provide a legal education for blacks as soon as it provided it for whites. *Sipuel* v. *Oklahoma State Board of Regents*, 332 U.S. 631 (1948).

[82]Philip B. Kurland, "The Supreme Court, 1963 Term—Foreword: 'Equal in Origin and Equal in Title to the Legislative and Executive Branches of the Government,'" *Harvard Law Review* 78: 1 (November 1964): 143-176, at 145.

[83]*Brown* v. *Board of Education*, 349 U.S. 294 (1955), (hereinafter *Brown II*). See also J. Harvie Wilkinson III, *From Brown to Bakke: The Supreme Court and School Integration, 1954-1978* (New York: Oxford University Press, 1979), especially ch. 4, " 'All Deliberate Speed': Brown II," pp. 61-77. Wilkinson ended this chapter stating:

> Human nature, the Southerner believed, was like a roadside mule that could be prodded, cajoled, sweet-talked, and downright cussed but not pushed infinitely against his will. "All deliberate speed" accepted, a bit too completely, this southern view. The mule came too close to lying down in the road. Thus, *Brown II* can be justified, but just barely. Deliberate speed was better at first for the nation than full speed ahead. Yet the Court's true-to-life politics imposed terrible moral costs. Those who bore the costs of prudence were those who pay the toll for much political compromise — the poor and powerless. In the South of the recent past, this meant those black schoolchildren who, like Mary Jones, began their education in that fall of 1954. Ibid., p. 77.

[84]The writer of this chapter stated the following at the Washington University School of Law symposium, "The Quest for Equality," about public school desegregation:

> For reasons of culture, social relations and economics, *Brown* could have been more easily enforced at the time it was decided than it could be today. And in that respect, I suppose, I agree with Professor Kurland that instead of the "all deliberate speed" proposition, the Court should have required desegregation immediately. Today, because of uneven development and certain economic gaps that expand and narrow between between blacks and whites in the North and the South, it seems that the spirit of *Brown* is more difficult to enforce than in 1955. It is my feeling that because of the delay, evolution of the *Brown* principles into *Green*, *Swann*, *Keyes* and *Milliken* had to come to counter past evasion. Although those latter decisions do seem to suggest an overreaching— maybe even an imperial—judiciary, those expansive remedies are necessary because of the failure to properly enforce *Brown* when it was first enunciated.

Kenneth S. Tollett, "Disenchantment with the 'Egalitarian Revolution,' " *Washington University Law Quarterly* 1979: 2 (Spring 1979): 421-429 at 423.

Professor Kurland critically reviewed *Brown* and its progeny at the above symposium. Philip B. Kurland, " '*Brown* v. *Board of Education* Was The Beginning': The School Desegregation Cases in the United States Supreme Court: 1954-1979," *Washington University Law Quarterly* 1979: 2 (Spring 1979): 309-405.

[85]Richard A. Wasserstrom, "Racism, Sexism, and Preferential Treatment: An Approach to the Topics," *UCLA Law Review* 24: 3 (February 1977): 581-622. Wasserstrom strikingly observes:

> [C]onceptual racism . . . holds that the claims of black children were worth less than the claims of white children in those cases in which conflict is inevitable. It seems to me that any minimally fair solution would have required that during the interim process, if anybody had to go to an inadequate school, it should have been the white children, since they were the ones who had previously had the benefit of good schools. Ibid., pp. 600-601.

See also Kenneth S. Tollett, "Justice is the Reversal of Discrimination," in Cynthia J. Smith, ed., *Equality of Opportunity: A Matter of Justice, Proceedings from the National Invitational Conference* (Washington, D.C.: Institute for the Study of Educational Policy, 1978), pp. 27, 33-34.

[86]It took President Dwight D. Eisenhower nationalizing Arkansas' National Guard, sending in the federal troops, and a unanimous decision of the United States Supreme Court, signed by each member of the Court, to overcome Faubus' defiance. *Cooper* v. *Aaron*, 358 U.S. 1 (1958).

[87]*Griffin* v. *County School Board*, 377 U.S. 218 (1964).

[88]In 1968, the Court struck down a "freedom-of-choice" plan in Virginia holding that de jure racial segregation imposed an affirmative duty on school systems "to take whatever steps might be necessary to convert to a unitary system in which racial discrimination would be eliminated root and branch." *Green* v. *County School Board*, 391 U.S. 430, 437-438 (1968). A "free-transfer" plan in Tennessee was struck down because it perpetuated the dual system and did not effectively move toward a unitary system by disestablishing state-imposed segregation. *Monroe* v. *Board of Commissioners*, 391 U.S. 450 (1968). A year later the Court held that "all deliberate speed" was no longer constitutionally permissible and every school district must terminate their dual systems "at once" and "operate now and hereafter only unitary schools." *Alexander* v. *Holmes County Board of Education*, 396 U.S. 19, 20 (1969). The Court sanctioned numerical ratios based upon racial composition and busing two years later. *Swann* v. *Charlotte-Mecklenburg Board of Education*, 402 U.S. 1 (1971). In a companion case the Court struck down a state statute which prohibited involuntary busing or assignments based upon race to produce racial balance. *North Carolina State Board of Education* v. *Swann*, 402 U.S. 43 (1971). Anything done which has the effect of impeding the desegregation of public schools, even if that was not the motive for creating a new school district, the Court held, violates the Equal Protection Clause. *Wright* v. *Council of City of Emporia*, 407 U.S. 451 (1972). This 5 to 4 decision of the Court was its first

nonunanimous disposition of a case designed to implement *Brown I* and *II*. All
of President Nixon's appointees dissented, foreshadowing things to come. For
a discussion of these and many other decisions of the Warren and Nixon-Burger Courts, see Kenneth S. Tollett, "The Viability and Reliability of the U.S.
Supreme Court as an Institution for Social Change and Progress Beneficial to
Blacks," Parts I and II, *The Black Law Journal* 2: 3 (Winter 1972): 197-219,
and 3: 1 (1973): 5-50. One of the conclusions of the latter article is that "The
Nixon-Burger Court probably will undo as much as it can, although incre-
mentally and sometimes circumspectly, of what the Warren Court has done
which was beneficial to Blacks." Ibid., Part II, pp. 48-49. Of course, as will be
seen below, the Reagan-Rehnquist Court has accelerated the movement away
from beneficial decisions for blacks.

[89]The effort to "desegregate" the public school systems outside the South
was almost as problematical as it was in the South. *Keyes* v. *School District No.
1, Denver, Colo.*, 413 U.S. 189 (1973) held that, although Denver never had a
statutory dual school system, intentionally segregating part of the district
placed the burden on the board to prove such de jure segregation did not affect
other parts of the system and, thus, was an isolated event. Four years later in
Board of Education v. *Brinkman*, 433 U.S. 406 (1977) (*Dayton I*), the Court
held that a systemwide remedy was "entirely out of proportion to the constitutional violations found by the District Court" (433 U.S. at 418), which held
that the Dayton School Board failed to correct racial imbalances, used op-
tional attendance zones, and rescinded its earlier resolution regarding its responsibility. In his opinion for the Court, Justice Rehnquist emphasized the
importance of finding "intentionally segregative action." (433 U.S. at 413.) On
remand the desegregation complaint was dismissed by the district court which
held that the plaintiffs did not prove present incremental segregative effects
which stemmed from prior constitutional violations. The court of appeals, as it
had done in *Dayton I*, reversed the district court's decision and ordered a systemwide remedy again. This time the Supreme Court affirmed the court of appeals by a 5 to 4 vote, seeing no reason to upset the appeal court's conclusion.
The board had operated purposefully segregated schools which constituted a
substantial violation of the Equal Protection Clause. *Dayton Board of Education* v. *Brinkman*, 443 U.S. 526 (1979) (*Dayton II*). On the day *Dayton II* was
decided, *Columbus Board of Education* v. *Penick*, 433 U.S. 449 (1979) upheld
another systemwide desegregation order. However, four years earlier in *Milliken* v. *Bradley*, 418 U.S. 717 (1974) (*Milliken I*), the Court had held that absent the finding of an interdistrict violation, federal courts lacked the power to
impose interdistrict remedies. Since the school system of Detroit was 70 percent black, racial balance reflecting even this percentage would have required
massive busing of white students from one black school to another, which the
district court did not require. However, the Court upheld the district court's
order for extensive education reform such as career guidance, remedial education and counseling. *Milliken* v. *Bradley*, 433 U.S. 267 (1977) (*Milliken II*).
Once a district court had "implemented a racially neutral attendance pattern
in order to remedy the perceived constitutional violation" by the board, the
court exhausted its remedial powers and did not need to make annual readjust-
ments of school boundary lines to avoid schools with a majority of minority
students. *Pasadena Board of Education* v. *Spangler*, 427 U.S. 424, 437 (1976).

[90]Derrick A. Bell, Jr., *And We Are Not Saved: The Elusive Quest for Racial Justice* (New York: Basic Books, Inc., 1987), especially ch. 4, "Neither Separate Schools Nor Mixed Schools: The Chronicle of the Sacrificed Black School Children," pp. 102-122; Alvin V. Adair, *Desegregation: The Illusion of Black Progress* (Lanham, MD: University Press of America, 1984); and Cruse, op. cit. note 38.

[91]Bell, ibid., p. 107.

[92]Derrick A. Bell, Jr., ed., *Shades of Brown: New Perspectives on School Desegregation* (New York: Teachers College Press, Columbia University, 1980), p. 90.

[93]Ibid., p. 95.

[94]Ibid., p. 101, citing Laurence Tribe, *American Constitutional Law*, p. 1022 (1978). (Footnote omitted.)

[95]Kenneth S. Tollett, "Black Institutions of Higher Learning: Inadvertent Victims or Necessary Sacrifices?," *Black Law Journal* 3: 23 (Winter/Spring 1974): 162-174 at 162-163.

[96]Kenneth S. Tollett, *Black Institutions of Higher Learning: Inadvertent Victims or Necessary Sacrifices?: With 1981 Prologue Update*, ISEP Reprint (Washington, D.C.: Institute for the Study of Educational Policy, 1981), p. 1; and Kenneth S. Tollett, *Black Colleges as Instruments of Affirmative Action* (Washington, D.C.: Institute for the Study of Educational Policy, 1982).

[97]Ibid., p. 4.

[98]For a discussion of "reverse discrimination" suits against predominantly black colleges and some recommendations on how to defend or avoid such suits, see Tollett, *Black Colleges as Instruments of Affirmative Action*, op. cit. note 96, pp. 56-61.

[99]See Kenneth S. Tollett, Jeannette Leonard and Portia James, "A Color-Conscious Constitution: The One Pervading Purpose *Redux*," *Journal of Negro Education* 52: 3 (Summer 1983): 189-212.

[100]Tollett, *Institutions of Higher Learning*, op. cit. note 96, p. 2.

[101]*Slaughterhouse Cases*, 83 U.S. (16 Wall.) 36, 71 (1873).

[102]Justice Powell wrote the following in *Bakke*, 438 U.S. at 291-292 (1978):

The Court's initial view of the Fourteenth Amendment was that its "one pervading purpose" was "the freedom of the slave race, the security and firm establishment of that freedom, and the protection of the newly-made freeman and citizen from the oppressions of those who had formerly exercised dominion over him.". . . The Equal Protection Clause, however, was "[v]irtually strangled in its infancy by post-Civil-War judicial reactionism." It was relegated to decades of relative desuetude while the Due Process Clause of the Fourteenth Amendment, after a short germinal period, flourished as a cornerstone in the Court's defense of property and liberty of contract. . . . In that cause, the Fourteenth Amendment's "one pervading purpose" was displaced. . . . It was only as the era of substantive due process came to a close . . . that the

> Equal Protection Clause began to attain a genuine measure of vitality. . . .
>
> By that time it was no longer possible to peg the guarantees of the Fourteenth Amendment to the struggle for the equality of one racial minority. During the dormancy of the Equal Protection Clause, the United States had become a Nation of minorities.

Cf. Kenneth S. Tollett, "Philosophical Reflections Upon Social Science, Law and Public Policy," in Jan M. Broekman, Kazimierz Opalek and Dzhangir Ali-Abbasovich Kerimov, eds., *Social Justice and Individual Responsibility in the Welfare State*, Proceedings of the 11th World Congress on Philosophy of Law and Social Philisophy (Stuttgart, W. Germany: Franz Steiner Verlag Wiesbaden GmbH, 1985), pp. 154-155.

[103]See brief discussion of *Green* and *Swann* in note 88.

[104]Erwin N. Griswold, "The *Bakke* Problem—Allocation of Scarce Resources in Education and Other Areas," *Washington University Law Quarterly* 1979: 1 (Winter 1979): 55-80 at 66.

[105]Edley and Sperling compendiously state what the Reagan-Rehnquist Court has wrought in 1989:

> Since the start of this year, Supreme Court decisions have: hobbled a century-old statute against discrimination in private contracts; undermined Congress' effort to encourage voluntary settlements in discrimination suits; imposed uncertain but surely great burdens on governments that seek voluntarily to use race-conscious remedies such as contract set-asides; and blunted the strongest tool against subtle job discrimination, implicitly overruling a unanimous 1971 Supreme Court holding.

Christopher Edley, Jr., and Gene B. Sperling, "Have We Really 'Done Enough' for Civil Rights?" *Washington Post* (June 25, 1989), p. B1.

[106]See William Julius Wilson, *The Truly Disadvantaged: The Inner City, the Underclass, and Public Policy*, op. cit. note 11.

[107]James E. Cheek, "If We Do Not, Then Who Will?: The Continuing Burden to Undo the Yoke of Bondage," *ISEP Monitor* 4 (December 1980)): 5.

PUBLIC POLICY AND THE AFRICAN-AMERICAN FAMILY

Wade W. Nobles

San Francisco State University

The debate over whether the African-American family is an organization inherently laden with problems and inadequacies has raged literally from the beginning of the twentieth century.[1] Scholarly debate about the reasons for the intrinsic weakness of the African-American family has paralleled and mirrored the wider society's negative and pejorative image of African-American people. The fact of the matter is that the school of thought which posited an exclusively pathological or negative African-American family system resulted from racist and ideological contamination of scientific analysis. The family *qua* family is an institution, and all family systems have a particular functional integrity and are influenced by their interactions with wider societal systems. The African-American family is no exception to this empirical generalization.

A sound understanding of the African-American family as an institution, with strengths and weaknesses resulting from both its functional integrity and its structural relationship with external societal forces (or "praxis"), as well as the way these conditions are affected by public policy, necessitates the unravelling of several commingling issues. As an institution, the African-American family is situated in a society characterized by the twin forces of social and political exploitation and racial and cultural dehumanization (domination).

The ongoing debate regarding the proper role of government and public policy in relation to society in general, and the African-American family in particular, must always be qualified by the historical experiences of African-Americans. This issue of the proper role of government has most often been couched in terms of the extent to which the public sector (i.e., government) and the private sector (i.e., individual initiative) ought to allocate society's resources and ensure the acquisition of basic necessities. In effect, the question becomes to what extent should command mechanisms (the authority of the government) rather than market mechanisms (the laws of commerce) be utilized to allocate societal resources and security.[2] This debate seems reasonable, and although in the United States there is a historical bias in favor of market/private sector allocation, command/public sector mechanisms have been utilized to direct and redistribute resources and services. In relation to African-Americans, however, the debate over public versus private sector resources is somewhat specious.

Two facts must be recognized if one is to observe clearly and distinctly the pervasive and insidious nature of the phenomena that negatively affect African-American families. One must first recognize that discrimination is an act designed to separate people for the purpose of allowing one group to receive preferential treatment and advantage; and second, that in a system characterized by racism and oppression, almost every element or process managed by the racist system is designed primarily to continue and secure the status of the "advantaged" by guaranteeing preference in all arenas. Consequently, the conceptual and empirical connection between sociopolitical exploitation and racial/cultural dehumanization makes the distinction between the public and private imperceptible.

The history of the public and private sector treatment of African-Americans and its consequences for the African-American family mirror the same image. The private sector, which has and should serve as the arena for bettering one's life chances and conditions, has never allowed African-American people the opportunity to benefit from full and open participation. The structure of discrimination, which is the foremost tool of the twin forces of exploitation and dehumanization, has served virtually to prevent African-American advancement. Discrimination in education and employment has restricted and continues to restrict, if not eliminate, the paths to development and security for African-American people. At the turn of the century, for example, the United States was becoming an urban, industrial-based society; by participating in the private sector, some people were able to gain economic independence and to guarantee that their children would move up the socioeconomic ladder. But at the same time African-American people, regardless of education, were generally considered to be inferior, and relegated to low-status, poorly-paid occupations in the private sector. In fact, the structure of racial discrimination was such that northern white industrialists looked to Europe for the labor needed to build the burgeoning urban-industrial economy, rather than recruiting African-American freedmen from the labor-intensive South.[3] From industrial/corporate ownership to union/labor membership, racism and prejudice in the private sector have, for the most part, formed for African-American people an impenetrable barrier to permanent personal advancement and long-term family security.

Norman Bell and Ezra Vogel[4] have posited that the family contributes its loyalty to the government in exchange for leadership and governance which will provide direct and indirect benefits to the family. The underlying assumption here is that governmental intervention will serve the family. There is little doubt that African-American people have been loyal to the United States, but, although citizens, they have derived few reciprocal benefits for their loyalty.[5] The public sector has the power to change positively the conditions affecting African-American family life. However, as Andrew Billingsley observes, when the public sector is contaminated by the philosophies of domination and control, the mechanisms it utilizes are by definition incapable of intervening positively on behalf of the disenfranchised and exploited (i.e., African-American people). To the contrary, the power of the public sector serves as an additional negative force in shaping the conditions under which African-American people live.[6] Almost from the very moment that Africans were captured and enslaved in the United States, the public sector has pursued and established policies which have partially contributed to or guaranteed the victimization of the African-American family.[7]

During the period of American slavery, for instance, the public sector legally defined the African as less than human. Subsequent laws and practices (e.g., enslaved Africans could make no binding contracts or have legal redress) established the precedent for and ensured the exploitation of the African-American family. Public sector acts of commission and omission (e.g., the slave commodity exchange was more valued than African-American family bonds) resulted in the government doing nothing to ensure stable African-American family life. In fact, the national government was committed to the institution of slavery and the dehumanization of the African. The public sector in the United States in effect defaulted on its responsibility to protect the integrity of the African-American family. More recent public sector initiatives ranging from AFDC to Social Security to the policies of "benign neglect" and "workfare" must be viewed in this historical context. In fact, to look at public sector initiatives ahistorically results in confusion and distortions regarding what they can or should do. Historical events and experiences place both public and private initiatives in context. The contextual framework of ideas, beliefs, attitudes and forces which shapes and determines human events is very important. The idea of "context," for example, helps to explain the difference in outcomes between one running on an asphalt track and one running in two feet of water. Just as asphalt and water are contextual variables influencing both time and distance in running, the ideas held about African-American people and beliefs about reasonable use of command mechanisms influence and shape the development of public policy. Ideas and beliefs constitute an intellectual—and contextual—atmosphere which reflects the society's conceptual universe. This same context or intellectual atmosphere also, predictably, influences the scientific examination and understanding of African-American family dynamics.

One must examine the issue of the African-American family and public policy in terms of both the African-American family's functional integrity and its structural relationship to the set of ideas and beliefs constituting America's political context. For example, many scholars reject the idea of "the African-American family," arguing that the phenomenon known as the African-American family is not monolithic; African-American families do not march in lockstep and do not exhibit the same features, structures or practices. The same scholars then argue that there is no such thing as "the African-American family"; rather there are many different types of African-American families. Although not accepting the myopic, monolithic steroeotype of the African-American family, this author does not reject the appropriateness and applicability of the idea of the African-American family as an institution, especially in regard to its relevance to public policy.

The appropriateness of the concept of the African-American family as opposed to African-American families relates directly to how one defines the constellation of beings, ideas, values, beliefs, attitudes and practices which represent a family system. When one works with and studies African-American families thoroughly over an extended period of time, one cannot help but recognize that many different family forms and structures exist in African-American communities. However, scientific investigation of the African-American family also teaches one that in conjunction with the diversity of forms and structures, much similarity can be found among the "different" types of African-American families.

As social systems, families are products of society. Thus the recognizable specialness of a particular kind of family emerges as a function of the family's culture and its relationship with the larger society. Hence, the communality or "special sameness" found among African-American families is the result of their common historical experiences, and the relationship between the group (the roots of which rest in sociopolitical exploitation and racial/cultural dehumanization) and its common cultural ancestry (the base of which is African). Technically, therefore, the term African-American family has utility because the phenomenon so named has definable parameters which allow it to be located in time and space, recognized by the senses, and distinguished from other like phenomena. In effect, African-American family is a term used to classify the social and human organization of a group of people of African descent who are biologically and spiritually bonded, and whose relation to each other and the outside world are governed by a particular set of cultural beliefs, historical experiences and behavioral practices.

Institutions share a key attribute with organisms; as both weaken, their abilities to resist the ill effects of their environments diminish correspondingly. The African-American family is no different; the ill effects of American society, in the form of sociopolitical exploitation and racial/cultural dehumanization, constantly bombard African-American families, both directly and indirectly. Yet, the societal problems experienced by the African-American family and its members are often viewed as personal character flaws or indicators of racial inferiority. It is important, however, to note that the perception and definition of African-American family problems are influenced by the same societal values and forces. African-American family "problems" are not isolated, individualized and personal problems experienced by racially inferior people. The problems have their moorings in societal causations. Teenage pregnancy, for example, emanates not only from teenage sexuality and immaturity, but also from a larger array of societal influences. Substance abuse is not just a problem of individual character flaws, but is also a societal problem. Interpersonal violence is not only the failure of individual problem solving and coping strategies. The feminization of poverty is clearly a problem of the devaluation of women in this society. Educational failure is grounded in the inability of schools to teach the young. The criminalization of African-American youth ultimately results from this society providing only limited options for their development, thus narrowing if not eliminating their choices for adult productivity. And finally, the clearest example of societal problems masking themselves as family problems is "economic dependency." Economic dependency and unacceptable levels of African-American unemployment are without question the results of a society whose core value system is corroded and unjust. Hence, economic dependency is also a societal problem.

The problems experienced by the African-American family result from its structural relationship with American society, leading to a weakening of the former's functional integrity. This weakening is best revealed in the area of culture. The delegitimization/defamation of African culture, in fact, has been the principal instrument in the negative transformation of the African-American family institution. From its very origin American society articulated the racist and unsubstantiated opinion that African people were innately inferior. Purportedly,

Africans and those of African descent had no culture worthy of respect, or, at best, had a deviant culture deserving of ridicule and rejection.

Unfortunately, and probably in consequence of our socialization to judge a culture by its material artifacts and affluence, many African-American people have come to believe in the lie that African-American culture either is nonexistent or deviant. But culture is more than its material representations. Culture is a process which gives people a general design for living and patterns for interpreting reality. As such, culture emerges as a dynamic human system of features, factors and functions with sets of guiding principles, assumptions, codes, conventions, beliefs and rules which permit and determine how members of a group relate to each other and develop their creative potential. Accordingly, nothing human happens outside of the realm of culture. Most cross-cultural psychologists now recognize that when the symbols, rituals and rites of a culture lose their legitimacy and power to compel thought and action, disruption occurs within the cultural orientation and reflects itself as a pathology in the psychology of the people belonging to that culture.

Given that American society has often, via public policy and private action, attacked and denigrated African culture, and given that culture serves as the social cement for familial and societal functioning, the question becomes how the government can direct and redistribute resources and services in such a way so that the functional integrity of the African-American family system can be maintained and enhanced. In order to make this determination, one must fully understand and appreciate the concrete reality of African-American family life as well as the antecedent and consequential conditions in relation to that reality.

The African-American family has been a subject of study and investigation for over one hundred years, and for almost the total duration of that period, scientists, scholars and commentators have put forth the opinion that there is something intrinsically wrong with it. Nathan and Julia Hare[8] and Benjamin Bowser[9] call attention to the problem of African-American family analyses, pointing to the confusion surrounding the importance of culture and class, as well as to the influences of internal versus external factors. In spite of the difficulty in assessing accurately the African-American family, there are data to support the observation that African-American families across this nation are experiencing an ever-increasing weakness in their ability to function as viable human organizations. The emerging weaknesses in the African-American family are clear: decreasing self-reliance; the perpetuation of intergenerational dependency (the so-called welfare syndrome); increasing alienation and violence among the young; social isolation of the elderly; and, most important, a loss of spiritual values, or at least an exchange of spiritual values for materialist ones. These factors are all both causes and symptoms of the erosion of African-American family integrity.

In 1987, the estimated 29.6 million African-American people living in the United States represented 12.2 percent of an estimated total population of 242.8 million, or approximately one in every eight persons in the society. This number comprised 7.1 million African-American families. Structurally, the African-American family has undergone distressing and predictable change since the mid-twentieth century. In 1960, two-parent families nationally accounted for 80 percent of all African-American families. Almost three decades later in 1987, this state of affairs had been reversed, and single-parent families constituted 58.5 percent of all African-American families (55.3 percent were headed by women and 3.2 percent by men), while 41.5 percent were traditional two-parent (intact) families.[10] Approximately three-fifths of all African-American families reside in New York, California, Texas, Illinois, Georgia, Florida, North Carolina, Louisiana, Michigan and Ohio. In 1985, these ten states, in addition to Alabama, Maryland, New Jersey, Pennsylvania, South Carolina and Virginia, each had an African-American population in excess of one million.[11]

At a time when the wider society is popularizing the idea of African-American progress, census data indicate that the relative position of the African-American population is becoming worse and that the "image" of progress is more real than the "reality" of progress. For example, across the nation the ratio of the median African-American family income to the white family median fell from .61 in 1970 to .58 in 1980 and .56 in 1987.[12] In 1987, then, the African-American family had only fifty-six cents for every dollar the white family had to obtain the same necessities of life.

Moreover, unemployment continues to be a more common experience of African-Americans than their white counterparts. It is well-known that since the Korean War, the unemployment rate of African-Americans has remained roughly 2 to 2.5 times greater than that of whites, regardless of whether the economy was expanding or contracting. In 1972, for example, the white unemployment rate was 5.1 percent, but for African-Americans it was 10.4 percent. In 1982 (at the height of the 1981-1983 recession), they were 8.6 percent and 18.9 percent, respectively, and in 1987 the figures were 5.3 percent for whites and 13.0 percent for African-Americans.[13] Also, national data indicate that African-Americans remain unemployed longer than whites, and tend to become discouraged from seeking to join the work force at higher rates. The longevity of the condition suggests that for many

African-American families, the basic lifestyle is one of unemployment and economic dependence. In 1983, 48.5 percent or nearly one out of every two African-American teenagers was unemployed, a figure that had decreased to a still unacceptable 34.7 percent in 1987.[14] Sensitive to the historical context mentioned earlier, one can project that a significant proportion of African-American youth—i.e., the next generation of parents—will grow into adulthood and most likely parenthood without having had the experience of working and the feeling of self-reliance. It is known that unemployment during adolescence follows the African-American throughout his/her life cycle, making it more difficult to gain employment as an adult. One result of this is that the African-American family feels and experiences the negative consequences of unemployment far more often and in more different forms than the white family.

Turning to personal security and safety, it is known that African-Americans experience violent crimes, both as victims and offenders, at an overall rate higher than that of any other racial/ethnic group. Nationally, African-American people represent approximately two-fifths of the total arrests for violent crimes (i.e., murder, rape, robbery, etc.). Of the murder victims in 1980, 95 percent were killed by someone in their own social network. In terms of victimization, African-American families are more likely to suffer from residential burglary than other groups, and overall, crime tends to be intraracial, with most of the crimes committed by African-Americans against other African-Americans. Given African-American youths' involvement with the criminal justice system at an increasingly younger age, it appears that criminalization is becoming a major pattern of socialization for African-American youth, especially males, across the country.

The implication this has for the African-American family is almost beyond imagination, but lamentably not beyond reality. Crime, poverty, unemployment and violence are becoming synonymous with the urban experience, which is the single most important aspect of the contemporary conditions affecting African-American families. Until the mid-twentieth century, most African-American families were from rural southern areas. For some time now, though, the migratory pattern has been from the rural South into the urban central city, where limited employment opportunities, environmental pollutants, adverse mobility and decrepit housing, poor recreational facilities and unhealthy living conditions all affect negatively the life chances and quality of life of the African-American family.

Furthermore, education, which is so essential to the well-being of the African-American family, must be mentioned here, if only briefly. At a time when success demands a college education or technical training, the failure of African-American youngsters to go on to college is all too troublesome. In 1987, the American Council on Education reported that

> since 1976, Black high school graduates have been enrolling in college at a substantially lower rate. College enrollment rates for Blacks increased from 29.2 percent of high school graduates in 1971 to 33.5 percent in 1976. . . . [H]owever, between 1976 and 1985 the percentage dropped to 26.1 percent. . . . [T]his decline is *particularly alarming* since during this same period the number and rate of Blacks graduating from high school increased significantly. In 1976 just over two-thirds, or 67.5 percent, of the 3.3 million 18-24-year-old Blacks graduated from high school. In 1985, those figures had increased to 75.6 percent and 3.7 million, respectively.[15]

Concerning health, it is known that the generally poorer and environmentally inferior conditions of the inner-city urban experience directly affect the health status and psychological well-being of African-American families. Within the urban environment, most African-Americans live in neighborhoods with crowded living quarters of poor quality, depleted of community services and resources, and lacking viable business infrastructures. African-American people, as urban dwellers, also encounter an inordinate and inestimable amount of environmental hazards, with constant exposure to high levels of automobile emissions, a lack of open space, and high noise levels. These conditions may be associated with a higher death rate in the African-American community from heart diseases, strokes and cancers. Since the mid-1960s, the cancer incident rate in African-Americans has increased by 34 percent. The consequence of this is that three out of every four African-American families will have a cancer victim, and that one out of six African-American deaths is attributable to cancer each year.

Teenage pregnancy and parenting, though not exclusively health issues, must also be mentioned. The problem of teenage pregnancy is severe and appears to strike at the very basis of the African-American family's ability to provide education and training to its young members. In 1981, 562,000 or 16 percent of all births in the United States were to teenagers; 27 percent of those teenage births, or 152,000, were to African-American teenagers. One out of every four African-American births in the United States in 1982 was to a teenager and one out of every two first births was to a teenager. In addition, the majority of these births were to unmarried women. This suggests that African-American women begin the process of childbearing at very young ages. Over the long term, early childbearing results in undesirable life conditions for the teenage parent. It is also generally acknowledged that infants born to teenage parents are an at-risk population in terms of both social and emotional development, as well as physical abuse and neglect. Hence, lower levels of education, arrested career development, greater dependency on public assistance and a host of other vexations are becoming the norm for these children.

It is extremely important, however, that in addressing the teenage pregnancy and parenting problem, we are conscious of the fact that it is not simply the girl's problem. There is a male side to the equation that must be addressed as well. Sensitive and sound adult interaction with teenage males as well as females is critical to the prevention of teenage pregnancy, which is a social and cultural phenomenon, and not simply one of gender.

Nationally, drug-related behavior and drug trafficking have become the newest and most dangerous problem confronting African-American families. Few understand the full implications of the drug culture and drug lifestyles which are emerging as the standard and model of African-American community life. Also, the tie between drugs and crime is obvious. Recent research on the mental health impact of drugs and drug trafficking on African-American children and families in Oakland[16] suggests that the emerging drug culture may be responsible for the ultimate destruction of the African-American family.

Lawford L. Goddard, a sociologist and demographer associated with the Institute for the Advanced Study of Black Family Life and Culture and the Drew-King Medical School at UCLA, subscribes to the observation that were the past and present socioeconomic trends to continue, we would witness the establishment of a permanent African-American underclass in the United States. He believes that basic demographic changes have affected the structure of the African-American population. In 1980, the African-American population of 26.7 million people comprised 11.8 percent of the nation's population. Of this group, 45 percent of the males and 34 percent of the females were under twenty years old. There were ninety males for every one hundred females. The African-American population is a relatively young one with a median age of 23.6 years for males and 26.2 for females. This population is projected to increase to 33 million by 1995 and 35 million by the year 2000.[17] This population will, of course, age somewhat. It is projected that by 2000, 35 percent of the males and 31 percent of the females will be under twenty years of age. In spite of this aging, the African-American population will continue to be a young one relative to the national population.

The most significant demographic change in the African-American population has been the change in the sex ratio. It has declined steadily throughout the twentieth century, although it is projected to be ninety-one males for every one hundred females at the onset of the twenty-first century. The decline in the sex ratio has been a consequence of three fundamental processes affecting African-American males.[18] First, there was a significant loss of African-American males in the Korean and Vietnam Wars, resulting in noteworthy shortages of African-American males in the middle-age group, thirty-five to forty-nine years old. Second, African-American males have been incarcerated disproportionately in relation to their white counterparts. Prison data indicate that African-Americans accounted for 46.5 percent of the federal and state prison population in 1980 and 45.9 percent in 1985. Moreover, of the 227,137 African-Americans incarcerated in these prisons in 1985, only 10,793 or 4.75 percent were females.[19] African-Americans are also more likely to receive longer prison terms than whites for the same crimes, which is consistent with a long-established historical pattern. Finally, the African-American sex ratio is affected by violence. African-American males are more likely to be the victims of violent crime than any other group in the society. In 1980, the African-American male homicide rate of 66.6 per 100,000 was nearly five times the rate of 13.5 for African-American females, six times the rate of 10.9 for white males, and twenty times the rate of 3.2 for white females. (In 1986, the figures were 55.0, 12.1, 8.6 and 3.0, respectively.)[20] In the age group of twenty-to-twenty-four years, homicide is the leading cause of death among African-American males. Among African-American male teenagers, violence (i.e., suicide, accidents, homicide) is the leading cause of death.

These social processes affect the African-American male population in that age range (twenty-to-forty years old) which is most significant in the process of family formation. This basic demographic change has affected the composition of the African-American population to such an extent that the single-parent household has become a common form of family structure. If demographic shifts such as the sex ratio continue, the single-parent household is likely to be the major form of African-American family organization in the twenty-first century.

The structure and composition of the African-American family has changed to such an extent that the proportion of families maintained by a woman with no husband present has more than doubled since the 1960s. African-American female-headed families increased from 22 percent of families in 1960 to 45 percent in 1983. Along with this increase in female-headed African-American families has been a relative decline in the proportion of childless African-American families, which fell from 44 percent in 1960 to 40 percent in 1983. A significant factor in the decline of African-American childless families has been the pattern of early childbearing among African-American women. In 1983, 50 percent of all African-American women between the ages of eighteen and twenty-four had given birth to at least one child. The data also indicate that by age twenty-seven, most African-American women have completed their childbearing experience. The consequence of this early childbearing pattern and the decline in the sex ratio is that the proportion of female-headed African-American families with children has increased. The proportion of African-American single-parent families increased from 44 percent in 1960 to 72 percent in 1983, and the proportion of African-American children living with both parents has declined from 80 percent in 1960 to 42 percent in 1987.

The ability of these single-parent units to provide adequate care and sustenance for their children is taxed severely given the changing national economy, patterns of employment, and the changing value system in the African-American community. In this context, the eroding economic well-being of the African-American family is of great concern. The United States has long begun a transition from an industrial- and manufacturing-based economy to one based on providing services and processing information. This shift increases the probability of the continued erosion of the economic viability of the African-American family. Already some of the gains made by African-Americans in acquiring skilled and semi-skilled occupations (blue-collar jobs) have been lost as a result of structural changes in the prime manufacturing sector of the economy (steel, automobile, rubber, etc.). As the American economy retools its technology to increase productivity and maintain a competitive edge in world markets, new technological and scientific advances (robots, lasers, computers, etc.) will continue to be introduced into the workplace. As this process unfolds, African-American workers will be disproportionately displaced because a service and information-producing economy requires a different pool of skilled workers (e.g., computer programmers, analysts, media specialists, etc.). Generally, African-American workers do not now have these skills and are not being trained for them in sufficient numbers.

The displacement of the African-American worker was most evident in the period from 1972 to 1982, when the unemployment rate of the African-American population increased by 140 percent. Although as of 1987 the unemployment rate of African-Americans had declined to 13.0 percent from 18.9 percent in 1982, it was still intolerably high.[21] A significant factor that is often overlooked in considering the unemployment rate is the withdrawal of the African-American male from the work force. The work force participation rate of African-American males declined from 83 percent in 1960 to 70 percent in 1982. Among African-American females the opposite trend occurred, with the work force participation rate increasing from 48 percent in 1960 to 54 percent in 1982.

The participation of the African-American woman in the work force has allowed the African-American family to maintain some semblance of economic solvency and even to approximate, in many cases, middle-class living. This point needs to be stressed. In the mid-1970s, 48 percent of African-American women were in the work force as compared to 35 percent of white women. The comparative data prior to this period are very similar to these, suggesting that, historically, African-American women participated in the work force alongside African-American men before it was fashionable as an expression of self-actualization or sex equity. This is also a fairly strong indicator of racism as a contextual variable in African-American reality. (That is, because of racism and economic exploitation, the solvency of the African-American family has almost always depended upon two wage earners.) Given the changing family structure and the withdrawal of the African-American male from the work force, it is not unsound to suggest that the future African-American family is likely to have only one worker—and that worker will be a woman.

The current pattern of employment makes it unlikely that African-American females will be able to provide for their children in the way they would no doubt desire. African-American female employment has traditionally been concentrated in the lower echelons of the economic system (e.g., service and white-collar occupations such as teachers, counselors, health technologists, nurses, secretaries, food service workers, custodians, etc.), characterized by low pay, high turnover rates, greater incidence of unemployment, and limited opportunities for occupational mobility. Predictably, the African-American single-parent family has and will continue to have a difficult time economically. The median income of African-American single-parent families was only $7,501 in 1981, down from the 1971 figure of $8,185 to which it still had not rebounded in 1987 when it was $7,981.[22] More than half of African-American single-parent families are living below the poverty level, and in 1987, 45.1 percent of all African-American children lived in poverty.[23] The implication of this state of affairs is that the next generation of African-American adults is likely to be less economically capable than their parents, marking a troublesome retrogression in the economic progress of the African-American population.

Given the preceding observations and the analytical distinctions between public and private sector initiatives, the question of public policy capability to address the needs of African-American families becomes even more critical. However, before one can evaluate public policy's impact on African-American family functioning, one must un-

derstand what constitutes authentic African-American family functioning, as distinct from "praxis problems" in the African-American
family system.

In order to understand what constitutes authentic African-American family functioning, and thereby appreciate fully the intrinsic integrity of African-American family life, close attention must be paid to
culture. Asa Hilliard[24] has observed that family systems cannot exist
in the absence of a cultural base. Yet, a good deal of orthodox scholarship on the African-American family has accepted the notions that (1)
African culture and the retention of cultural residuals from Africa were
radically destroyed and eliminated during the slave trade and
America's period of slavery; and (2) the American experience ultimately determined and shaped the reality of African-American family
life. In accepting these two notions, those who subscribe to the orthodox examination and understanding of African-American family life
have erroneously bound themselves to an autogenous analysis of the
existential development of African-American families in American
society.

The common themes which run through most non-African-American analyses of the African-American family are that (1) the original
African cultural and philosophical heritage of African-American people was destroyed or modified qualitatively; (2) African-American families are products of the American experience; (3) American society is
homogeneous (a melting pot); and (4) to differ from the standard (i.e.,
white) American family form is an indicator of deviancy. Thus, the
African-American family has been depicted as a disorganized and pathological form of social organization and functioning.

In stating that this perception is wrong, one does not wish to imply
that African-American family life is without problems. The family life
of African-American people is marked by a range of adversities which,
for the most part, emerges from its relationship with a racist and oppressive social structure. To recognize this, while simultaneously calling into question the character of the scientific paradigm which misdi-
rects analyses and overwhelmingly defines African-American family
life as negativistic, problem-laden and pathological, is not inconsistent.
It is, in fact, necessary in order to explain the difference between problems in the African-American family and problems in the *study* of the
African-American family.

Culture is important. In fact, many students of liberation struggles[25] have noted that culture serves as a weapon in a people's struggle
because the suppression or denial of their culture is a part of their enslavement. Culture is the process that gives people a general design for
living and patterns for interpreting their reality.[26] It provides a people

with their indigenous definition and with the meaning of human processes. Because each culture has its own vision or conception of the human experience (its social psychology of humanity), each will also have its own intrinsic conception of how to function as "a family." Through its implicit philosophy of family, each culture asks what the family is, what the family's purpose should be, and how individuals and society as a whole should behave in response to the family. Culture also defines the criteria for providing answers to these critical questions. Unfortunately, in most instances, members of a given society or culture ask and answer these questions without being conscious of the process.

It is, in part, because of the importance of public policy that one must detail and explicate African and African-American peoples' cultural vision regarding family. The cultural vision (or world view) of any group of people functions like a special set of lenses which, in focusing upon a given slice of objective reality, perceives and is aware of those situations which are meaningful and excludes those which are not. It is primarily through this special set of lenses that the myriad of sensory impressions received by an individual is filtered, organized and transformed into mental impressions and behavioral dispositions and responses. In a very real sense, culture provides a code or set of instructions which organizes the reception of "sensory" data. It occasions the rejection of what is perceived to be inappropriate information, and the acceptance of whatever is deemed to be appropriate. It taps the reservoir of past associations, ideas and knowledge in defining problems and constructing their solutions.

The African-American culture in the United States is the result of a special mixture of continued African orientation operating within another cultural milieu, which is defined primarily by the philosophical assumptions and underpinnings of the Anglo-American community.[27] It is the African perspective that is at the base of the African-American cultural milieu. And so, it is the continuation of that African vision which is at the root of the special features in African-American family lifestyles. It is, in effect, the continuation of the African orientation that, in part, helps to define the "general design for living and the patterns for interpreting reality" for, or characteristic of, African-American people. In order to demonstrate this contention, a brief discussion of traditional African belief systems, particularly as they relate to family, is necessary.

When considering the African-American family, it is important to understand the African philosophical, ontological and cosmological conception of the universe. The implicit African cosmological (oneness of the origin and being) and ontological (the nature of being is as a spirit) conceptions, along with the particular definitions of time and space within these cosmological and ontological constructs, suggest that the family constitutes the center of one's being or existence. Individual consciousness is such that the family constitutes the reference point wherein one's existence is perceived as being interconnected to the existence of all else. On this point, John Mbiti[28] observes that for Africans, the individual owes his very existence to all the members (living, dead and yet unborn) of the family, tribe or clan. Mbiti further notes that the individual does not and cannot exist alone. The individual is an integral part of the collective unity, i.e., the family.

Ontologically, the African belief system understands that the nature of all things in the universe is "force" or "spirit."[29] It is logical, or at least consistent, that in believing that all things, including man, are endowed with the same supreme force, Africans would also believe that all things are "essentially" one. This notion is referred to as the ontological principle of consubstantiation.

For the African, a natural feature of the universe is the multiplicity of forms and moments. What characterizes African peoples' understanding of the universe is, consequently, a simultaneous respect for the concrete detail in the multiplicity of forms and the rejection of the possibility of an absence or vacuum of forms. The African conception of the world and all of the phenomena within it amounts to a set of syntheses (connections) and contradictions (antagonisms) linked to a particular classification of beings as differential quantifications of force. Combined, these "connectual" and "antagonistic" participatory sets form the whole of universal relations, and, thereby, family relations.

The notion of "self" is based on one's individual consciousness, taking as its reference point the family, wherein one's existence is perceived as being interconnected to the existence of all else. More specifically, one can note that the traditional philosophical notion of oneness of being requires that man conceptualize his own existence as an awareness of his universal connectedness, that is, man is an indispensable, integrated and interdependent part of the universe. The notions of interdependence and oneness of being allow for a conception of self which transcends, throughout the historical consciousness of one's people, the finiteness of the physical body, space and time. The notion of self, or more specifically, the awareness of self within African peoples, is, therefore, not limited to just the cognitive awareness of one's own uniqueness, individuality and historical finiteness. The most compelling property of the traditional notion of self is the process of cosmologically grounding oneself in the collective, social and spiritual sense of the history of one's people or family.

Across African family systems the clan is believed to be a sort of total entity, of which its members—like the elemental structure of the universe—are integral and interconnected parts. The family, which includes the living, the dead and the yet unborn,[30] is thought to be the center or focal point, wherein the essence of the community or peoplehood is kept alive. The family is based on the unity and diversity of people and processes. It is at the very heart of one's existence, and serves as the center of the universe. In recognition of this kind of self-awareness, one can note that the traditional African view of "self" (and the view of most contemporary African descendants) is contingent upon the existence of family.

When one examines intrinsic African-American family functions as distinct from examples of structural breakdown (e.g., single-parent households), the retention of the cultural vision articulated above is quite evident. It is in terms of family functions (i.e., organizational purpose, social organization, interpersonal relations and role relations) and the meanings attributed to these that authentic and positive African-American family functioning is evidenced.

A number of African-American family researchers[31] have suggested that the functional integrity of African-American family systems remains influenced by African cultural perceptions. Thus, authentic, intrinsic family functioning has to be examined in its own right. Organizational purpose, for instance, refers to the primary purpose of the existence of the family organization. In effect, organizational purpose selects and determines what is of importance to a given family system. As such, the organizational purpose of African-American families is best described as "child-centered." By this is meant that the purpose of the African-American family focuses on, even if it does not require, the presence of children. The family system exists for the affirmation of life. It literally exists for the growth and development of children, rather than for the self-actualization of the adult members of the unit.

Social organization pertains to the organized pattern of functions and relations within the family organization. In a general sense, the social organization reflects the ethos or set of guiding principles by which the family organization operates and by which its members must abide. Thus, the social organizational quality of the African-American family reveals a close network of relationships within and between families. This "family networking" in the African-American community, though being seriously eroded by the vicissitudes and imperatives of urban life, has served as an unrecognized cohesive force in the community and has been the basis of many services (e.g., child care, financial aid, counseling) which are otherwise not readily available to African-American people. The special aspect of this family networking worth highlighting is the "elastic" nature of the family structurally. The African-American family, in effect, essentially "stretches" to accommodate new members (i.e., non-blood relatives) into the network. The importance of these "social relatives," or "para-kin," is almost indistinguishable from that of biological or legal relatives. The close intrafamily relations as well as the cohesive interfamily network serve both pragmatic and psychological functions.[32]

Many African-American families comprise several individual households, with the family definition and lines of authority and decision-making transcending any one household unit in the "family."[33] In terms of interpersonal relationships, one of the most striking qualities of African-American family life is the presence of "multiple parentage." Historically, parents in African-American families have invariably received help in rearing their children from other members of the clan or community. In a similar way, older siblings perform significant child rearing or parenting functions in the African-American family. In addition, it is not unusual for African-American children to be allowed to visit other relatives for long periods of time as "members" of their relatives' immediate households. These temporary and periodic "interfamilial consensual adoptions" must have a real and profound effect on the child's development.

Children in African-American families are also exposed to several kinds of roles, both in and out of their immediate households. Role relations within the African-American family are flexible and interchangeable. In terms of intentional or specific roles, however, African-American parents make a clear distinction between "role definition" and "role performance." Role definitions are sex-linked, while roles are performed regardless of sex. African-American parents generally feel it to be very important for their male children, for example, to learn what it means to be masculine and possess "manly" qualities, while for their female children, the emphasis is on understanding and acquiring "feminine" qualities. This pattern of socialization, though, is in relation to definition and not performance. Research data on role performance attest overwhelmingly to the belief of African-American parents that their children, regardless of sex, should be equipped with the pragmatic skills and psychological attitudes to support themselves and their families. Finally, as is true in African families, in African-American families the elderly play a crucial role in the affairs of family life. They serve the critical function of instilling in the young a sense of family, and they provide an important source of psychological support in easing the traumas of family transitions or crises.

The African-American family clearly represents a complex human phenomenon with recognizable strengths and weaknesses both intrinsically and in terms of its relationship with external forces. It is in fact this complexity that must be captured and considered in the development of public policy.

Public Policy and African-American Family Life

Public policy ultimately must address itself to both the intrinsic functional integrity of African-American family systems and the external structural relation between the African-American family and the wider sociopolitical reality. This is especially important in the context of the observation of William Darity and Samuel Myers that private and public sector forces are in open competition for the control of American society.[34] The private sector forces represent the business establishment and its vested interests, while the public sector forces represent the governmental establishment and its. Each of these forces, in turn, utilizes its intelligentsia in articulating and defending its interests. However, when it comes to the interests of the African-American family, the distinction between the vested interests of the private and public sectors seems to fade. This distinction, in fact, disappears when one examines the philosophical foundation and conceptual universe upon which each is built. Parenthetically, it probably should be noted that the distinction in actuality does not exist, and it is only upon applying the public/private dichotomy to the area of African-American family life that the illusory nature of the distinction is revealed.

In science, the conceptual universe takes the form of paradigms which, technically speaking, serve as formalized frameworks that guide descriptions, explanations and evaluations of the empirical world. A paradigm is an instrument for knowing. At the center of the conceptual universe lies a core set of ideas which gives the conceptual universe its particular focus and/or orientation. A people's understanding of the world is guided by its conceptual universe, which in turn not only determines the people's perception of human capabilities, but also guides the development of new human inventions.[35] How a people define and classify both regular and irregular patterns of social interactions, behavior and development is determined and guided by their conceptual universe. It defines and determines the meaning and purpose of human (social) relationships and experiences. In the United States, both public and private sector interests are filtered through a single conceptual universe that is grounded in the same philosophical and cultural traditions. Hence, in the determination of public policy, the public and private sectors approach the issue of understanding societal problems and clarifying, justifying and defending solutions from a common conceptual universe. This is illustrated well in the area of the intellectual or scholarly treatment of the African-American family.

The core idea at the center of the conceptual universe of American society regarding African-American people is the notion of inferiority and annihilation.[36] The paradigms for understanding African-American reality, especially African-American family life, have been governed by this particular conceptual universe. Syed Khatib[37] notes, for instance, that from this perspective scientific examination of African-American people takes as its interpretative framework that of non-African-American people. The overweighted emphasis on "the study of negativity" in African-American family research is thus understandable as a methodological and epistemological artifact when one reflects upon the centrality of race in American social relationships. In further recognition of the social and racial grounding of knowledge concerning the African-American family, Robert Staples[38] observes that the imposition of ethnocentric (white) values on the analysis of African-American family life precludes the application of much of the nontraditional research and theory concerning the African-American family. Several African-American scholars[39] have in fact concluded that the major reason why African-American family life studies yield negative conclusions lies not with the intrinsic family functioning, but rather with the inappropriateness and inapplicability of the conceptual universe utilized by the intelligentsia to guide the studies. A conceptual universe which accepts as a basic tenet the innate inferiority of African peoples has real limitations for explicating the true problems associated with African-American family life.

The private and public sectors draw equally from the same intellectual source. Thus, their definitions of problems and solutions in relation to African-American family life do not differ. Only the techniques and agents of change, or source of solution, differ. Consequently, it is not surprising that public policy thus far has directed itself at solving "perceived" intrinsic family functioning problems. However, as noted previously, African-American family problems, upon closer examination, are observed to be related to the position of African-Americans in American society, and not intrinsic functioning problems.

The issue of public policy as it affects African-American families, therefore, must be viewed very carefully, since it is clouded by the complexity of public and private sector interests as well as by the intellectual tradition utilized by both to argue for or against public policy initiatives. There is a direct connection between the establishment of "laws of the land" (i.e., public policy) and the findings of the intelligentsia (i.e., social scientific information). The social scientist, in effect, provides the facts and the "truths" upon which policies are based. Obviously, to the extent that these policies are based on incorrect or inaccurate "facts," national policy is likely to become more of a problem than an aid to the people. Since the social scientific community historically has viewed the African-American family as deviant, pathological and weak organizationally, it follows both conceptually and empirically that public policies have been based on these perceptions.

Metropolitan population growth, for instance, is a basic feature of the social and economic transformation of American society. The growth and dispersion of the metropolitan population have created new and intensified old problems of social organization, and have affected several social institutions. In the case of African-Americans, the process of urbanization occurred at a dramatic pace. In 1900, the vast majority of the African-American population (77 percent) lived in rural areas, and only 23 percent lived in the urban areas. Within the short span of eighty years, the figures were completely reversed. Now, 75 percent of African-Americans live in urban/metropolitan areas, and only 25 percent live in rural areas. Several public policy programs and laws have been introduced to alleviate or solve some of the crucial problems facing urban areas. Since 1937, for example, the U.S. Congress has passed eighty-three housing laws. In 1949, public policy in the form of a housing act was passed, the purpose of which was to provide "a decent home and a suitable living environment for every American family."[40] That this program and subsequent housing laws did not solve the housing problem is evidenced by the fact that in 1974, another housing and community development act was passed. The purpose of that new act was "the development of viable urban communities, by providing decent housing and a suitable living environment and expanding economic opportunities, principally for persons of low and moderate income."[41]

In the field of employment, public policy resulted in the Employment Act of 1946. The purpose of this law was "to promote maximum employment, production, and purchasing power."[42] However, in 1964 more legislation (i.e., the Economic Opportunity Act) was still needed to "eliminate the paradox of poverty in the midst of plenty."[43] In the same year, the Civil Rights Act of 1964 was enacted in order to eliminate discrimination and provide equal employment opportunities for all.[44] In 1965, public policy in the form of the Elementary and Secondary Education Act was established "to strengthen and improve educational quality and educational opportunities in the Nation's elementary and secondary schools."[45] Eight years later, the Comprehensive Employment and Training Act was passed "to provide job training and employment opportunities . . . and enhance self-sufficiency by establishing a flexible and decentralized system of Federal, State, and local programs."[46]

An examination of public policy thus calls out the importance of the theoretical framework guiding the intellectual study of the African-American family. A review of the literature completed in the early 1980s revealed, for instance, that the "victimization orientation" prevailed in African-American family analyses in the 1940s.[47] This occurred at a time of massive migrations of African-American people to urban areas in the North, with the consequent dislocation and disruption of their family structure. Public policy initiatives emphasizing housing and urban life predictably rose in this period. Similarly, in the 1960s when the policy emphasis was on housing and urban development, African-American family research was characterized by the orientation which suggested that the internal dynamics of the African-American family were the primary factors in its decline and decay. Later, when scientific research on the African-American family was guided by the "poverty-acculturation" orientation, which emphasized economic conditions as the primary causal factor for the observed features of the purportedly dysfunctional African-American family, public policy emphasized employment issues.

The clearest example of the way in which public policy, based on incorrect social science research, has negatively affected African-American families is seen in the Moynihan[48] and Coleman[49] reports. Both studies, based on the deficit model of African-American culture, implied that some internal features of the African-American family and community were weak and had to be corrected. Consequently, policies such as Head Start, Upward Bound, cultural enrichment, school integration, the Work Incentive Program and Operation Mainstream were all introduced with the intention of improving the quality of life for the "deficient" African-American population. However, by failing to provide an accurate representation of African-American family dynamics or African-American reality in the United States, the analyses of Moynihan and Coleman led to the emergence of public policies that were based upon misconceptions and "mistakes of meaning." These policies failed to occasion any positive and permanent transformations in the African-American community.

The well-being of a people is contingent upon the family system's ability to satisfy or accomplish a number of things: (1) a set of human imperatives which include procreation, protection, sustenance, rest and education; (2) specific cultural requirements, which include sociocultural traditions, the family's sense of being, and rites, rituals and protocols; and (3) the relational essences which reflect the particular biological integrity, sense of efficacy, intimacy and permanence of the members of the family system.[50] As has been said earlier, the well-being of a people in society is contingent upon how effectively the family system functions internally and externally. Internally, the family process should result in a sense of personal worth, individual dignity and family unity. Externally, the family process should result in economic self-sufficiency, political efficacy and sociocultural integrity. When the family system or process is weakened, public policy must be devised that aims at restrengthening the family's internal and external capacities.

However, in the United States public policy solutions have, for the most part, been designed to remedy perceived weaknesses in the intrinsic functioning of the African-American family. With the exception of a few examples (e.g., the 1954 *Brown* decision and the Thirteenth, Fourteenth and Fifteenth Amendments), public policy has seldom been used as an instrument to change problems in African-American families resulting from their structural relationship with American society.

In helping to satisfy the human imperatives and cultural requirements of a community, public policy mechanisms must respect the reality of African-American family life. To do so means that in the utilization of societal mechanisms to respond to the needs of African-American families, the framers and administrators of public policy must be sensitive in providing aid and resources in ways that neither disturb nor damage the authentic functional integrity of the family system. The challenge will be to design public policy that responds not only to the legitimate interests of public and private sector mechanisms, but also to the distinction between the intrinsic functioning of the African-American family and its structural relationship with societal institutions and forces. Recent public policy initiatives in the areas of maternity and paternity leave and benefits, childcare, equal employment and pay equity, maternal and child health care, and flexible working conditions must, therefore, be reviewed in relation to their impact on the African-American family. Similarly, the twenty recommendations which emerged from the 1980 White House Conference on Families,[51] and which may yet serve as a blueprint for future family policy decisions, must be reevaluated relative to the African-American family.

Public policy designed to meet the challenges of the twenty-first century must be broad and extensive enough to allow for the expression of the varied and different features of American families in a multicultural society. We must constantly remind ourselves that national policy, as it affects family features, historically has not allowed for the expression of that diversity. For example, most health care legislation works against the process of elasticity in African-American family structures, such as interfamilial consensual adoptions, in that these intrinsic cultural behaviors are not recognized by law. Similarly, the organizational purpose of African-American families, which centers on the procreation and development of children, is devalued by the wider society. This is evidenced by the heavy emphasis on family planning, the use of fertility as an index which depresses the quality of life, and the stigma attached to recipients of Aid to Families with Dependent Children. Assuming that only one form of family structure is normal, and then viewing all differences from this conceptual model as deviations, impels one to ignore the cultural diversity of American society. Public policy based on the implicit definition of a single homogeneous family type results in the underdevelopment and oppression of families belonging to different ethnic and racial groups in the society.

Future public policy will therefore have the dual responsibility of preserving the cultural integrity of the African-American family, while protecting it from the harmful consequences of social structures built upon sociopolitical exploitation and racial and cultural dehumanization. Public policy formation presupposes certain economic, political and social constraints, proceeding from these to develop methods and mechanisms which make resource distribution and service delivery systems more efficient, effective and, hopefully, equitable. However, when the American political process is viewed as a zero-sum game and power as absolute, Marguerite Ross Barnett correctly notes that African-American people historically have been "external" to the American creed and left out of the rewards of the American dream.[52] Accordingly, the only type of public policy which will in fact assist African-Americans is one which necessitates them to confront and define for themselves their unique position in American society. Public policy concerning African-American families must be filtered through their own self-definition. As long as public policy initiatives are not openly responsive to the cultural integrity and objective conditions of African-American people, the goals and objectives of the initiatives will fail and the conditions of African-American family life will continue to worsen. African-Americans will then truly become a permanent and irreversible underclass in American society.

NOTES

[1] Wade W. Nobles and Lawford L. Goddard, *Understanding the Black Family: A Guide for Scholarship and Research* (Oakland, CA: Black Family Institute Publications, 1984), pp. 1-10.

[2]John Wanat, *Introduction to Budgeting* (Scituate, MA: Duxbury Press, 1978), pp. 14-25.

[3]Joel S. Kovel, *White Racism: Psychohistory* (New York: Vintage Books, 1971, © 1970). Kovel argues that racism is deeply embedded in the white psyche, an essential part of white American culture which is indistinguishable from the rest of American life. Hence, even with "business decisions," racism plays a central role.

[4]Norman Bell and Ezra Vogel, eds., *A Modern Introduction to the Family*, rev'd ed. (New York: Free Press, 1968, © 1960), pp. 14-16. Bell and Vogel note that in every society, the family submits to the rulership of government and exchanges its loyalty to governmental constraints for greater leadership and benefits in the form of direct and indirect services and security. In regard to the specific case of African-American families, however, they note that historically the exchange principle has been violated.

[5]Robert Staples, "Public Policy and the Changing Status of Black Families," in Robert Staples, ed., *The Black Family: Essays and Studies*, 2d ed. (Belmont, CA: Wadsworth Publishing Co., 1978), pp. 263-269.

[6]Andrew Billingsley, *Black Families in White America* (Englewood Cliffs, NJ: Prentice-Hall, 1978), pp. 177-181. Billingsley points out that when the public sector is contaminated by the philosophies of domination and control, then the control mechanism society utilizes or invents will by definition be incapable of effectively intervening on behalf of the dominated and exploited. Accordingly, he notes, in the case of African-American families, the control mechanism of this society too often serves as an additional negative force in guaranteeing their disenfranchisement.

[7]Staples, op. cit. note 5, p. 264.

[8]Nathan Hare and Julia Hare, *The Endangered Black Family: Coping with the Unisexualization and Coming Extinction of the Black Race* (San Francisco: Black Think Tank Publishers, 1984), pp. 7-19. The Hares discuss the sociopolitical aspects of research on the black family and note that due to political and not scientific considerations, some black and most white intellectuals adopted a theoretical approach which misdirected the analyses of black family life, drawing attention away from analyzing the conditions imposed on black families by an oppressive and racist society.

[9]Benjamin Bowser, "Community and Economic Context of Black Families: A Critical Review of the Literature, 1909-1985," *Journal of Social Psychiatry* 6: 1 (Winter 1986): 17-26.

[10]U.S. Bureau of the Census, *Statistical Abstract of the United States: 1989*, 109th ed. (Washington, D.C.: U.S. Government Printing Office, 1989), p. 50.

[11]"Minority Population State by State," *New York Times* (June 21, 1989).

[12]U.S. Bureau of the Census, op. cit. note 10, p. 445.

[13]Ibid., p. 393.

[14]Ibid.

[15]American Council on Education, Office of Minority Concerns, "Minorities In Higher Education" (Washington, D.C.: American Council on Education, 1987), p. 3. (Author's italics.)

[16]Wade W. Nobles, et al., "The Mental Health Impact of Drugs and Drug Trafficking on African-American Children and Families in Oakland: Alameda County Final Report" (Oakland, CA: Black Family Institute Publications, 1987), pp. 57-89. Rather than focusing on drug use and abuse as a social, economic, legal or health problem, the Nobles team examined the impact of an emerging drug culture and value system on the mental health of African-American families and children. They concluded that if left unattended, the drug culture is capable of inflicting irreversible damage on the African-American family.

[17]U.S. Bureau of the Census, op. cit., note 10, p. 14.

[18]Lawford L. Goddard, "The Future of the African-American Family," *Southern Christian Leadership Conference National Magazine* 15: 2 (May/June 1986): 82-85. Goddard views the decline in the sex ratio between African-American males and females as the consequence of three fundamental processes specifically affecting African-American males: inordinate loss of life in the Korean and Vietnam wars; differential patterns of institutionalization; and the effects of community-based violence.

[19]U.S. Bureau of the Census, *Statistical Abstract of the United States: 1988*, 108th ed. (Washington, D.C.: U.S. Government Printing Office, 1988), p. 175.

[20]U.S. Bureau of the Census, op. cit. note 10, p. 168.

[21]Ibid., p. 393.

[22]Ibid., p. 442.

[23]Ibid., p. 454.

[24]Asa Hilliard, "The Maroon in the United States: The Lessons of Africa for the Parenting and Education of African-American Children," *Journal of African-American Studies* (San Francisco State University) 1: 2 (Fall/Winter 1983): 14-22. According to Hilliard, no family system can exist in the absence of a cultural base; the reclamation of their indigenous cultural base is the necessary foundation of effective African-American parenting.

[25]Africa Information Service, ed., *Return to the Source: Selected Speeches [of Amilcar Cabrall]* (New York: Monthly Review Press, 1974, © 1973), pp. 75-92.

[26]Wade W. Nobles, *Africanity and the Black Family: The Development of a Theoretical Model* (Oakland, CA: Black Family Institute Publications, 1985), p. 54. The problem of imposing inappropriate ethnocentric analyses on the black family is addressed, an act which, it is argued, results in the false depiction of the African-American family as an "illegitimate white family." In calling for a more appropriate theoretical model, the article further highlights the implications of the epistemological shift in the study of the African-American family.

[27]Ibid., p. 55.

[28]John S. Mbiti, *African Religions and Philosophy* (Garden City, NY: Doubleday, 1970), pp. 33-45.

[29]Placide Tempels, *Bantu Philosophy* (Paris: Presence Africaine, 1959), pp. 3-34.

[30]Pierre Erny, *Childhood and Cosmos: The Social Psychology of the Black African Child* (Washington, D.C.: Black Orpheus Press, 1973), pp. 183-197.

[31]Wade W. Nobles, "A Formulative and Empirical Study of Black Families: Final Report" (Washington, D.C.: U.S. Department of Health, Education and Welfare, Pub. No. OCD-90-C-255, 1976), pp. 14-42. In this federally funded research, the operative relations and residuals of African psychocultural behavioral practices and beliefs in the contemporary African-American family were documented empirically. See also Janice Hale, "Black Children: Their Roots, Culture, and Learning Styles," *Young Children* 36: 2 (January 1981): 37-50. Professor Hale's research not only supports the retention of Africanisms in the black family process, but also supports the recognition that cognitive styles and the way black children learn are a direct result of their culturally specific family process. The Hale findings have strong implications for any discussion of public policy, particularly the interface of public and private initiatives in education.

[32]See Herbert G. Gutman, *The Black Family in Slavery and Freedom, 1750-1925* (New York: Vintage Books, 1976), especially pp. 185-229.

[33]See Harriette Pipes McAdoo, "Black Kinship," *Psychology Today* 12: 12 (May 1979): 67-70, 79; and Elmer P. Martin and Joanne M. Martin, *The Black Extended Family* (Chicago: University of Chicago Press, 1978), pp. 5-16.

[34]William A. Darity, Jr., and Samuel L. Myers, Jr., "Public Policy and the Condition of Black Family Life," *The Review of Black Political Economy* 13: 1-2 (Summer/Fall 1984): 165-187.

[35]Wade W. Nobles, "The Reclamation of Culture and the Right to Reconciliation: An Afrocentric Perspective for Developing and Implementing Programs for the Mentally Retarded Offender," in Aminitu R. Harvey and Terry L. Carr, eds., *The African-American Mentally Retarded Offender: A Holistic Approach to Prevention and Rehabilitation* (New York: United Church of Christ, Commission for Racial Justice, 1982), pp. 39-63.

[36]F. Cress Welsing, *The Cress Theory of Color Confrontation and Racism (White Supremacy)* (Washington, D.C.: Frances Welsing, 1970), pp. 4-5.

[37]Syed Khatib (aka Cedric X. Clark), "African-American Studies and the Study of African-American People," in Reginald L. Jones, ed., *African-American Psychology*, 2d ed. (New York: Harper and Row, 1980).

[38]Robert Staples, "Toward A Sociology of the Black Family: A Theoretical and Methodological Assessment," *Journal of Marriage and the Family* 33: 1 (February 1971): 119-138.

[39]See Robert B. Hill, ed., *The Strengths of Black Families* (New York: Emerson Hall Publ., distributed by Independent Publishers Group, 1972); Joyce A. Ladner, *Tomorrow's Tomorrow: The Black Woman* (New York: Anchor Press, 1972), pp. 1-43; Wade W. Nobles, "African Root and American Fruit: The

Black Family," *Journal of Social and Behavioral Sciences* 20: 2 (Spring 1974): 52-64; and Lewis M. King, "The Assessment of Afro-American Families: Issues in Search of Theory," in Barbara Ann Bass, Gail Elizabeth Wyatt and Gloria Johnson Powell, eds., *The Afro-American Family: Assessment, Treatment, and Research Issues* (New York: Grune and Stratton, Inc., 1982), pp. 101-117.

[40]Housing Act of 1949, P.L. 171 (81st Congress, 1st Session), sec. 2.

[41]Housing and Community Development Act of 1974, P.L. 93-383 (93d Congress, 2d Session), sec. 101(c).

[42]Employment Act of 1946, P.L. 304 (79th Congress, 2d Session), sec. 2.

[43]Economic Opportunity Act of 1964, P.L. 88-452 (88th Congress, 2d Session), sec. 2.

[44]See Civil Rights Act of 1964, P.L. 88-352 (88th Congress, 2d Session), Title VII, Equal Employment Opportunity.

[45]Elementary and Secondary Education Act of 1965, P.L. 89-10 (89th Congress, 1st Session), subtitle.

[46]Comprehensive Employment and Training Act of 1973, P.L. 93-203 (93d Congress, 1st Session), sec. 2.

[47]Wade W. Nobles, *Critical Analysis of Scholarship on Black Family Life: Final Report* (New York: United Church of Christ, Commission for Racial Justice, 1983), pp. 12-19.

[48]Daniel P. Moynihan, *The Negro Family: The Case for National Action* (Washington, D.C.: U.S. Department of Labor, Office of Policy Planning and Research, March 1965).

[49]James S. Coleman, *Equality of Educational Opportunity* (Washington, D.C.: U.S. Department of Health, Education and Welfare, Office of Education, 1966), pp. 3-9.

[50]Wade W. Nobles, *Km Ebit Husia: Authoritative Utterances of Exceptional Insight for the Black Family* (Oakland, CA: Black Family Institute Publications, 1986), p. 4.

[51]White House Conference on Families, *Listening to America's Families: Action for the 80's, Report to the President, Congress and Families of the Nation* (Washington, D.C.: U.S. Government Printing Office, October 1980).

[52]Marguerite Ross Barnett, "A Theoretical Perspective on American Racial Public Policy," in Marguerite Ross Barnett and James A. Hefner, eds., *Public Policy for the Black Community: Strategies and Perspectives* (Port Washington, NY: Alfred Publishing Co., Inc., 1976), pp. 1-54 at 13.

RESIDENCE AND RACE: 1619 TO 2019

Karl E. Taeuber

University of Wisconsin-Madison

In the United States today, political rhetoric and many public policies promote racial integration in public settings and in the workplace. But at the end of the day, blacks go home to black neighborhoods and whites go home to white neighborhoods. Late in the twentieth century, racial separation prevails in family life, playgrounds, churches and local community activities.

Segregation of housing is a key mechanism for maintaining the subordinate status of blacks. Persisting residential segregation is a hindrance to the attainment of the educational dreams inspired by the Supreme Court in its 1954 *Brown* decision.[1] Housing policies and practices have been a leading cause of the nation's decaying central cities and fractured metropolitan communities. Restrictions on residential choice have hampered the efforts of black workers to find accessible and desirable employment, and locked many black children into environs of low opportunity and lost hope.

The National Advisory Commission on Civil Disorders, appointed to examine the racial disorders in American cities in the summer of 1967, reported that "our nation is moving toward two societies, one black, one white — separate and unequal."[2] The members of the commission attracted attention with these blunt words. They intended to. They hoped their cry of warning would be heard: "This deepening racial division is not inevitable. The movement apart can be reversed. Choice is still possible."[3]

Twenty years after the "disorders" of 1967, race relations in our nation's cities continue to be disorderly. The "long, hot summers" of the late 1960s have been supplanted by attention-gaining episodes occurring sporadically in all seasons. In the Howard Beach incident of winter 1986, three blacks who chanced to be in a "white neighborhood" in New York City were beaten and one was killed. In the Bensonhurst incident of summer 1989, a black youth was shot and killed for being in the "wrong" neighborhood — a white neighborhood — in Brooklyn, New York. Similar manifestations of racism and racial conflict repeatedly but irregularly pop into the limelight of the mass media, and serve as public symbols of continuing disgruntlement, despair and disorder.

This chapter discusses racial housing patterns and the nation's limited efforts to achieve open access to quality housing. It looks back over the route to the present and looks forward to the future we are making for ourselves. Its focus is on racial separateness and togetherness in where people live, and gives little attention to the physical condition of the housing they occupy. More attention will be given to looking back than to looking forward, for the past is immanent in the present and is our best guide to the emergent future.

Beginnings: 1619-1865

Africans were in servitude in Europe before the exploration and settlement of the New World, and blacks almost invariably accompanied the explorers. As an arbitrary date for the title of this chapter, 1619 has been chosen, when twenty black indentured servants were brought to Jamestown. Indenture for blacks was often permanent, and colonial legal codes were gradually amended to provide for a formal system of slavery. When the colonies gained independence, slavery continued. The retention and expansion of slavery were debated during the Constitutional Convention, and the final compromise provided for the continued importation of slaves until 1808. After this deadline, slavery continued to be legal and profitable, and some importation occurred illegally. During the entire period from 1619 to 1863, perhaps half a million blacks entered the American colonies or the new nation as slaves.[4]

The legal code of slavery designated the children of slaves as property of the mother's owner. Natural reproduction soon prevailed over importation as the main source of growth of the slave population. At the time of the Civil War, most of the four million slaves in the southern states had been born in the United States of parents born in the United States.

In the southern slave society, blacks often lived in proximity to whites. Whites who held few slaves—one or two and perhaps some children — were in frequent close contact with their chattel. Owners of large numbers of slaves typically employed them in agricultural enterprises. All or most of the slaves lived in separate quarters, often out of daily view of the owner.

Proximity of residence and employment sometimes led to close nurturing relationships between black women and white children, play among young black children and white children, daily interaction be-

tween white families and black house servants, and sexual liaisons between white men and black women. Contemporary social scientific
studies of the nature of prejudice conclude that interracial contact is
unlikely to lead to the reduction of prejudice, unless that contact is on
an equal basis. Personal proximity in a society with rigid racial structures of domination and subordination did and do not often lead to a
decline of prejudice or stereotypical racial thinking. Frequent contacts
of whites with blacks was hardly likely to subvert the racist social
order.

Colonial settlement and the employment of slaves began in the
southern coastal states. Slaves were moved to the interior and west-
ward as agriculture spread to new crops and new land. Black participation in the settling of new territories depended on the kind of farming
and its social and economic organization. The current diversity of racial composition among southern counties, from majority black to
overwhelmingly white, often reflects the persistence of patterns established during the antebellum decades.

A review of antebellum residential patterns must acknowledge this
variety of racial settings for whites and for blacks. Images prevalent in
the late twentieth century feature enormous plantations with aristo-
cratic white families served by hundreds of healthy slaves. These
images, gathered from *Uncle Tom's Cabin, Gone with the Wind, Song of
the South* and other fictions, invoke a form of agricultural enterprise
that was in fact unusual. Large-scale plantations with many slaves
probably increased in number with the growth of cotton agriculture
during the later stages of slavery, but they were not everywhere suitable and profitable. Plantations never prevailed throughout the South.
Racial residential arrangements varied greatly with time and place.

Most southern whites were not slaveholders. Many lived in parts of
the South where slaves were seldom encountered in the daily routine.
Other whites, while not themselves slaveholders, regularly hired slaves
or free blacks for unskilled or craft jobs. In regions of the South where
slave ownership was more common, most of the whites who possessed
slaves were small holders. In the white social structure, the large-scale
slaveowners struggled to obtain and maintain political and economic
power to further their interests, and much of the political and economic
history of the South reflects these conflicts among whites.

The demographics of the situation assigned a greater role for plantations in the experience of blacks than of whites. Each large slave plan-
tation contained many blacks and few whites. Thus a much higher proportion of the black population than of the white lived on plantations.
Southern blacks were concentrated in those geographic regions where
slave-based agricultural production prospered. Whether on or off plan-

tations, the majority of blacks were given few opportunities to develop skills, although some were allowed to develop and practice specialized crafts. Skilled black workers were sometimes hired out to other whites for temporary work, and some blacks gained a more varied experience of white society. A few were able to keep a portion of their earnings and eventually to purchase freedom, while others gained freedom by gift or escape.

The proportion of free blacks among the nation's black population fluctuated around 10 percent throughout the period from 1790 to 1860. Many free blacks lived in the North, but a majority remained in the South. Clusters of free blacks grew in several large cities in each region, but because people had to walk to scattered worksites, there was no large-scale residential segregation.

Between the Wars: 1865-1913

The Emancipation Proclamation (1863) nominally ended slavery, but it was not self-implementing. The Civil War years brought economic difficulties to much of southern agriculture, but the subordination of blacks was generally maintained. Areas directly affected by battle experienced more severe disruption. Some blacks sought freedom by trying to attach themselves to northern troops. Thousands of black migrants moved to Washington, D.C., and others made their way farther north. Many southern blacks wanted to celebrate their new freedom by migrating, but opportunities were severely constrained. In the economically devastated rural South, most blacks faced a struggle to maintain life. Former slaves owned no land, no livestock, no tools. Despite the good intentions of abolitionists, the efforts of many black and white Reconstructionists, and the hopes and struggles of the newly freed people, the nation and its states and communities failed to adopt effective programs to enhance economic opportunity. Most black workers had to continue to provide farm labor and menial services to white landowners. Forty acres and a mule were beyond reach. Southern agriculture was not reorganized to make room for blacks as independent farmers, nor were the nation's frontiers opened to provide blacks a viable chance to carve out a livelihood.

As the years and decades went by, forms of tenancy were developed in southern agricultural regions so that blacks could eke out a living and whites could retain control and gain the profit. After Reconstruction, and with the development of new patterns of legislated Jim Crow, black sharecroppers were bound ever more tightly to tenancy. Whites maintained strict dominance of credit systems as well as legal, political, educational and economic institutions. Many of the blacks who were fortunate enough in the Reconstruction years to acquire ownership of land or to find an economic niche in skilled trades were later displaced by the rampant white supremacy movements.

During the postbellum years, the rapidly expanding northern industrial economy absorbed millions of white workers from the American and European countryside and from Europe's cities and villages. Blacks were neither sought nor welcomed for most of the burgeoning jobs, but thousands nonetheless made their way north and found laboring and service positions at the bottom of the pay and status scales. Between 1860 and 1910, the black population of the North and West tripled, from 345,000 to 1,078,000. Still, northern migration was the exception. More prevalent was remaining in place. During these fifty years, natural increase brought a gain of 4,652,000 blacks to the southern population. In 1910, 89 percent of all blacks lived in the South. Fewer than 2 percent of the northern population were blacks, compared to 36 percent of the southern population.[5]

The most striking feature of black residential patterns during the five decades following emancipation was persistence. Some changes occurred in southern population distribution, but these changes merely perpetuated traditional racial patterns. As new land was brought into more intense agricultural use, whites and blacks moved west within the southern region and brought along racially discriminatory farm tenancy and labor relations.

The pace of southern urbanization lagged far behind that in the North, where the 1910 census recorded a majority of the population as urban. Rural residence still accounted for four-fifths of southerners of each race. Blacks and whites both participated in the slow expansion of the southern urban economy, but southern cities, mostly small, were not seedbeds of racial change.

Most blacks, North and South, remained economically dependent on whites, and had to live close to their place of employment. In the cities, most blacks served white households or small businesses rather than laboring in factories. Black settlements had to be scattered throughout the urban areas, often in low-valued locations near dumps, railyards, marshes or other deterrents to white residential occupancy. In the rural areas also, small settlements for each race were common. Where both races were present in a county, large-scale geographic separation was likely to be economically impractical. Racial propinquity was a practical necessity.

The Great Migration and Great Depression: 1914-1941

The "Great Migration" of blacks from the South to northern cities began during the early years of this period. Like most social transformations, this movement had many causes and its effects cannot be
bounded. The boll weevil repeatedly devastated cotton production in
portions of the South. Many black tenants lost their livelihoods and
had to seek other means of survival. Other agricultural calamities
caused local disruptions. Repression of civil liberties and restriction of
social and economic opportunities were continuing features of life for
southern blacks, but perhaps their intensity was greater in some counties and thus spurred more blacks there to seek out the better conditions rumored to be found in the North. Or perhaps it was not so much
a worsening of racism as an increasing awareness of the possibility of
escape to the North. As any pattern of migration gathers force, people
and information flow in both directions. As migrants return, temporar-
ily or permanently, more information spreads person-to-person within
the places of origin. In the early years of this century, without elec-
tronic mass media or widespread literacy, personal communication
played an essential role. Adventurous early migrants established paths
and support systems that made it easier for others to follow.

Events in the North also played a causal role in the Great Migration. Urbanization was proceeding at a rapid pace, and World War I
and much of the 1920s were periods of economic expansion. Although
northern blacks had been subject to some of the Jim Crow restrictions
and displacements from skilled jobs that occurred in the South, several
hundred thousand black workers in the North were filling menial and
domestic positions for which there was increasing demand. The European war cut the transatlantic flow of workers to northern industry.
Postwar xenophobia against the "new immigration" from southern
and eastern Europe spurred tight legal restrictions. Although the
prejudices against Italians and Jews, Poles and Greeks, were more than
matched by prejudices against blacks, some northern employers in
search of strikebreakers or simply a new supply of unskilled workers
found that southern blacks could meet their needs. Labor recruiters
were sent to the South with train tickets and promises of jobs. Political
controversy over the rights of recruiters to "steal" blacks from the
South helped to spread the word.

Fifty years after emancipation, the simultaneity of these many
causes finally spurred a mass exodus from the South. In large-scale labor migrations, it is often young adult males who lead the way. Among
black men in Georgia who were between the ages of fifteen and thirty-
four in 1920, 45 percent were gone by 1930. (We do not have direct

statistical information on the migrations, but we can learn much indirectly; for this datum about Georgia, the numbers aged fifteen to thirty-four in 1920 were compared to the numbers aged twenty-five to forty-four in 1930.) In some Georgia counties, nearly all the young men and many of the young women moved north. In Alabama, one-fifth of young black men left during the 1910-1920 period, and one-fifth of the oncoming generation left during the 1920-1930 period.[6]

At the northern arrival points, the demographic changes were also striking: there were gains in the numbers of young men measuring 138 percent in Michigan, 67 percent in Illinois, and 54 percent in New York from 1910 to 1920, and not dissimilar increases continued during the 1920s.

Conditions in the North proved to be vastly different in many ways, not all of them positive in the view of the migrants. Many blacks found higher wages in the North than were available in the South, and certain kinds of freedoms were more prevalent. But northern blacks also encountered bitter winters, unfamiliar big-city life, expensive tenements and crowded housing. They found prejudice and restricted opportunities at work, at school, in "public" places and institutions, and in everyday life. Some of the jobs offered them were as replacements for white workers on strike, thus bringing the charge of scabs and fueling prejudice against blacks. Many blacks lost their jobs when strikes were settled, when wartime labor shortages eased, and when organized white opposition insisted on restricting competition from blacks. As is the case with every migration stream where return is possible, some unhappy or unsuccessful migrants moved back. Other maintained ties in the North and South and moved repeatedly in both directions.

Housing for blacks in the cities was already a problem before this migration. W.E.B. DuBois wrote of the wretched housing conditions facing Philadelphia's blacks in the 1890s.[7] The growth of streetcars and public transportation made possible increased separation of residential location from job location. This facilitated racial segregation; new housing developments could be for whites only and previously dispersed blacks could be displaced without losing their access to their places of employment. Every city developed its sections where blacks were allowed to live, but in many cases other urban poor of low social status were also housed in these sections. With a rapid influx of newcomers, many of whom were unfamiliar with urban ways and only able to earn low incomes, the situation deteriorated. An increased demand for low-rent housing with access to unskilled work was channeled into the areas that already had blacks.

The steering of blacks to selected areas and the growing scale of racial and lower-class enclaves were partially conditioned by the tendency of newcomers to begin their housing search by seeking relatives or acquaintances already in the city. But these relatives and acquaintances were themselves confined by the racial prejudices of the times. The increasing numbers of blacks attracted attention and aroused concern among longer-term residents, black and white. Some established blacks were worried by the newcomers, fearful of an aroused white prejudice that would lead to new racial restrictions and obliterate the economic and social status they had struggled to attain. Other blacks sought to help the newcomers, to use their plight to call attention to the need for greater access to jobs, housing and public services. Recently, an increasing number of "ghetto histories" have been calling attention to the efforts made by black lodges, churches, organizations, politicians and occasional white groups to combat the forces of discrimination and neglect at that time.

The power, of course, laid predominantly with whites. Their racial prejudices were deep, and many whites profited from exploiting the new labor force and its need for housing. The real estate industry quickly organized to impose control and predictability. The means chosen was confinement of blacks to housing in "Negro areas." To accommodate the increasing black population, limited expansion was controlled by designated blocks being added to the Negro areas. Thus it became unethical for whites in the business to sell or rent housing to blacks outside of the agreed-upon Negro areas. Accompanying this official code was an unwritten gray market, whereby neighboring white areas could selectively be targeted for blockbusting and then become part of the openly-marketed Negro area. White and black owners and renters in the transition zones often were especially exploited, with speculators and their financial backers reaping extraordinarily large profits.[8]

In his famous 1925 article, "The Growth of the City," Ernest W. Burgess described the concentric changes in urban land use in response to growth at the commercial and industrial center.[9] He used concepts chosen from studies of plant communities, and made analogies to biotic invasion and succession. Growing urban systems displayed many systematic patterns of structure and of change that could be described and examined using the insights provided by Burgess and other "Chicago School" sociologists and their successors in urban planning and urban economics. The idea of "natural areas," whatever its applicability in plant ecology, took on a life of its own far removed from biological analogy. This concept often degenerated into an ahistorical and nonsociological conception of social change. What got lost to view in much of the literature on urban form and structure was the deliberate manipulation of these processes by financiers, politicians and other human actors.

The idea of natural areas took hold without the juxtaposition of a presumed opposite; there is not even a term for "unnatural" areas. The assumptions of an unfettered marketplace for urban land, with multiple participants and no monopolies, oligopolies or other restraints of trade, were accepted with little notice of the role of deliberate human action and embedded racism.

One of the devices used by the real estate industry to ensure the orderly functioning of the real estate market was the racially restrictive covenant. Covenants are an overtly de jure device, to use a term made familiar in more recent times in policy debates over school segregation. In the school segregation context since 1954, the notion of state action (de jure) is contrasted with the idea of segregation arising de facto. Many have taken these terms as opposites, without recognizing that governmental action and public policy may influence racial patterns in schools even if there is no state law mandating racial separation. A narrow jurisprudential perspective often obscures the underlying similarities. In the housing segregation context, restrictive covenants illustrate the confounding of de jure and de facto acts.

Racially restrictive covenants are private actions sanctioned by law. Consider the following examples of restrictions recorded in deeds for residential property:

- This land shall never be occupied by or conveyed to a colored person. (1925)

- None of the buildings erected upon or in this subdivision shall be used to house either for business purposes or residence purpose any colored persons or others outside the Caucasian race, and the conveyance of any lot or lots in violation of the restriction shall ipso facto constitute a forfeiture. (1927)

- At no time shall any portion of said subdivision . . . be occupied by or sold, conveyed, mortgaged, pledged, rented or leased . . . to any persons of Negro or Ethiopian descent, provided however, this is not intended to include or prevent occupancy of such persons as a domestic servant or while actually employed in or about the premises by the owner or occupant thereof. (1928)

- At no time shall any lot or building thereon be purchased, owned, leased, occupied or used by any person other than a citizen of the United States of America, of the White Race. This provision shall not apply to domestic servants. . . . (1937)

• No race other than the Caucasian race shall use or occupy any
  building or any lot in said subdivision; however, this covenant
  shall not prevent the occupancy of domestic servants of a different race employed by an owner or tenant. (1945)

• No Persons other the white race shall own or occupy . . . .
  (1953)[10]

These examples are taken from suburbs around the city of Milwaukee, and they are quite typical. During the 1920s and 1930s, much of
the property in the major subdivisions of many central cities and their
suburbs was restricted by such racial covenants. The case of Milwaukee is particularly interesting because there seems to have been no reasonable likelihood of substantial black in-movement to any of these
subdivisions. Milwaukee was not a major destination for blacks during
this migration; at the time of the 1920 census, 2,200 blacks lived in the
city and fewer than 200 lived in the entire suburban territory. At the
time of the 1940 census, the city's black population numbered 8,800.
Outside the city, in the four counties that today comprise the Milwaukee metropolitan area, there were 376 black residents. Milwaukee had
yet to experience the ghetto expansion pressures and racial succession
like that which occurred in Chicago and Detroit. No census tract in the
city was predominantly black. Black residents were concentrated near
downtown, far from the city's borders, in Milwaukee's traditional "inner core" area. Even within this core there were many whites. The
"threat" of black invasion to most city and suburban residential sections was nonexistent, yet much of the city and suburbs had long since
been protected by these covenants.[11]

That racially restrictive covenants were written and recorded on
such a large scale demonstrates that these clauses were not simply a
protective response to reasoned concerns about actual threats to property values. Covenants had become a canon of normal bureaucracy and
business practice. Developers and brokers inserted one or another of
these racially restrictive clauses in their contracts and deeds, whether
or not that language was essential to the particular circumstances.

During the New Deal, President Franklin Roosevelt characterized
one-third of the nation as ill-housed. The federal government began
several programs to increase the supply and reduce the cost of safe and
sanitary housing. The Federal Housing Administration, a new agency
charged in part with providing mortgage guarantees to home buyers,
prepared an underwriting manual for its personnel throughout the
country. The FHA wanted to gain the confidence of the public and the
housing industry, as well as protect its program from excessive losses
through defaults. The manual, modeled on existing texts and practices,

promulgated conservative business standards for property evaluation and lending practices. The bound version of the manual, published in 1938, contains several sections on the need to look beyond the individual house and buyer and assess the economic prospects of the neighborhood.[12] "Protection from Adverse Influences" is the title of one section, and paragraph 932 identifies this as "one of the most important features" to assess. The manual identifies zoning and restrictive covenants as techniques that developers and political jurisdictions may use to ensure such protection. Restrictive covenants are said to work best if they cover a broad area, and among the desirable covenants is "Prohibition of the occupancy of properties except by the race for which they are intended."[13]

Appraisers were advised to consider the existence of physical or artificial barriers that would help prevent "infiltration of inharmonious racial groups."[14] Surrounding areas were to be examined, and if incompatible racial groups were present, the appraiser was to include in his report a prediction of the probability of "being invaded."[15]

The code of ethics of the National Association of Real Estate Boards for many years included the following article:

> A Realtor should never be instrumental in introducing into a neighborhood . . . members of any race . . . whose presence will clearly be detrimental to property values in that neighborhood.[16]

In Wisconsin, this code took on state sanction. The Wisconsin Real Estate Broker's Board, a state agency responsible for licensing brokers, published the full NAREB Code in its 1940 manual, "A Legal Guide for Wisconsin Real Estate Brokers."[17]

There is little evidence of the frequency with which courts or administrative agencies of federal, state or local governments were asked to enforce racially restrictive covenants. The widespread recording of covenants testifies to their acceptance as sound and conservative business practice, and is symbolic of the prevailing belief that blacks should not be allowed to live in white neighborhoods. Covenants were not always effective in preventing sales to blacks, though. Some areas covered by such covenants, especially central city ones close to expanding black neighborhoods, experienced rapid racial turnover.

During the 1920s, '30s, and '40s, many public and private agencies thought covenants were important. The propagation of covenants is an example of how private discrimination and public discrimination are confounded historically. Covenants are an object lesson in the difficulties of maintaining a clear distinction between de facto and de jure effects. There is no satisfying way to disentangle the role of private action.

The Great Migration and the period between the wars brought rapid change for the nation and for its black population. Rapid change is disruptive and turbulent. The accommodation of northern cities to expanding numbers of blacks was not merely a matter of subtle racism and the development of new bureaucratic and legalistic tools of white resistance. There was also overt social turmoil and violent upheaval. In 1919 a black youth swimming at a "white beach" on Chicago's south side was stoned, and a full-scale riot grew out of the incident. A study of the riot headed by sociologist Charles S. Johnson documented the scope and depth of racism and racial conflict in Chicago.[18] Riots and other violent incidents occurred throughout the nation, with lynchings continuing in the South and the Klan having a resurgence and spreading to the North. The many books, essays and editorials by W. E. B. DuBois, historian-scholar, one of the founders of the NAACP and editor of its journal, *Crisis*, exposed the pervasive character of racism in American society.[19] The "Harlem Renaissance" of black intellectual, artistic, and social life produced poetry, drama, novels and reports on the human condition in America. Black newspapers, which chronicled the precarious political and economic status of blacks in several major cities, circulated throughout the country. The Marcus Garvey movement was an enduring symbol of the creation of a new black national consciousness. The evolving debate between accommodationists such as Booker T. Washington and activists such as DuBois demonstrated the intensity of efforts by the subordinated group to combat domination despite its limited power and the strength and fierceness of the opposition.

In the rural South, which remained the location of most southern blacks, the spread of commercial agriculture and agricultural credit systems, augmented in the 1930s by New Deal programs, benefited the whites, while Jim Crow retained its strong grip on southern race relations. Anthropological and social psychological studies document the rigid character of the rural tenancy systems and the small-town caste systems.[20]

In the mid-1930s, the Carnegie Foundation commissioned a massive social scientific study of American race relations, with Gunnar Myrdal, a Swedish social economist and later winner of the Nobel Prize in economics, as director. The thousand-page book which resulted, *An American Dilemma*, together with other books and reports prepared by the distinguished staff, provides a detailed picture of rural economic stagnation and urban struggle.[21] The study was conducted during the depths of the depression. It provides endless evidence of the web of discrimination and the vicious cycle of multiple causation regarding the subordinate status of America's blacks. Yet Myrdal's text emphasizes his faith in American democracy.

Publication delays caused by the onset of World War II afforded Myrdal opportunity to observe that the nation was finally moving beyond the depression, that wartime was stimulating an economic revival, a renewed urban migration, and a new political climate. Myrdal's book offers a meticulous recording of Jim Crow racism, the tight grip of white power, and the Sisyphean burden of the vicious circle. Yet the book attracted attention and became a best seller in part because Myrdal retained an underlying tone of optimism. Whether his faith in American democracy and the efficacy of political change was justified is still being debated, but he was certainly correct that the war was spurring a new cycle of change in American race relations.

Civil Rights Era to the Present: 1941-1989

The nation's mobilization for World War II accelerated the transformation of American race relations from a regional to a national issue. Changing agricultural policies and economic circumstances pushed millions of blacks out of their special niche in southern agriculture and into the industries and cities of every region. Major civil rights events occurred with increasing frequency. A. Philip Randolph's threatened march on Washington came early in the war years, and the Fair Employment Practices Commission was created. Pressure increased for putting more equality into "separate but equal" programs such as public and war housing. President Harry Truman's announcement that the armed forces would be desegregated demonstrated that direct attacks on segregation in major organizations and institutions were now politically thinkable. Implementation of new civil rights programs was typically limited and slow, but the very idea of cumulative progress in race relations was a striking change.

The resumption of a great migration to the cities was a result not only of wartime industrial expansion, but also of the cessation of immigration of new workers from Europe and the diversion of millions of American men into the military. Blacks participated in this new urbanization to a far greater extent than in the earlier Great Migration. Between 1940 and 1950, nearly one-half of Mississippi's young blacks aged fifteen to thirty-four left the state and moved north. Detroit, New York and Chicago were again major destinations, but other cities bypassed by the earlier migration, such as Milwaukee and Los Angeles, now attracted thousands of black workers.[22]

The new migration continued twice as long as the original. During the thirty years from 1940 to 1970, the net migration of blacks from the South to the North and West averaged over 100,000 persons per year. The northern and western share of the nation's total black population jumped from 23 percent in 1940 to 47 percent in 1970. The southern transformation was twofold. Not only were millions leaving the region, but the social and economic structure of the South itself was changing. The percentage of southern blacks living in cities rather than in rural areas reached 67 percent in 1970, nearly double the prewar ratio.

Blacks moving into the cities encountered a variety of discriminatory actions by employers and unions to maintain occupational segregation and keep blacks out of the better-paying sectors. In the housing market, landlords, speculators, financial and insurance agencies, and governmental officials conspired to contain blacks in traditional residential areas and channel the demand for additional housing into limited ghetto expansion.

Whites were also flocking to the cities, and housing was in short supply. In the depression, housing construction had dropped to very low levels. During the war, military demands on the economy meant shortages in supplies for civilian uses and prolonged restrictions on the supply of new housing. Individuals and families moving to the cities piled up in the existing central city housing stock. The racial dynamics imposed on urban housing during the earlier pre-WW I migration were revitalized. Access to living quarters was structured as a competition between whites and blacks. The real estate industry, including its financial arms, continued to foster rigid residential segregation. To help the nation fill its role as the arsenal for democracy, the federal government launched a new program of war housing for defense workers. Even in this program, customary patterns of racial separation prevailed.

Racial conflict intensified in many cities, with riots and other major disturbances. Black organizations vigorously publicized the irony of fighting for democracy abroad while racism flourished in the armed forces and on the home front. This perspective meshed perfectly with the overarching theme in Myrdal's study, which carried the subtitle, "The Negro Problem and Modern Democracy."[23] Myrdal saw a continuing conflict throughout American history between American ideals and American racial practices. He was optimistic that the war would be a spur to a new cycle of positive social trends. Other studies of the period were more gloomy. *Black Metropolis* portrayed the pervasive racial organization of life in Chicago.[24] *The Negro Ghetto* documented that governmental action was a contributing cause to the racial polarization of the nation's cities.[25]

When the war ended, the veterans came home, bringing a temporary worsening of overcrowded housing conditions. A surge in marriages and the beginnings of the baby boom meant that even more families desired housing of their own. The new Veterans Administration home mortgage program, together with a growing FHA program, changed the traditional rules for residential mortgages. Young families with little cash could, if their skin color were white, obtain long-term financing. A boom in new housing construction spread single-family homes, duplexes and garden apartments over the suburban landscape where large tracts of inexpensive land were available.

Federal and private financing encouraged new developments of economically homogeneous housing. Conflict over racial discrimination in the housing programs of the federal government was endemic. The executive branch had shown itself susceptible to pressure. In the federal judiciary, educational desegregation cases were being pursued and won, laying the foundations for the 1954 *Brown* decision. In 1948, the U.S. Supreme Court ruled in *Shelley* v. *Kramer* that judicial enforcement of racially restrictive covenants was improper.[26] But, in a reflection of the Court's persisting caution on racial matters, the covenants themselves were ruled to be mere private agreements and not illegal. One of the Milwaukee-area covenants quoted earlier was first recorded in 1953, five years after the *Shelley* decision. Most of the covenants specified a duration during which they would be in force, often twenty-five years, but many had a provision for renewal. Racially restrictive covenants are still recorded in the registries of deeds in county offices throughout the nation, and public figures are periodically embarrassed by revelations that they own property with such provisions. More than sixty years after covenants came into widespread use, and forty years after their judicial enforcement was ruled illegal, debate continues about their symbolic meaning, the likelihood that homeowners ever read the fine print in their deeds, and the costs and benefits of purging covenants from the cumbersome files.

By the mid-1950s, the FHA underwriting manual had been revised to exclude explicit reference to racial groups as being undesirable or inharmonious, but the rest of the language about the desirability of protecting neighborhoods from adverse influences remained. Social and economic similarity was explicitly mandated. Everyone knew, though it was less commonly written on official documents or spoken at public meetings, that the intrusion of blacks into white neighborhoods was to be avoided.

Chicago stands as the prototypical city for the vigorous maintenance of racial residential separation during a period of rapid black population growth. Chicago's segregation was not unique, but it was

extensively documented.[27] Despite high demand by blacks for housing, and higher rents offered by blacks than by whites, most housing
remained closed to blacks. "Blockbusting" was a prime technique for
opening new residences to blacks. Although it offered enormous profits
to speculators willing to violate the public norms against allowing
blacks into residential areas designated for whites, blockbusting was
only in part a free market response to an artificially restricted market.
It was never completely unfettered, but operated as a socially constrained process. It served as a market pressure valve, a mechanism for
selecting some of the areas adjacent to existing ghetto boundaries as
the ones to be turned over to blacks. Other border areas, and housing
farther from the ghetto, were highly desirable to blacks, and in a freely
functioning market would have brought profit to anyone willing to sell
or rent to them. But these areas were not targets for blockbusting.
Ghetto expansion continued throughout the 1940s and 1950s as a
highly structured process. The "invasion" of a "white neighborhood"
by a few blacks led inexorably to the succession of whites by blacks, to
consolidation as a predominantly black area, and eventually to the so-
lidification of new "established Negro areas." The overcrowding and
high costs of housing in Negro areas were repeatedly documented in
Chicago and many other cities with a growing black population.

In Chicago, even during the periods of extreme restriction in the
housing supply, there was a strong pattern of social and economic dif-
ferentiation within the ghetto. Blacks with education, better jobs and
stable incomes continually sought to improve their housing by moving
away from central city areas with their older and poorer quality units.
Their efforts were repeatedly frustrated by their inability to obtain decent housing except in invasion areas, which were subject to rapid transition from racially mixed to solidly black. Areas in racial transition
often experienced rapid decline in neighborhood quality-of-life. Popular opinion blamed the victims for the decline, overlooking the fact
that city services were cut back as neighborhoods shifted from white to
black, that the subdividing of units and high prices contributed to
overcrowding, and that the owners of homes and apartments cut back
on maintenance in a speculative grab for short-term profits. As a neighborhood became increasingly black, the initial in-movers and other upwardly mobile blacks launched a new search for better housing.

Residential segregation thus became a defining feature of American
society in the postwar period. The white population embarked on a
surge of family formation, childbearing, improvement of housing, a
shift from renting to owning, and relocation to the suburbs. For blacks,
urban migration and the baby boom replenished the demand for housing, but most cities ardently emulated the constraining tactics that had

succeeded so well in creating and maintaining racial segregation in Chicago, Detroit, Cleveland and elsewhere during the 1940s. Public housing programs were launched to help cities deal with burgeoning numbers of poor, but these, like the war housing programs, served to further reinforce racial segregation. Massive urban renewal programs cleared many slums, but inadequate aid was offered to those displaced and the consequence was usually to intensify the concentration of the minority poor elsewhere.

The growing civil rights movement achieved gradual gains in expanding public housing for blacks and improving relocation programs, but desegregative housing policies were vigorously and effective resisted at all levels of government and the shelter industry. Not until deep into President John Kennedy's term did the federal government renounce discrimination in federal housing programs. Even then, change was slow and administrative actions did little to foster desegregation. Legislative approaches were similarly resisted. The 1964 Civil Rights Act did not include fair housing provisions. Dr. Martin Luther King, Jr.'s open housing marches in Chicago were generally regarded as failures. Throughout the mid-1960s, only a few state and local legislatures were able to pass any kind of open housing laws.

The urban racial disorders of the last half of the 1960s called dramatic attention to the nation's segregated cities. The 1968 report of the National Advisory Commission on Civil Disorders stands as the clarion call to the nation to become aware of the underlying issues.[28] Those who interpret the commission's imagery of two societies as a call for change, rather than a prophecy of perpetual segregation, can find support in the ensuing history. Within months, Congress incorporated prohibitions against housing discrimination into the body of civil rights laws, and the Supreme Court held that all racial discrimination in housing was illegal.[29] The national government's efforts to overcome institutionalized discrimination in federal housing programs showed occasional activist sparks, even after the Nixon administration succeeded the Johnson administration. Sporadic attacks were made against racial discrimination in home insurance and financing, and suits alleging patterns of discrimination were prosecuted successfully against private sales and rental companies. Many state and local governments and private agencies launched their own fair housing programs.

A decade after the commission forewarned of a nation of two societies, William Julius Wilson proclaimed "the declining significance of race."[30] He claimed that the economic status of blacks had become less attributable to blatant racial discrimination and increasingly so to transformations in the economic structure. Differential opportunities, he said, are now based on class more than on race.

To apply this perspective to racial housing patterns, attention has to be directed to patterns of change rather than to current levels of segregation. It would be simplistic to suggest that racial residential segregation already has been eliminated from American society; obviously it has not. What should be apparent, if class and economic status rather than race are becoming the prime determinants of residential location, is a slowing pace of transition of racially mixed neighborhoods to all-black. Neighborhood population composition should shift toward increasing class homogeneity and racial heterogeneity. A significant increase should occur in the scattering of black families in predominantly white neighborhoods. Neighborhoods that were all black should be attracting whites of a similar economic level.

Is there evidence that these patterns of change have a reality beyond abstract sociological theory? Attitude surveys report declining levels of racial prejudice, specifically on the willingness of whites to accept a black neighbor of similar economic status.[31] If these data are taken at face value, and if post-1968 legal challenges to housing discrimination have had significant effect, one would expect to find a reduction in the white violence and panic selling that were once such commonplace responses to the appearance of a few black families in a neighborhood. The news media still report sporadic incidents of violence against blacks moving into white neighborhoods, and panic selling occurs often enough that there are continuing legislative efforts to prohibit or regulate it. Still, many observers of the housing scene report that traditional modes of intimidation and induced racial turnover are less common than two or three decades ago. These pieces of evidence, and many others, make it necessary to give serious attention to the notion of declining racism, particularly when trying to peer into the future.

A belief in the persistence of racism leads to a different set of expectations about recent and future trends in racial residential segregation. Many observers believe that the proclamation of the nation's drift into "two societies" was an insightful forecast.[32] Simultaneously, they believe the commission's call to action was ineffective. Actions such as the 1968 fair housing law are seen as symbolic rather than practical. For twenty years, efforts to amend it in order to add meaningful enforcement powers and accessible remedies failed repeatedly, until the 1988 amendments to the Civil Rights Act of 1968. During most of the time since 1968, the federal government has been controlled by administrations viewed by activists as hostile to civil rights. Rapid white departure from central cities to suburbs has continued. Blacks remain concentrated in the central cities. Institutional forces that promote and maintain racial segregation in housing may have become better hidden, but subtlety and sophistication only mask, not replace, institutional racism. The attitudinal studies are a case in point. Public expressions of racial tolerance are belied by numerous studies that include careful testing of the behavior of real estate personnel.[33] Overt prejudice is less likely to be manifest in direct statements, but testers encounter racially differential treatment. Discriminatory outcomes continue.

Discrimination is lessening; discrimination persists. The cup is half-full and half-empty. In every domain of American race relations, the observer may choose to emphasize progress or deterioration. The scholar who marshals objective evidence is not freed of this choice. Evidence does not speak out; it must be interpreted.

Considerable empirical evidence on segregation trends has accumulated in scholarly studies that use the highly detailed geographic data provided by the decennial censuses. Several kinds of analyses have been undertaken for various intercensal periods. In a study of neighborhood racial change in the period 1940-1960, it was found that the prototypical racial succession process was not the result of some unbreakable law of race relations, but was very much affected by demographic circumstances.[34] Census tracts are geographically contiguous population areas of about four thousand, delineated by the Census Bureau to facilitate the study of change in small sub-areas of cities. Census tract data were examined for ten cities with large black populations. Taking each city and each decade as a separate observation, ten observations were made for 1950-1960, ten for 1940-1950, and seven for earlier decades. Of this set of twenty-seven city-decades, twenty were characterized by low or negative rates of white population growth and high rates of black population growth. For these twenty observations, there was much invasion of white residential tracts by blacks and rapid residential succession toward their establishment as all-black neighborhoods.

In the other seven city-decade observations, black population growth did not exceed white population growth. In cities experiencing these circumstances, instances occurred of whites displacing blacks as well as blacks displacing whites. Census tracts that began a decade with mixed racial composition often retained their racial diversity throughout the decade without movement toward becoming all black. Prototypical racial succession, Chicago-style, was infrequent.

These data demonstrate the dependence of the racial invasion and succession process on a central city experiencing a rapidly increasing black population and a declining white population. This demographic pattern was more likely in cities that lacked available land for residential development. In some northern cities before World War II and in some southern cities even in the postwar period, the demographic demands on the housing market were less intense, new housing developments were still being located within the central city, and racial succession did not become the dominant mode of accommodation.

These historical observations provide an insight that this chapter will use for its projection of trends into the twenty-first century. The future is likely to bring a prevalence of slow growth for black and white populations in most urban areas. In such demographic circumstances, the prototypical Chicago model of racial succession may be an inappropriate guide.

In another phase of the aforementioned comparative study of residential segregation, trends were assessed using a segregation index.[35] This segregation index is technically an index of dissimilarity. The more dissimilar the distribution of black households is from the distribution of nonblack households, the higher the index. These index values are calculated using the smallest available geographic area, individual city blocks. If all city blocks are occupied only by black households or only by nonblack households, the index value would be at its maximum — one hundred. If every city block has the same ratio of black to nonblack households as every other city block (the ratio that characterizes the entire city population), the index value would be at its minimum — zero. Scores between zero and one hundred can be interpreted as the percentage of either race that would need to move in order to obtain a zero score.

In 1940, the first census year for which the necessary data were available, the mean segregation score for a group of 109 large cities was eighty-five. This is near the high end of the scale, indicative of the prevailing pattern of racial residential separation. In 1950, segregation scores for most cities were about what they had been in 1940. The mean score increased to eighty-seven, largely because of increasing scores in many southern cities. During the 1950s, segregation scores again increased in many southern cities, but in other regions declining scores prevailed. In the 1960s and 1970s, declining scores were common for cities in all parts of the country. It became clear that these declines represented a genuine and persistent change from the upward trend in residential segregation that prevailed in the first half of this century. These declines were too consistent to be attributable to the temporary racial mixture that occurs at the ghetto periphery as succession is occurring. Yet the data remain open to interpretation. Those of the "half-full" persuasion can focus on the remarkably broad character of the declines from the peak levels of segregation around 1950 or 1960.

Those of the "half-empty" persuasion can rest assured that index values for most cities remain very high on the scale.

The distinctive trend for southern cities provides another instructive note for anyone who wishes to peer into the future. Social and economic patterns are in continual flux, and no pattern or trend persists forever. In older southern cities, those which had a sizable black population early in the twentieth century, blacks originally lived in most areas of the city, close to their places of employment as domestic servants and casual laborers. These cities grew up with a strong "etiquette of race relations" and a political economy that did not depend on residential separation. Racial propinquity, persisting from an earlier period and only gradually declining as transportation systems grew, did not entail that blacks lived in the same kinds of housing or acquired the social status that a neighborhood conferred on its white residents. As these southern cities became more tightly integrated into the national industrial economy, as they grew and entered the suburban era, they rid themselves of the scattered racial pockets, developed large-scale concentrations of blacks, and increased their residential segregation.

Many crucial questions about segregation pertain to patterns of suburbanization and the metropolitan racial structure. The trend analysis of segregation indices from 1940 to 1980 was based on city block data and excluded the suburbs. The kinds of census data available do not permit such a long series of segregation indices using data for suburbs as well as cities. Using data for census tracts rather than city blocks, similar analyses can be undertaken for metropolitan areas beginning with the year 1960.

Two studies reported on trends in racial residential segregation in metropolitan areas for the decade 1960-1970. According to one, average segregation levels changed little.[36] The other concluded that metropolitan segregation levels increased during the 1960s.[37] The two studies used different indices of segregation, and calculated their averages over different groups of metropolitan areas. Despite these differences, the two studies were in agreement in failing to find for metropolitan areas evidence of the pervasive declines in segregation that characterized large central cities during the 1960s.

Prior to analysis of 1980 census data, social scientists had contrary perspectives on the trend of the 1970s regarding metropolitan racial residential segregation. Those who emphasized the persistence of racism and the maintenance of barriers to integration could point to the increasingly metropolitan basis of social organization in urban territories, the continuing predominance of whites in the suburban migration flows, and the prevailing "lily white" character of most suburban communities. Those who emphasized the decline of racism and the opening up of opportunity for a growing middle-class black population could point to the declining central city segregation indices and to new, highly visible suburban movements of blacks in metropolitan areas such as Washington, D.C., Atlanta, New York and Los Angeles.

A study completed in 1984 calculated segregation scores (indices of dissimilarity) from 1980 census data for the thirty-eight metropolitan areas with populations of one million or more.[38] For thirty-six of these, comparable scores for 1970 were available from the prior studies. The empirical evidence for the 1970-1980 period showed pervasive declines in metropolitan racial residential segregation. Every one of the thirty-six large metropolitan areas had a lower segregation score in 1980 than in 1970. The average decline was nine points; twenty-five of thirty-six declined by at least five points. Declines were especially great in metropolitan areas in the West and South. But the evidence, as usual, was not uniform. In Chicago and several other large northern metropolitan areas with high black percentages, the declines were small.

Suburbanization of metropolitan populations proceeded at a rapid pace during most of this century, spurred first by trolleys and systems of mass transportation and more recently by widespread car ownership and expanding commuter highway networks. Throughout most of this period, suburbanization was more rapid for whites than for blacks, but the pattern changed during the 1970s. Numerically, whites continued to be far more numerous than blacks, but the rate of the black suburban population increase was well above that which obtained for whites. The aggregate number of suburban blacks grew by nearly 50 percent in the ten years from 1970 to 1980. The ratio of black to total suburban population increased from 4.8 percent in 1970 to 6.1 percent in 1980.

Suburbanization of the black population has been quite varied. It is occurring rapidly in some metropolitan areas, but is still outpaced by white suburbanization in others. In earlier decades, much of the black movement to suburbs was restricted to three types of suburb: older suburbs with their own industrial and "central city" character; lower-cost residential suburbs whose attractiveness to whites had declined; and new developments marketed originally to blacks. Still, the census data demonstrate a new pattern in the 1970s of black migration spread widely into many suburbs that had formerly been almost exclusively occupied by whites. The suburbs were opening up on an unprecedented scale.

The declines in metropolitan segregation indices and the surge of black suburbanization seem consistent with the view that the nation is on a path of residential desegregation. But not all the evidence points in this direction. The persistence of many instances of extreme racial segregation is an indication of an inertia in the residential system. A decade or two of desegregative trends has not sufficed to transform the essentially segregated character of housing. At the time of the 1980 census, the suburbs surrounding Gary-Hammond-East Chicago were more than 99.75 percent white, while the suburbs surrounding Milwaukee were more than 99.5 percent white. In those metropolitan areas where blacks were moving to the suburbs in large numbers, the opening of formerly all-white suburbs was accompanied by growth in predominantly black suburbs and rapid racial succession in other suburbs. The possibility exists that the declines in the metropolitan index result from temporary features of an underlying process that is still essentially segregative. Data for a single decade are insufficient to permit a judgment on whether increased integration is only a transitional situation. Perhaps the 1980 census happened to catch the process at a middle stage that gives the appearance of integration. Many racially mixed suburbs may be on the way from predominantly white to predominantly black.

Evidence on black suburbanization during the 1970s in more than one thousand individual suburbs can be interpreted to give support to either perspective.[39] First, consider evidence of a rapid pace of change at the very low end of the black suburban presence. In 1970, the great majority of suburbs throughout the country had fewer than 0.5 percent blacks among their residents. Of these "lily white" suburbs, about four of every ten had more than 0.5 percent blacks among their residents in 1980. Most of these suburbs were in the early stages of token integration, but the change is still dramatic. If in the 1980s and again in the 1990s, 40 percent of "lily white" suburbs move into the ranks of a more noticeable black presence, there will soon be few remaining white havens. The initial opening of the suburbs to the first few black families may be well advanced and nearly complete by the end of the century. Among those suburbs with black percentages in the above-zero but low range in 1970, increases in black population and percentage were common, but most were still less than 10 percent black in 1980. The number of suburbs experiencing pronounced racial succession, with black percentages moving sharply upward to 50 percent or higher, was small. Predominantly black suburbs exist, but their number is not yet large.

This examination of suburban areas provides clear evidence of widespread decline in the practice of complete exclusion of blacks. Although many of the newly opened suburbs have only token numbers of blacks, the number of suburbs that are 3 percent, 10 percent and 20 percent black has also increased. There is little indication, so far, that large numbers of suburbs will repeat the prototypical central-city pattern of racial succession proceeding through the full sequence from the first black family to the last white family.

The same data on suburban population trends from 1970 to 1980 give a different impression when assessed from the perspective of black persons rather than individual suburbs. Many suburbs moved upward in black percentage within the range from zero to 10 percent, but each such suburb accomplished this without taking in very many black residents. A few suburbs with large black populations and high black percentages absorbed large numbers of new black residents. These two groups of suburbs accounted for roughly similar numbers of suburbanizing blacks during the 1970s. The ongoing suburbanization process includes components of both desegregation and relocation of the ghetto. Which of these is likely to prevail in coming decades?

Back to the Future: 1990-2019

If the beginnings of black America can be traced to the landing at Jamestown in 1619, only three decades remain until the four hundredth anniversary of that event. Whether or not 1619 is the appropriate date of origin, 2019 is a convenient date for ending this account, It is far enough in the future to suit the theme of the "Twenty-First Century Prognoses," yet close enough to the present that some of its features and possibilities are discernible. Peering into the distant future requires science fiction or prophecy, but visions of the near future come through extrapolation. The future is emergent, yet the task of prognosis shall begin with a backward look.

With the segregation index scores for 1940 to 1970, a statistical projection was attempted. Recall that the average score for the set of 109 cities was 85 in 1940, 87 in 1950, 86 in 1960 and 82 in 1970. A simple demographic model was constructed based on findings of previous studies that black and white population growth and racial composition were key determinants of change in segregation. There were three observations of change over three ten-year periods. The initial question addressed, with help from the model, was whether the changes observed for 1960 to 1970 were compatible with the 1940-to-1950 and 1950-to-1960 changes, or whether the evidence supported the idea of a fundamental shift in the process of change.

> We have presumed that the equilibrium state of American cities is one of nearly complete segregation. . . . Our paper suggests that the environment in which that process . . . operates is changing. Segregation has been going down. A projection of segregation using our second order model suggests a value of about 75 by 1980. Further, if our interpretation of the data is correct,

then consolidation is proceeding more slowly and many neighborhoods are remaining desegregated for longer periods of time. If whatever process is operating has high values of segregation as a stable equilibrium, then the change will be only temporary. . . . If the process has high levels of segregation as an unstable equilibrium — a saddle point if you will — then the trends presently under way may move segregation far enough away from their high values to start them on a new trajectory of change. The process under way in the 1960s, then, may foretell more dramatic changes in the future.[40]

Based only on the statistical model and census data for 1970 and earlier years, it was projected that the mean segregation index for the 109 cities would decline from 82 in 1970 to 75 in 1980. Eight years later, when the appropriate data from the 1980 census had been put through the computer, the mean index was 76.

Accuracy of projection lends credence to a model, but no model should be presumed to be the true version of the actual causation. Many other models might also yield accurate projections. The model cited here used only demographic data for 1970 and earlier dates. It did not take into explicit account the various social, economic and political changes that contributed to intensified or diminished residential segregation. Despite all these qualifications, the results of the model can be taken as additional evidence for the perspective that things are changing, that old patterns of segregation do not persist forever.

In the late 1970s the nation experienced a "nonmetropolitan turnaround." Many counties beyond the suburban zone of our big cities reversed a long trend of population decline, while growth in metropolitan counties slowed and in many cases turned downward. A century-long pattern of continual massive concentration in metropolitan areas came to an end. In the 1980s the turnaround itself turned around and metropolitan growth resumed, but the rate of growth has been slow and is unlikely to return to high levels. The nonmetropolitan areas of the country no longer have the population numbers and the high fertility rate required to fuel sustained, rapid increases in the metropolitan portion of the population. The numerical role of the central cities in metropolitan patterns has also diminished. Many cities which had lost white population for decades have recently begun to lose black population.

Racial patterns occur in social, economic and demographic contexts, and there is no way to be sure of the underlying causes of change. Reductions in the rapidity of racial succession were interpreted earlier as consistent with the perspective of declining racism. Other explanations are available that do not depend on the two racial perspectives which have been contrasted in this chapter. For example, in many cities the pent-up demand for housing caused by rapid black urbanization and the slow pace of housing construction in the 1930s and 1940s was finally satisfied during the 1960s (at least in terms of simple quantity, ignoring quality and location). Contributing to lessened black demand for additional housing were the demographic transition to lower fertility and the near completion of the migration flows from country to city. As the decades-long pressures for additional housing finally abated among urban blacks, the conditions for rapid racial succession diminished. Thus whatever perspective one takes on racism, one should avoid projecting into the future the 1940s-style Chicago racial succession model.

The connection between processes of racial segregation and of class segregation must also be assessed by the seer. Consider the regional difference noted for the 1940s and 1950s:

> In southern cities . . . there is little relationship between the characteristics of whites and Negroes living in the same neighborhood — high-status Negroes are as likely to live near low-status whites as near high-status whites. Furthermore, there is a tendency for high-status Negroes to live in predominantly Negro areas, whereas in the North high-status Negroes are more likely to live outside of the core of the ghetto.[41]

These regional differences, like the others previously discussed, have been in transition. Older southern cities are moving from their traditional functions as regional trade centers and becoming integrated, demographically as well as economically, into the national economic system. "New" southern cities have emerged, such as Houston and Dallas, whose main growth has occurred in the contemporary period. Older northern cities are now adapting to growing second- and third-generation urban black populations. Cities in every region are experiencing rapid growth of first- and second-generation Hispanic and Asian immigrants. The residential sorting out of this new melange of classes and minority groups defies easy analysis or projection into the future.

A common pattern for black middle-class families has been to seek housing away from the core of the ghetto. They were not always successful, especially in the 1960s and earlier, in obtaining residence in homogeneous middle-class neighborhoods. Because of the relatively small size of the black middle classes and the constraints of segregation, their residential neighborhoods had far greater proportions of lower-class neighbors than were found in the white middle-class neighborhoods.[42] If there is future growth in the size of the black middle classes, their ability to dominate entire neighborhoods will increase.

Metropolitan areas differ in the rate of growth of the black middle classes and in the degree to which outlying city and suburban neighborhoods have become open to blacks. There are wide variations among metropolitan areas in the degree to which the pattern observed by Brigitte Erbe is true of places other than Chicago and times other than the 1970s. Because today's metropolitan landscape is variegated, it is plausible to envision a future in which metropolitan areas are not all alike. As the North-South differences of the past are dissipating, a diversity of patterns is emerging. The crystal ball is too dim for one to discern a single new pattern.

If class will increasingly prevail over race in determining residential location, continued and even accelerated metropolitan desegregation may be in store. The complexities of personal choice may confound such an easy extrapolation, though. Inertia and vested interests help maintain the ghetto. The new political power recently gained by blacks in many central cities may facilitate the retention of middle-class blacks. Historical traditions in particular cities may explain distinctive patterns of racial location that then persist for decades into the future.

Many of the blacks moving to "black suburbs" rather than "white suburbs" are making a deliberate choice to live with plenty of black neighbors. This choice may be viewed in light of America's tradition of racism or in light of America's cultural pluralism. In any case, an opening up of suburban choice for blacks does not necessarily lead to lessened segregation. It may lead to a much greater freedom of choice of locations, kinds of housing and racial compositions. One certainly does not foresee in the next three decades that race will lose all of its influence on residential location. It may, however, operate as much less of a barrier.

Racial housing patterns are potentially affected by any policies and trends that affect household location decisions and restrictions. Many of these cannot be projected confidently into the future. Consider school desegregation, which has occurred in most cities during recent years. Research attention to the residential effects of school desegregation has so far focused on the segregative effects of white flight, but a few studies suggest other possibilities. In Louisville, the metropolitan school desegregation plan included specific incentives for families to seek racially integrated housing.[43] School desegregation programs elsewhere may also have been conducive to housing desegregation.[44] A recent study suggests that the metropolitan school desegregation plans implemented in some localities have already had strong desegregative effects on housing.[45]

As a demographer, this author is well aware of the profession's history of failing to predict the baby boom, failure to recognize it until it was well under way, failure to foresee the baby bust, and repeatedly failing to have actual census results fall within the wide intervals projected in the most careful forecasts. Thus one readily pleads professional incompetence to project or predict the future precisely, but one can review the past and identify some changes that may prove important.

This discussion has emphasized social forces that have reduced the intensity of racial residential segregation and that are likely to facilitate a degree of desegregation. It may, however, have exaggerated the significance of the statistical evidence of scattered residential integration occurring in many urban and suburban neighborhoods, under-emphasized the formation of new racial concentrations in the suburbs, downplayed the overwhelming forces of inertia perpetuating the ghetto and residential segregation, and avoided the complications imposed by the changing numbers and character of America's other minority groups.

Occurrences of desegregation may be epiphenomenal rather than forerunners of a coming era. The persistence of racist structures is emphasized in a recent history of the civil rights movement:

> Perhaps the least change of all since *Brown* came in residential segregation. Despite court rulings and legislation outlawing discrimination in housing, such discrimination persisted. . . . Whites of every class continued to resist housing integration if it involved anything other than token numbers of blacks. . . . The majority of America's [26.7] million blacks in 1980 had been confined to the inner cities of a score of metropolitan areas . . . , fulfilling the prophesy, and not heeding the warning, of the National Advisory Commission on Civil Disorders in 1968: "Our nation is moving toward two societies, one black, one white — separate and unequal."[46]

But let us not yield too much. Persistence is only part of history. Old trends never go on forever; they have to fade away. The period of rapid metropolitanization of the nation's population is over. It has been completed for blacks as it was earlier for whites. Many central cities have lost so much population, black and white, that they are far below their peak numbers, thus changing their residential character. No substantial migration continues long without changing the conditions that gave rise to it at its places of origin and the conditions that promoted it at its places of destination. The energy crisis of the 1970s made us aware of the possibility of renewed population centralization, and the gentrification of declining neighborhoods alerts us to the fact that neighborhoods are not forever. You can go home again, but home most likely will not be the same.

During the last fifty years, blacks have played the more active role in the desegregation that has occurred. More blacks have moved to predominantly white and racially mixed areas than vice versa. Whites have played a limited role, increasingly receiving some blacks as neighbors and showing a reduced tendency to flee or avoid small numbers of black families. But there has been little active white movement into predominantly black areas. Gentrification has so far been of modest statistical dimensions, and has oftentimes been resegregative rather than integrative.

Without change in the all-black character of central city ghettoes, desegregation can proceed only slowly. Perhaps such change will occur. A 1987 news item reported a plan in Dallas to break up housing for the poor.[47] Similar reports have come from other cities. If more aging and decaying public housing projects are razed or converted to other uses, opportunity is created for the transformation of portions of the central city landscape. During the urban renewal and highway construction programs of the 1930s through 1960s, large-scale remaking of the central city landscape was a commonplace. Those efforts were notable for preserving and intensifying the racial residential pattern. The lesson, however, is that change is possible. Central city black ghettoes were created over many decades, and their dismantlement, if it happens, could take decades. If they are undone, will it occur while new suburban ghettoes are growing to massive scale?

The dual trends regarding suburbanization (most suburbs desegregating, but the few heavily black suburbs absorbing much of the black population) lead to an indeterminacy about the future. In the jargon of high politics, we may be confronting a "window of opportunity." Thousands of urban and suburban neighborhoods have moved or will soon move into the token integration stage. If they continue to receive black families and to move steadily toward proportional racial representation, the movement of a few hundred suburbs toward all-black status will be slowed. But if suburban ghettoization becomes the norm during the rest of this century and the early years of the next, the opportunity will have been lost. If racial concentration persists in the central cities and increases in the suburbs, the pattern for the twenty-first century may be gilded, but it will still be segregated. A few blacks and many whites will be able to live in neighborhoods with a token degree of integration, those blacks who prefer black neighborhoods will have more choice than in the past, and those whites and blacks who would like racially diverse neighborhoods will be frustrated as in the twentieth century.

The emphasis on altered processes of racial change and the feasibility of declining residential segregation is in part a research strategy. I am more comfortable as a researcher than as a seer. Alertness to the possibility of change can be a warning against the careless application of generalizations and models from the past, and a spur to thoughtful and thorough analysis from new perspectives. Whatever the speculations and hypotheses, it is the data that will let us know what has happened. The answers will continually be surprising to social scientists, and thus satisfy our urge to ask more questions, seek better data, and increase understanding.

There also is a political strategy. The notion of a window of opportunity should be taken seriously. It is not too late for governmental programs and private decisions/actions to influence the racial and residential patterns that will prevail in the next century. Notable examples include the 1988 amendments to the Civil Rights Acts of 1968; the Kentucky Commission on Human Rights working in the Louisville area; the Cuyahoga Plan in the Cleveland area; National Neighbors, seeking to coordinate and encourage fair housing advocates around the country; and individuals such as Morris Milgram, pioneer developer of open housing, whose experiences are described in his book, *Good Neighborhood*.[48] We are in a crucial stage of transition from old patterns to new ones. Once the new patterns are set, inducing change will be much more difficult. The opportunity must be seized to increase the availability of integrated residential life for all Americans. To accommodate only those who cherish neighborhood racial homogeneity would be to prolong America's enduring dilemma.

NOTES

[1] *Brown v. Board of Education*, 347 U.S. 483 (1954).

[2] National Advisory Commission on Civil Disorders, *Report of the National Advisory Commission on Civil Disorders* (New York: Bantam Books, 1968), p. 1.

[3] Ibid.

[4] Karl E. Taeuber and Alma F. Taeuber, "The Black Population in the United States," in Mabel M. Smythe, ed., *The Black American Reference Book* (Englewood Cliffs, NJ: Prentice-Hall, Inc., 1976), pp. 161-162.

[5] Ibid., pp. 162-167.

[6] Ibid., pp. 169-175.

[7] W.E.B. DuBois, *The Philadelphia Negro* (New York: Benjamin Bloom, 1967; first published in 1899), pp. 287-309.

[8] Rose Helper, *Racial Policies and Practices of Real Estate Brokers* (Minneapolis: University of Minnesota Press, 1969).

[9] Ernest W. Burgess, "The Growth of the City," in Robert E. Park, Ernest W. Burgess and Roderick D. McKenzie, *The City* (Chicago: University of Chicago Press, 1925), pp. 47-62. See also Ernest W. Burgess, "Residential Segrega-

tion in American Cities," *Annals of the American Academy of Political and Social Science* Publication No. 2180 (November 1928): 1-11.

[10]Metropolitan Integration Research Center, *Racially Restrictive Covenants* (Milwaukee: Metropolitan Integration Research Center, 1979).

[11]Joe William Trotter, *Black Milwaukee* (Urbana, IL: University of Illinois Press, 1985), pp. 20-25.

[12]U.S. Federal Housing Administration, *Underwriters Manual* (Washington, D.C.: U.S. Federal Housing Administration, 1938).

[13]Ibid., Sec. 980.3.

[14]Ibid., Sec. 935.

[15]Ibid., Sec. 937.

[16]Helper, op. cit. note 8.

[17]Wisconsin Real Estate Brokers Board, *A Legal Guide for Wisconsin Real Estate Brokers* (1940), Ch. X, Article 34.

[18]Chicago Commission on Race Relations, *The Negro in Chicago* (Chicago: University of Chicago Press, 1922).

[19]See especially W.E.B. DuBois, *The Souls of Black Folk* (Chicago: A. C. McClurg, 1903).

[20]Hortense Powdermaker, *After Freedom: A Cultural Study in the Deep South* (New York: The Viking Press, 1939); John Dollard, *Caste and Class in a Southern Town* (New Haven, CT: Yale University Press, 1937); and Arthur F. Raper, *Preface to Peasantry* (Chapel Hill, NC: University of North Carolina Press, 1936).

[21]Gunnar Myrdal, *An American Dilemma* (New York: Harper & Brothers, 1944).

[22]Taeuber and Taeuber, "The Black Population," op. cit. note 4, pp. 171-181.

[23]Myrdal, op. cit. note 21.

[24]St. Clair Drake and Horace R. Cayton, *Black Metropolis: A Study of Negro Life in a Northern City* (New York: Harcourt, Brace, 1945).

[25]Robert C. Weaver, *The Negro Ghetto* (New York: Harcourt, Brace, 1948).

[26]*Shelley* v. *Kramer*, 334 U.S. 1 (1948).

[27]Otis Dudley Duncan and Beverly Duncan, *The Negro Population of Chicago: A Study of Residential Succession* (Chicago: University of Chicago Press, 1957). See also Helper, op. cit. note 8, and Drake and Cayton, op. cit. note 24.

[28]National Advisory Commission on Civil Disorders, op. cit. note 2, pp. 1-2 and 483.

[29]*Jones* v. *Mayer*, 392 U.S. 409 (1968); Title VIII of the Civil Rights Act of 1968, codified at 42 U.S.C. 3601 et seq.

[30]William Julius Wilson, *The Declining Significance of Race* (Chicago: University of Chicago Press, 1978).

[31]Howard Schuman, Charlotte Steeh and Lawrence Bobo, *Racial Attitudes in America: Trends and Interpretations* (Cambridge, MA: Harvard University Press, 1985), ch. 3, pp. 71-138.

[32]National Advisory Commission on Civil Disorders, op. cit. note 2, p. 1.

[33]See, for example, Ronald E. Wienk, Clifford E. Reid, John C. Simonson and Frederic J. Eggers, *Measuring Racial Discrimination in American Housing Markets: The Housing Market Practices Survey* (Washington, D.C.: U.S. Department of Housing and Urban Development, 1979).

[34]Karl E. Taeuber and Alma F. Taeuber, *Negroes in Cities: Residential Segregation and Neighborhood Change* (Chicago: Aldine Publishing Co., 1965), ch. 5, pp. 99-125.

[35]Ibid., ch. 3, pp. 28-68.

[36]Thomas L. Van Valey, Wade Clark Roof and Jerome E. Wilcox, "Trends in Residential Segregation: 1960-1970," *American Journal of Sociology* 82: 4 (January 1977): 826-844.

[37]Ann B. Schnare, "Trends in Residential Segregation by Race: 1960-1970," *Journal of Urban Eonomics* 7: 3 (May 1980): 293-301; Ann B. Schnare, *Residential Segregation by Race in U.S. Metropolitan Areas: An Analysis Across Cities and Over Time*, Contract Report No. 246-2 (Washington, D.C.: The Urban Institute, 1977).

[38]Karl E. Taeuber, et al., "The Trend in Metropolitan Residential Segregation," paper presented at the Annual Meeting of the Population Association of America (Minneapolis: 1984).

[39]Elaine L. Fielding, *Black Suburbanization and Racial Change, 1970-1980*, CDE Working Paper 87-24 (Madison, WI: Center for Demography and Ecology, University of Wisconsin–Madison, 1987).

[40]Halliman H. Winsborough, Karl E. Taueber and Annemette Sorensen, *Models of Change in Residential Segregation, 1940-1970*, CDE Working Paper 75-27 (Madison, WI: Center for Demography and Ecology, University of Wisconsin–Madison, 1975), pp. 20-21.

[41]Taeuber and Taeuber, *Negroes in Cities*, op. cit. note 34, pp. 5-6.

[42]Brigitte Mach Erbe, "Race and Socioeconomic Segregation," *American Sociological Review* 40: 6 (December 1975): 801-812.

[43]Kentucky Commission on Human Rights, "Housing Desegregation Increases As Schools Desegregate in Jefferson County," (Louisville, KY: Kentucky Commission on Human Rights, 1977).

[44]Karl E. Taeuber, "School Desegregation and Racial Housing Patterns," in Daniel J. Monti, ed., *Impact of Desegregation*, New Directions for Testing and Measurement Series (San Francisco: Jossey-Bass, June 1982), pp. 53-65.

[45]Diana M. Pearce, Robert L. Crain, Reynolds Farley and Karl E. Taeuber, "Lessons Not Lost: The Effect of School Desegregation on the Rate of Residential Desegregation in Large Central Cities" (unpublished manuscript, 1986).

[46]Harvard Sitkoff, *The Struggle for Black Equality, 1945-1980* (New York: Hill and Wang, 1981), ch. 7, pp. 233-234.

[47]John Herbers, "Breakup of Housing for Poor Is Backed in Integration Move," *New York Times* (April 28, 1987), pp. A1 and A22.

[48]Morris Milgram, *Good Neighborhood: The Challenge of Open Housing* (New York: W.W. Norton, 1977).

INEQUALITY AND AFRICAN-AMERICAN HEALTH STATUS: POLICIES AND PROSPECTS *

Leith Mullings

City University of New York Graduate School

Introduction

Over the last century, there has been a significant improvement in the overall health status of African-Americans. Life expectancy has increased dramatically, the principal causes of death have shifted from infectious diseases to chronic ones, and the absolute prevalence of many diseases has decreased. However, if one compares the health of African-Americans to that of Euro-Americans, the relative disadvantages in terms of mortality and morbidity have, for many diseases, remained the same, or in some cases increased. African-Americans as a population have higher rates of morbidity and mortality for most diseases and die younger than Euro-Americans.

This chapter will examine the changes that have occurred in health status and access to treatment in the last century, and attempt to situate these within the context of changing social conditions. In doing so, it will take the position that health status is significantly influenced by the conditions of daily life. The first part of the chapter will examine trends in African-American health in the last century and some of the contemporary health issues of concern to African-Americans.[1] It will then examine critically the models that have been developed to explain racial/ethnic disparities in health and the way in which these models underlie policy directions. The chapter will conclude with a discussion of policy options.

---

*I would like to thank June Jackson Christmas, M.D., H. Jack Geiger, M.D., and Stephen Robinson, M.D., for their helpful comments.

Trends in African-American Health in the Twentieth Century

This section will begin by discussing social conditions, access to treatment, and selected aspects of morbidity and mortality in the first half of the century. Although reliable data are relatively scarce prior to 1940, it is nevertheless possible to get a general sense of health conditions. After examining some of the changes that occurred as the African-American struggle for equal opportunity culminated in the civil rights movement, contemporary access and health conditions will be examined.

The First Five Decades

At the turn of the century, African-Americans had been out of slavery for less than fifty years. Radical Reconstruction in the South had been defeated and legal segregation was being solidified. Most African-Americans lived in the South where the majority worked as sharecroppers or in domestic service, and for the most part received very low remuneration for their labor. As David Swinton points out in this volume, the African-American migrations from the South—resulting in the transformation of the work force from one engaged in predominantly agricultural pursuits to one more involved in the industrial economy—significantly improved social conditions and, some scholars argue, health status.

For many years following slavery, biomedicine was to a great extent inaccessible to African-Americans. There were few African-American health professionals and institutions, and most mainstream health institutions and personnel were off-limits to them (although access in the North and South differed). One response to this was to depend upon traditional medicine. "Root work," synthesizing classical medicine and European and African beliefs, became part of the folk medical system of both the recently emancipated African-Americans and poor Southern whites.[2]

Following the dismantling of Reconstruction, de jure segregation in the South and de facto segregation in the North extended into all spheres of life. Given the devaluation of the lives of African-Americans, such access as did obtain could be dangerous. In addition to the inferior facilities, denial of more extensive diagnostic procedures and treatments, and medical stereotyping—all of which persist to this day—no one knows how many incidents of more dramatic abuse, such as the infamous Tuskegee experiments carried out by the U.S. Public Health Service, occurred. Between 1932 and 1972, despite the fact that penicillin became widely available in the early 1950s, four hundred African-American men were left untreated for syphilis so that the natural history of the disease could be observed.[3]

At the same time that medical care through Euro-American institutions was generally unavailable, there were major barriers to the training of African-American medical practitioners. At the turn of the century, virtually all of the 152 medical schools in the United States barred African-Americans from attendance. Howard Medical School, Meharry Medical College, and five other African-American medical schools were established during the post-Reconstruction period through the efforts of African-American self-help groups and Euro-American philanthropic organizations.

Shortly after the turn of the century, a national committee was formed to examine medical education. The *Flexner Report*, published in 1910, had a far-reaching effect on medical education. As a consequence of the widespread deficiencies described in the report, only about seventy medical schools remained open. While the manifest purpose of the report was the standardization and professionalization of medical education, an additional result was to make medicine virtually the preserve of wealthy Euro-American males and to further limit the access of African-Americans and women to medical education.

Abraham Flexner argued that given the tendency of African-Americans to avoid cleanliness and sanitation, the education of African-American physicians should emphasize "hygiene rather than surgery. . . ," and that since "the practice of the Negro doctor would be limited to his own race," only two African-American medical schools were needed.[4] In 1900 there were seven predominantly African-American medical schools; Howard and Meharry were the only ones to survive the reform.

This fixed the pattern of African-American entry into medical education for the next fifty years; this in turn significantly affected African-American access to medical care and health status. For each year between 1920 and 1964, only 2 to 3 percent of students entering U.S. medical schools were African-American; the vast majority of those attended Howard and Meharry. Discriminatory patterns were encouraged by the national medical associations. For example, in 1945 the American College of Surgeons turned down an admittedly qualified African-American physician in his application for membership, stating that "fellowship in the college is not to be conferred to members of the Negro race at this time."[5] As late as 1963, the American Medical Association refused to prohibit racial discrimination by affiliated county and state societies.[6]

Throughout most of the century, then, the training of African-American physicians has been restricted. In 1920, when the African-American population was approximately 10.5 million, there were only 3,855 African-American physicians. By 1942 the population had grown to 12.9 million, but the number of physicians had decreased to 3,810, and by 1948 it had further decreased to 3,753. In New York City, for example, there were only 305 African-American physicians, 2 percent of all the physicians in the city in 1954—making the ratio of African-American physicians to the population 1:2754, as compared to 1:480 for Euro-Americans.[7]

The health status of African-Americans reflected the conditions of daily life and their lack of access to biomedical care, as well as the state of medical knowledge and technology. At the turn of the century, the leading causes of death were influenza, pneumonia, tuberculosis and gastritis.[8] The death rate among African-Americans from tuberculosis was over 450 per 100,000—three times the Euro-American rate.[9] At this time, the life expectancy for African-Americans at birth was approximately 36.5 years.[10] John Reid and his co-authors make the interesting point that the expectations a parent would die early made the extended family necessary to ensure the survival of children during this period.[11] By 1940, life expectancy at birth was approximately 54 years.[12] Although there was a gradual narrowing of the difference in life expectancy at birth between African-Americans and Euro-Americans from 14.6 years in 1900 to 8.3 years in 1950,[13] African-American life expectancy remained below that of Euro-Americans.

Much of the improvement in life expectancy was attributable to reductions in child and infant mortality. Enslaved African-American infants died at a rate of approximately four times that of Euro-American infants.[14] And although between 1900 and 1940 the infant and child (to age five) mortality rate among African-Americans declined from 264 per 1,000 to 90 per 1,000, it remained approximately 70 percent above that of Euro-Americans.[15]

What accounts for the improvements in health status and decreases in mortality during this period? All researchers recognize the role of medical advances, but some suggest that the improvements in socioeconomic status were decisive, particularly in light of the fact that in some periods African-American gains in life expectancy were proportionately greater than those for Euro-Americans. The wartime economy, which created a market for African-American labor and allowed them to leave the tenant farms of the South and thereby improve their socioeconomic status;[16] changes in childfeeding practices; and improved sanitation and housing (particularly in relation to infectious diseases)[17] were among the significant developments. Douglas Ewbank points to the importance of socioeconomic status and household conditions. The data on infant mortality in eight cities between 1911 and 1915 show that for those African-Americans with incomes under $550 per year, the infant mortality rate was 60 percent higher than for those with incomes of $650 to $849. Controlling for income, African-American infant mortality rates were 10 percent higher than rates for native Euro-Americans and 5 percent higher than rates for foreign-born whites. However, this appears to be related to differences in the proportion of mothers who worked outside the home. Where mothers were not employed away from home, and holding income constant, African-American infants had slightly lower mortality rates than their Euro-American counterparts.[18]

In the first half of the century, then, one observes major transformations in the socioeconomic status of African-Americans, and coupled with that, improvements in health status, specifically a reduction in the mortality rate for infectious diseases and an increase in life expectancy. During this period, one can discern at least three major strategies which African-Americans employed to cope with health problems. First, they made use of the "popular" sector. This included the use of home remedies, traditional medicines, folk healers and healing churches.[19] Second, within the constraints of institutional discrimination, they participated in the biomedical system and made major contributions to mainstream biomedicine. For example, it was the African-American physician Charles Drew who developed a method for preserving blood plasma in 1939-40 and pioneered the establishment of blood banks. Finally, African-Americans confronted the institutional constraints that limited both their conditions of existence and their access to biomedicine. To the extent that health is significantly influenced by social conditions, it was probably this last strategy that had the greatest consequences.

The Impact of the Civil Rights Movement

These struggles against institutional discrimination culminated in the civil rights movement of the mid-1950s through the mid-1970s. While not accomplishing all of its goals, the civil rights movement played a major role in improving the conditions of life for African-Americans. It stimulated legislation that removed legal barriers to voting rights and to equal access to public accommodations. To a limited degree it mitigated occupational and educational segregation, and it influenced public policy to make health care more accessible to larger numbers of people. Several scholars argue that it had a major impact on health status.

As the civil rights struggle challenged segregated medical education, the number of African-Americans entering medical schools increased dramatically. By 1974, 7.5 percent of all entering students were African-American (as compared to 2 percent between World War II and the mid-sixties.)[20] Gains were almost entirely a result of the increased entry of African-Americans into predominantly Euro-American schools. Before 1968, less than one percent of the total entering class of predominantly Euro-American medical schools was African-American, whereas between 1967 and 1974, the proportion of African-Americans in the entering class of these schools increased approximately eightfold, from 0.8 to 6.3 percent.[21]

The civil rights struggle clearly had an impact on health services. While there seems to be ample evidence documenting continuing racism in the health care system,[22] and many African-Americans continue to perceive the medical care system as less accessible to them,[23] some of the more overt and manifest aspects of racial discrimination were curtailed. From the mid-sixties to the seventies, there were approximately seventy-five pieces of federal legislation directed at providing broader access to health services. The "War on Poverty" promoted increased access to health care through Medicaid, the Comprehensive Health Planning Act and the Community Health Centers Act, among others.[24] Community primary care programs grew, and numerous studies document their effectiveness.[25]

The introduction of Medicaid and Medicare, despite their shortcomings, was important in expanding access to health care for Americans of all races. By 1976, studies indicated that with the exception of hospital utilization among southern African-Americans without chronic health problems, African-Americans and Euro-Americans made equal use of chronically ill and ambulatory care medical services under Medicaid.[26] In 1978, the Robert Wood Johnson Foundation was able to report a nearly equal percentage of African-Americans and Euro-Americans seeing a physician during a twelve-month period, even controlling for increased need.[27]

While there are difficulties in drawing a causal relationship between changes in health status and a particular set of events in a limited period of time, several scholars argue convincingly that some improvements in health can be directly related to "the antiracist struggle."[28] Researchers have noted that between 1968 and 1978 the differential in life expectancy improved in favor of nonwhites, with a drop in death rates from coronary heart disease and a steep drop in deaths from stroke;[29] that in approximately the same decade the number of excess deaths among African-Americans dropped from 73,000 to 59,000, with 65 percent of the drop occurring in African-American women; and that the death rates among African-Americans for accidents and infant mortality also decreased.[30] These and other data suggest that progress can be achieved when social, economic and health care resources are made available.[31]

Examining the improvements in health status in the third quarter of the twentieth century, Haynes Rice and LaRah Payne predicted in the 1981 edition of *The State of Black America* that if improvements were to continue at the same rate, rapid gains in relative health status should be evident. For example, they suggested that differentials between African-Americans and Euro-Americans in pneumonia and influenza should close in another ten to twenty years.[32]

Contemporary Conditions, Access and Health Status

Given the fact that many of the achievements of the civil rights era have been eroded over the decade of the 1980s, it is unclear whether the gains in health status will be maintained, particularly if the policies begun during the Reagan administration were to continue. While African-Americans have virtually eliminated the racial disparity in secondary school completion, current economic policies have prevented this from translating into an overall income gain. (See Swinton's chapter in this volume.) Class differences within the population have widened. Though the small African-American middle class has moved into a wider range of professions and higher income brackets, poverty has increased for a growing number of African-Americans. By 1987, African-American income was 56.1 percent of Euro-American income (down from 61 percent in 1970), and 33.1 percent lived in poverty (up from 24 percent in 1974).[33]

Unemployment rates for African-American workers have remained devastatingly high, at over twice the rates of Euro-Americans throughout the 1970s and 1980s. In 1983, the unemployment rate was 9.6 percent nationally; 8.4 percent for Euro-Americans and 19.5 percent for African-Americans. Among African-American youth, unemployment was 48.5 percent, more than twice the 22.4 percent rate among all teenagers.[34] In 1988, the official unemployment rate was 4.0 percent for Euro-Americans, but 10.0 percent for African-Americans.[35] Regarding unemployment, it is interesting to examine M. Harvey Brenner's provocative hypothesis that for every one percent increase in national unemployment, suicide increases by 4.1 percent, admissions to mental hospitals by 3.4 percent, admissions to state prisons by 4.0 percent, homicide by 5.7 percent, cirrhosis of the liver by 1.7 percent, and cardiovascular-renal disease mortality by 1.9 percent.[36]

In a fee-for-service health system such as that in the United States, the ability to pay for service depends on income or access to health insurance. Employment-based, third-party insurance is the major source of health insurance for those under age sixty-five. Thus, as unemployment increases, access to health insurance decreases. In 1982, 9 percent of the U.S. population had no health insurance coverage of any kind, and African-American and Hispanic uninsured rates were two to three times higher than those of Euro-Americans. By 1985, 22 percent of all African-Americans—and 15 percent of all others—had no form of health insurance, including Medicaid.[37] While Medicaid is an important source of health insurance for the poor (20 percent of African-American families use Medicaid as their only source of health insurance[38]), it is clear that the eligibility requirements of Medicaid severely limit its availability. Moreover, funding for neighborhood health centers has been reduced and some services have been dismantled.[39]

The Reagan administration policy of creating block grants altered the amount of money available for health programs. In 1982, ninety programs were consolidated into four block grants to the states, including two in health—with a 25 percent reduction in funds. The 1982 funding level for programs in maternal and child health services, nutrition for children, rehabilitative services, genetic disease and adolescent health services was 13 percent below the funding for those individual categories in 1981. Similarly, drug abuse, alcohol treatment and community mental health programs were reformulated into block grants and cut 25 percent over fiscal year 1981, leading Woodrow Jones, Jr., and Mitchell Rice to suggest that block grants had resulted in increased mortality.[40] The Reagan administration also virtually eliminated the National Health Service Corps scholarships which offered stipends for medical school in return for a period of service in underserved areas.

What is now commonly referred to as a crisis in health care, characterized by constantly rising costs and the relative ineffectiveness of health care interventions, has implications for the entire population, but disproportionately so for African-Americans. Although in the early 1980s a surplus of physicians was projected for the next decade, many of the twenty-seven million people living in primary-care manpower shortage areas were nonwhites, who constituted most of the 80 percent of those utilizing neighborhood health centers.[41] Alan Sager's study of forty years of hospital closings concluded that the racial composition of the hospital's neighborhood, rather than the economic conditions of the hospital, determined whether a hospital closed or was relocated. The study predicted that "in the next 10 to 15 years there will be no hospitals in the inner city except tertiary care centers,"[42] which are often less accessible than community hospitals.

Race continues to be a factor in determining the type of medical care people receive. For example, a recent study of Massachusetts patients with cardiovascular problems demonstrated that after controlling for age, sex, socioeconomic status, insurance status and clinical characteristics, Euro-Americans had substantially higher rates of certain cardiac procedures than African-Americans. These were procedures that if "used appropriately . . . can have substantial health benefits."[43]

As could be expected, a 1986 national telephone survey of the self-reported health status of more than ten thousand people led researchers to conclude that African-Americans were "worse off than whites in terms of access to physician care."[44] In spite of the fact that serious illness was far more common among African-Americans, their average annual number of physician visits was considerably lower than that for Euro-Americans—3.4 per year as compared to 4.4 per year.[45] Furthermore, African-Americans were less likely to have medical insurance, less likely to receive dental care, more likely to use hospital clinics and emergency rooms, and more likely to prefer to go to a different provider than the one they saw on their last visit.

Despite these conditions, the number of new African-American physicians has been curtailed in the post-civil rights period. Between 1974 and 1983 the proportion of African-Americans in the entering classes of U.S. medical schools fell from 7.5 percent to 6.8 percent (even though the applicant pool share increased from 5.6 percent in 1974 to 7.3 percent in 1978),[46] and by 1985, African-American first-year medical students represented only 6.6 percent of first-year enrollment.[47] In 1983, African-American physicians represented only 3 percent of the total physician population.[48] It appears that the shortage of trained African-American physicians will continue; in 1985 the Task Force on Black and Minority Health, commissioned by the secretary of the Department of Health and Human Services, found that:

> The proportion of Blacks among health professionals is relatively low and not likely to change appreciably in the near future. In virtually none of the States surveyed for this report do the number of Black graduates of medical, dental, or pharmacy schools even approach the proportions of Blacks in the population. If the number of Black graduates continues to rise, as it has during the past two decades, it is still unlikely that the proportion of Black professionals will significantly increase in the near future.[49]

Because African-American physicians continue to comprise a significant proportion of the providers of health care to African-Americans, this shortage has serious implications for the availability of health services. While access to medical care is not as strictly segregated by race as it was in the past, "physicians are most likely to practice among members of their own ethnic group."[50] Furthermore, existing studies indicate that "health professionals who are from the same cultural background as their patients may be able to communicate better and thereby have a [more] positive influence on many of the factors that affect health outcome."[51]

In the last decades of the century, one observes a continuing discrepancy between the health status of African-Americans and that of Euro-Americans. In 1983 the life expectancy for Euro-Americans was 75.2 years; for African-Americans it was 69.6 years, or 5.6 years less. This figure for African-Americans approximates the life expectancy reached by Euro-Americans in the 1950s, a lag of approximately 30 years.[52] Life expectancy for African-Americans is lower than life expectancy for Euro-Americans except at advanced ages, when the former actually have a higher life expectancy. Known as the "crossover" effect, this is thought to be a result of differential early mortality whereby the least robust of the disadvantaged population die at earlier ages, providing that population with proportionately more robust individuals at later ages.[53]

African-Americans experience greater morbidity and mortality than Euro-Americans from certain cancers, hypertension, diabetes and other occupational and chronic diseases, with the leading causes of death being heart disease and malignant neoplasms. There is an 11 percent higher incidence of cancer among African-Americans, with an age-adjusted incidence 25 percent higher among African-American men compared with nonminority men, and 4 percent higher among African-American women compared with nonminority women.[54] African-Americans are two to four times more likely to report hypertension; they have a twofold excess risk of diabetes and other chronic diseases, such as arthritis.[55]

In its 1985 report on black and minority health, the U.S. Department of Health and Human Services calculated the excess death rate and the relative risk for several diseases. The concept of excess death "expresses the difference between the number of deaths actually observed in a minority group and the number of deaths that would have occurred in that group if it experienced the same death rates for each age and sex as the White population."[56] Relative risk is "the ratio of the minority death rate to the White death rate."[57] Analyzing the mortality data from 1979 to 1981, the task force found that 42.3 percent of all deaths of African-Americans who died before the age of seventy could be considered excess deaths.[58]

Death from cancer, cardiovascular disease, stroke, cirrhosis, diabetes, homicide, accidents and infant mortality accounted for 80 percent
of the excess deaths.[59] Excess deaths were most pronounced for infants
and for adults through middle age, representing 47 percent of the total
annual deaths of people age forty-five or less, and 42 percent of the
total annual deaths of people age seventy or less. For African-Americans between the ages of forty-five and sixty-nine, excess mortality was
due primarily to cancer, heart disease, stroke, diabetes and cirrhosis.
African-Americans under the age of forty-five have a relative risk of
dying from all causes that is nearly twice that of Euro-Americans; for
the same group, relative risk of death is the highest for tuberculosis,
hypertension, homicide and anemias. For African-Americans between
the ages of twenty-five and forty-four, homicide was the major cause of
excess deaths.[60]

Differences in nondisease mortality and morbidity rates such as accidents and housefires were found to diminish when adjusted for income.[61] Similarly, a 1971 study of homicide rates among African-
American men in Atlanta demonstrated the significance of socioeconomic status. It found that a sizeable difference in comparative homicide rates remained if education was held constant; if one controlled for
income the difference narrowed; but if one controlled for occupants per
room as a direct estimate of purchasing power, the racial difference in
domestic homicide disappeared.[62] An analysis of national statistics
supports these findings; racial differences disappear or become much
smaller when socioeconomic status is controlled for, and the majority
of homicides are concentrated in urban areas characterized by low socioeconomic status, bad housing and high density.[63]

As the national government has been increasingly unable or unwill-
ing to prevent the influx of illegal drugs into the country, and treatment facilities continue to be inadequate, drug abuse has reached epidemic proportions in some African-American communities. With the
growth of intravenous drug abuse [64] and as those addicted to "crack"
barter sex for drugs, the risk of contracting and dying from acquired
immunodeficiency syndrome (AIDS) has increased dramatically. Of
the 66,464 cases of AIDS reported to the Centers for Disease Control
from June 1, 1981 to July 4, 1988, most (60 percent) occurred among
non-Hispanic Euro-Americans. But African-Americans and Hispanics
were disproportionately represented with 26 percent and 13 percent of
the cases, respectively;[65] African-Americans constituted 53.6 percent
of all women with AIDS[66] and 76 percent of all children with AIDS.[67]
As AIDS follows the pattern of many other diseases in becoming a
marker of poverty,[68] the AIDS epidemic will have widespread ramifi-

cations in poor communities. In addition to the direct effects on the victims, their families and communities, the additional load on the health care system is likely to further limit the provision of health services in communities that are already underserved.

Increasingly, people in the United States also are dying from work-related conditions. Annually, 100,000 people die from such conditions and four million people contract occupational diseases.[69] African-Americans are especially vulnerable. African-American workers with the same level of education as Euro-American workers find themselves in substantially more dangerous occupations; thus it is not surprising that, writing in 1984, James Robinson found that the average African-American worker is in an occupation 37 to 52 percent more likely to produce serious accidents or illnesses than his/her Euro-American counterpart.[70] In 1980 Morris Davis observed:

> We enter the 1980s with the following statistics. Fifteen percent of the black work force (one to one and one-half million) are unable to work due to permanent or partial job-related disabilities. Black workers have a 37 percent greater chance than whites of suffering an occupational injury or illness. Black workers are one and one-half times more likely than whites to be severely disabled from job injuries and illnesses and face a 20 percent greater chance than whites of dying from job-related injuries and illnesses. [Citations omitted.][71]

There is, though, some cause for optimism in James Robinson's findings that between 1968 and 1986 the excess risk of disabling occupational injury faced by African-American men in relation to Euro-American men declined by 50 percent.[72] He attributes this decline to the successes of the struggle for equal opportunity in the workplace. However, there were absolute increases in occupational injury rates for both African-Americans and Euro-Americans, and the excess rate of disabling occupational injury increased by 20 percent among African-American women, giving them the same injury risk as Euro-American men.[73]

As one leaves the 1980s and looks back over the first nine decades of the century, one observes that the absolute health status of African-Americans has improved. This has been a result of both advances in medical technology and the struggle of African-Americans to improve their conditions of life and access to these advances. At the same time, though, significant differentials in health status remain that should not be underestimated.

Policy and Prognosis

Interpretations of the Health Differential

At the core of health policy is a judgment about why racial differentials in health status exist. Hence, health policy cannot be understood without addressing the theoretical biases that underlie both research decisions and health services policy, specifically assumptions about what are the critical determinants of health status.

In the literature on medicine, epidemiology and public health, as well as in popular thought, two explanatory models dominate: the first can be called the racial/genetic model and the second the cultural model.[74] The racial/genetic model, particularly as used to explain health inequality, suggests that significant aspects of the health differential between African-Americans and Euro-Americans—the higher rates of illness and death for the former—are largely attributable to biological and/or genetic differences. Even where attribution is not stated explicitly, assumptions of genetic susceptibility implicitly underlie the categories that structure the collection of data, as well as the way in which findings are reported. After sex and age, mortality and morbidity data are most consistently categorized by race,[75] with the underlying assumption that race is as *biologically* fundamental a predictor of disease as are age and gender.[76]

The concept of race is no longer used as crudely as it was at the turn of the century. At that time, some southern doctors called for a separate branch of "negro medicine," arguing that the racial differential in disease was a result of biological and physiological differences based on African-Americans having smaller brains, less developed nervous systems, and larger livers, glands and kidneys.[77] Nevertheless, race, as it is now used in the medical literature, tends to assume homogeneity within groups and heterogeneity between groups. This is based on the typological approach to human variation that became popular at the turn of the century when biblical rationalizations for slavery were replaced by purportedly scientific ones. Thus Nancy Krieger and Mary Bassett note that the 1968 handbook of the International Epidemiological Association defined race as "persons who are relatively homogeneous with respect to biological inheritance."[78] These kinds of interpretations of racial correlations often tend to explicitly or implicitly rely on alleged biological or genetic differences to explain differential disease rates.

There is the tendency, as well, to minimize the importance of the social context. Many anthropologists, recognizing the range of human variation and the thousands of human traits which vary in different ways, would suggest that the choice of one such trait, skin color, as a marker tells us more about society than about biology. In other words, it is an analysis of the social context—in which the trait of skin color is isolated and used to divide and identify human groups—that gives one an indication of why race is such an important predictor of health status in the United States.

What is important, then, is not the inherent "biological" significance of these traits, *but the meaning they are ascribed within a particular historical and social context*. It is because Africans were enslaved and their descendants subjected to racism and discrimination that skin color in the United States has become a major determinant of life chances and therefore bears a relationship to health. It is not the biological variation itself, but the meaning that such variation carries in a given society that makes it a predictor of health status. The medical literature, however, often contains the implicit assumption that there is an important link between those genetic elements that determine the relative presence or absence of melanin (or, more accurately, self-reports based on genealogical interpretations of such, as is done in the decennial census) and what are often hypothetical genetic elements that are alleged to determine the presence or absence of disease. As Richard Cooper puts it, "[m]ost public health analysis based on racial categories adopts this false analogy—that a 'package' of genetic differences exists—and is thus fatally flawed."[79]

There are many diseases that occur more frequently within specific populations. However, once a statistical relationship between a particular race and a disease has been demonstrated, it is first necessary to establish a functional relationship between the biological attributes of the individuals of that race and the disease. Thereafter, a causal relationship must be proven.[80] For the most part, these steps have not been carried out for diseases where genetic relationships are implied.

There are, of course, some cases where genetic differences have been demonstrated to have a direct bearing on health and disease. Evolutionary adaptation to West Africa, for example, favored increased frequency of the sickle-cell gene, where heterozygotes seem to have a relative immunity to, or contract a less severe form of, falciparum malaria. In the popular view, and often in the biomedical community, sickle-cell disease in the United States is considered to be a "racial" disease confined to Africans and African-Americans. Yet, hemoglobin S is not found in all African populations, and sickling appears to have emerged independently in West Africa and in other parts of Africa and Asia. As

Anthony Polednak suggests, what appears to be a racial/ethnic concentration of a disease may be part of a broader pattern of adaptation.[81] But most important is that those diseases with a clear genetic component, such as sickle-cell anemia, have a relatively small impact on the overall health status of the African-American population: Of the eighty thousand "excess deaths" among African-Americans in 1977, only 277 or 0.3 percent of the total excess could be attributed to hemoglobinopathies.[82]

Although the utility of the concept of race may diminish as methods of population genetics define more specific features of human biological adaptation, the assumption that the health differential is attributable to biological differences continues to have important consequences for both research and public policy. Krieger and Bassett report that of over five hundred recent articles in medical journals on hypertension, fewer than one dozen explored social factors.[83] Similarly, the rise of genetic screening of employees by industry is one indication of the policy ramifications of this model. James Bowman, a Chicago physician, has documented the way in which insurance and other companies, state governments, the armed forces and others have used genetic screening improperly to discriminate against African-Americans.[84] By 1982, forty-nine major industrial companies had informed the congressional Office of Technology Assessment that they intended to begin genetic screening of employees in the next five years; seventeen began carrying out such tests in the five years previous and more than five were in the process of doing so.[85] Reports in the mass media indicate that insurance companies increasingly propose the use of genetic screening to determine insurability.

That social conditions are a major determinant of health has been evident since the Middle Ages, when "it was clear that wealth could mitigate, and poverty exacerbate, the distribution of disease."[86] As early as the 1660s, when bad harvests, famines and war prompted the migration of the rural poor to overcrowded, rat-infested urban areas, the 1665 Great Plague of London clearly demonstrated the class implications of disease. The prosperous inner-city residents, who could flee the city, suffered only one-seventh of the mortality, the bulk of which was borne by the poor.[87]

Nonetheless, even where it is recognized that health is significantly influenced by social status, there is disagreement about the ways in which social conditions relate to disease. The second major model found in the literature emphasizes cultural traits, often described as lifestyle characteristics, as a major factor in explaining disparities in health. Predominant in the public health literature, for example, is a "culture of poverty" model which calls attention to harmful personal, cultural and lifestyle traits as determinants of health status.

Although this approach has recently resurfaced in the political sphere, interpretations of health status that focus on deleterious lifestyle differences as major risk factors are not new. The process of industrialization, the emergence of the factory system, the migration of rural populations to crowded urban centers and the consolidation of capitalist relations in England produced social conditions that set the stage for the resurgence of epidemics, rampant infanticide, and deteriorating conditions in the cities. The dominant official interpretation was represented by Edwin Chadwick, author of the Public Health Act of 1848. He described those inhabiting the working-class sector as "short-lived, improvident, reckless, and intemperate, with habitual avidity for sensual gratification . . . ," and noted that disease leaves in its wake "a population that is young, inexperienced, ignorant, credulous, irritable, passionate and dangerous, having a perpetual tendency to moral as well as physical deterioration."[88] Similarly, physicians in the United States interpreted the postslavery health crises among African-Americans as an indication of their biological and cultural inferiority. African-Americans were thought not only to be a threat to themselves, but an epidemiologic menace to Euro-Americans.[89]

In the late 1960s, the "culture of poverty" approach was synthesized and popularized by the anthropologist, Oscar Lewis. Briefly, Lewis suggested that certain poor people develop a subculture, characterized by approximately seventy negative traits, such as unemployment, matriarchy, alienation, provincial outlook, minimal social organization, and so forth. Children were thought to absorb this culture by the age of six or seven and were then unable to change despite new opportunities.[90] This approach has been criticized by anthropologists who have noted that Lewis' notion of culture as a list of unchangeable traits was antiquated, that Lewis' own data contradicted his conclusions, that his methodology was faulty, and that his observations were inaccurate.[91] Still, the "culture of poverty" perspective continues to hold sway in the practice disciplines such as social work and health.

In the field of health, this approach implies that attitudes, beliefs, habits, customs and lifestyle characteristics are the chief determinants of health and illness. Vulnerability to illness because of social conditions, utilization of medical services, and availability and accessibility of health services are presented as secondary to lifestyle changes in transforming health status. Irwin Rosenstock summarizes this view as follows:

> The culture of poverty may originally have been based on a history of economic deprivation, but it seems to be a culture exhibit-

ing its own rationale and structure, and reflecting a way of life that is transmitted to new generations. It is therefore suggested that while financial costs may serve as barriers to obtaining health services, their removal would probably not have the effect of creating widespread changes in the health behavior of the poor, at least not in the foreseeable future.[92]

The Reagan administration enthusiastically embraced this model. Emphasis on lifestyle characteristics as a major determinant of health is evident in the 1985 *Report of the Secretary's Task Force on Black and Minority Health*. In it, health education is promoted as a major solution to the 42.3 percent of excess deaths among African-Americans.[93]

While there has been a great deal of debate and disagreement about the role of culture in health care utilization, most of the concrete studies of controlled social change demonstrate that when conditions of health care delivery—accessibility, efficiency, cost, beliefs and attitudes—are improved, people change to take advantage of those conditions. An experimental study of 6,297 children enrolled in a primary care program is representative. The researchers concluded that in a system that sought to decrease barriers to health care, African-American children made about equal use of the services. They further suggested that system-related factors are significant determinants of the use of health services, rather than culture or belief issues.[94] These findings are in keeping with the more modern anthropological understanding of culture, where culture is conceptualized as dynamic, evolutionary and everchanging as people react to their conditions and act upon them.

It is important to note that critics of the "culture of poverty" approach would agree that health education may be beneficial in changing certain detrimental cultural characteristics and, further, that education may empower people. But they would argue that cultural traits are not independent of the larger social system; that the emphasis on lifestyles obscures the fact that lifestyle characteristics are not fully "voluntary" choices; that options for employment, recreation, nutrition and such are shaped by the social structure; and that analysis of the structural aspects of society, in particular class and racial hierarchies, tells one more about much of the health differences between African-Americans and Euro-Americans than does an examination of genetic or individual differences.

Cancer presents an interesting example of the complexities of this issue. There is general agreement that the overall incidence and mortality rates for cancer have been increasing in the last thirty years,[95] and that "excess" rates are disproportionately high for African-Americans, particularly for men.[96] Genetic and lifestyle interpretations of the disproportionate African-American cancer rate abound and seem to have the most impact on policy and funding. The search for genetic explanations of the racial differential continues despite the fact that comparative studies have consistently found that African-Americans have higher incidence rates for most cancers than Africans,[97] and that African-American cancer rates are more like those of Euro-Americans than of the African populations from which they were drawn.[98] Indeed, some researchers suggest that apart from those cancers such as skin and lip cancers where African-Americans show distinctly lower rates than Euro-Americans, it is unlikely that the differences in rates between African-Americans and Euro-Americans are due primarily to genetic as opposed to environmental factors.[99]

Similarly, the growing emphasis on lifestyle explanations for cancer tends to treat behavioral traits as though they are entirely voluntary or culturally-based choices, without sufficient attention to the way in which forces external to the individual influence lifestyle characteristics and constrain choices. A few examples will suffice. Diet may be a major factor in a high proportion of cancers.[100] High-fat diets seem to be implicated in cancers of the breast, colon and, perhaps, others. It has been argued that the growing reliance on fast foods—which depend heavily on meat and fat products—is a result of the monopolization of food production and the demanding pace of contemporary life.[101] Thus, though education about the role of diet is important, its potential cannot be realized unless healthful foods are available and people have the money to purchase them as well as the conditions of life that allow their utilization. Low-income working mothers are, regrettably, among the major consumers of fast food.

Similarly, smoking has a major impact on the rate of cancer,[102] and is generally treated as a lifestyle issue requiring education.[103] A few decades ago African-Americans had lower rates of smoking than Euro-Americans, but smoking rates among African-Americans now exceed those among Euro-Americans and death rates from lung cancer are considerably higher.[104] In this case it might be useful to examine the relationship of this behavioral trait to larger historical trends, including the relationships between social class, occupation, smoking, and the role of tobacco companies in targeting African-American communities for intensive advertising campaigns.[105]

The issue here is not that an analysis of genetic and cultural characteristics has no place in understanding and trying to prevent cancer, but that their roles are often exaggerated while the effects of larger environmental and social factors are correspondingly minimized. Greenberg and Randall conclude that the American Cancer Society "has shown scant interest in the carcinogenic effects of air and water pollution, drugs and food additives."[106] Similarly, the role of involuntary exposure to occupational carcinogens receives relatively little treatment in the literature or in public policy. During the Reagan administration, for example, the Occupational Safety and Health Administration was almost dismantled, all but destroying the enforcement of occupational health and safety laws.

This is particularly significant for African-Americans who, as a result of discriminatory practices, are disproportionately represented in the more hazardous jobs and occupations—even after controlling for racial differences in years of education and work experience. Morris Davis argues that increased exposure to carcinogens began during the early 1900s when African-Americans migrated in large numbers to urban industrial areas. They were recruited for the most strenuous and hazardous jobs that exposed them to carcinogenic chemicals and physical agents. The combination of exposure, long working hours and other unhealthful conditions significantly contributed to the high rates of cancer among African-Americans.[107] Several studies lend support to this analysis.[108]

There are certainly biological/genetic elements being discovered everyday, such as human histocompatibility antigens, that have a bearing on cancer morbidity and mortality. However, these do not necessarily have a clear connection to racial groups as defined in the medical literature. There are cultural traits such as dietary factors that may increase or reduce the risk of cancer; but there is a complex interaction between culture/lifestyle "choices" and the structure of differential distribution of jobs, rewards and resources.

For researchers, the task at hand is to find out why racial disparities in disease exist. This requires distinguishing analytically the influence of socioeconomic factors from genetic differences, and elucidating the interaction of the socioeconomic structure with both cultural traits and genetic differences. It appears that, in a significant proportion of cases, the racial differentials in disease which are perceived as genetic in origin have more to do with the position of African-Americans in the social hierarchy than with genetic factors or with cultural "choices." For example, one finds that with adjustment for socioeconomic status, the racial disparities in rates of lung cancer[109] and survival rates for breast cancer[110] just about disappear. Adjustment for socioeconomic factors will not, however, give the full picture of the way in which racism influences health status. While racism may be a product of socioeconomic relations, it is not confined to class categories. Thus, racism may produce health disparities that cannot be predicted by socioeconomic status alone.

Options and Prognosis

The major challenge for policymakers is to confront the implications of the interrelationships of social conditions and health status. The data presented in this chapter, as well as the experience of the British health system,[111] suggest that achieving equity in health status requires closing the gap in socioeconomic status. This would necessitate significant social structural changes, including, as Milton Terris puts it,

> full employment and adequate income, decent housing, good nutrition, greater financial support for public education and the elimination of financial barriers to higher education, increased cultural and recreational opportunities, and affirmative action to end discrimination against minorities in all areas of our national life.[112]

The United States is the only industrialized country other than South Africa that does not provide guaranteed access to health services for its citizenry. With spiraling costs and inadequate services, it is now generally recognized that health care is a major problem that affects most Americans. Between 1950 and 1960, health expenditures went from $12 billion to $25.9 billion. In the 1970s, these costs doubled in five years.[113] By 1983, health expenditures accounted for $355.4 billion, or 10.8 percent of the gross national product.[114] As of 1988, 11.5 percent of the gross national product was being spent on health.[115] Despite these costs, American citizens are not assured access to health care.

The health care options under discussion at the end of the 1980s included employer-mandated health insurance, expanding Medicaid eligibility, and allowing eligible people to buy into Medicaid. None of these solutions, however, would sufficiently meet the needs of the uninsured, particularly African-Americans, although some combination might have a more balanced effect. If disproportionate unemployment continues, African-Americans would benefit from employer-mandated insurance significantly less that Euro-Americans. The disadvantages of Medicaid, including its limited coverage of medical services, are well known.

Another option is national health insurance as proposed in the Kennedy-Corman Bill, first introduced in 1967. A national insurance plan would improve the situation for those without insurance by guaranteeing payment to doctors and hospitals. Yet, national health insurance, like the insurance schemes discussed above, does not address the fundamental problem of skyrocketing health care costs. Because the private practice of medicine would continue, and drug and hospital equipment companies would still be privately owned, these options would not necessarily contain costs. Rather, they would simply result in the transfer of funds from the public to the private sector.

On the other hand, a national health service, as proposed in a bill introduced by Representative Ronald Dellums (Dem.—CA), would provide comprehensive health care coverage and guarantee access to quality health care to all citizens and residents of the United States. It would "expand the availability of health and medical services and improve the health status of the nation's people, [and maintain] the delivery of health and medical care . . . as a public service . . . ."[116] The bill proposes to restructure and rationalize services and facilities, pay salaries to all personnel, emphasize primary and preventive services, and abolish the fee-for-service medical system. Jesse Jackson was the only presidential candidate in 1988 to propose a national health program along these lines. While this bill does not appear to have a good chance of being passed by Congress in the near future, it represents a direction that could have a major impact on the racial disparities in health status and access to health services. Given poll results indicating that the majority of Americans favor establishment of a health care program that would guarantee the right to health care, and the expanding support which was evidenced by the Jesse Jackson campaign in 1988 (see the chapter by Ronald Walters in this volume), the development of a broad coalition for national medical care is not inconceivable.

As one reflects upon the twentieth century in the context of medical advances, it seems clear that African-Americans have improved their health status considerably. This has been occasioned in no little measure by their use of strategies designed to change their social conditions, as well as by confronting the exclusionary attributes of the health institutions in the society. Nonetheless, not only do racial disparities remain, but many of the gains show signs of being reversed. The prognosis for the next century will depend on the extent to which people are able to organize effectively to address the inequalities of the larger social system, and not just those of access to health care.

NOTES

[1] Because I will be primarily concerned with drawing, in broad strokes, the social context in which illness patterns and access to health care have changed over the past century, much of my analysis relies on secondary sources.

[2] Jacquelyne Jackson, "Urban Black Americans," in Allan Harwood, ed., *Ethnicity and Medical Care* (Cambridge, MA: Harvard University Press, 1981), p. 37.

[3]Allan M. Brandt, "Racism and Research: The Case of the Tuskegee Syphilis Study," *Hastings Center Report* 8: 6 (December 1978): 21-29.

[4]David McBride, "Inequality in the Availability of Black Physicians," *New York State Journal of Medicine* 85: 4 (April 1985): 139-142 at 139; citing Abraham Flexner, *The Flexner Report on Medical Education in the U.S. and Canada, 1910—A Report to the Carnegie Foundation for the Advancement of Teaching*, Bulletin 4 (New York: Carnegie Foundation, 1910), pp. 180-181.

[5]Steven Shea and Mindy Thompson Fullilove, "Entry of Black and Other Minority Students into U.S. Medical Schools: Historical Perspectives and Recent Trends," *The New England Journal of Medicine* 313: 15 (October 10, 1985): 933-940 at 934; citing Herbert M. Morais, *The History of the Negro in Medicine* (New York: Publishers Company, Inc., 1968).

[6]Shea and Fullilove, ibid., p. 934.

[7]McBride, op. cit. note 4, pp. 141-142.

[8]John D. Reid, Everett S. Lee, Davor Jedlicka and Yongsock Shin, "Trends in Black Health," *Phylon* XXXVIII: 2 (Summer 1977): 105-116 at 112.

[9]Kenneth Kiple and Virginia King, *Another Dimension to the Black Diaspora: Diet, Disease, and Racism* (London: Cambridge University Press, 1981), p. 191.

[10]Douglas C. Ewbank, "History of Black Mortality and Health Before 1940," *The Milbank Quarterly* 65: Supplement 1 (1987): 100-128 at 105.

[11]Reid, et al., op. cit. note 8, p. 108.

[12]Ewbank, op. cit. note 10, p. 125.

[13]Kyriakos S. Markides, "Mortality Among Minority Populations: A Review of Recent Patterns and Trends," *Public Health Reports* 98: 3 (May-June 1983): 252-260 at 253.

[14]Kiple and King, op. cit. note 9, p. 192.

[15]Ewbank, op. cit. note 10, p. 108.

[16]Reid, et al., op. cit. note 8, p. 109.

[17]Ewbank, op. cit. note 10, pp. 117-121.

[18]Ibid., p. 117.

[19]Ezra H. Griffith and Marie A. Methewson, "Communitas and Charisma in a Black Church Service," *Journal of the National Medical Association* 73: 11 (November 1981): 1023-1027; and Jeffery S. Levin, "The Role of the Black Church in Community Medicine," *Journal of the National Medical Association* 76: 5 (May 1984): 477-483.

[20]Shea and Fullilove, op. cit. note 5, p. 935.

[21]Ibid., p. 936.

[22]Haynes Rice and LaRah D. Payne, "Health Issues for the Eighties," in *The State of Black America 1981* (New York: The National Urban League, 1981), pp. 119-151 at 127.

[23]U.S. Department of Health and Human Services, *Report of the Secretary's Task Force on Black and Minority Health* (Washington, D.C.: U.S. Government Printing Office, 1985), Vol. 1, p. 114.

[24]Rice and Payne, op. cit. note 22, p. 121.

[25]Karen Davis, Marsha Lillie-Blanton, Barbara Lyons, Fitzhugh Millan, Neil Powe and Diane Roland, "Health Care for Black Americans: The Public Sector Role," *The Milbank Quarterly* 65: Supplement 1 (1987): 213-246 at 237.

[26]Charles R. Link, Stephen H. Long and Russell F. Settle, "Access to Medical Care Under Medicaid: Differentials by Race," *Journal of Health Politics, Policy, and Law* 7: 2 (Summer 1982): 345-365.

[27]See Frank Karel, ed., and William Walch, assoc. ed., *Special Report: A New Survey on Access to Medical Care*, No. 1, 1978 (Princeton, NJ: The Robert Wood Johnson Foundation, 1978), pp. 6-7; see also Davis, et al., op. cit. note 25, pp. 217-218.

[28]Richard Cooper, Michael Steinhauer, Arthur Schatzkin and William Miller, "Improved Mortality Among U.S. Blacks, 1968-1978: The Role of Antiracist Struggle," *International Journal of Health Services* 11: 4 (1981): 511-522.

[29]Ibid., Tables 2 and 3, p. 513.

[30]Kenneth G. Manton, Clifford H. Patrick and Katrina W. Johnson, "Health Differentials Between Blacks and Whites: Recent Trends in Mortality and Morbidity," *The Milbank Quarterly* 65: Supplement 1 (1987): 129-199 at 164. "Excess deaths" is defined as the number of actual deaths less the number of expected deaths, where expected deaths equals the white death rate times the black population up to age seventy. See also William P. O'Hare, who notes that between 1970 and 1980, the average annual increase in life expectancy at birth was 0.42 for African-American women and 0.38 for African-American men. Between 1980 and 1985, the average annual increase was 0.3 years for African-American males and 0.24 years for African-American females. Between 1984 and 1985, life expectancy at birth decreased for African-American males. William P. O'Hare, "Black Demographic Trends in the 1980s," *The Milbank Quarterly* 65: Supplement 1 (1987): 35-55 at 47, including Table 7.

[31]Much of this improvement seems to be attributable to hypertension control. In addition to the introduction of new drugs, the 1972 national hypertension control initiative resulted in greater access to health care and active intervention programs. The gains made in this period against cardiovascular disease "reinforce the theory that the cause is environmental, i.e., social and preventable." Cooper, et al., op. cit. note 28, p. 518. This thesis is supported by data from Chicago, where between 1967 and 1971 only 5.8 percent of men were adequately treated for hypertension, whereas by 1977-78, 43 percent were. Ibid., p. 517.

[32]Rice and Payne, op. cit. note 22, p. 129.

[33]U.S. Bureau of the Census, *Money Income and Poverty Status in the U.S.: 1987*, Advance Report, Series P-60, No. 161, Current Population Reports (Washington, D.C.: U.S. Government Printing Office, 1988), Table 3, p. 16, and Table 15, p. 27; and U.S. Bureau of the Census, *Statistical Abstract of the United States: 1972*, 93rd ed., (Washington, D.C.: U.S. Government Printing Office, 1972), Table 525, p. 323.

[34]U.S. Bureau of the Census, *Statistical Abstract of the United States: 1985*, 105th ed. (Washington, D.C.: U.S. Government Printing Office, 1984), Table 680, p. 406.

[35]U.S. Bureau of the Census, *Statistical Abstract of the United States: 1989*, 109th ed. (Washington, D.C.: U.S. Government Printing Office, 1988), Table 649, p. 394.

[36]M. Harvey Brenner, "Personality Stability and Economic Security," *Social Policy* 8: 1 (May-June 1977): 2-4.

[37]Stephen H. Long, "Public versus Employment-Related Health Insurance: Experience and Implications for Black and Nonblack Americans," *The Milbank Quarterly* 65: Supplement 1 (1987): 202-212 at Table 1, pp. 202-203.

[38]*Secretary's Task Force*, op. cit. note 23, p. 190.

[39]Rice and Payne, op. cit. note 22, p. 122.

[40]Woodrow Jones, Jr., and Mitchell F. Rice, "Black Health Care in an Era of Retrenchment Politics," in Mitchell F. Rice and Woodrow Jones, Jr., eds., *Contemporary Public Policy Perspectives and Black Americans* (Westport, CT: Greenwood Press, 1984), pp. 157-171 at 169.

[41]Rice and Payne, op. cit. note 22, p. 124.

[42]Presentation by Alan Sager at the 1980 meeting of the American Public Health Association (Detroit: October 21, 1980), cited in Rice and Payne, ibid., p. 132.

[43]Mark B. Wenneker and Arnold M. Epstein, "Racial Inequalities in the Use of Procedures for Patients with Ischemic Heart Disease in Massachusetts," *Journal of the American Medical Association* 261: 2 (1989): 253-257 at 253. Wenneker and Epstein analyzed the records of all patients with principal diagnoses indicating cardiovascular problems who had been discharged from short-term hospitals in Massachusetts during fiscal year 1985. Noting that Euro-Americans underwent one-third more coronary catheterizations and twice as many coronary artery bypass grafts as compared to African-Americans (ibid., p. 255), the authors concluded that "racial inequalities exist in the provision of cardiac care in Massachusetts." Ibid., p. 257.

[44]Robert J. Blendon, Linda H. Aiken, Howard E. Freeman and Christopher R. Corey, "Access to Medical Care for Black and White Americans: A Matter of Continuing Concern," *Journal of the American Medical Association* 261: 2 (1989): 278-281 at 279.

[45]Ibid., p. 279.

[46]Shea and Fullilove, op. cit. note 5, pp. 936-937.

[47]Ruth S. Hanft and Catherine C. White, "Constraining the Supply of Physicians: Effects on Black Physicians," *The Milbank Quarterly* 65: Supplement 2 (1987): 249-269 at 253.

[48]Ibid., p. 250.

[49]*Secretary's Task Force*, op. cit. note 23, p. 192.

[50]A. H. Strelnick, R. J. Massad, W. B. Bateman and S. D. Shepherd, "Minority Students in U.S. Medical Schools," *New England Journal of Medicine* 415: 1 (1986): 67-68.

[51]*Secretary's Task Force*, op. cit. note 23, p. 191.

[52]Ibid., p. 2.

[53]Markides, op. cit. note 13, p. 253, quoting Kenneth G. Manton, "Sex and Race Specific Differentials in Multiple Cause of Death Data," *Gerontologist* 20: 4 (August 1980): 480-493. Manton, et al., however, question the reality of the crossover effect. Manton, et al., op. cit. note 30, pp. 142-143.

[54]Manton, et al., ibid., p. 158.

[55]Ibid., pp. 169-171.

[56]*Secretary's Task Force*, op. cit. note 23, p. 63.

[57]Ibid., p. 64. Manton, et al. argue that the concept of excess death, using the Euro-American death rate as the standard, may not be the best measure, noting the ambiguity of suicide or certain cancers where rates of death are higher for Euro-American men and women respectively. They suggest that a better standard might be the lowest mortality rate achieved for a disease globally. Manton, et al., op. cit. note 30, p. 132.

[58]*Secretary's Task Force*, op. cit. note 23, p. 70.

[59]Ibid., p. 4.

[60]Ibid., pp. 74-75.

[61]Ibid., p. 52.

[62]See Richard R. Cooper, "A Note on the Biological Concept of Race and Its Application in Epidemiologic Research," *American Heart Journal* 108: 3, Part 2 (September 1984): 715-723 at 721. The author suggests that this is a reflection of the fact that, with identical education, African-Americans receive lower wages. Further, their purchasing power is well below that of Euro-Americans in that a comparable standard of housing will cost approximately 30 percent more in an African-American neighborhood.

[63]Centers for Disease Control, "Perspectives in Disease Prevention and Health Promotion: Homicide Among Young Black Males—United States, 1970-1982," *Morbidity and Mortality Weekly Report* 34: 41 (October 18, 1985): 629-633 at 632.

[64]Beny J. Primm, "Drug Use: Special Implications for Black America," in *The State of Black America 1987* (New York: The National Urban League, 1987), pp. 145-158.

[65]See Centers for Disease Control, "Distribution of AIDS Cases, by Racial/ Ethnic Group and Exposure Category, United States, June 1, 1981—July 4, 1988," *CDC Surveillance Summaries*, July 1988; and *Morbidity and Mortality Weekly Report* 37: SS-3 (July 1988): 1-10 at 1.

[66]*Morbidity and Mortality Weekly Report*, ibid., p. 9.

[67]Ibid., p. 10.

[68]See Roderick Wallace, "A Synergism of Plagues: 'Planned Shrinkage,' Contagious Housing Destruction, and AIDS in the Bronx," *Environmental Research* 47: (1988): 1-33, for an analysis of the relationship between urban policy, housing destruction and AIDS in a New York City neighborhood.

[69]Vicente Navarro, *Crisis, Health, and Medicine: A Social Critique* (New York: Tavistock, 1986), p. 36.

[70]James C. Robinson, "Racial Inequality and the Probability of Occupation-Related Injury or Illness," *The Milbank Quarterly* 62: 4 (Fall 1984): 567-590 at 587.

[71]Morris E. Davis, "The Impact of Workplace Health and Safety on Black Workers: Assessment and Prognosis," *Labor Law Journal* 31: 12 (December 1980): 723-732 at 724.

[72]James C. Robinson, "Trends in Racial Inequality and Exposure to Work-related Hazards, 1968-1986," in David P. Willis, ed., *Health Policies and Black Americans* (New Brunswick, NJ: Transaction Publishers, 1989), pp. 404-420 at 417.

[73]Ibid., p. 417.

[74]This analysis is an elaboration of a paper published in 1984 in which I suggested that these explanatory models were dominant in the health status literature on minority and low-income populations. See Leith Mullings, "Minority Women, Work, and Health," in Wendy Chavkin, ed., *Double Exposure: Women's Health Hazards on the Job and at Home* (New York: Monthly Review Press, 1984), pp. 121-138. In a 1984 article, Richard Cooper elaborated the genetic model. See Cooper, op. cit. note 62. Since then, the ideas in both these articles have been amplified by Krieger and Bassett. See Nancy Krieger and Mary Bassett, "The Health of Black Folk: Disease, Class, and Ideology in Science," *Monthly Review* 38: 3 (July-August 1986): 74-85. I will draw on the analysis in each of these papers.

[75]David P. Willis, "Introduction" to an issue on black health care, *The Milbank Quarterly* 65: Supplement 1 (1987): 1-8 at 2.

[76]Krieger and Bassett, op. cit. note 74, p. 75.

[77]Kiple and King, op. cit. note 9, pp. 61 and 183.

[78]Krieger and Bassett, op. cit. note 74, p. 75.

[79]Cooper, op. cit. note 62, p. 717.

[80]Elizabeth S. Watts, "The Biological Race Concept and Diseases of Modern Man," in Henry Rothschild, ed., *Biocultural Aspects of Disease* (New York: Academic Press, 1981), pp. 3-23 at 19-21.

[81]Anthony P. Polednak, *Host Factors in Disease: Age, Sex, Racial and Ethnic Group, and Body Build* (Springfield, IL: Charles C. Thomas, 1987), p. 99.

[82]Cooper, op. cit. note 62, p. 719.

[83]Krieger and Bassett, op. cit. note 74, pp. 75-77.

[84]James E. Bowman, "Genetic Screening Programs and Public Policy," *Phylon* XXXVIII: 2 (Summer 1977): 117-142 at 122.

[85]Women's Occupational Health Resource Center, "Fifty-nine Major Companies Will Begin Screening for Genetic Traits," *WOHRC News* 4: 4 (September 1982): 2.

[86]Mervyn Susser, William Watson and Kim Hopper, eds., *Sociology in Medicine*, 3d ed. (New York: Oxford University Press, 1985), p. 213.

[87]Ibid., p. 214.

[88]Sir Edwin Chadwick and Michael W. Flinn, eds., *Report on the Sanitary Condition of the Labouring Population of Great Britain* (Edinburgh: University Press, 1965 [originally published 1842]), p. 370.

[89]Kiple and King, op. cit note 9, p. 189.

[90]Oscar Lewis, "The Culture of Poverty," *Scientific American* 215: 4 (October 1966): 19-25.

[91]See the following articles in Eleanor Leacock, ed., *The Culture of Poverty: A Critique* (New York: Simon and Schuster, 1971): Eleanor Leacock, "Introduction," pp. 9-37; Anthony Leeds, "The Concept of the 'Culture of Poverty': Conceptual, Logical, and Empirical Problems, with Perspectives from Brazil and Peru," pp. 226-284; and Charles Valentine, "The 'Culture of Poverty': Its Scientific Significance and Its Implications for Action," pp. 345-363. See also Michael Lewis, *The Culture of Inequality* (Amherst, MA: University of Massachusetts Press, 1978).

[92]Irwin M. Rosenstock, cited in Catherine Kohler Riessman, "The Use of Health Services by the Poor," *Social Policy* 5: 1 (May-June 1974): 41-49 at note 12.

[93]*Secretary's Task Force*, op. cit. note 23, pp. 9-45.

[94]Suezanne Tangerose Orr, C. Arden Miller and Sherman A. Jones, "Differences in Use of Health Services by Children According to Race: Relative Importance of Cultural and System-Related Factors," *Medical Care* 22: 9 (September 1984): 848-853. See also Gary W. Shannon, Rashid L. Bashshur and Carl W. Spurlock, "The Search for Medical Care: An Exploration of Urban Black Behavior," *International Journal of Health Services* 8: 3 (1978): 519-530.

[95]H. Hall, "Cancer and Blacks: The Second-Leading Cause of Death," *The Urban League Review* 9: 2 (Winter 1985-86): 26-31 at 26; Manton, et al., op. cit. note 30, pp. 157-158.

[96]Hall, ibid; Manton, et al., ibid.

[97]See I. S. Thind, R. Najem, J. Paradiso and M. Fuerman, "Cancer Among Blacks in Newark, New Jersey, 1970-1976: A National and International Comparison," *Cancer* 50: 1 (July 1982): 180-186 at 185. Young, et al. found that rates among African-American men were three times those of men in Ibadan, Nigeria, and that rates for African-American women were twice those of African women in the same study. John L. Young, Jr., Susan S. Devesa and Sidney J. Cutler, "Incidence of Cancer in United States Blacks," *Cancer Research* 35: 11 (November 1975): 3523-3536 at 3536.

[98]Richard Doll and Richard Peto, *The Causes of Cancer* (New York: Oxford University Press, 1981), p. 1200.

[99]Alfred Goldson, Ulrich Henschke, LaSalle D. Leffall and Roy L. Schneider, "Is There A Genetic Basis for the Differences in Cancer Incidence Between Afro-Americans and Euro-Americans?," *Journal of the National Medical Association* 73: 8 (August 1981): 701-706; Doll and Peto, ibid.

[100]Doll and Peto, ibid., p. 1235.

[101]Richard Cooper, Michael Steinhauer, William Miller, Richard David and Arthur Schatzkin, "Racism, Society, and Disease: An Exploration of the Social Biological Mechanisms of Differential Mortality," *International Journal of Health Services* 11: 3 (1981): 389-414 at 393.

[102]Doll and Peto, op. cit. note 98, p. 1220.

[103]In 1987, six universities were awarded federal grants to find out why African-Americans smoke and to introduce smoking prevention programs. Commenting on the project, Dr. Edward Hailes, president of the NAACP chapter in Washington, asserted that the grant money should be used to confront more pressing issues like education, unemployment, housing and racism, and that the project was "ill targeted." "Study to Look at Why So Many Blacks Smoke," *The New York Times* (February 24, 1987), p. A19.

[104]Cooper, et al., op. cit. note 101, pp. 398-399.

[105]Centers for Disease Control, "Topics in Minority Health: Cigarette Smoking Among Blacks and Other Minority Populations," *Morbidity and Mortality Weekly Report* 36: 25 (July 3, 1987): 404-407; Ronald M. Davis, "Current Trends in Cigarette Advertising and Marketing," *New England Journal of Medicine* 316: (1987): 725-732; and Linda Williams, "Tobacco Companies Target Blacks With Ads, Donations and Festivals," *The Wall Street Journal* (October 6, 1986), sec. 2, p. 1.

[106]Cited in Navarro, op. cit. note 69, p. 56.

[107]Davis, op. cit. note 71, p. 727.

[108]For example, a study of 6,500 rubber workers in a tire manufacturing plant in Akron, Ohio, found that African-American workers were concentrated in the more dangerous compounding and mixing areas. Of the study popula-

tion, 27 percent of African-American workers, but only 3 percent of Euro-American workers, had worked in this area of the plant. The strongest associations with cancer elevations tended to be in the mixing and compounding area, where workers were most exposed to the dusts, chemical ingredients and vapors that contained toxic early-reaction byproducts. Davis, ibid.

Similar studies in steel plants demonstrated higher rates of cancer associated with coke oven operation. Again, African-American workers were concentrated in this area. A 1959 study of employment patterns found 89 percent of nonwhite coke plant workers employed at the coke ovens, while only 32 percent of the Euro-American workers were employed at this job. Not surprisingly, nonwhite workers were found to experience double the death rate from malignant neoplasms as compared to Euro-American workers. Ibid., p. 728.

In 1980, 40.4 percent of all clothing ironers and pressers and 23.3 percent of all laundry and dry cleaning operators were African-American women. Diane Nilsen Westcott, "Blacks in the 1970s: Did They Scale the Job Ladder?," *Monthly Labor Review* 105: 6 (June 1982): 29-38 at Table 3, p. 32. A study conducted by the National Cancer Institute compared the death rates of laundry and dry cleaning workers to those of the general population, using records kept by a St. Louis trade union local from 1957 to 1977. Analysis of the distribution of deaths found a predominance of women—particularly nonwhite women—and excess rates of cancers among the workers, particularly of the lungs, cervix, uterus and skin. Most significantly, the death rate for African-American males and females was double that for Euro-American males and females. The study suggests that elevated cancer risks result from multiple exposures to various dry cleaning fluids. Aaron Blair, Pierre Decoufle and Dan Grauman, "Causes of Death Among Laundry and Dry Cleaning Workers," *American Journal of Public Health* 69: 5 (May 1979): 508-511.

[109]Susan S. Devesa and Earl L. Diamond, "Socioeconomic and Racial Differences in Lung Cancer Incidence," *American Journal of Epidemiology* 118: 6 (December 1983): 818-831 at 818.

[110]Mary T. Bassett and Nancy Krieger, "Social Class and Black-White Differences in Breast Cancer Survival," *American Journal of Public Health* 76: 12 (December 1986): 1400-1403.

[111]Richard G. Wilkinson, ed., *Class and Health: Research on Longitudinal Data* (London and New York: Tavistock, 1986).

[112]Milton Terris, "The Components of Care," *Health/PAC Bulletin* 17: 5 (November 1987): 12-17 at 13. (Editor's note: See note 32 of Boxill's chapter in this volume in relation to the Supreme Court's assault on affirmative action at the end of the 1980s.)

[113]Rice and Payne, op. cit. note 22, p. 121.

[114]U.S. Bureau of the Census, op. cit. note 34, Table 142, p. 96.

[115]Andrew H. Malcolm, "In Health Care Policy, The Latest Word Is Fiscal," *New York Times* (October 23, 1988), p. E3.

[116]Committee for a National Health Service, *A National Health Service for the U.S.* (New York: Committee for a National Health Service, 1976), unpaginated.

BLACKS IN THE U.S. MILITARY: TRENDS IN PARTICIPATION

Richard O. Hope

Massachusetts Institute of Technology

Introduction

Mankind has gone to war since the beginning of civilization. The concepts of the noble warrior and elites are prominent in the annals of war. The nobility are typically represented in the leadership or officer class, and the lower classes are generally depicted as the masses who charge into battle. Slaves captured in battle were often conscripted to continue fighting for their conqueror in future campaigns. The class structure of the combatants in war has had a profound impact on the sociological organization of the United States military.

This class structure has affected black participation in the armed forces of the United States since the country's very first war. Being brought to this country as slaves or indentured servants, blacks generally were relegated to support roles in its early wars. Such concepts as democracy and community responsibility played nominal roles in determining the daily lives of blacks in the military. The writings of Niccolò Machiavelli, Baron de Montesquieu, Thomas Jefferson and others concerning the responsibilities of the citizen-soldier, as well as full societal participation in war, did not resonate for those blacks who were often forced or "persuaded" to join the army when white enlistments were down.

This chapter will analyze the social structure of the military in relation to black involvement in the armed forces. Discussions of this subject have typically reviewed statistical information about representation by rank and service and the extent of unit, base and community desegregation. These data are usually presented as measures of the extent and magnitude of full and successful integration of blacks into the armed forces. This approach is of some value in determining participation rates, but does not provide a framework for understanding the significance of the racial atmosphere in which black soldiers must live and work on a daily basis. It is the purpose of this presentation to analyze both participation rates and racial atmosphere in the military. Although blacks have experienced unprecedented participation in recent years, there are nonetheless very disturbing trends which could have disastrous effects on future successful participation if they are allowed to go unchecked.

In order to understand the present state of blacks in the armed forces, it is essential that one grasps the historical context in which it is grounded; for there are patterns of utilization which continue to this day.

Blacks in U.S. Military History

It is now known that blacks served with honor and distinction in all wars waged by the United States. Since the American Revolution, the use of blacks has been of pivotal importance in the success of these wars. Over five thousand blacks served in the colonial army and fought in almost every engagement, north and south.[1] Although George Washington did attempt to exclude blacks from the army, the need for manpower, and the threat of blacks being enlisted by Lord Dunmore of the British army, provided sufficient impetus to motivate him to repeal his stance to the Continental Congress on January 16, 1776.

As in the Revolutionary War, black Americans played a crucial role in the Civil War. Although President Abraham Lincoln did not want blacks to be recruited into the Union army, because it "would drive the slaveholding border states into the Confederacy,"[2] they did become an integral part of the Union forces. It was first assumed that the conflict would be of short duration. When it became clear that the war would be protracted and the number of northern white volunteers waned, the president and the War Department accepted the necessity of having blacks enlist in the Union army. As was true in the Revolutionary War, the need for manpower convinced the field commanders that blacks could be used effectively in labor gangs for construction of fortifications, and as foot soldiers. Their skillful execution of the many roles to which they were assigned impressed a range of observers at that time, most notably Lincoln:

> Lincoln and others commented most favorably on the performance of the nearly 200,000 blacks who served as volunteers during the Civil War and asserted that without their aid, the Union could not have won. . . . Blacks suffered extremely high casualties during the war. Some 38,000 black soldiers lost their lives, a mortality rate that was proportionately 35 percent greater than among other troops, notwithstanding their late entrance into the armed forces.[3]

During the Spanish-American War, the black troops of the Tenth Cavalry won considerable praise for their courage in the Battle of Las Guasimas:

> They further distinguished themselves at El Caney, where after costly battle, the 25th Infantry along with the 12th Infantry captured the village. The 24th Infantry played its part in the famous assault on San Juan Hill. . . . [T]he commander of the 24th declared, "Too much cannot be said of their [blacks'] courage, willingness and endurance."[4]

The army awarded five Medals of Honor and twenty-six Certificates of Merit to blacks for their heroism in the Cuban campaign. Theodore Roosevelt spoke of the black regulars as "brave men, worthy of respect. . . . I don't think any rough rider . . . will ever forget the tie that binds us to the Ninth and Tenth Cavalry."[5]

By the time of World War I there was again the realization that blacks would be needed to serve in all aspects of battle. There were 106 battalions, out of 213, consisting of black soldiers. Blacks comprised over one-tenth of the nation's population, one-eighth of the armed forces, one-thirtieth of the combat strength, but one-third of the military's noncombat labor force. In spite of the considerable historical evidence pertaining to their effectiveness in combat, where deeds of heroism are recompensed in national honor, blacks were still relegated to largely noncombat roles. Nonetheless, the black soldier in World War I did receive some recognition for bravery in battle. General John J. Pershing, in a tribute to black soldiers of World War I, stated, "I cannot commend too highly the spirit shown among the colored combat troops, who exhibit fine capacity for quick training and eagerness for the most dangerous work."[6]

As in earlier wars involving the United States, there was great reluctance to permit blacks to enlist in the service during World War II. The Roosevelt administration relented only after pressure from the black community, specifically the black press. Finally, in December 1942, President Franklin Roosevelt issued an executive order requiring all services to enlist their men through the draft and accept blacks on an equal basis.[7]

Most of the blacks inducted into the military at this time were assigned to the service branches, where they performed such unskilled jobs as road building, stevedoring, laundry and fumigating. More than 1.15 million blacks were to serve in World War II, but by 1945, 75 percent of them had been given only menial jobs. This was, of course, quite consistent with the historical pattern of the underutilization of the combat skills of blacks.

Despite the large number of black soldiers who participated in World War II, none received this county's highest award for bravery, the Congressional Medal of Honor. This does not mean, however, that there were not innumerable acts of bravery, some of which were most heroic. For example, Dori Miller, working in the laundry aboard the USS *Arizona* in Pearl Harbor, shot down six Japanese fighters. Charles Jackson French towed fifteen men on a raft for hours away from enemy fire at the Battle of the Coral Sea. Private Ernest Jenkins alone captured fifteen Germans.

The broader military and national significance of such acts of bravery was lost not only to those in decisionmaking roles, both civilian and military, who were disinclined to place blacks in combat roles, but also to those in the society who believed that the filling of menial roles should be the lot of blacks in life. The latter was instantiated ever so strikingly by the savage acts of racial violence that were waged against returning black veterans of World War II, all too reminiscent of what occurred after World War I and earlier wars. House burnings, snipings and the killing of black families began to increase. Harold Hinton, a *New York Times* reporter, wrote that the Ku Klux Klan had committed the murders to terrorize returning black veterans who "were getting out of their place."[8]

At the end of World War II, Lieutenant General Alvan C. Gillem, Jr., headed a board of officers which conducted a study of black participation in the war and made recommendations for the peacetime utilization of black soldiers. The final report supported increased opportunities for blacks within the military, yet reaffirmed a quota system. Not surprisingly, the sole recommendation that was implemented was the one calling for a quota system. This report was condemned by the black press. Roy Wilkins, then executive director of the NAACP, wrote, "The basic policy is still Jim Crow units."[9]

In July 1948 President Harry Truman signed Executive Order No. 9981, declaring a policy of equality of treatment and opportunity in the military services. An enforcement commission, which became known as the Fahy committee, was appointed in 1949. It publicly came out against the quota system, contrary to the Gillem report. It was Fahy's belief that the quota system would perpetuate discrimination.[10]

The elimination of a recruiting quota in 1950 resulted in a rapid increase of 28 percent in the number of black enlistees within a few months. The Korean War saw a marked increase in the number of blacks in combat roles, and, correspondingly, it produced the first black men to be awarded the nation's highest military decoration since the Spanish-American War. Private William H. Thompson and Sergeant Cornelius H. Charlton both received the Congressional Medal of Honor posthumously.

The period between the Korean War and the Vietnam War was one in which the high career aspirations of blacks in the armed forces did not materialize. Racism was thought to have been solved with the integration of troop units. It was assumed that the normal processes of job mobility would occur, and blacks, like their white counterparts, would be rewarded for superior performance. But this assumption was all too ahistorical, for it failed to come to grips fully with the ramifications of the need to reduce the number of personnel at the end of the Korean War. As in previous postwar periods, the reduction affected blacks and other minorities disproportionately: "In 1957 and 1958 alone," as Jack Foner observes, "blacks accounted for more than 40 percent of the new reduction in army personnel."[11]

The aspirations of blacks for a military career were not rejuvenated until draft calls began to increase in 1965 because of the escalating conflict in Vietnam. As the need for manpower increased, blacks were inducted, especially into the combat arms, in numbers that were disproportionate to their presence in the population. In 1965 about 27 percent of black inductees were assigned to the infantry, as compared to about 18 percent of whites. In 1967, 20 percent of all army fatalities were black.[12]

As this pattern continued into the late 1960s, younger blacks entered the services who had been influenced profoundly by the civil rights movement. Many were aware of Martin Luther King, Jr.'s, public opposition to the Vietnam War in 1967, and were troubled by the disproportionate number of blacks on the front line. In a very real sense, then, the Vietnam War reversed a long-standing historical pattern in relation to blacks in the combat arms. But the putative glory of the combat arms was tainted by the moral conflicts and societal divisions that accompanied the war, and the black soldier felt all too rudely the hurt, if not contempt, of this taint. And so, as has been the bitter experience of blacks all too often in the society, in the very cross section of historical time when the black soldier should have benefited from the national purpose of full participation in the combat arms, he/she suffered the indifference of a society that was at war with itself morally.

As the war continued, black soldiers started to immerse themselves in symbols of racial pride by wearing the "Afro" hair style, listening to "soul" music in mess halls and clubs, and reading books by Eldridge Cleaver and Malcolm X. The Afro hair style became a major issue in the Pentagon since regulations forbade longer hair styles. A few violent racial confrontations occurred in mess halls and clubs because blacks wanted to hear soul music while whites preferred the country western music that was usually played in a given hall or club. With increasing frequency, racial conflicts and riots occurred at bases in Vietnam, Germany and the United States. Black troops also protested being used for riot control duty to combat other blacks.

This state of affairs impelled President Richard Nixon in August of 1970 to send an investigative team, headed by Frank Render II, to Europe to determine the reason for the growing number of racial incidents. In December the team reported "acute frustration" and "volatile anger" among black troops. A major cause of this frustration, according to the investigative team, was "the failure in too many instances of command leadership to exercise the authority and responsibility" they had for monitoring the equal opportunity provisions that were already a part of military regulations. It was noted that

> Blacks assembling in groups of three or four or more were viewed as a threat, and in many cases these groups were dispersed without provocation. . . . The mission also found overwhelming discrimination in military justice, military policy, work assignments, promotions, the management of clubs, and housing. Discrimination by club owners frequently resulted from white threats of economic boycott if discriminatory policies were not maintained.[13]

As a result of the Render Report, the Department of Defense ordered the army in December of 1970:

- To establish an "equal opportunity" or human relations officer and a human relations council at major units;

- To develop numerical goals and timetables to increase utilization of minorities in occupations;

- To remove or reassign officers, noncommissioned officers, and civilians who fail to act against discrimination;

- To give base commanders power to declare housing within the United States "off limits," without prior Pentagon approval, if landlords practice racial discrimination.[14]

The results of the Render Report were corroborated by a separate investigation conducted by the NAACP. The NAACP team found inequities in career assignments and promotion practices for both black enlisted men and officers.[15] There was "deep dissatisfaction" among black commissioned officers because few were given command positions.[16] The disaffection of blacks was also observed in the military justice system, which they perceived to be "discriminatory and unjust." The use of nonjudicial punishment and pretrial confinement constituted major sources of grievance among black servicemen. These findings were supported by a blue-ribbon Task Force on the Administration of Military Justice, appointed a year after the NAACP investigation.

Recognizing the critical importance of the behavior of its middle and lower ranks to its effectiveness in executing its purpose and mission, the armed forces instituted compulsory race relations seminars, which all military personnel were to attend. The scope and widespread effect of this program made it comparable in significance to the order for the integration of the armed forces under President Truman. Believing strongly that much more needed to be done to blot out the inequities of racial discrimination in the military, on January 28, 1970, Secretary of Defense Melvin Laird issued a memorandum creating the Interservice Task Force on Education in Race Relations. It was charged with the development of a program to be put into effect throughout the armed forces.

Black Participation in the Military in the Post-Vietnam War Era

Contrary to what occurred after previous wars, the military did not experience a decline in the proportion of black officers or enlisted personnel in the years immediately following the withdrawal of the United States from Vietnam. This can be observed in Table 1, which shows a steady increase from 1976 through 1981. Black army enlistments rose to 33.2 percent, with an accompanying officer rate of 7.8 percent. These figures were unprecedented.

The significant postwar increase in the number of blacks in the armed forces, and especially in the army, was due largely to the All-Volunteer Force (AVF) which President Nixon initiated. This program changed the course of history for blacks in military service. In 1969, Nixon commissioned a study of an all-volunteer force. After almost a year of study, the Gates Commission issued its recommendation:

> We unanimously believe that the nation's interest will be better served by an all-volunteer force. . . . We have satisfied ourselves that a volunteer force will not jeopardize national security, and we believe it will have a beneficial effect on the military as well as the rest of our society. [17]

This proposal for an all-volunteer force was a radical departure from the draft, which had been the only means of national conscription in the United States. The proposal was radical because it seemed to set

TABLE 1

BLACKS AS A PERCENTAGE OF THE ARMED FORCES,
BY SERVICE, SELECTED FISCAL YEARS, 1942-1981[a]

Fiscal Year	Army			Navy			Marine Corps			Air Force			All Services		
	Enlisted	Officer	Total	Enlisted	Officer	Total	Enlisted	Officer	Total	Enlisted	Officer	Total	Enlisted	Officer	Total
1942[b]	6.2	0.3	5.8	n.a.	n.a.	n.a.	n.a.	n.a.	n.a.	b	b	b	n.a.	n.a.	n.a.
1945[b]	9.3	0.8	8.4	4.8	0.0	n.a.	n.a.	n.a.	n.a.	b	b	b	n.a.	n.a.	n.a.
1949	11.1	1.9	10.1	4.4	*	4.0	2.5	*	2.3	6.1	0.6	5.3	7.5	0.9	6.7
1964	11.8	3.3	10.9	5.9	0.3	5.3	8.7	0.3	7.9	10.0	1.5	8.6	9.7	1.8	8.7
1968	12.6	3.3	11.5	5.0	0.4	4.5	11.5	0.9	10.7	10.2	1.8	8.9	10.2	2.1	9.2
1970	13.5	3.4	12.1	5.4	0.7	4.8	11.2	1.3	10.2	11.7	1.7	10.0	11.0	2.2	9.8
1971	14.3	3.6	12.9	5.4	0.7	4.8	11.4	1.3	10.4	12.3	1.7	10.5	11.4	2.3	10.2
1972	17.0	3.9	15.0	6.4	0.9	5.7	13.7	1.5	12.5	12.6	1.7	10.8	12.6	2.3	11.1
1973	18.4	4.0	16.3	7.7	1.1	6.8	16.9	1.9	15.4	13.4	2.0	11.5	14.0	2.5	12.4
1974	21.3	4.5	19.0	8.4	1.3	7.5	18.1	2.4	16.5	14.2	2.2	12.1	15.7	2.8	13.9
1975	22.2	4.8	19.9	8.0	1.4	7.2	18.1	3.0	16.7	14.6	2.6	12.5	16.1	3.1	14.3
1976	24.3	5.3	21.9	8.1	1.6	7.3	17.0	3.5	15.6	14.7	2.8	12.7	16.9	3.5	15.1
1977	26.4	6.1	23.9	8.7	1.9	7.9	17.6	3.6	16.2	14.7	3.2	12.7	17.9	4.0	16.0
1978	29.2	6.4	26.3	9.4	2.2	8.5	19.0	3.7	17.6	14.9	3.6	13.0	19.3	4.3	17.3
1979	32.2	6.8	28.9	10.7	2.3	9.7	21.5	3.9	19.8	15.8	4.3	13.8	21.2	4.7	19.0
1980	32.9	7.1	29.6	11.5	2.5	10.4	22.4	3.9	20.6	16.2	4.6	14.1	21.9	5.0	19.6
1981	33.2	7.8	29.8	12.0	2.7	10.8	22.0	4.0	20.2	16.5	4.8	14.4	22.1	5.3	19.8

Source: Martin Binkin and Mark J. Eitelberg, with Alvin J. Schexnider and Marvin M. Smith, *Blacks and the Military* (Washington, D.C.: The Brookings Institution, 1982), Table 3-1, p. 42, citing the following sources: Data for 1942 and 1945 from Ulysses Lee, Jr., *The United States Army in World II, Special Studies: The Employment of Negro Troops* (Washington, D.C.: Office of the Chief of Military History, U.S. Army, 1966), p. 415; data for 1949-70 from Department of Defense, *The Negro in the Armed Forces: A Statistical Fact Book* (Washington, D.C.: Office of the Deputy Assistant Secretary of Defense for Equal Opportunity, 1971); data for 1971-80 provided by the Department of Defense, Defense Manpower Data Center.

n.a.—Not available

* Less than 0.05 percent

a Percentage computations are based on the total active force in June for 1943, 1945, 1949 and 1971-1975; in December for 1964, 1968 and 1970; and in September for 1976-1981. Officers include commissioned and warrant officers.

b Army computations for 1942 and 1945 include Air Force personnel.

aside a principle of societal organization that had withstood the test of time by serving both ancient Rome and the United States well; namely, the citizen-soldier, with its accompanying duties, rights, responsibilities and obligations. Were not all of the citizenry responsible for the defense of the country? Would the United States suffer the fate of Rome when it ceased being defended by citizen-soldiers and came to rely on professional soldiers? These are questions of the greatest historical significance, but their substance largely misses the mark when applied to blacks in the United States.

First, blacks were not included in the grand constitutional scheme of universal participation. They were recruited neither for the officer nor the enlisted corps on a regular basis, even during the period when James Madison and Benjamin Franklin were drafting the Constitution and setting policies for the national militia. Although examples of individual heroism by blacks abound, slaves served in the Continental Army for only a short time to meet the demand for manpower.

Second, and extremely important in relation to the questions asked above, the Gates Commission found that the draft was not working on a democratic basis as planned. Sons of wealthy families were receiving preferential treatment by draft boards around the country. Blacks, other minorities, and individuals from low-income families were the ones who had become the source of manpower that swelled the enlisted ranks in times of military crisis.

Thus, on July 1, 1973, Congress approved the elimination of the president's induction authority and the enactment of the AVF. One of the early criticisms of this program was that it encouraged the rise of a "mercenary" mentality—which was, of course, the case in ancient Rome. It was also argued that the AVF would encourage low-income and minority young men to seek the military as a career in disproportionate numbers to their white and upper-income counterparts. Many disagreed with these prognoses, however. In point of fact, Nixon, in proposing an end to the draft during the 1968 presidential campaign, characterized as "sheer fantasy" the notion that "a volunteer army would be a black army."[18]

Concern about the AVF was also expressed by well-known scholars of the military such as Morris Janowitz and Charles Moskos, Jr., who argued that it was contrary to the democratic principle of universal participation in the country's defense. They observed that: 1) a national fighting force should be broadly representative if it were to enjoy democratic and political legitimacy; 2) a force that is disproportionately black could discourage white recruits; 3) a force that is disproportionately black could lead to excessive black casualties in times of war;

and 4) a force that is disproportionately black could prove to be unreliable.[19]

Yet it seems that much of the concern expressed about the overrepresentation of blacks was overdrawn, given the pattern of black enlistment that has emerged since the authorization of the AVF. While the proportion of black enlisted volunteers reached an all-time high of almost 37 percent in 1979 (i.e., almost three times the proportion of blacks in the general youth population), there has been a noticeable decline since then in the number of blacks who have been admitted into the army, for example. Table 2 shows that from 1979 to 1980, black enlistments had dropped from 36.7 percent of total enlistment to 29.7 percent. The decline continued into 1981, when 27.4 percent of total enlistees were black. The decline was even greater for black males, who by 1981 had dropped to 25.7 percent of the total from a high of 36.1 percent in 1979.

TABLE 2

BLACK ENLISTED ENTRANTS[a] TO THE ARMY, BY SEX,
SELECTED FISCAL YEARS, 1954-1981

Fiscal Year	Male		Female		Total	
	Number	Percent	Number	Percent	Number	Percent
1954[b]	34,617	9.9	n.a.	n.a.	n.a.	n.a.
1964[b]	30,534	14.0	n.a.	n.a.	n.a.	n.a.
1971	41,326	14.1	1,161	20.7	42,487	14.2
1972	26,599	15.1	1,055	17.7	27,654	14.2
1973	38,159	19.6	1,574	18.9	39,733	19.6
1974	46,250	28.0	2,987	19.8	49,237	27.4
1975	37,491	23.2	3,558	19.2	41,049	22.8
1976	40,170	25.0	2,810	17.8	43,520	24.3
1976[c]	14,619	30.1	955	22.4	15,574	29.5
1977	44,900	30.1	3,163	21.6	48,063	29.4
1978	36,624	34.9	5,239	30.3	41,863	34.2
1979	40,030	36.1	7,010	40.9	47,040	36.7
1980	37,790	28.0	8,775	39.6	46,565	29.7
1981	25,328	25.7	6,635	36.6	31,963	27.4

Source: Martin Binkin and Mark J. Eitelberg, with Alvin J. Schexnider and Marvin M. Smith, *Blacks and the Military* (Washington, D.C.: The Brookings Institution, 1982), Table 3-2, p. 45, citing the following sources: Data for 1954 and 1964 Army accessions from Bernard D. Karpinos, *Male Chargeable Accessions: Evaluation by Mental Categories, 1953-1973* (Alexandria, VA: Human Resources Research Organization, January 1977), Special Report ED-75-18, pp. 33-36. All other data derived from information provided by the Department of Defense, Defense Manpower Data Center.

n.a.—Not available

[a] Enlisted entrants include inductees and enlistees without prior service.

[b] Data for 1954 and 1964 include blacks and other nonwhite minorities who entered
   military service between January and December of each of these years.

[c] Fiscal 1976 transition quarter (July through September).

In the early 1980s the white enlistment pool increased, perhaps as a corollary of the worsening job market. The economy began to rebound late in the summer of 1983, entering a peacetime expansion that lasted throughout the remainder of the decade, yet more and more whites continued to compete with blacks for enlistment. Substantial increases in enlistment pay in conjuction with a range of other incentives, most particularly a set of generous educational benefits, were designed to attract "quality" enlistees. Many in the black community interpreted "quality" enlistees to mean "white" enlistees. Also, Martin Binkin and Mark Eitelberg note that "the possibility that 'special efforts' were made by Army recruiters to bring in white enlistees, in response to criticism about the racially unbalanced Army and the declining quality of the force (as measured by aptitude tests), should not be discounted."[20]

There does appear to be a shift of recruiting stations away from areas where there are heavy concentrations of blacks. In 1981 the army announced that, in an effort to obtain "better" recruits, it would shift recruiters from urban locations to suburban ones near high school and college campuses. [21] Congress also enacted legislation in 1981 which affected black enlistment. Reacting to what appeared to be declining test scores, the Defense Authorization Act provided that:

- • . . . for fiscal year 1981, the Army can enlist or induct no more than 35 percent non-high school graduates among the male non-prior service accessions in the Army;

- • . . . for fiscal year 1981, the services *as a whole* may not enlist or induct more than 25 percent of the new accessions from personnel who score between the 10th and 30th percentile on the entrance examinations;

- • . . . for fiscal year 1983 and each fiscal year thereafter, each service may not enlist or induct more than 20 percent of its new accessions from personnel who score between the 10th and 30th percentile on the entrance examination.[22]

Paper and pencil test scores have long been used to control the number of blacks in American institutions. For example, since 1958 the army has required that recruits who have a score on the standardized entry test, the Armed Forces Qualification Test (AFQT), above the minimum requirement but below the 31st percentile (category IV), must also attain particular scores on the Army Qualification Battery (AQB), a test designed to measure specific occupational aptitudes. The

standards for qualification have changed radically at different periods
of time, depending on the army's manpower needs. Table 3 demonstrates vividly these erratic changes.

TABLE 3

PERCENT QUALIFYING UNDER
ARMY QUALIFICATION BATTERY (AQB)

Period	Percent in Category IV Who Qualified under AQB Requirements
Before August 1958	100.0
August 1958—May 1963	68.1
May 1963—November 1965	31.2
November 1965—April 1966	42.9
October 1966—December 1966	72.0
December 1966	85.1

Source: Bernard D. Karpinos, *AFQT: Historical Data (1958-1972)*, Special Report ED-
75-12 (Alexandria, VA: Human Resources Research Organization, 1975), p. 21,
cited in Martin Binkin and Mark J. Eitelberg, with Alvin J. Schexnider and
Marvin M. Smith, *Blacks and the Military* (Washington, D.C.: The Brookings
Institution, 1982), p. 137, note 28.

The use of tests is usually justified by the military in terms of probability of job success: "While aptitude tests are not perfect predictors,
they do enhance the probability that the service[s] will select the best
people from the pool of applicants and will assign them jobs in which
they are likely to succeed."[23] Many studies, however, have raised serious questions about the value of these tests as the primary criteria for
predicting success in the military.[24]

The issue of recruit selection is accompanied by the matter of reenlistment. What are the chances of black enlistees remaining in the services after their first tour of duty? By the early 1980s the army, for
example, had increased the stringency of its requirements for reenlistment. Under the new rules, a soldier could not reenlist if he/she failed to
make E4 (corporal or specialist four) during the first three years of service. In addition, first-term personnel who 1) acquired two or more
AWOLs (absent without leave), 2) had one AWOL in excess of five days
during his/her previous twenty-four months of service, or 3) failed to
score at least ninety-five on any three components of the standardized
aptitude tests used for classification, became ineligible for
reenlistment.[25]

This change impelled Binkin, et al., to observe that "intended or not, the tighter criteria will probably have a disproportionate impact on blacks, who in recent years have been reenlisting at about 1.6 times the rate for whites."[26] Although blacks have been affected by the more rigid reenlistment requirements, they have not experienced in the 1980s the sort of separation en masse from the military that was true of, say, the 1940s and 1950s. Indeed, as of 1989 they constituted 28 percent of the army, 15.2 percent of the air force, 14.7 percent of the navy, 19.2 percent of the Marine Corps, and 20.1 percent of total personnel in the armed forces.[27] It is intriguing that ten years earlier (1979), blacks comprised 28.9 percent of the army, 13.8 percent of the air force, 9.7 percent of the navy, 19.8 percent of the Marine Corps, and 19 percent of the armed forces' total personnel.[28] These figures make at least two compelling points: 1) blacks are slowly being "institutionalized" in the armed forces, and 2) fears concerning black overrepresentation in the AVF have been confounded empirically.

Interracial Atmosphere

What are the racial attitudes of military personnel? Can or do these attitudes produce an atmosphere which discourages black participation in the armed forces? Race relations have varied considerably from time to time and base to base. The atmosphere immediately following the end of the Vietnam War was relatively tranquil compared to what preceded it, but the transition to an all-volunteer force quickly gave way to what one senior Pentagon official termed "a new racism."[29] By 1978, Moskos was able to observe that:

> The recent improvement in the racial climate of the Army, however, must be qualified by a potentially calamitous omen. I detected a degree of latent klanism among some white enlisted men. A few would show me klan cards in their wallets . . . .[30]

The term "white backlash" has been used to name a set of sentiments and behaviors grounded in white resentment towards blacks in consequence of perceived—though not necessarily real—advantages accruing to blacks from a range of policies, most notably ones pertaining to affirmative action. In spite of the cost of white backlash, the Department of Defense has, over the years, taken some of the more farsighted and bold policy steps in this area of any major institution in the United States. It acted with dispatch to implement President Truman's executive order mandating the desegregation of the services after the Second World War. During the Vietnam era, it established compulsory attendance at human relations seminars designed to improve the racial atmosphere at every U.S. military installation around the world. And from its ranks came the first black national security advisor to a president of the United States, namely General Colin Powell, who was President Ronald Reagan's assistant for national security affairs from 1987 to 1989.

The sensitivity of the Department of Defense towards the lot of the black soldier was no doubt heightened in 1949 by the release of a study by Samuel Stouffer, et al., concerning the American soldier, conducted during World War II.[31] As might be expected, racial discrimination was an overriding concern of blacks as compared to whites. Participants in the study were asked the following question: "If you could talk with the President of the United States, what are the three most important questions you would want to ask him about the war and your part in it?" Fifty percent of the black or "Negro Soldiers" suggested questions about some aspect of race relations or discrimination in the army. By contrast, the white respondents did not perceive these as compelling issues. The concerns of black soldiers were grounded in such questions as:

- Will I as a Negro share this so-called democracy after the war?

- Why don't he stop so much lynching? Our life is worth as much to us as the white's life is to them.

- Why aren't Negro troops allowed to fight in combat as much as white troops?

- Why aren't Negro soldiers given the same chance for advancement as white soldiers?[32]

In June of 1945 the question was asked: "In general, do you think that you yourself have gotten a square deal from the Army?" The percentage for the response, "yes, in most ways, I have," was relatively low for blacks and whites alike, but black troops were somewhat less likely than whites to say that they had received a square deal from the army. Open-ended comments on this question revealed that "racial discrimination" was the number one reason for this belief. On questions unrelated to race, black troop morale and "adjustment" were considered equal to and slightly higher than those of most white soldiers: "Indeed . . . in some respect—as in pride in outfit or in sense of importance of Army job and expressed interest in it—the Negro attitudes were somewhat more favorable than those of whites."[33]

This study of World War II soldiers finds corroboration in a later investigation of troops during the Korean War. The later research was conducted to determine the effectiveness of integrated units. The Korean War provided the first opportunity to test under actual battlefield conditions the assumptions of Truman's order to desegregate the military. The questions asked in this study were similar to the ones asked by Stouffer's team during World War II. As was true of their counterparts in World War II, black servicemen were more supportive of racial integration than white servicemen. Still, among white troops, opposition to desegregation decreased from 84 percent in 1943 to 44 percent in 1951, and among black military personnel it decreased from 36 to 4 percent over the same time period.

The above study, conducted by Johns Hopkins University, is now known by its code name, "Project Clear." It reached the following conclusions:

- There is virtually complete agreement throughout the Army that Negroes should be given the same kinds of jobs as white soldiers.

- Integration of white and Negro troops has proceeded smoothly, without incidents or major problems, in those units where it is in effect.

- It is the consensus among officers that Negroes perform most efficiently in mixed (integrated) units.

- White officers and enlisted men who have experienced integration are more favorable to it than are those who have not.

- Integration eliminates some of the strain on leadership which is present in the all-Negro unit (since most leaders of these units tended historically to be white).

- White enlisted men follow the directions of Negro leaders in mixed units, without the appearance of any special problems.

- Under conditions of integration, the attitudes of white soldiers are most favorable when Negroes are in a minority, as they normally are in the population. Where Negroes are actually in a majority, the attitudes of whites are least favorable.

- Difference of opinions on racial questions are more pronounced between Northern and Southern white soldiers in the U.S. than in the combat zone.[34]

Decades later, in 1975, another study, conducted for the Army Research Institute, observed the persistence of noteworthy differences in the perceptions of blacks and whites. This study compared the results of surveys done in 1972 and 1974. Highlights of the findings include the following:

- The sharp and pervasive difference which exists between the perceptions held by blacks and whites regarding race relations and equal opportunity in the Army in 1972 were still substantially present in 1974, although almost all changes which had occurred were in the direction of reducing the differences.

- Although less than in 1972, blacks continued in 1974 to see a great deal of racial discrimination, especially in regard to their opportunities for promotion and in the administration of military justice.

- The vast majority of whites continued to see little or no evidence of discrimination against blacks in the Army.

- Blacks continued to see considerably more racial prejudice in the civilian communities surrounding their posts than [did] whites.

- Most enlisted personnel, black and white, still do not see their officers and NCOs (noncommissioned officers) as accepting race relations and equal opportunity as part of their leadership responsibilities.

- There is an indication that feelings of "white backlash" may be becoming somewhat more widespread, although they are still confined to a minority of whites. This occurs even as many blacks are just beginning to see progress in equal treatment as a result of the equal opportunity and treatment programs.[35]

The study concluded by noting: "It appears that although the goal of equal opportunity in the Army is still far from being achieved, there has been real progress toward it during the past two years."[36] The study, then, shared a number of common themes with previous research, including: 1) a major concern by blacks regarding the persistence of discrimination in the armed forces; 2) white soldiers' lack of consciousness of racial discrimination; and 3) a growing resistance by white soldiers to an overemphasis on racial issues, just as black soldiers began to become more comfortable with perceived improvements in race relations.

Another major study in the 1970s compared three selected years, 1972, 1974 and 1976.[37] These longitudinal data provide a rare glimpse into some of the realities of the racial atmosphere in the army. Black soldiers and white soldiers answered the same question at three different times: "Which of the following statements is closest to your opinion? 1) In general, race relations in the Army are good; 2) In general, race relations in the Army are fair; or 3) In general, race relations in the Army are poor." Table 4 presents changes in the respondents' perceptions of race relations in the army. It shows a consensus among white soldiers and black soldiers that race relations had not improved between 1974 and 1976. The proportion of both blacks and whites who saw race relations as poor actually increased from 1974 to 1976, while there was no change in the proportion of whites who perceived race relations as good. The proportion of blacks and whites who perceived race relations as fair declined from 1974 to 1976.

TABLE 4

PERCEPTIONS OF ARMY RACE RELATIONS

Whites	1972	1974	1976
Race relations are good.	20%	23%	23%
Race relations are fair.	55%	55%	48%
Race relations are poor.	25%	22%	29%
Blacks			
Race relations are good.	10%	20%	23%
Race relations are fair.	50%	52%	45%
Race relations are poor.	39%	27%	32%

Source: Robert L. Hiett and Peter G. Nordlie, *An Analysis of the Unit Race Relations Training Program in the U.S. Army* (McLean, VA: Human Sciences Research, Inc., December 1976), prepared for the U.S. Army Research Institute, Contract DAHC 19-76-C-0015, p. 30.

Another question measured perceived changes in the trend of race relations. It asked: "Over the past year, race relations in the Army: 1) have been getting better; 2) have not changed; or 3) have been getting worse." Table 5 presents changes in the perception of the trend in race relations by blacks and whites. An increasing proportion of black troops and white troops saw no change in race relations. This increase is related significantly to a decrease in the proportion of whites and blacks who perceived race relations as getting better. In 1974, 41 percent of whites and 48 percent of blacks felt race relations were improving; two years later, the figures were 29 percent and 38 percent, respectively.

TABLE 5

PERCEPTIONS OF THE TREND IN RACE RELATIONS

Whites	1972	1974	1976
Race relations are getting better.	39%	41%	29%
Race relations have not changed.	36%	41%	55%
Race relations are getting worse.	24%	18%	16%
Blacks			
Race relations are getting better.	42%	48%	38%
Race relations have not changed.	39%	39%	48%
Race relations are getting worse.	18%	11%	13%

Source: Robert L. Hiett and Peter G. Nordlie, *An Analysis of the Unit Race Relations Training Program in the U.S. Army* (McLean, VA: Human Sciences Research, Inc., December 1976), prepared for the U.S. Army Research Institute, Contract DAHC 19-76-C-0015, p. 30.

These last two longitudinal tables represent another dramatic turning point in the history of race relations in the military. Most of the studies of the post-Vietnam War racial atmosphere depict an improving state of affairs until 1975. The results of the 1976 study reflected a retrogression in the racial climate of the army, and seemed to prefigure the racial atmosphere of the 1980s in the society as a whole. The researchers reached the following conclusions:

- Most black members of the Army continue to see racial discrimination against nonwhites in virtually every important aspect of Army life.

- Most whites see little evidence of discrimination against minorities.

- Each racial group perceives the other racial group as behaving in the more dysfunctional way and having more negative attitudes than [its] own group.

- The frequency of positive interracial interactions is quite low.

- The overall quality of race relations in the Army, which improved between 1972 and 1974, has stabilized at a level described as somewhere between "poor" and "fair."

- Voluntary racial separation is reported by all groups both on and off duty. Each group perceives the other group doing more voluntary racial separation.

- A substantial frequency of negative verbal behavior is still reported. Each racial group tends to see the other as doing more.[38]

In summary, studies on the racial atmosphere in the military from World War II through the post-Vietnam War era present contrasting themes. On the one hand, since 1945, these investigations have called out blacks' continuing perception of racial discrimination, and whites' lack of consciousness of discriminatory practices. On the other hand, they have also shown that racial separation decreased and positive racial attitudes and relations improved until 1974, only to begin a decline in 1976. The stabilization of black participation in the military in the 1980s calls out the value of, and need for, both continued study and concerted action in relation to the racial atmosphere of the armed forces.

Positive race relations in the military historically have not been the general pattern. While some progress in equal opportunity across the board can be acknowledged,[39] one should nonetheless approach cautiously any presumption pertaining to a decline in discrimination and an improvement in racial atmosphere. Black soldiers remain sensitive to the continued existence of what they perceive to be discrimination. Despite the lower frequency of cases of interracial violence, race-related tensions persist. It appears that a sort of "interracial detente" now obtains, above an undercurrent of suppressed interracial suspicions and tensions. A primary source of tension seems to emanate from the continued frustration and bitterness of blacks. A second source is the anger of a growing number of white soldiers who believe that they are being victimized by the "reverse discrimination" of preferential treatment programs for blacks. (See Table 6.) The use of concepts such as "black overrepresention" masks such sentiments.

This chapter has discussed the status of twentieth-century blacks in the military. The analysis of trends in the military suggests that although a modest increase in black participation in the armed forces was observed between 1979 and 1989, it would be unsound to conclude from this that historical patterns discussed earlier have been reversed irrevocably. Policies are now in place that could presage a period in the twenty-first century which replicates previous ones pertaining to the participation of blacks in the military. Given current financial and educational incentives, the needs of the AVF could probably be met largely through white enlistments, especially if the strong economy of the 1980s were to weaken over the course of the 1990s, and the racial climate of the society at large were to worsen. Indeed, the apparent worsening of race relations is a matter of no little concern.

TABLE 6

PERCEPTIONS OF REVERSE RACISM

Statement: *Non-whites get away with breaking rules that whites are punished for.*

	Higher-Quality Program Units			Lower-Quality Program Units		
	Blacks	Whites	Others	Blacks	Whites	Others
Strongly Agree/Agree	4%	40%	26%	7%	51%	30%
Neither Agree Nor Disagree	13%	18%	17%	10%	18%	26%
Disagree/Strongly Disagree	83%	42%	57%	83%	31%	45%

Statement: *There is racial discrimination against whites on this post.*

	Higher-Quality Program Units			Lower-Quality Program Units		
	Blacks	Whites	Others	Blacks	Whites	Others
Strongly Agree/Agree	21%	31%	20%	25%	45%	44%
Neither Agree Nor Disagree	26%	28%	28%	33%	29%	35%
Disagree/Strongly Disagree	53%	41%	52%	42%	27%	21%

Statement: *The Army's RR/EO [race relations/equal opportunity] program helps minorities get ahead at the expense of whites.*

	Higher-Quality Program Units			Lower-Quality Program Units		
	Blacks	Whites	Others	Blacks	Whites	Others
Strongly Agree/Agree	6%	25%	9%	6%	32%	19%
Neither Agree Nor Disagree	21%	30%	28%	27%	35%	46%
Disagree/Strongly Disagree	74%	45%	63%	67%	33%	35%

Statement: *White middle-class Americans are giving up too many of their own rights for the rights of others.*

	Higher-Quality Program Units			Lower-Quality Program Units		
	Blacks	Whites	Others	Blacks	Whites	Others
Strongly Agree/Agree	9%	33%	11%	10%	39%	19%
Neither Agree Nor Disagree	33%	31%	31%	29%	35%	54%
Disagree/Strongly Disagree	58%	37%	58%	62%	26%	27%

Source: Table 6 is excerpted from Robert L. Hiett and Peter G. Nordlie, *An Analysis of the Unit Race Relations Training Program in the U.S. Army* (McLean, VA: Human Sciences Research, Inc., December 1976), prepared for the U.S. Army Research Institute, Contract DAHC 19-76-C-0015, p. 75.

Both attitudinally and behaviorally, key indicators signal significant changes in the relationship of blacks and whites. After a disproportionate loss of life in the Vietnam War, black military personnel continue to be frustrated by racial discrimination. White soldiers, on the other hand, all too often believe that equal opportunity and affirmative action programs have impinged unduly on their rights. They also worry about the "overrepresentation" of blacks in the services. This tension could well lead to violence similar to that observed in the 1960s and 1970s, and/or to a dramatic exodus of blacks from the military. Without interventions such as expanded human relations education and strong implementation of a military justice program, the military could lose the leadership role it has held since the mid-twentieth century as the most supportive agency in the United States for black opportunity and mobility.

NOTES

[1]Richard J. Stillman, *Integration of the Negro in the U.S. Armed Forces* (New York: Praeger Publishers, 1968), p. 7.

[2]Jack D. Foner, *Blacks and the Military in American History: A New Perspective* (New York: Praeger Publishers, 1974), p. 32.

[3]Ibid., p. 48.

[4]Ibid., p. 77.

[5]Ibid., p. 79.

[6]Emmett Jay Scott, *Scott's Official History of the American Negro in the World War* (Chicago: Homewood Press, 1919; reprinted Arno Press, 1969), p. 16.

[7]Foner, op. cit. note 2, p. 144.

[8]Ibid., p. 179.

[9]Ibid., p. 177.

[10]Ibid., pp. 183-188.

[11]Ibid., p. 202.

[12]Ibid., p. 204.

[13]Ibid., p. 220.

[14]U.S. Department of Defense, *Equal Opportunity*, Render Report (Washington, D.C.: U.S. Government Printing Office, December 1970).

[15]National Association for the Advancement of Colored People, *The Search for Military Justice: Report of an NAACP Inquiry into the Problems of the Negro Serviceman in West Germany* (New York: NAACP Special Fund, 1971).

[16]Foner, op. cit. note 2, p. 223.

[17]Gates Commission, *The Report of the President's Commission on an All-Volunteer Armed Force* (New York: Macmillan Co., 1970), p. 1.

[18]Richard M. Nixon, "The All-Volunteer Armed Force," address given over the CBS radio network, October 17, 1968, quoted in Gerald Leinwand, ed., *The Draft* (New York: Washington Square Press, 1970), p. 190.

[19]Morris Janowitz and Charles C. Moskos, Jr., "Racial Composition in the All-Volunteer Force: Policy Alternatives," *Armed Forces and Society* 1: 1 (Winter 1974): 109-123.

[20]Martin Binkin and Mark J. Eitelberg, with Alvin J. Schexnider and Marvin M. Smith, *Blacks and the Military* (Washington, D.C.: The Brookings Institution, 1982), p. 44.

[21]Larry Carney, "Recruiters Will Move Nearer Campuses," *Army Times* (September 7, 1981), p. 23.

204 RACE: DILEMMAS AND PROGNOSES

[22]*Department of Defense Authorization Act, 1981*, Conference Report, Title III, sec. 302.

[23]U.S. Department of Defense, *Aptitude Testing of Recruits*, Report to the House Armed Services Committee (Washington, D.C.: Office of the Assistant Secretary of Defense for Manpower, Reserve Affairs, and Logistics, 1980), p. 73.

[24]See, for example, John S. Butler and Kenneth L. Wilson, "*The American Soldier* Revisited: Race Relations and the Military," *Social Science Quarterly* 59: 3 (December 1978): 451-467; Alvin J. Schexnider and John S. Butler, "Race and the All-Volunteer System: A Reply to Janowitz and Moskos," *Armed Forces and Society* 2: 3 (Spring 1976): 421-432; and Alvin J. Schexnider, "Review: The Black Experience in the American Military," *Armed Forces and Society* 4: 2 (Winter 1978): 329-334.

[25]Larry Carney, "Re-up Bar Tightened for 18-Year Troops," *Army Times* (January 4, 1982), p. 3.

[26]Binkin, et al., op. cit. note 20, p. 138.

[27]The data were obtained via a telephone conversation with Major David Super of the Defense Manpower Data Center of the Department of Defense on July 21, 1989.

[28]Charles C. Moskos, Jr., "Racial and Educational Composition of the All-Volunteer Army," in Winston A. Van Horne, ed., and Thomas V. Tonnesen, man. ed., *Ethnicity and Public Policy*, Vol. 1 (Milwaukee: University of Wisconsin System American Ethnic Studies Coordinating Committee, 1982), pp. 121-133 at 122.

[29]Comments attributed to M. Kathleen Carpenter, Deputy Assistant Secretary of Defense for Equal Opportunity, in "Pentagon Official Reports 'a New Racism' in Military," *New York Times* (July 24, 1979), p. A10.

[30]Charles C. Moskos, Jr., "The Enlisted Ranks in the All-Volunteer Army," in John B. Keeley, ed., *The All-Volunteer Force and American Society* (Charlottesville, VA: University Press of Virginia, 1978), pp. 39-80 at 65.

[31]Samuel A. Stouffer, Edward A. Schman, Leland C. DeVinney, Shirley A. Stan and Robin M. Williams, Jr., *The American Soldier: Adjustments During Army Life*, in two volumes (Princeton, NJ: Princeton University Press, 1949).

[32]Ibid., Vol. I, pp. 402-407.

[33]Ibid., Vol. I, pp. 511-514.

[34]Leo Bogart, ed., *Social Research and the Desegregation of the U.S. Army: Two Original 1951 Field Reports* (Chicago: Markham Publishing, 1969), p. 1.,

[35]Dale K. Brown and Peter G. Nordlie, with James A. Thomas, *Changes in Black and White Perceptions of the Army's Race Relations/Equal Opportunity Program—1972 to 1974* (McLean, VA: Human Sciences Research, Inc., January 1975), prepared for the U.S. Army Research Institute, Contract DAHC 19-74-C-0047, p. 4.

[36]Ibid., p. 5.

[37]Robert L. Hiett and Peter G. Nordlie, *An Analysis of the Unit Race Relations Training Program in the U.S. Army* (McLean, VA: Human Sciences Research, Inc., December 1976), prepared for the U.S. Army Research Institute, Contract DAHC 19-76-C-0015.

[38]Ibid., p. 13.

[39]See, for example, Charles C. Moskos, Jr., "Success Story: Blacks in the Army," *Atlantic Monthly* 257 (May 1986): 64-72.

RACIAL PARITY UNDER LAISSEZ-FAIRE: AN IMPOSSIBLE DREAM

David H. Swinton

Jackson State University

Introduction

As the twentieth century began, the economic, political and social sub-ordination of the black population was an established pattern in all regions of the United States. Blacks were only thirty-seven years away from the Emancipation Proclamation. Reconstruction in the South had come to an end, and most of the rights that blacks had won after the Civil War had been effectively overturned. The notorious Jim Crow laws had been enacted in the South, reestablishing white supremacy. Moreover, as the nineteenth century drew to a close the Supreme Court issued its infamous "separate but equal" doctrine, which effectively legalized segregation and discrimination against blacks.[1] Thus, blacks started their twentieth-century quest for economic equality in a very restrictive environment.

There can be little question that blacks were severely disadvantaged economically at the time. Although data are limited, there is enough information to leave little doubt that blacks had low incomes, high poverty rates and little wealth accumulation, both absolutely and relative to whites. They owned few businesses and were, therefore, generally dependent on selling their labor to white-owned enterprises to earn a living. The overwhelming majority of blacks lived in the South, where they could gain employment only in low-wage agricultural and domestic service pursuits. In the North, blacks had been pushed out of much skilled work by European immigrants and, for the most part, had difficulty obtaining employment except in lines of work that others did not want.

The economic disadvantages confronting blacks at the beginning of the twentieth century were the result of several factors. First, and perhaps most important, was the fact that blacks were almost entirely a laboring class as the century opened. No reparations or other forms of compensation were ever awarded to the newly-freed slaves. As such, they were wholly dependent upon others for employment and other economic opportunities. Second, black workers were concentrated in the rural areas of the South where they were largely restricted to working in the low-wage agricultural sector, work not unlike what many performed under slavery. Third, because of the legacy of slavery and the practice of discrimination, blacks were severely disadvantaged educationally. Fourth, perhaps because of their limited ownership, blacks were subject to severe discrimination in the North and the South in gaining access to economic opportunities. Thus, as the twentieth century began, blacks had limited prospects for improving their situation through their own independent activities.

This chapter discusses the evolution of black economic status during the 1900s. A principal objective is to examine the record of progress in overcoming the high degree of racial inequality in economic life that existed at the turn of the century. This will be done through a review of enough of the available data to paint a general picture of trends in the twentieth century. This laborious but necessary task will be undertaken in the next section.

After describing twentieth-century trends, attention will be turned to explaining the patterns and assessing the extent of progress that have been observed. It will be maintained here that the pace of blacks' progress in overcoming economic disadvantages has depended on several factors. First, the position of blacks has been contingent on general developments in the economy as a whole, and especially in the labor market. Second, progress for blacks has depended on the pattern and extent of racial discrimination. Third, black gains have been dependent on the extent of their cumulative disadvantages in the ownership of human and material resources. Fourth, black advance has depended on black self-help activities. And, finally, the policies and activities of the government have played an important role. The interplay of these factors during this century has produced periods of significant economic progress for blacks, and other periods of stagnation and retrogression. However, the net result taken for the century as a whole has been improvement in the economic status of blacks in relation to its pre-twentieth-century level. Yet blacks are still far short of achieving economic parity, and the erosion of gains since the mid-1970s suggests that blacks remain economically vulnerable as they approach the next hundred years.

The final section of the chapter will include a brief prognosis of prospects for black economic progress in the next century. Here it will be argued that the same factors that have determined the pace of progress in the twentieth century will also obtain in the twenty-first. The prospects for black economic progress over the next century depend crucially on developments in the marketplace and on the effectiveness of black self-help activities in establishing and maintaining equal conditions and equal opportunities for blacks to compete in the American economy.

Trends in Black Economic Status during the Twentieth Century

As has been mentioned previously, the start of the twentieth century found blacks with little economic ownership and as participants in the economy primarily as low-wage agricultural and domestic service workers. The participation of the black work force in nonagricultural pursuits other than domestic service was minimal. Government-supported social welfare programs were also limited. Thus, blacks had to procure the necessaries of life with whatever income they could obtain from selling their labor or from private philanthropy. Although statistics on income are limited and the poverty index had not yet been defined, it is clear that blacks were in a severely disadvantaged economic position both absolutely and relative to whites.

The major change in the economic position of blacks during this century has been the transformation of the black work force from one employed preponderantly in southern agriculture and domestic service to one which is engaged predominantly in nonagricultural pursuits more evenly dispersed across the four census regions. There has also clearly been an expansion in black access to social welfare programs. Black participation in such programs has grown sharply since the 1960s along with the general expansion in the social welfare activities of the federal government and the states. The changes in other measures of the position of blacks in the American economy have been less pronounced. There has been some growth in relative black business ownership, but current ownership is still very limited. Black wealth holdings are also low in relation to those of whites.

Nevertheless, there can be little doubt that the economic well-being of the black population has improved in both absolute and relative terms. Incomes are higher and poverty rates are undoubtedly lower than they were at the turn of the century. Improvement in the labor market status of blacks has been the major factor in increasing incomes and in decreasing poverty rates. In comparison to the economic state of blacks at the turn of the century, the overall gains have been impressive.

The pace of progress has not been even, though, either over time or across geographic regions. In fact, since the late 1970s progress has ground to almost a complete halt. There have even been some erosion of income gains and an increase in poverty rates over this period. Moreover, although black labor market status has improved, blacks are still a long way from labor market parity, and recent trends suggest a deterioration in some aspects of black labor market position. These recent developments call into question the permanency of black gains. The remainder of this section will review briefly some of the highlights of twentieth-century trends in black economic status.

Labor Market Developments

Changes in Region and Sectors of Employment

Two major themes have dominated developments for blacks in the labor market during the twentieth century. The first is the redistribution of the black work force from the South to the North; the second is the transformation of the work force from one engaged in agricultural and domestic service occupations to one engaged primarily in other pursuits. These two trends are obviously interrelated, since the migration of blacks to the North was tantamount to leaving agriculture for nonagricultural pursuits. However, even within the South a dramatic industrial transformation has occurred, albeit at a somewhat slower pace.

TABLE 1

BLACK EMPLOYMENT BY REGION, 1890-1984

	Number Employed (In Thousands)			
	South	North & West	Total U.S.	Percent in South
1890[a]	2,746	327	3,073	89.4
1910[a]	4,592	600	5,193	88.4
1930[a]	4,210	1,293	5,504	76.5
1940[b]	3,571	908	4,479	79.7
1960[b]	3,537	2,560	6,097	58.0
1970[b]	3,799	3,562	7,361	51.6
1981	5,012	4,177	9,189	54.5
1984	5,575	4,544	10,119	55.1

Source: Figures for 1890 to 1970, inclusive, are derived from the U.S. Bureau of the Census, *The Social and Economic Status of the Black Population in the United States: An Historical View, 1790-1978* (Washington, D.C.: U.S. Government Printing Office, 1979), Tables 52 and 53, pp. 73-75. Figures for 1982 and 1984 are from the U.S. Bureau of Labor Statistics, *Geographic Profile of Employment and Unemployment, 1982 and 1984*, Bulletins No. 2170 and 2234, respectively

(Washington, D.C.: U.S. Government Printing Office, 1983 and 1985), Table 4, pp. 12-14 and 13-16, respectively.

[a]Figures are for employed people ten years old and older.

[b]Figures are for employed people fourteen years old and older.

The dramatic nature of the regional shift in black employment is revealed by the facts displayed in Table 1. In 1890 nearly 90 percent of the employed black population worked in the South, while only 10 percent worked in the North and West. By 1970, only about 52 percent of employed blacks worked in the South, while 48 percent worked in the other regions. The proportion of blacks working in the South has declined by over 40 percent since the beginning of the century, while the proportion working in the other regions has more than quadrupled. As the data in Table 1 clearly show, the shift of the locus of black employment to regions outside of the South occurred in two spurts. The first occurred between 1910 and 1930, a period that corresponded to World War I and the general prosperity of the 1920s. During these two decades, total employment of blacks in the South actually declined by about 382,000, while total employment of blacks in the North and West increased by about 700,000 workers. Thus, the proportion of employed blacks residing in the South declined from over 88 percent in 1910 to about 76.5 percent in 1930.

During the depression decade of the 1930s, blacks actually lost employment at about the same rate both in the North and West and in the South. Hence, there was very little change in the regional distribution of black employment during that decade.

The second major spurt in the relocation of black employment occurred between 1940 and 1970. During this period black employment remained almost constant in absolute numbers in the South, while blacks gained about 2.7 million jobs in the North and West. The proportion of blacks employed in the South declined from 79.7 to 51.6 percent during this thirty-year period. Since 1970, black employment has grown in both the South and the non-South, but growth has been faster in the South. As a consequence, the proportion of blacks employed in the South has increased modestly since 1970.

TABLE 2

WHITE EMPLOYMENT BY REGION, 1890-1984[a]

	Number Employed (In Thousands)			
	South	North & West	Total U.S.	Percent in South
1890[b]	6,754	12,788	19,542	34.6
1910[b]	12,295	20,479	32,774	37.5

1930[b]	14,310	28,274	42,584	33.6
1940[c]	10,207	30,480	40,687	25.1
1960[c]	15,079	43,464	58,543	25.8
1970[c]	18,998	50,194	69,192	27.5
1982	27,601	60,302	87,903	31.4
1984	29,251	62,869	92,120	31.8

Source: Figures for 1890 to 1970, inclusive, are derived from the U.S. Bureau of the Census, *The Social and Economic Status of the Black Population in the United States: An Historical View, 1790-1978* (Washington, D.C.: U.S. Government Printing Office, 1979), Tables 51 and 54, pp. 72 and 75. Figures for 1982 and 1984 are from the U.S. Bureau of Labor Statistics, *Geographic Profile of Employment and Unemployment, 1982 and 1984*, Bulletins No. 2170 and 2234, respectively (Washington, D.C.: U.S. Government Printing Office, 1983 and 1985), Table 4, pp. 12-14 and 13-16, respectively.

[a]"White" does not include Hispanics.

[b]Figures are for employed people ten years old and older.

[c]Figures are for employed people fourteen years old and older.

The decline in the proportion of blacks employed in the South between 1940 and 1970 was much more dramatic than for whites. Data for the distribution of white employment by region are shown in Table 2. This table, juxtaposed with Table 1, enables one to observe that while black employment in the South grew by only about 200,000 jobs between 1940 and 1970, white employment grew by about nine million jobs. Indeed, while the proportion of blacks employed in the South declined by about 25 percent between 1930 and 1970, the proportion of whites working in the South declined by only about 6 percent. It is thus apparent that during the first seventy years of the twentieth century, blacks were being displaced from the southern work force in large numbers.

The second major trend of the twentieth century — the shift of black workers out of domestic service and agriculture into other sectors of the economy — has been even more dramatic. Table 3 presents data which summarizes this trend. The shift has occurred in both the North and West and in the South. In 1890, for the nation as a whole, about eighty-eight of every one hundred black workers were employed either in agriculture or in domestic and personal service; the corresponding figures were 79 percent in the North and West and 90 percent in the South. These proportions declined every decade after 1890, and by 1982 the proportion of blacks employed in agriculture and domestic service reached an all-time low of 4.8 percent nationally — composed of 7 percent in the South and 2.1 percent in the North and West.

TABLE 3

EMPLOYMENT IN AGRICULTURE AND DOMESTIC SERVICE INDUSTRIES, BY RACE (PERCENT)

	White	Black		
	Total U.S.	Total U.S.	South	North & West
1890	54	88	90	79
1910	38	77	80	56
1930	28	66	71	46
1940	20	54	61	30
1960	7	23	32	11
1970	4	10	17	6
1982	3.7	4.8	7	2.1
1984	5	6	8.3	3.1

Source: Figures for 1890 to 1970, inclusive, are from the U.S. Bureau of the Census, *The Social and Economic Status of the Black Population in the United States: An Historical View, 1790-1978* (Washington, D.C.: U.S. Government Printing Office, 1979), Tables 51, 52 and 54, pp. 72, 73 and 75. Figures for 1982 and 1984 are from the U.S. Bureau of Labor Statistics, *Geographic Profile of Employment and Unemployment, 1982 and 1984*, Bulletins No. 2170 and 2234, respectively (Washington, D.C.: U.S. Government Printing Office, 1983 and 1985), Table 4, pp. 12-14 and 13-16, respectively.

For the nation as a whole, the decline in the concentration of black employment in the agricultural and domestic service sectors proceeded at a fairly rapid pace throughout the century. Between 1890 and 1940 this proportion fell from 88 percent to 54 percent, and between 1940 and 1982 it declined from 54 to 4.8 percent. In the South, the period when the decline in employment in these two sectors was most rapid occurred after 1940. In the North and West it was between 1890 and 1940.

The transformation of the black work force from one heavily concentrated in the agricultural and domestic service sectors corresponds to a national trend of diversification of employment away from agriculture. As Table 3 shows, although only 54 percent of the white population worked in agriculture and domestic service in 1890, the proportion of whites employed in these sectors also declined each decade, reaching 3.7 percent by 1982. The differences that obtained between black workers and white workers vis-à-vis sectors of employment over the first half of the twentieth century have decreased steadily since 1940, and had almost vanished completely by 1982 in all regions of the country. This convergence of sectors of employment accounts for most of the relative gains for black workers during this century. The shift of black workers from the South and out of the agricultural and domestic service sectors has had a major impact on their occupational distribution, employment rates, wage rates and earnings. The next three sections of this chapter will discuss the changes that have occurred in each of these areas of black labor market status.

Occupational Changes

As one might expect, the dramatic changes in blacks' sectors of employment were accompanied by equally striking shifts in their occupational distribution. Table 4 summarizes available occupational data for 1890, 1910 and 1930. Between 1890 and 1930 the proportion of blacks employed in domestic service and agricultural occupations declined from about 88 percent to about 66 percent. In 1890 only about 11 percent of the black work force was engaged in what might be roughly classified as blue-collar occupations in the nonagricultural sector; by 1930 this figure had increased to 26 percent. Similarly, about 9 percent of blacks worked in white-collar pursuits in 1930 as compared to only about one percent in 1890. Thus, there were large absolute gains in the occupational status of black workers.

TABLE 4

DISTRIBUTION OF WORKERS BY OCCUPATION AND RACE, 1890-1930 (PERCENT)

	1890		1910		1930	
	Black	White	Black	White	Black	White
Professional	a	a	1.3	4.7	2.1	6.7
Managers and Administrators	a	a	0.8	7.3	1.0	8.4
Clerical	a	a	0.8	11.7	1.5	19.2
Manufacturing and Mechanical	6.0	25.0	13.0	30.0	19.0	30.0
Transportation and Communication	5.0	16.0	5.0	7.0	7.0	8.0
Domestic and Personal Service	31.0	17.0	22.0	8.0	29.0	8.0
Agriculture	57.0	37.0	55.0	30.0	37.0	20.0
Other	1.0	5.0	3.1	1.0	4.4	0.0

Source: Figures for blacks in the first three categories are based on data in Gunnar Myrdal, *An American Dilemma: The Negro Problem and Modern Democracy*, 3d ed., Vol. 1 (New York: Harper & Row, 1962, printed 1969), Table 1, p. 306. All other figures are from the U.S. Bureau of the Census, *The Social and Economic Status of the Black Population: An Historical View, 1790-1978* (Washington, D.C.: U.S. Government Printing Office, 1979), Table 51, p. 72.

^aIncluded in the category "Other."

However, relative black gains were limited because similar occupational changes also occurred for whites during the first part of the century. Between the beginning of the century and 1930, the increase in white employment in nonagricultural pursuits actually proceeded at a faster pace than that of blacks. As shown in Table 4, the proportion of whites employed in agricultural and domestic or personal service occupations decreased from 54 percent in 1890 to 28 percent in 1930. The proportion classified as white-collar workers (the "Other" category in 1890) increased strikingly from about 5 percent to around 34 percent.[2]

Thus, during the early part of the century the occupational roles of blacks and whites diverged. The relative occupational status of blacks during this period actually may have declined despite the absolute gains in occupational status. For example, while blacks were about 1.6 times as likely as whites to be in the traditional agricultural and domestic service occupations in 1890, by 1930 they were about 2.4 times as likely to be in these occupations. A gap in white-collar occupations in 1890 of roughly 4 percent increased to 25 percent by 1930. Only in blue-collar occupations did the figures for the proportional employment of blacks and whites converge. And so, during the first three decades of the twentieth century, as blacks diversified out of the traditional occupations, the pattern of disadvantageous occupational distribution, which had always existed in the traditional sectors, was also established in nontraditional ones.

In the agricultural sector, for example, blacks had always been concentrated in the least advantageous roles. In 1930, for example, blacks employed in agriculture were almost twice as likely to be sharecroppers or wage laborers as whites (64.9 percent versus 33.5 percent).[3] On the other hand, whites were more than three times as likely as blacks to be owners and managers (42.4 percent versus 13.1 percent).[4] As can be observed from the data in Table 4, a similar pattern of underrepresentation in the more advantageous occupations characterized the occupational distribution of blacks in the new industrial work force. In 1930, only 9 percent of blacks working in sectors other than agriculture or domestic service were managers or professionals. In comparison, 21 percent of whites working in the nontraditional sectors were employed in such occupations.

The transformation of the occupational structure of the employed black work force accelerated after 1940, and continued through the 1980 decennial census in both the North and West and in the South. This was especially true for black females. Occupational data for females for the years 1940 and 1980 are displayed in Table 5. Between 1940 and 1980, the share of employed black women working in farm and domestic service occupations declined sharply from about 75 percent to about 6 percent. The proportion of black women employed in every other major occupational group increased during this period. Hence, there was an acceleration of the occupational upgrading of the black female labor force during this period. The most impressive gains occurred in the clerical occupations. The proportion of black women employed as clerical workers rose from roughly one percent in 1940 to about 26 percent in 1980. The proportion of black females working in professional and technical jobs, service occupations other than domestic service, and operative jobs also increased significantly. On the other hand, black females continued to have a low rate of employment as managers and officials, which increased from one percent to 4.7 percent, and as sales workers, which increased from less than one percent to 6.1 percent.

TABLE 5

DISTRIBUTION OF EMPLOYED WOMEN BY OCCUPATION AND RACE, 1940 AND 1980 (PERCENT)

	1940			1980		
	Black	White	Ratio Black:White	Black	White	Ratio Black:White
Professional and Technical	4.3	14.7	.29	15.2	17.7	.86
Managerial	0.7	4.3	.16	4.7	7.8	.60
Clerical	0.9	24.7	.04	25.8	32.2	.80
Saleswomen	0.5	8.1	.06	6.1	12.0	.51
Craft Workers	0.2	1.1	.18	2.3	2.3	1.0
Operatives	6.2	20.3	.31	13.2	8.8	1.5
Farm Laborers	12.9	1.2	10.75	0.5	0.6	.83
Other Laborers	0.8	0.9	.89	2.9	2.0	1.45
Service Workers	10.4	11.5	.90	24.3	15.4	1.58
Domestic Service	59.5	10.9	5.46	5.0	0.8	6.25
Farmers & Farm Managers	3.0	1.1	2.73	0.1	0.4	.25

Source: Data for 1940 are from the U.S. Bureau of the Census, *1940 Census: Population*, Vol. III, Part 1, U.S. Summary (Washington, D.C.: U.S. Government Printing Office, 1943), Table 62, pp. 88-90; data for 1980 are derived from the U.S. Bureau of the Census, *1980 Census: Detailed Population Characteristics*, Part 1, U.S. Summary, Report No. PC 80-1-D1-A (Washington, D.C.: U.S. Government Printing Office, 1984), pp. 1-196 — 1-215.

The telling nature of the post-1940 occupational upgrading of black women is revealed by the fact that in 1940, two major occupational groups, operatives and nonhousehold service workers, accounted for about 71 percent of all black female employment outside of the agricultural and domestic service sectors. By 1980 the share of these two sectors had dropped to about 43 percent. The major increase was for clerical workers whose share among industrial workers rose from 3.8 percent to 31.8 percent.

Occupational data for males, both black and white, for this period are shown in Table 6.

TABLE 6

DISTRIBUTION OF EMPLOYED MEN BY
OCCUPATION AND RACE, 1940 AND 1980 (PERCENT)

| | 1940 | | | 1980 | | |
	Black	White	Ratio Black:White	Black	White	Ratio Black:White
Professional and Technical	1.8	5.9	.31	7.9	14.5	.54
Managerial	1.3	10.6	.12	5.7	13.5	.42
Clerical	1.2	7.1	.17	9.3	6.6	1.41
Salesmen	0.8	6.8	.12	3.9	9.8	.40
Craft Workers	4.4	15.6	.28	15.5	21.4	.72
Operatives	12.5	18.8	.66	25.8	16.0	1.61
Farm Laborers	19.8	7.0	2.83	2.9	2.0	1.45
Other Laborers	21.2	7.5	2.83	11.5	5.7	2.02
Service Workers	12.3	5.8	3.32	16.8	8.2	2.05
Domestic Service	2.9	0.2	14.50	0.2	-	-
Farmers & Farm Managers	21.1	14.0	1.51	0.5	2.3	.22

Source: Data for 1940 are from the U.S. Bureau of the Census, *1940 Census: Population*, Vol. III, Part 1, U.S. Summary (Washington, D.C.: U.S. Government Printing Office, 1943), Table 62, pp. 88-90; data for 1980 are derived from the U.S. Bureau of the Census, *1980 Census: Detailed Population Characteristics*, Part 1, U.S. Summary, Report No. PC 80-1-D1-A (Washington, D.C.: U.S. Government Printing Office, 1984), pp. 1-196 — 1-215.

The changes for black males after 1940 were less notable because only about 44 percent of them worked in agricultural or domestic service occupations in 1940. Nevertheless, there was substantial absolute upgrading in the occupational status of employed black males. The largest increases in employment shares occurred in the skilled craft and operative occupations. The shares of employed black males working in these two occupations increased from 4.4 to 15.5 percent and from 12.5 to 25.8 percent, respectively. The proportion of black males employed in white-collar occupations also increased. In total, 26.8 percent of employed black males held white-collar jobs in 1980 as compared to only 5.1 percent in 1940. All of the white-collar occupations also increased as a share of the total black nonagricultural employment. The proportion of black males employed in service occupations other than private household workers increased from 12.3 percent in 1940 to 16.8 percent in 1980. The proportion of black males employed as laborers outside of the agricultural sector actually declined from 21.2 percent in 1940 to 11.5 percent in 1980. In 1940, two occupational groups (laborers and service workers outside of the household sector) accounted for 60 percent of black male industrial employment. The proportion of black industrial workers employed in these occupations declined to about 30 percent in 1980.

The data in Tables 5 and 6 show that the occupational structure for the white population also changed over the forty years from 1940 to 1980. However, because whites already had relatively low representation in the agricultural and domestic service sectors, the changes for blacks were more conspicuous. Between 1940 and 1980 the proportion of white men working in agricultural, domestic service and industrial laborer occupations declined from 28.7 percent to 10 percent, while the proportion of black males so employed declined from 65 to 15.1 percent. Similarly, only about 14 percent of employed white women worked in such occupations in 1940, compared to about 76 percent of employed black women. For white women, the major change in the distribution of industrial workers was an increase in clerical and nonhousehold service workers and a decline in the proportion working as operatives. Most of the decline in the agricultural and domestic service sectors for white males was offset by gains in white-collar occupations, where their share of jobs increased from about 30 percent to about 44 percent. For white males, the proportion of blue-collar jobs only increased by about three percentage points, and the proportion of service jobs also increased by about the same.

The changes in the occupational structures for blacks and whites reflect the changing demand for labor in the economy. Because blacks were more heavily concentrated in the occupations for which demand was declining, occupational changes for blacks have been more dramatic. As a result of these changes, there has been a convergence in the occupational structures for both blacks and whites. Moreover, the structures have converged even if one only considers those employed in the nontraditional occupations. The relative proportion of black males and black females employed in the better occupational categories has increased, while the relative proportion employed in the less desirable occupations has decreased.

For example, black males employed in nontraditional sectors were about three times as likely to be employed as laborers or service workers in 1940, but only about two times as likely to be so employed in 1980. For the white-collar occupations (professionals, managers, and sales), black males were about 43 percent as likely as white males to hold such jobs in 1980, compared to 13 percent in 1940.[5]

The relative gains for black females were similar, though less vivid, because of more similar distributions of nondomestic service workers in 1940. However, the large numerical advantage of white females in clerical work in 1940 had been significantly reduced by 1980, as the relative likelihood of black female employment increased from 13 percent to 85 percent over this period. Also, black females not in the traditional sectors were 3.3 times as likely as white females to work as nonhousehold service workers in 1940, but only 1.7 times as likely in 1980. Curiously enough, the relative likelihood of a black female nondomestic worker being in a professional or managerial occupation actually dropped slightly between 1940 and 1980.

The major part of the occupational transformation for black males occurred between 1940 and 1960.[6] The bulk of the movement out of agriculture and into craft and operative positions took place during this period. Between 1960 and 1980 most of the increase in white-collar employment occurred as the share of farm workers continued to decline, and the share of laborers started to fall as well. For black females, the changes occurred more evenly across the forty-year period. Most of the decline in the share of agricultural occupations, and about 40 percent of the decline in the proportion of domestic service workers, occurred between 1940 and 1960. During this period there were significant increases in the proportion of black women working as operatives, clericals and nonhousehold service workers. The major decline between 1960 and 1980 was in the proportion employed in domestic service occupations; the primary increase was in the share of black women working in clerical jobs.

Trends in occupational transformation also differed across regions.[7] In general, the primary development between 1940 and 1960 for black males in the North and West (where there was little agricultural employment for blacks in 1940) was a movement out of service and laborer occupations and into clerical, operative and craft ones, with very little penetration into the higher white-collar occupations. Between 1960 and 1980 the occupational structure for black males outside of the South continued to evolve. Most of the shift was away from laborer and operative occupations. The proportion of black males employed in higher white-collar occupations did increase during this period. In the South, on the other hand, the major change between 1940 and 1960 was a movement out of agricultural occupations. The proportion of employed blacks increased not only in the craft and operative occupations, but in the laborer and nonhousehold service occupations as well. During the next twenty years (1960-1980) the proportions working in agricultural and laborer occupations continued to fall, while there were gains in the white-collar as well as the blue-collar occupations.

The occupational status of working black males has improved relative to white males within each region in the post-1940 period. But, as of 1980, black males continued to have substantially unequal labor market positions in each region. In general, black males are underrepresented in the best occupations (professionals, managers, sales and crafts) and overrepresented in the other occupations in each region. Employed black males are still slightly less than 50 percent as likely as whites to be sales or managerial workers in the North, and a little less than 60 percent as likely in the West and one-third as likely in the South. In the North and West, blacks are from 60 to 67 percent as likely to be professional workers as whites and in the South they are about 50 percent as likely. In general, occupational distributions are closest to parity in the West, and furthest from parity in the South.

The pattern of occupational change also has varied among regions for black females. It has been similar to that of black males, except that the movement was from domestic service and agriculture instead of from laborers and agriculture. Again, the changes between 1940 and 1960 were greater outside the South. Within the South, the changes were greater between 1960 and 1980. It is also the case that the movement into higher-valued, white-collar occupations was greater between 1960 and 1980.

The occupational convergence of blacks and whites has been greater for employed black females than for black males in all regions during this century, but inequality still exists. Black females generally are overrepresented in blue-collar and service occupations, and underrepresented in white-collar ones. Moreover, as is true of black males, the greatest inequalities continue to exist in the South. The proportion of black females with professional or technical occupations is over 82 percent as large as the proportion of white females holding such occupations in every region, a figure which points to increasing progress. The proportion of black females holding clerical occupations is practically at parity in every region except the South. Employed black females have also gained in their representation within managerial positions. The greatest remaining disparities are black females' underrepresentation among sales workers and their overrepresentation among domestic workers.

Employment Rates

The occupational distribution of employed blacks is only one aspect of the labor market status of black workers. Occupational statistics do not take any account of joblessness. Occupational data thus provide an incomplete picture of the evolving status of black workers whenever there are absolute or relative changes in employment rates. Still, they are a useful measure of how well blacks are faring in the labor market.

The employment rate measures the proportion of the population that has a job at a point in time, regardless of the occupation. Being employed is, for most working-age persons, necessary for having earnings. For much of the twentieth century, though occupationally disadvantaged, blacks have had higher rates of employment than whites. This employment advantage has been particularly marked for black women. However, the employment rates of black men have declined significantly since the 1960s, and the gap between black female and white female employment rates has narrowed. As a result, the historical advantage for blacks has been completely eroded and whites currently have higher employment rates than blacks.

TABLE 7

EMPLOYMENT TO POPULATION RATIO, BY
RACE AND SEX, 1910-1985[a] (PERCENT)

	Both Sexes		Male		Female	
	Black	**White**	**Black**	**White**	**Black**	**White**
1910	71.0	51.4	87.4	80.6	54.7	19.7
1920	59.9	49.3	81.1	77.9	38.9	19.2
1930	59.2	48.5	80.2	75.8	38.9	20.2
1940	48.3	44.3	65.5	67.5	31.8	21.0
1950	53.7	52.4	73.3	78.1	35.4	27.8
1960	54.0	54.6	69.3	77.3	40.0	33.1
1970	53.8	55.9	65.5	74.7	43.8	38.7
1980	52.6	58.6	58.8	71.7	47.3	46.6
1985	53.4	61.0	60.0	72.3	48.1	50.7

Source: Figures for 1910 through 1930 are derived from Charles E. Hall, *Negroes in the United States, 1920-1932* (Washington, D.C.: U.S. Bureau of the Census, 1935, reprinted New York: Arno Press, 1969), Table 1, p. 288. Figures for 1940 through 1980 are derived from the U.S. Bureau of the Census, *General Social and Economic Characteristics, 1980 Census of the Population*, Report No. PC 80-1-C1 (Washington, D.C.: U.S. Government Printing Office, 1983), Table 86, pp. 1-26 — 1-30. Figures for 1985 are from the U.S. Bureau of Labor Statistics, *Geographic Profile of Employment and Unemployment, 1985*, Bulletin No. 2266 (Washington, D.C.: U.S. Government Printing Office, 1986), Table 1, pp. 3-7.

[a]Figures for 1910 to 1930 refer to gainful workers aged ten years and older, whether or not employed. Figures for 1940 are for workers aged fourteen years and older, and for 1950 and later, workers aged sixteen years and older. For 1910 through 1930, "White" refers to all "non-Negro" workers; for 1940 through 1960, "Black" includes nonwhite workers.

According to the decennial censuses (see data in Table 7), roughly 60 percent of blacks over age ten were gainfully employed in 1920 and 1930 and over 70 percent were gainfully employed in 1910. Both black males and black females were more likely to be classified as gainfully employed than their white counterparts during these early decades. However, the differential varied from only four to seven percentage points for males, while black females were between two and three times as likely to hold jobs as white females. Thus, the historically higher employment rates for blacks were due in large measure to the high rates of employment among black females. The high rates of employment for blacks during the first part of the century partially offset the income lost due to their less advantageous occupational distribution.

At the national level, blacks continued to have higher employment rates than whites until about 1960. Since 1960, though, whites have had higher employment rates than blacks. In 1940, as the nation was about to emerge from the depression, the census numbers indicate that the employment rates for both blacks and whites were lower than in 1930, although blacks continued to have a higher employment rate than whites (48.3 vs 44.3 percent). Between 1940 and 1980 black employment rates fluctuated, but never rose more than six percentage points above the 1940 level. But, white employment grew faster, and by 1980 was about fourteen percentage points higher than it was in 1940. And so, while the black employment rate was 4 percent higher in 1940 than the figure for whites, by 1980 it was 6 percent lower than that for whites.

The erosion in the employment rates of blacks was caused by a sharp decline in the employment levels of black males in relation to white males, and a sharp rise in the employment rate of white females relative to black females. By the 1960s black males had already fallen below white males in their rate of employment. For example, in 1960 only about 69 percent of black males over age sixteen were employed com-

pared to about 77 percent of white males. By 1980 the black male employment rate had fallen to about 59 percent of the black population,
while the white male employment rate had fallen only to about 72 percent of the white population. Hence, while black males were 90 percent
as likely as white males to be employed in 1960, they were only 82 percent as likely to be so in 1980.[8]

The erosion of the relative position of black females was occasioned
largely by the growth in the white female employment rate. While only
about 20 percent of white females were employed prior to World War
II, the proportion of white women employed had increased to 33.1 percent by 1960 and to about 47 percent in 1980. In the meantime, the
proportion of black women employed increased only from 40 percent to
about 47 percent between 1960 and 1980. The employment rate for
white women actually exceeded the employment rate among black
women for the first time in 1975, and has been higher nearly every year
since. Thus, black women's status has changed; while they were up to
twice as likely to be employed as white women prior to World War II,
they are now less than 95 percent as likely to be employed.

The trend in black employment rates has varied regionally. (See Table 8 for the regional data.) In general, employment rates declined in
the Northeast and the Midwest subsequent to 1950, and held relatively
steady in the South and the West through 1980. They have increased
slightly in the South and the West since 1980. White employment
rates, however, have increased faster than black employment rates in
all regions: black employment rates were higher than those for whites
through 1960, but since then have fallen below white employment rates
in all regions. The largest relative declines have been in the Midwest
and the Northeast. Between World War II and 1970, blacks in the
South had the lowest absolute employment rates of all regions. Since
the mid-1970s the rates of employment in the Northeast and the Midwest have fallen below the rates in the South. In 1985 only about 47
percent of blacks in the Midwest were employed, compared to 62 percent of whites. Since the mid-1970s, blacks have experienced the lowest absolute and relative employment rates on record outside of the
depression.

TABLE 8

EMPLOYMENT TO POPULATION RATIO, BY RACE, SEX AND REGION, 1950-1985^a (PERCENT)

| | **MALES** | | | | | | | |
| | Northeast | | Midwest | | South | | West | |
	Black	White	Black	White	Black	White	Black	White
1950	67.7	76.2	69.6	79.8	76.1	79.1	68.8	75.8
1960	71.8	77.2	67.2	78.0	68.6	76.4	71.9	78.0
1970	67.4	b	66.0	b	64.6	b	65.8	b
1980	57.0	70.1	54.5	71.8	60.4	71.9	62.7	72.6
1985	58.6	71.5	51.9	72.8	62.9	72.4	62.8	72.4

| | **FEMALES** | | | | | | | |
| | Northeast | | Midwest | | South | | West | |
	Black	White	Black	White	Black	White	Black	White
1950	40.8	30.1	32.6	27.7	34.9	25.3	34.5	27.6
1960	45.0	34.5	36.8	32.8	39.6	31.6	39.5	33.6
1970	45.4	b	43.8	b	43.1	b	44.7	b
1980	47.0	45.9	45.4	47.0	47.6	45.7	50.1	48.4
1985	47.4	49.6	43.5	51.8	49.4	49.8	52.0	51.9

Source: Figures for 1950 through 1980 are derived from the U.S. Bureau of the Census, *General Social and Economic Characteristics, 1980 Census of the Population,* Report No. PC 80-1-C1 (Washington, D.C.: U.S. Government Printing Office, 1983), Table 86, pp. 1-26 — 1-30. Figures for 1985 are derived from the U.S. Bureau of Labor Statistics, *Geographic Profile of Employment and Unemployment, 1985* (Washington, D.C.: U.S. Government Printing Office, 1986), Table 1, pp. 3-7.

^{a}Figure are for workers aged sixteen and older. For 1950 and 1960, "Black" includes all nonwhite workers.

^{b}Not available.

The decline in relative black employment is a consequence of trends in participation and unemployment rates. The national participation rate data are shown in Table 9. Participation rates for blacks have held at about 58 to 60 percent of the working-age population since the end of World War II. In contrast, the white participation rate has risen during the same period from about 55 percent to about 62 percent. Until the end of the 1960s, blacks participated at higher rates than whites. In 1910, for example, blacks age ten and older were about 40 percent more likely to participate in the labor force than whites.[9] This participation advantage declined steadily, though, until by 1970 blacks participated at about the same rate as whites. Subsequent to 1970, whites have participated at higher rates than blacks.

TABLE 9

LABOR FORCE PARTICIPATION RATE,
BY RACE, 1910-1980[a]

	Black	White	Black:White
1910	71.0	51.3	1.384
1920	59.9	49.2	1.217
1930	59.2	48.4	1.223
1940	58.1	51.6	1.126
1950	58.2	54.8	1.062
1960	58.9	57.2	1.030
1970	57.7	58.2	.991
1980	59.4	62.2	.955

Source: Figures for 1910 through 1930 are derived from Charles E. Hall, *Negroes in the United States, 1920-1932* (Washington, D.C.: U.S. Bureau of the Census, 1985, reprinted New York: Arno Press, 1969), Table 1, p. 288. Figures for 1940 through 1980 are derived from the U.S. Bureau of the Census, *General Social and Economic Characteristics, 1980 Census of the Population,* Report No. PC 80-1-C1 (Washington, D.C.: U.S. Government Printing Office, 1983), Table 86, pp. 1-26 — 1-30.

[a]Figures for 1910 through 1930 refer to gainful workers aged ten years and older, whether or not employed. Figures for 1940 are for workers aged fourteen years and older, and for 1950 and later, are for workers aged sixteen years and older. For 1910 through 1930, "White" refers to all "non-Negro" workers; for 1940 through 1960, "Black" includes all nonwhite workers.

As shown in Table 10, the patterns have been different for males and females. The participation rate for black males was 80.8 percent in 1962, which was already slightly lower than the 82.1 percent participation rate for white males. Between 1960 and 1980, the participation rate for black males declined steadily and at a faster rate than was the case for white males. Thus, the 2 percent gap in participation rates that existed in 1960 grew to an 8 percent gap by 1980, as only 70.3 percent of black males versus 78.2 percent of white males participated in the labor force. The obverse was true for black females.

The participation rate for black females actually increased after 1962, from 48 percent to 53 percent by 1980. The rate for white females over the same period rose faster though, from 37 percent to 51 percent. Hence, the 11 percent advantage for black females which existed in 1962 had declined to a 2 percent advantage by 1980.

TABLE 10

CIVILIAN LABOR FORCE PARTICIPATION RATE,
BY RACE AND SEX, 1962-1985

	Males			Females		
	Black	White	Black:White	Black	White	Black:White
1962	80.8	82.1	.98	48.0	36.7	1.31
1966	79.0	80.6	.98	49.3	39.2	1.26
1970	76.5	80.0	.96	49.5	42.6	1.16
1974	72.9	79.4	.92	49.0	45.2	1.08
1978	71.5	78.6	.91	53.1	49.4	1.07
1980	70.3	78.2	.90	53.1	51.2	1.04
1985	70.8	77.0	.92	56.5	54.1	1.04

Source: Figures for blacks from 1962 through 1970 are from the U.S. Bureau of Labor
Statistics, *Handbook of Labor Statistics*, Bulletin No. 2070 (Washington, D.C.:
U.S. Government Printing Office, 1980), Table 4, pp. 13-15. Figures for 1974
through 1980, and for whites from 1962 through 1970, are from the U.S. Bureau
of Labor Statistics, *Handbook of Labor Statistics*, Bulletin No. 2217 (Washington, D.C.: U.S. Government Printing Office, 1985), Table 5, pp. 19-21. Figures
for 1985 are from the U.S. Bureau of Labor Statistics, *Geographic Profile of Employment and Unemployment, 1985*, Bulletin No. 2266 (Washington, D.C.: U.S.
Government Printing Office, 1986), Table 1, pp. 3-7.

Regional trends in participation are shown in Table 11. The greatest
relative declines have occurred in the Northeast and the Midwest, even
though, in fact, black participation rates were actually higher in all
regions in the 1980s than they were prior to 1980, except the Northeast.
The major reason for the relative decline has been the faster growth of
white participation rates. The sex pattern in each region mirrors the
pattern discussed in the national data.

TABLE 11

LABOR FORCE PARTICIPATION RATE,
BY RACE AND REGION, 1950-1985[a]

	Northeast		Midwest		South		West	
	Black	White	Black	White	Black	White	Black	White
1950	59.9	53.3	57.0	55.1	57.9	53.5	60.7	55.3
1960	62.9	57.6	58.2	57.2	57.4	55.8	61.6	58.7
1970	58.7	b	58.9	b	56.5	b	60.6	b
1980	58.4	61.2	59.0	63.0	59.3	61.1	63.2	64.0
1985	59.5	63.4	60.7	66.4	64.5	64.2	65.5	66.4

Source: Figures for 1950 through 1980 are from the U.S. Bureau of the Census, *General
Social and Economic Characteristics, 1980 Census of the Population*, Report No.
PC 80-1-C1 (Washington, D.C.: U.S. Government Printing Office, 1983), Table
86, pp. 1-26 — 1-30. Figures for 1985 are from the U.S. Bureau of Labor Statis-

tics, *Geographic Profile of Employment and Unemployment, 1985*, Bulletin No. 2266 (Washington, D.C.: U.S. Government Printing Office, 1986), Table 1, pp. 3-7.

[a]Figures are for workers aged sixteen years and older. For 1950 and 1960, "Black" includes all nonwhite workers.

[b]Not available.

In addition to the decline in relative participation rates, there have also been absolute and relative increases in the black unemployment rate since World War II. These data are shown in Table 12 for the nation as a whole and in Table 13 by region. The unemployment rate fluctuates with the business cycle, but for blacks it has generally been drifting upwards. Their 1980 unemployment rate of 14.3 percent was twice the 1970 rate of 7.0 percent. Since 1970 the unemployment rate for blacks seemingly increases with each downturn in the cycle and decreases less with each recovery. The unemployment rate for blacks averaged 15.0 percent between 1975 and 1986. In comparison, white unemployment rates, which were between 4.1 and 4.7 percent in the decennial censuses from 1950 to 1970, had increased only to 6.3 percent by the 1980 census. Over the period during which blacks averaged 15.0 percent unemployment, whites averaged only 6.7 percent unemployment.[10] Prior to 1970, the black unemployment rate generally fluctuated from 1.7 to 2.1 times the white rate. Since 1976, the black rate has fluctuated from 2.3 to 2.5 times the white rate.

TABLE 12

**UNEMPLOYMENT RATE BY RACE,
1940-1985[a]**

	Black	White	Black:White
1940	16.9	14.2	1.19
1950	7.9	4.5	1.76
1960	8.6	4.7	1.83
1970	7.0	4.1	1.71
1975	14.8	7.8	1.90
1980	14.3	6.3	2.27
1985	15.1	6.2	2.44

Sources: Figures for 1940 through 1970 are from the U.S. Bureau of the Census, *General Social and Economic Characteristics, 1980 Census of the Population,* Report No. PC 80-1-C1 (Washington, D.C.: U.S. Government Printing Office, 1983), Table 86, pp. 1-26 — 1-30. Figures for 1975 and 1980 are from the U.S. Bureau of Labor Statistics, *Handbook of Labor Statistics,* Bulletin No. 2217 (Washington, D.C.: U.S. Government Printing Office, 1985), Table 25, p. 64. Figures for 1985 are from the U.S. Bureau of Labor Statistics, *Geographic Profile of Employment and Unemployment, 1985,* Bulletin No. 2266 (Washington, D.C.: U.S. Government Printing Office, 1986), Table 1, pp. 3-7.

[a]Figures for 1940 are for workers aged fourteen and over; for 1950 through 1985, figures are for workers aged sixteen and older. For 1940 and 1950, "Black" includes all nonwhite workers.

The data in Table 13 show that black unemployment rates have gone up in absolute and relative terms in all regions. The sharpest absolute increases have occurred in the Midwest. Through much of the 1980s, black unemployment rates in the Midwest averaged over 22 percent. Unemployment rates in the other three regions have been somewhat lower, but are still substanstially above their historical norm. Racial inequality is also greatest in the Midwest when measured by ratio; black-to-white unemployment rates have hovered slightly over 3:1. The degree of inequality is also very high in the South, averaging close to 2.5:1 during the 1980s. In both the Northeast and the West, the level of inequality also increased during the 1980s; generally the black unemployment rate has been over twice the white unemployment rate.

TABLE 13

UNEMPLOYMENT RATE BY REGION AND RACE,
1950-1985[a]

	Northeast		Midwest		South		West	
	Black	White	Black	White	Black	White	Black	White
1950	10.9	5.6	11.0	3.4	5.8	3.5	13.3	6.7
1960	8.8	4.9	11.9	4.3	7.3	4.4	9.2	5.6
1970	6.0	b	8.2	b	6.4	b	10.0	b
1980	12.2	6.0	16.2	6.6	10.1	4.7	11.0	6.1
1985	12.0	5.6	22.2	6.7	14.0	5.7	13.0	6.9

Source: Figures for 1950 through 1980 are from the U.S. Bureau of the Census, *General Social and Economic Characteristics, 1980 Census of the Population*, Report No. PC 80-1-C1 (Washington, D.C.: U.S. Government Printing Office, 1983), Table 86, pp. 1-26 — 1-30. Figures for 1985 are from the U.S. Bureau of Labor Statistics, *Geographic Profile of Employment and Unemployment, 1985*, Bulletin No. 2266 (Washington, D.C.: U.S. Government Printing Office, 1986), Table 1, pp. 3-7.

[a]Figures are for workers aged sixteen years and older. For 1950 and 1960, "Black" includes all nonwhite workers.

[b]Not available.

The pattern of increasing unemployment rates has affected both black males and black females evenly, as shown by the data in Table 14. For both sexes, the unemployment rate has drifted upward since the mid-1970s in both absolute and relative terms. In fact, black females generally had an unemployment rate less than two times the white female rate prior to the mid-1970s, but since then the differential has generally been substantially above two to one. Black males have also experienced greater relative inequality. The absolute gap between black male and white male unemployment rates never exceeded 7.1 percent between 1960 and 1975, but has exceeded that figure every year since and stood at roughly 10 percent in the first three years of the 1980s.[11]

TABLE 14

UNEMPLOYMENT RATE, BY RACE AND SEX, FOR SELECTED YEARS

	Males			Females		
	Black	White	Black:White	Black	White	Black:White
1962	10.9	4.6	2.37	11.0	5.5	2.0
1966	6.3	2.8	2.25	8.6	4.3	2.0
1970	7.3	4.0	1.75	9.3	5.4	1.72
1974	9.8	4.4	2.23	11.3	6.1	1.85
1978	11.8	4.6	2.57	13.8	6.2	2.23
1980	14.5	6.1	2.38	14.0	6.5	2.15
1985	15.3	6.1	2.51	14.9	6.4	2.33

Source: Figures for blacks from 1962 through 1970 are from the U.S. Bureau of Labor Statistics, *Handbook of Labor Statistics*, Bulletin No. 1825 (Washington D.C.: U.S. Government Printing Office, 1974), Table 63, pp. 151-153. All figures for 1974 through 1980, and those for whites from 1962 through 1970, are from the U.S. Bureau of Labor Statistics, *Handbook of Labor Statistics* (Washington, D.C.: U.S. Government Printing Office, 1985), Table 27, pp. 69-73. Figures for 1985 are from the U.S. Bureau of Labor Statistics, *Geographic Profile of Employment and Unemployment, 1985*, Bulletin No. 2266 (Washington, D.C.: U.S. Government Printing Office, 1986), Table 1, pp. 3-7.

The employment disadvantages for blacks are greatest for the youngest members of both sexes. However, since the mid-1970s the experience of serious unemployment problems has drifted up the black age distribution.[12]

Wages and Earnings

Data on wage rates and earnings are scarce prior to the 1960s. Still, it is widely believed that the wages and earnings of blacks were considerably lower than those of whites during the first half of this century. Data reported in a study by James Smith and Finis Welch suggest that the wages of employed blacks have risen significantly since 1940.[13] This should be expected given the massive migration of blacks from low-wage southern labor markets to higher-wage nonsouthern ones, as well as the significant occupational transformation that has occurred. According to Smith and Welch, the wages of black males rose both absolutely and relatively in relation to their white counterparts. They observe that black male wages rose from 43 percent of white male wages in 1940 to 73 percent in 1980, and that wages increased every decade from 1940 to 1980, with the greatest rate of increase occurring between 1940 and 1950.

TABLE 15

RATIO OF BLACK-TO-WHITE MEDIAN USUAL WEEKLY EARNINGS OF FULL-TIME WAGE AND SALARY WORKERS, BY SEX
1967, 1969-1987

	Male	Female
1967	.69	.80
1969	.72	.83
1970	.72	.85
1971	.73	.85
1972	.75	.92
1973	.77	.91
1974	.77	.94
1975	.77	.94
1976	.78	.94
1977	.78	.94
1978	.78	.95
1979	.75	.92
1980	.77	.91
1981	.75	.93
1982	.75	.88
1983	.75	.91
1984	.75	.92
1985	.73	.90
1986	.73	.89
1987	.72	.90

Source: Figures for 1967 through 1978 are derived from the U.S. Bureau of Labor Statistics, *Handbook of Labor Statistics*, Bulletin No. 2070 (Washington, D.C.: U.S. Government Printing Office, 1980), Table 60, p. 118. Figures for 1979 through 1983 are derived from the U.S. Bureau of Labor Statistics, *Handbook of Labor Statistics*, Bulletin No. 2217 (1985). Figures for 1984 are derived from the U.S. Bureau of the Census, *Statistical Abstract of the United States: 1986*, 106th ed.

(Washington, D.C.: U.S. Government Printing Office, 1985), Table 704, p. 419.
Figures for 1985 through 1987 are derived from the *Statistical Abstract of the
United States: 1989*, 109th ed. (1989), Table 666, p. 406.

A closer examination of data from 1967 through 1987, shown in Table 15, suggests that progress for employed black males in obtaining
wage equality reversed after 1976, and that by 1985 the degree of wage
equality for employed black males had declined to the 1971 level. In
1976 the median usual weekly earnings for black males working full
time was 78 percent that of white males; by 1985 this figure had
dropped to 73 percent. Thus, while the wages and salaries of working
black males have risen considerably since the beginning of the century,
a large gap still obtains in relation to the wages and salaries of white
males, and the trend since the late 1970s has been towards increasing
wage inequality.

TABLE 16

RATIO OF BLACK-TO-WHITE, MEDIAN ANNUAL EARNINGS, BY SEX, 1967, 1969-1984

	Male	Female
1967	.57	.80
1969	.59	.85
1970	.60	.92
1971	.60	.90
1972	.62	.96
1973	.63	.93
1974	.64	.92
1975	.63	.92
1976	.63	.95
1977	.61	.88
1978	.64	.92
1979	.65	.93
1980	.63	.96
1981	.63	.92
1982	.64	.90
1983	.64	.88
1984	.63	.91

Source: All figures are derived from the U.S. Bureau of the Census, *Money Income of
Households, Families, and Persons in the United States: 1984*, Report P-20, No.
151 (Washington, D.C.: U.S. Government Printing Office, 1986), Table 28, pp.
99-101.

The wage data shown earlier in Table 15 do not reflect the impact of employment differences. Discussions of wages in the literature usually focus on those who work full time for the entire year. Earnings data take unemployment into account only to a limited extent. The data on the ratio of black-to-white median annual earnings shown in Table 16 suggest that labor market inequality is somewhat higher than what is indicated by wage ratio data. Between 1967 and 1984 the median earnings of all black male workers never exceeded 65 percent of the median earnings of white males. Moreover, by 1984 the ratio of black male to white male median earnings had fallen to 63 percent.

Yet, even these data understate the real disadvantage of black males in earning a living, because those individuals who have zero earnings during the year are excluded from the calculation. Since the late 1960s, the proportion of black males with earnings has been falling. In 1969, for example, 77.6 percent of working-age black males had some earnings. But by 1984, this was true for only 65.8 percent of them. In contrast, the proportion of white males with earnings only declined from 81.9 percent to 78.6 percent over this same period. Thus, while black males were 95 percent as likely as white males to have earnings in 1969, they were only 84 percent as likely to have earnings in 1984. Taking this factor into account, one observes that earnings for black males have not improved at all in relation to their white counterparts since the end of the 1960s.[14]

The picture for working black females shown by the data in Table 15 is somewhat different. Median usual weekly wages for black female full-time wage and salary workers had reached 95 percent of white wages by 1978. Although this ratio had declined to 90 percent by 1985, it was still considerably higher than it was for black males. Correspondingly, the wage inequality for black females was much lower than wage inequality for black males. Moreover, within particular occupations black females have achieved parity in wages. The difference in the overall wage rate arises primarily from differences in the distribution of blacks and whites across occupations. However, since the end of the 1970s, the trend has been towards declining relative wages for black females.

Unlike the case for black males, the median annual earnings for employed black females have roughly equalled the median annual earnings of white females since the early 1970s. This has occurred despite the fact that the relative employment of black females has declined. The apparent reason for this phenomenon is that employed black females are more likely to work full time for the entire year, and are also more likely to be prime-age experienced workers.

Business Ownership

As indicated in the introduction to this chapter, black business ownership has been very limited through most of the twentieth century.
Data on black business ownership prior to 1969 are limited, but those
that are available clearly establish that blacks have owned a relatively
small share of total American businesses throughout the century. The
businesses that blacks own have been small and marginal and heavily
concentrated in retail and service establishments.[15] Moreover, most of
the businesses have had no paid employees.

Since 1969 better data have become availabe which describe the
characteristics of black-owned businesses. All four censuses taken by
the Census Bureau since 1969 confirm that the black business sector
remains small and marginal. Information about the black business sector is shown in Table 17, and selected data for all American businesses
are shown in Table 18. The census suggests that blacks owned roughly
339,000 business firms in 1982, which had total receipts of 12.4 billion
dollars. This amounts to about 12.4 firms per 1000 black persons, and
about $456 in gross receipts per black person. Black businesses ac-
counted for 2 percent of all businesses and handled less than 0.2 percent
of all receipts. Blacks owned about 17 percent as many firms per capita
as the total population, and these firms generated only about 1.4 percent of the per capita receipts.

The marginality of the black business sector is also seen in the limited amounts of employment provided by black businesses. In 1982, for
example, only 11.2 percent of the 339,239 black businesses had paid
employees. The average number of paid employees per firm was only
4.3. All together these businesses employed only 165,765 workers. In
contrast, total black employment in 1982 was 9,189,000.[16]

The small black business sector remains overconcentrated in the retail trade and service area. In 1982, for example, more than 68 percent
of black businesses were in these two sectors. Black business ownership
is limited in each sector. In 1982 blacks owned almost as many service
firms per capita as whites — 98 percent as many. Yet, these firms generated fifteen times less receipts per capita. In the manufacturing and
wholesale sectors blacks owned fewer than one-tenth as many firms as
whites, and these generated 250 times less receipts per capita. In the
construction sector blacks had roughly 43 percent as many firms as
whites, and in the retail trade sector they had about 37 percent as
many. The construction sector receipts per capita were thirty-eight
times smaller and those in the retail trade sector were thirty times
smaller than the comparable figures for white firms. It is obvious that
black businesses carry little weight in every industrial sector.

TABLE 17

GROWTH IN BLACK FIRMS AND RECEIPTS FOR SELECTED INDUSTRIES IN 1972, 1977 AND 1982
(RECEIPTS IN MILLIONS OF 1982 DOLLARS)

Industry	1972		1977		1982		% Change in Number of Firms		% Change in Sales Receipts	
	Total Firms	Receipts	Total Firms	Receipts	Total Firms	Receipts	1972-77	1977-82	1972-77	1977-82
Total	187,602	$12,767	231,203	$13,771	339,239	$12,444	23.2%	46.7%	7.9%	- 9.6%
Construction	19,120	1,446	21,101	1,207	23,061	995	10.4	9.3	-16.5	-17.6
Manufacturing	3,664	840	4,243	978	4,171	988	15.8	- 1.7	16.4	1.0
Transportation & Public Utilities	21,356	826	23,061	811	24,397	795	8.0	5.8	- 1.8	- 2.0
Wholesale Trade	1,708	750	2,212	1,058	3,651	859	29.5	65.1	41.1	-18.8
Retail Trade	53,924	5,548	55,428	5,340	84,053	4,119	2.8	51.6	- 3.7	-22.9
Finance, Insurance & Real Estate	7,669	909	9,805	1,021	14,829	748	27.9	51.2	12.3	-26.7
Selected Services	66,521	2,062	101,739	3,011	147,263	3,249	52.9	44.7	46.0	7.9
Other	13,640	388	13,614	346	37,814	691	- 0.1	177.8	-10.8	99.7

Source: William O'Hare and Robert Suggs, "Embattled Black Businesses," *American Demographics* 8: 4 (April 1986): 26-29, 48-49, at table, p. 29, citing the U.S. Bureau of the Census, *1977 Survey of Minority-Owned Business Enterprises: Black*, Report No. MB 77-1, and *1982 Survey of Minority-Owned Business Enterprises: Black*, Report No. MB 82-1.

TABLE 18

TOTAL GROWTH IN FIRMS AND RECEIPTS FOR SELECTED INDUSTRIES IN 1972, 1977 AND 1982
(RECEIPTS IN BILLIONS OF 1982 DOLLARS;[a] FIRMS IN THOUSANDS)

Industry	1972 Firms	1972 Receipts	1977 Firms	1977 Receipts	1982 Firms	1982 Receipts	% Change in Number of Firms 1972-77	% Change in Number of Firms 1977-82	% Change in Sales Receipts 1972-77	% Change in Sales Receipts 1977-82
Construction	438	357.7	480	377.9	457	324.5	9.6	-10.5	5.7	-16.5
Manufacturing	321	1738.9	360	2164.9	358	1960.2	12.2	- 0.6	24.5	-10.4
Wholesale Trade	370	1596.9	383	2004.6	416	1997.9	3.5	8.6	25.5	- 3.4
Retail Trade	1780	1050.7	1855	1151.9	1923	1065.9	- 8.1	3.7	9.6	4.2
Selected Services	684	237.1	725	261.6	1262	427.0	59.9	74.1	10.3	63.2

Source: U.S. Bureau of the Census, *Statistical Abstract of the United States, 1986*, 106th ed. (Washington, D.C.: U.S. Government Printing Office, 1985), Table 1286, p. 719; Table 1334, p. 744; Table 1387, p. 774; Table 1402, p. 783; and Table 1406, p. 786; and *Statistical Abstract of the United States: 1980*, 101st ed. (1980), Table 1513, p. 851.

[a]The Consumer Price Index was used to convert all receipts to 1982 dollars.

It is also evident that even "large" black businesses are small relative to large national businesses. In fact, in 1985 the combined sales of the top one hundred black businesses of all types were only equal to the sales of the firm ranked 228th on the Fortune 500 list. Moreover, the total number of employees of the one hundred largest black businesses would only rank them at number 259.[17]

Finally, it should be noted that there are no noteworthy trends pointing toward any significant growth in black-owned businesses. Although the numbers of black-owned firms recorded in the Census Bureau's *Survey of Black Businesses* have increased in all four surveys taken since 1969, much of the increase is due to broader survey coverage.[18] Furthermore, even including the additional businesses as indicated in Table 17, receipts actually declined between 1972 and 1982 after adjusting for inflation. It thus appears that the number of more marginal black businesses is actually increasing. In short, black business ownership is still very limited in the U.S. economy, and there are no signs that this will change soon.

Income, Poverty and Wealth

Income

The consequences of black disadvantages in economic participation are reflected in statistics on income, poverty and wealth. Data on income are not generally available prior to the 1940s. However, given the almost complete dependence of blacks on labor earnings, the overwhelming concentration of the black work force in the low-wage South, and the unfavorable occupational distributions of black workers in all regions of the country, it is reasonable to infer that blacks had low incomes absolutely and relative to whites during the first half of the twentieth century. Most of the following discussion will focus on data for the second half of the century, and is designed to corroborate earlier observations concerning the economic status of blacks based on their participation in economic activities.

TABLE 19

PER CAPITA MONEY INCOME, BY RACE,
1967-1984 (1984 DOLLARS)

	Black	White	Black:White
1967	4,362	8,101	.54
1968	4,717	8,610	.55
1969	4,992	8,993	.56
1970	5,000	8,972	.56
1971	5,288	9,223	.57
1972	5,711	9,852	.58
1973	5,892	10,193	.58
1974	5,725	9,851	.58
1975	5,736	9,788	.59
1976	5,996	10,138	.59
1977	6,126	10,456	.59
1978	6,423	10,822	.59
1979	6,359	10,838	.59
1980	6,056	10,378	.58
1981	5,858	10,255	.57
1982	5,768	10,252	.56
1983	6,000	10,556	.57
1984	6,277	10,939	.57

Source: U.S. Bureau of the Census, *Money Income of Households, Families, and Persons in the U.S.: 1984*, P-60/151 (Washington, D.C.: U.S. Government Printing Office, 1985), Table 27, p. 98.

Table 19 shows per capita income data from 1967 until 1984, which reinforce the earlier findings about black economic status during that time period. First, it is apparent that the economic gaps between blacks and whites are still very large. In 1984, per capita income for blacks was $6,277 compared to $10,939 for whites. Blacks thus received about fifty-seven cents for every dollar received by whites. The most striking thing about the income data, though, is the fact that by this measure little or no progress has been made in improving the relative economic status of blacks since the end of the 1960s. While the absolute level of per capita income in the mid-1980s was up from the levels of the early 1970s, the relative level was lower than it had been since 1972.

Although per capita income data are not readily available for earlier years, it seems likely that the current relative income of blacks is only slightly higher than it was during the 1950s. An earlier estimate by this author and Julian Ellison suggests that black per capita income was between 48 and 57 percent of the income of whites during the 1950s and early 1960s.[19] It is very likely that the income of blacks was in the range of 40 to 50 percent of the income of whites prior to 1950. It is therefore not unsound to observe that the gains have been quite modest for the century taken as a whole.

As shown in Table 20, the pattern for family income is similar to the pattern for per capita income. The median family income rose for blacks in the nation as a whole in both absolute and relative terms between 1959 and 1969. Even though the absolute level of family income probably rose during the 1950s, the ratio of black-to-white family income peaked in 1953 at 57 percent and declined to about 52 percent in 1959.[20] Since 1969, the absolute level of family income has fluctuated with the business cycle, but has clearly drifted downward since the mid-1970s. Moreover, the ratio of black-to-white family income has shown a decline since 1970, and has drifted back to the level attained in the mid-1960s and early 1950s.[21] Hence, the gains that were made in relative family income during the 1960s have been eroding since the mid-1970s.

TABLE 20

MEDIAN FAMILY INCOME, BY RACE,
1959-1985 (1985 DOLLARS)

	Black	White	Black:White
1959	10,758[a]	20,827	.517
1964	13,311[a]	23,785	.600
1965	13,614[a]	24,722	.551
1966	15,550[a]	25,938	.600
1967	15,707	26,530	.592
1968	16,574	27,634	.600
1969	17,604	28,740	.613
1970	17,395	28,358	.613
1971	17,106	28,347	.603
1972	17,650	29,697	.594
1973	17,596	30,489	.577
1974	17,465	29,249	.597
1975	17,547	28,518	.615
1976	17,465	29,361	.594
1977	16,976	29,717	.571
1978	17,939	30,287	.592
1979	17,153	30,292	.566
1980	16,546	28,596	.578
1981	15,691	27,816	.564
1982	15,155	26,420	.552
1983	15,722	27,898	.565
1984	15,982	28,674	.557
1985	16,786	29,152	.576

Source: U.S. Bureau of the Census, *Money Income of Households, Families, and Persons in the United States, 1985* P-60/156 (Washington, D.C.: U.S. Government Printing Office, 1986), Table 11, p. 33-35.

[a]Figures are for blacks and other nonwhite races.

Trends in median family income have also varied by region, as seen in Table 21. In each region real median family income, that is, income after adjustments for price changes, is currently higher than it was during the 1950s. Still, in the Midwest, the median family income of blacks declined to below the levels of the 1950s during the recession years of the 1980s. The gains of blacks relative to the early 1950s have been greatest in the South where their real family income has doubled. Most of the growth in their real income occurred in the 1960s, but since then their real income has declined in all regions. Indeed, even in the South their real income fell from the mid-1970s through the early 1980s.

TABLE 21

MEDIAN FAMILY INCOME, BY REGION AND RACE, 1953-1985 (1985 DOLLARS[a])

	Northeast		Midwest[b]		South		West	
	Black	White	Black	White	Black	White	Black	White
1953	13,531	18,744	14,268	18,710	7,316	14,960	15,277	18,680
1959	15,559	22,141	14,504	20,818	7,123	18,098	16,453	23,228
1964	17,189	25,738	17,506	24,285	10,068	20,432	20,073	25,699
1969	20,667	30,132	22,695	29,922	14,708	25,725	24,304	29,931
1974	21,527	31,256	22,508	30,580	15,130	26,546	24,986	29,186
1976	19,198	29,914	21,043	30,878	16,259	27,247	23,669	29,755
1977	18,259	30,711	18,975	30,585	15,908	27,905	17,603	30,148
1978	19,240	30,927	22,571	23,146	16,239	28,263	17,824	31,081
1979	17,814	31,611	19,301	31,252	15,910	27,979	19,439	31,177
1980	17,214	29,499	18,239	29,123	15,178	26,926	22,364	29,516
1981	15,666	29,196	17,545	28,246	14,525	26,076	19,621	28,764
1982	16,418	28,764	13,788	27,748	14,534	25,727	18,394	28,134
1983	16,987	29,995	14,203	27,690	14,998	26,507	19,660	28,129
1984	16,907	30,762	14,878	28,668	15,392	26,981	19,893	29,524
1985	18,085	31,491	15,956	28,964	15,816	27,104	24,453	30,239

Source: Figures are derived from the U.S. Bureau of the Census, *Money Income of Households, Families, and Persons in the United States: 1985*, Report P-60, No. 156 (Washington, D.C.: U.S. Government Printing Office, 1987), Table 9, pp. 26-28; *1984*, Report P-60, No. 151 (1986), Table 9, pp. 26-28; *1982*, Report P-60, No. 142 (1984), Table 13, pp. 32-40; *1980*, Report P-60, No. 132 (1982), Table 14, pp. 40-42; *Money Income of Families and Persons in the United States: 1978*, Report P-60, No. 123 (1980), Table I, pp. 16-18; *Money Income in 1976 of Families and Persons in the United States*, Report P-60, No. 114 (1978), Table 12, pp. 52-55.

[a]The Consumer Price Index was used to convert figures to 1985 dollars.

[b]For the years before and including 1976, the designation "North Central" was used in place of "Midwest."

As the data in Table 21 reveal, if one ignores the year 1985 in the West, racial inequality in family income has increased steadily in all regions outside of the South since the early 1950s. In both the Northeast and the Midwest, racial inequality in family income has been at all-time highs since the mid-1970s. In 1985 the ratio of black-to-white median family income was only about 57 percent in the Northeast and 55 percent in the Midwest. This compares to ratios above 70 percent in the 1950s and 1960s. In the West the ratio of black family-to-white family income has generally fluctuated between 60 and 70 percent since 1970, as compared to between 70 and 80 percent in the 1950s and 1960s. Only in the South has there been general improvement in the relative level of black family income since the 1950s. During the 1950s, relative black family income in the South actually fell from 50 percent to 40 percent. Most of the gain in the South since that time took place in the 1960s, when the ratio of black-to-white median family income rose to 57 percent by 1970. Since then, the ratio has fluctuated between 54 and 57 percent.

Poverty

Poverty data have been available only since 1959. Table 22 summarizes the available data. Poverty undoubtedly was higher prior to World War II. However, the level of poverty in 1960 for blacks was probably as high as it had been since World War II. The black poverty rate for the nation as a whole dropped sharply in absolute terms from 55.1 percent to 33.1 percent between 1959 and 1970. Black poverty rates declined from 36 to 40 percent in all regions during the 1960s. But the ratio of black-to-white poverty rates increased primarily because the white poverty rate decreased faster in the South. Thus, while blacks had been 2.5 times more likely to be poor than whites in 1960, they were nearly 3.5 times more likely in 1970. Racial inequality as measured by the ratio of black-to-white poverty rates increased in both the Midwest and the South during this period. Yet, in view of the much higher initial rates of poverty among blacks, the absolute decline in the poverty rate was much greater for blacks than for whites.

Between 1970 and this writing (1988), the drop in the black poverty rate has been nominal. Nationally, the black poverty rate of 33.1 percent in 1987 was equal to the rate for 1970. The trends have differed among the regions. Black poverty has declined most in the South, where the rate dropped from 42.6 percent in 1970 to 34.5 percent in 1987. Since 1970 the pace of decline in the South has been significantly slower than it was in the 1960s. In the West the black poverty rate remained fairly steady, reaching 24.3 percent in 1987 as compared

TABLE 22

POVERTY RATES, BY REGION AND RACE, 1959-1987

Region	1959			1970			1980			1987		
	Black	White	Black: White	Black	White	Black: White	Black	White	Black: White	Black	White	Black: White
U.S. Total	55.1%	18.1%	3.0	33.1%	8.1%	4.1	32.5%	10.2%	3.2	33.1%	10.5%	3.2
Northeast	n.a.	n.a.	n.a.	20.0	7.6	2.6	30.7	8.9	3.5	28.8	8.9	3.2
Midwest (N. Central)	n.a.	n.a.	n.a.	25.7	8.9	2.9	33.3	8.9	3.7	36.6	9.9	3.7
South	68.5	26.8	2.6	42.6	12.4	3.4	35.1	12.2	2.9	34.5	11.5	3.0
West	n.a.	n.a.	n.a.	20.4	10.6	1.9	19.0	10.4	1.8	24.3	11.5	2.1
Northwest	34.3	14.8	2.3	19.1	8.9	2.2	29.6	9.3	3.2	n.a.	n.a.	n.a.

Source: Figures for 1959 to 1980 are from the U.S. Bureau of the Census, *Characteristics of the Population Below the Poverty Level: 1980*, P-60/133 (Washington, D.C.: U.S. Government Printing Office, 1982), Table 4, pp. 19-20. Figures for 1987 are from the U.S. Bureau of the Census, *Money Income and Poverty Status in the United States: 1987*, P-60/161, using advance data from the March 1988 *Current Population Survey* (Washington, D.C.: U.S. Government Printing Office, 1988), Table 18, pp. 34-35.

n.a. = Not Available.

to 20.4 in 1970, while black poverty was up sharply in the Midwest and the Northeast. In both of the latter two regions, a good portion of the reduction in poverty that occurred during the 1960s was lost in the 1970s.

Racial inequality as measured by the ratio of black-to-white poverty rates has declined in the South but, relative to 1970 levels, is now higher in both the Midwest and the Northeast. Once again, the pattern of change in racial inequality has varied by regions. It should also be noted that despite the improvement in the South, racial inequality and absolute levels of poverty there generally have been higher than in any other region (though the Midwest has now overtaken the South as the region of greatest absolute and relative black poverty). The income and poverty trends thus mirror the labor market trends discussed earlier.

Wealth

Information concerning wealth holdings is scarce, and there are no meaningful trend data. However, a recent survey by the Census Bureau has provided an up-to-date picture of relative black wealth holdings. (See Tables 23 and 24.) Wealth has always been distributed more unequally than income. This continues to be the case today according to the Census Bureau report. While median black income equals about 57 percent of median white income, median net worth for blacks in 1984 was only $3,397, compared to $39,135 for whites. Thus, median black wealth was only about 9 percent of the median wealth holdings of whites.

TABLE 23

PERCENT OF HOUSEHOLDS OWNING, BY ASSEST TYPE AND BY RACE: 1984

	Black	**White**	**Black:White**
Number of Households (Thousands)	9,509	75,343	
Interest-Earning Assets at Financial Institutions	43.8	75.4	.58
Other Interest-Earning Assets	2.1	9.4	.22
Regular Checking Accounts	32.0	56.9	.56

Stocks and Mutual Fund Shares	5.4	22.0	.25
Equity in Business or Profession	4.0	14.0	.29
Equity in Motor Vehicles	65.0	88.5	.73
Equity in Own Home	43.8	67.3	.65
Equity in Rental Property	6.6	10.1	.65
Other Real Estate Equity	3.3	10.9	.36
Mortgages	0.1	3.3	.30
U.S. Savings Bonds	7.4	16.1	.46
IRA or KEOGH Accounts	5.1	21.4	.24
Other Assets	0.7	3.9	.18

Source: U.S. Bureau of the Census, *Current Population Reports: Household Wealth and Asset Ownership: 1984*, P-70/7 (Washington, D.C.: U.S. Government Printing Office, 1986), Table 1, pp. 8-11.

TABLE 24

MEDIAN VALUE OF HOLDINGS FOR ASSET OWNERS, BY RACE: 1984

	Black	White	Black:White
Number of Households (Thousands)	9,509	75,343	
Net Worth	$3,397	$39,135	.09
Interest-Earning Assets at Financial Institutions	739	3,457	.21
Other Interest-Earning Assets	a	9,826	—
Regular Checking Accounts	318	457	.70
Stocks and Mutual Fund Shares	2,777	3,908	.71
Equity in Business or Profession	2,054	7,113	.29

Equity in Motor Vehicles	2,691	4,293	.63
Equity in Own Home	24,077	41,999	.57
Equity in Rental Property	27,291	34,516	.79
Other Real Estate Equity	10,423	15,488	.67
U.S. Savings Bonds	200	305	.66
IRA or KEOGH Accounts	2,450	4,922	.50
Other Assets	a	13,089	—

Source: U.S. Bureau of the Census, *Current Population Reports: Household Wealth and Asset Ownership: 1984*, P-70/7 (Washington, D.C.: U.S. Government Printing Office, 1986), Table 5, pp. 22-25.

[a]Denotes base is too small

As the data in Tables 23 and 24 show, black wealth holdings are lower because blacks are less likely to own any given type of asset, and those blacks who do own a particular asset typically own less than whites. The ratio of the proportion of blacks holding a given asset to the proportion of whites owning the same type of asset varied from .18 to .73, that is, blacks owned none of these assets at the same rate as whites. Blacks came closest to equality in the ownership of assets related to everyday household needs. They were less likely to hold investment and business types of assets. The median value of black asset holdings relative to white holdings varied from a low of 21 percent to a high of 79 percent. The relative size of median black asset holdings was least in business and interest-bearing accounts, and greatest in real estate, stocks and mutual funds.

It is clear from the data that relative black wealth holdings are very small. In fact, aggregate black wealth in 1984 totaled only 192.5 billion dollars. If blacks had parity in the ownership of wealth, their total wealth would have been about 820.9 billion dollars.

Analysis of Twentieth-Century Trends

The twentieth century has been one of tremendous economic change for black Americans. The principal dynamic factor in this change has been the movement of the black work force out of its heavy concentration in low-wage agricultural and domestic service pursuits into higher-wage and more diversified industrial employment. Thus, the economic position of the black work force as the twentieth century draws to a close is entirely different from what it was at the outset of the century. Yet, substantial disadvantages remain.

In the introduction to this chapter, five major forces were identified as determinants in the evolution of black economic status during this century. These are market developments, racial inequality and discrimination, black ownership of human and material resources, black self-help activities, and the evolution of government policies. Each of these factors, alone and together, have helped to determine the path of black progress over the century.

The major factor influencing black economic status in the twentieth century has been the evolution of the economic structure, which, in large measure, has determined the range of opportunities in the society. The distribution of the available economic opportunities between blacks and whites has depended on the operations of markets, the competitiveness of blacks, and the extent of discrimination. Over the century, discrimination has influenced both the allocation of opportunities to earn income and the distribution of opportunities to acquire human capital. Black self-help efforts have operated through individual and collective efforts to gain human capital, develop businesses and combat discrimination. Finally, public policy has influenced the structure of opportunities as well as the rules of the game. A brief exposition of the role of each factor will clarify this presentation's explanation of twentieth-century trends.

Developments in the market have affected the range of opportunities within the society. In particular, growth and structural change in the economy alter the level and nature of demand for labor and other resources. Since the primary resource owned by blacks at the beginning of the century was labor, the evolving demand for labor was the major market development affecting black economic status. The decline in the relative demand for labor in the agricultural sector and an increase in the relative demand for labor in the industrial sector were the main engines driving the black labor market transformation. The dimensions of this transformation have been discussed already. The major cause of this change was technological progress in both the agricultural and nonagricultural sectors, which increased the productivity of labor. In addition, other developments which reduced the comparative advantage of southern agriculture also affected the demand for agricultural labor in the South. The net consequence of these evolving market forces was the wholesale displacement of black workers in southern rural agriculture. Simultaneously, there was an increase in the demand for black industrial workers in the South, North and West.

These developments in both agricultural and nonagricultural industries set the stage for a major black economic transformation. The wrenching uprooting of millions of blacks in the agricultural regions of the South is well-known. Having lost jobs in agriculture, these blacks had little choice except to seek to secure some of the expanding opportunities outside of the agricultural sector, most of which were outside the South. But in seeking employment opportunities in the nonagricultural sector, blacks faced tough competition from white labor, and had difficulty attaining equal access to jobs, especially good jobs, in the industrial sector.

The ability of blacks to move into industrial employment was hampered further by the discrimination they faced in both the North and the South, as well as by their lower levels of education and training. In the South, discrimination confined blacks to a lower caste, prohibiting their participation in many nontraditional roles. In the North, discrimination against blacks was less rigid: There were fewer absolute restrictions on black participation. Still, the effect of discrimination was to lower the probability of blacks gaining access to positions which were desired by white workers. Discrimination thus constrained the equal participation of blacks in the labor market, as well as limited their ability to gain the educational credentials and skills needed to compete on equal terms in an industrial setting.

The consequences of discrimination and inferior preparation are clear. First, because the South was more agricultural than the North and blacks in the South were overconcentrated in agriculture, the greatest need for new jobs was in the South. Agricultural jobs in the South for blacks not only declined as a share of jobs, but also declined in absolute numbers throughout most of the twentieth century. Although blacks did gain some jobs in the nonagricultural sector, their gains in the South were not nearly sufficient to offset their losses due to the decline of the agricultural sector.

In fact, the absolute level of black employment declined in the South. In 1910 about 4.6 million blacks were gainfully employed in the South; in 1970 only 3.8 million blacks were employed there, a decrease of about 800,000 jobs. (See Table 1.) White employment in the South increased by nearly 7 million over the same period from 12.3 million to about 19.0 million. (See Table 2.) Clearly, blacks were not succeeding in the competition with southern white workers. Blacks failed to make proportional gains in nonagricultural pursuits in the South throughout the first seventy years of the century. As a result, many blacks migrated North. Fortunately, they were more successful at finding jobs in the expanding industries of the North and West. Black employment in these regions grew substantially throughout the century, except for the depression years of the 1930s. Between 1910 and 1970, black employment outside of the South increased by almost three million jobs. However, this good fortune in the North came to an end in the early 1970s. The rate of black job growth in the North and West has declined significantly since 1970 as these regions have experienced economic decline and transformation.

White discrimination and inadequate preparation also restricted black access to better jobs in the North and South, although the restrictions on black industrial employment were greater in the South. As a consequence, black penetration into the industrial job market, especially in the early part of the century, was disproportionately into lower-level jobs. Nonetheless, the industrial and occupational transformation that occurred during the first twenty years of the century improved black living standards, since even low-level industrial workers were better off than low-wage agricultural and domestic service workers.

The willingness of industrial employers to hire blacks throughout most of the century appears to have depended on the tightness of the labor market. Whenever there have been labor shortages, employers usually have been willing to hire more blacks. In times of labor surplus, blacks have been hired at a lower rate and displaced at a higher rate. The cliche, "last hired, first fired," seems to have been a true characterization of black labor market status throughout most of the century.

Blacks have engaged in self-help activities throughout the century to improve their economic status. Such efforts have frequently met with collective and individual resistance from individual whites, white-controlled institutions and the government. Black self-help activities have taken two main forms. First, there have been individual efforts by members of millions of black families to prepare themselves and take advantage of whatever opportunities existed in society. These individual efforts, though encouraged by group norms, have, for the most part, been the result of individual blacks pursuing their own self-interest as best they could. One of the most noteworthy achievements of this individual self-help activity was the massive migration of southern blacks to the North and West. In every decade of the twentieth century up to 1970, substantial numbers of blacks have uprooted from their traditional southern homes to seek better opportunities in other regions. Net migration from the South averaged roughly 1.5 million blacks in each of the three decades following World War II. This remarkable movement, without any substantial government or other external support, permitted blacks to take advantage of the faster growth of demand for industrial labor in the North.

Another achievement of individual black self-help has been the conspicuous increase in black educational levels despite the hardships of poverty and inferior schools. Census Bureau data indicate that in 1890, fifty-seven out of every one hundred blacks were illiterate; by 1979 this figure had declined to under two of every one hundred.[22] Most of this improvement occurred before 1940. Since 1940 the median years of school completed by the adult black population have more than doubled, and the gap between black and white median attainment by 1987 had dropped from 3.1 years to three-tenths of a year.[23]

Individual black self-help efforts to create greater levels of business ownership and control have produced individual success stories, but have had only a limited impact on the aggregate ownership position of the black population as a whole. The small and marginal character of most black businesses has been called out already. This characteristic of black economic status has changed little over the course of the century, despite black self-help activities in this direction.

The second major form of black self-help has been collective action to change systemic barriers to progress. At the level of the individual, black self-help efforts essentially rely on one either accommodating oneself to the existing system or working out exceptions. At the collective level, black self-help efforts attempt to bring about systemic changes that will benefit the group as a whole. These collective activities have aimed at altering both internal and external barriers to black progress, with the main focus for most of the century on changing externally-controlled systemic barriers. The major thrust of these efforts has focused on reducing racial discrimination and racial inequality in all aspects of economic life. Such efforts have aimed at influencing the behavior of individuals as well as that of public and private sector institutions; at changing public policy, laws, attitudes, mores, regulations and conduct which permit discrimination; and at redistributing resources to end racial inequality in income, ownership and human capital.

As a result of self-help activities against discrimination, the most extreme forms of racist behavior by unions and public sector employers outside of the South was dampened by the 1950s. Some success was also achieved in getting favorable federal court rulings and executive orders against discrimination starting in the 1940s, but most of these successes occurred between the mid-1950s and the early 1970s. During this period, substantial progress was made in establishing laws and programs to address discrimination and to promote the attainment of equal treatment for blacks and other minorities.

Although substantial controversy surrounds the impact of these changes, it seems that they did help in relation to the economic status of blacks. Their major impact appears to have been the erosion of the caste system, especially in the South where it had been entrenched for generations. Thus, the major impact was probably felt in the South.

Indeed, the timing of black gains in the South corresponds to the period following the successful assault on the institutions that legalized and legitimized the system of Jim Crow. Yet the changes have so far proved inadequate to eliminate completely racial discrimination either in the North, the West or the South. After the initial success of establishing new, more aggressive equal opportunity programs such as affirmative action in the 1960s and early 1970s, a period of retrenchment in implementation and interpretation emerged in the late 1970s and continued throughout the 1980s.

Black self-help has had only limited success in promoting policies to eliminate racial inequality in ownership and human capital. Most of the limited success of this strategy occurred during the 1960s and 1970s with the implementation of the War on Poverty. A variety of educational and employment programs to increase black human capital were implemented during this period. Much smaller efforts under the general rubric of black capitalism were also begun. Employment, training and educational programs clearly had some initial success at increasing black human capital. Educational gaps have closed significantly, for example. However, the programs have never been implemented in sufficient magnitude to eliminate undue human capital differences. The programs to promote black capitalism were so marginal, relative to the existing capital gaps, that they have had very minimal impact on overall relative ownership by blacks. Given the severe curtailment of both types of programs in the 1980s, the relative gaps in ownership are no doubt on the rise again. Ownership gaps remain extremely large as the end of the twentieth century approaches; consequently, blacks remain vulnerable and dependent on the good will of whites.

As one peers back across the century, one observes that the government has played a secondary and reactive role in the evolution of the economic status of blacks. Throughout the century, government has essentially followed a laissez-faire policy in relation to the evolution of the economic structure. Accordingly, there have been only minimal efforts to assist blacks in adjusting to the disruption caused by economic transformation and growth. In general, few explicit attempts have ever been made to direct economic development to provide opportunities for blacks who have been displaced or passed over by economic change. Little help was provided to those blacks displaced by the agricultural decline in the rural South, or to the blacks who have experienced great difficulties in consequence of the technoindustrial transformation occurring at the century's end. Blacks experiencing economic difficulties have been left to fend for themselves.

Moreover, the government generally has played a marginal role in dealing with the social cost created by the economic dislocation of blacks. Prior to 1930, nothing of note was done about such problems in a systematic fashion. The Great Depression did lead to the provision of a variety of what are now called "safety net" programs. Blacks who had been excluded from economic participation did benefit from some of these programs, but they were not structured to have a major impact on blacks. The War on Poverty of the 1960s did add to the number of safety net programs and also resulted in more equitable black participation in existing programs. But even with the changes of the 1960s, the efforts in this regard must be judged as minimal. The assistance afforded has been inadequate, and has usually been provided begrudgingly and in ways that stigmatize.

For most of the century, government generally has also not supported black efforts to eliminate discrimination. In fact, in the South until the late 1960s, state and local governments supported the system of racial discrimination. For a brief shining moment during the late 1960s and early 1970s, the federal government was actively engaged in promoting equal opportunity for blacks. This effort ended in the mid-1970s, though, and government has once more become at best a passive actor. Many of the activist policies of the all-too-brief civil rights era have been placed on hold.

Finally, it should be noted that government efforts on behalf of blacks generally have been in response to demands placed before the government through the self-help efforts of blacks and their allies. The general posture of government in the absence of such pressure from civil rights advocates has been to give low priority to the collective advancement of blacks. In the normal course of events, laissez-faire is actively promoted, and government actively has fostered the interests of the white population without regard to the impact this would have on blacks.

In summary, the five major forces affecting black economic status during the twentieth century have been economic growth and transformation, white racism, black ownership of human and material resources, black self-help efforts and government policies. Economic growth by and large has responded to market forces. Economic growth and transformation created the conditions which permitted changes in the structural character of black participation in the American economy by displacing blacks in agriculture and creating opportunities for their employment in nonagricultural pursuits. White racism and discrimination have served to block the equal allocation of opportunities to blacks when these opportunities were desired by whites. The role and impact of white racism have varied with the overall state of the economy. White racism and discrimination have decreased over the century, especially in the South, but they continue to be substantial obstacles. Black self-help activities have been instrumental in enabling blacks to gain access to opportunities. The migration north and the educational upgrading of the black population have played major roles in permitting blacks to penetrate nonagricultural employment sectors. Antidiscrimination efforts have had major impacts on permitting occupational upgrading, especially in the public sector. Increasing the level of black ownership and economic development efforts has been less successful, though. Finally, the self-help movement had some temporary success during the 1960s in getting the federal government to play an active role in improving the economic status of blacks.

As one scrutinizes the role of government, one cannot but conclude that it has not been a major initiating force in improving the economic status of blacks. In general, the government has adopted a laissez-faire policy in relation to economic change, which negatively affects blacks. It has, for the most part, simply reacted to broad sociopolitical forces in formulating and implementing its policies. For much of the century, government at the state and local levels resisted black efforts for advancement. Nonetheless, black self-help efforts did have some success in turning this situation around.

Prospects for the Twenty-First Century

Taken as a whole, blacks have made notable economic progress during the twentieth century. Incomes are higher, poverty rates are substantially lower, and occupational status has improved. They have also made substantial educational gains, and a government policy of supporting discrimination has been reversed. Still, blacks remain a long way from attaining parity, and their economic status has improved only in the South in recent decades. In the North, black economic status has actually deteriorated in absolute and relative terms since the mid-1970s. Indeed, industrial transformation is currently displacing blacks in the North just as agricultural transformation displaced them in the South in earlier decades of the century. Moreover, just as southern blacks had limited success in obtaining jobs created by the new economic structure which replaced agriculture, northern blacks are also having difficulties obtaining a proportionate share of the newly-emerging jobs that are replacing blue-collar employment.

Prospects for the twenty-first century will depend on the same forces that have operated in the twentieth century. The current transformation is eroding the living standards of a great many American workers. Highly-paid, goods-producing jobs are being replaced by low-paying service and trade jobs. Professional and technical jobs requiring a high

degree of education and/or training are being created, but only in sufficient numbers to employ a minority of the work force. The overall rate
of jobs creation has been inadequate to accommodate the growth in the
population, as well as increases in labor force participation by youth
and women. These developments suggest that there will be substantial
economic pressures on blacks in the future as a result of the economic
changes that have accompanied the emergence and continued matura-
tion of technologic society. And so, the prospects for blacks in the
twenty-first century will depend, in no little measure, on the success of
the economy in reversing the emerging patterns in the current economic transformation.

White racism and discrimination also will continue to play an important role. Over the 1980s, whites have once again revealed a preference for a reduction in efforts to achieve racial equality. White interest
in maintaining the status quo has had an adverse effect on efforts to
give blacks a fair share of scarce opportunities. In the absence of countervailing pressure, one can expect a tendency for white selfishness to
rise if economic trends do not improve. If developments in the North in
the 1980s are indicative of things to come, the increasing conservatism
of whites could well have a devastating impact on black economic status if the economy were to contract severely.

Self-help efforts will thus remain crucial to the success of blacks in
the twenty-first century. At present, black self-help is focused primarily on individual efforts to acquire education, attain good opportunities
and start small businesses. These efforts are unlikely to be sufficient to
bring about black progress in the next century, if current economic and
social trends were to continue. The two major impediments affecting
blacks at the end of the 1980s are white conservatism and inadequate
opportunities. These will not be changed substantially by individual
black self-help efforts.

Collective self-help will be required if blacks are to improve their
chances of making progress. These efforts should focus primarily on
addressing important, externally-controlled systemic barriers to black
progress. Three important barriers must be addressed. First, more effective affirmative action efforts by the government should be sought.
These efforts should emphasize *results*, and should focus on eliminating
the glaring and increasing disparities between blacks and whites in education as well as in the ownership of the country's businesses. This
affirmative action effort may be thought of as reparations for the severe
cost imposed on blacks by centuries of racism and discrimination.
Blacks will have little prospect of attaining economic parity in the
early part of the twenty-first century without a considerable effort to
eliminate the existing disparities in ownership of human capital and

material resources. Second, a concerted effort should be made to reduce the overall level of unwarranted inequality in the economy. This should include improving the wage structure, drastically reducing unemployment, providing an adequate social safety net, and eliminating the persisting disparities in wealth and ownership. Finally, blacks also should increase their efforts to ensure that government policy leads to a better economic future. Blacks should aim at encouraging the government to adopt policies that will permit the evolution of a technologic structure which will permit full utilization of all human resources at adequate levels of compensation. This implies a government policy which is activist rather than laissez-faire. Put differently, much of the thrust of black self-help efforts should focus on utilizing the government as a more effective instrument to promote progressive social policies.

If blacks can once more find the internal energy to organize the self-help effort to bring about effective national policies, then prospects for the twenty-first century can be bright. Should this not happen, blacks will continue to be battered by the forces of laissez-faire, much as they have been since their sojourn in America began. The increasing complexity and interdependence of the world suggest that laissez-faire policies may be more ineffective in the future than they have been in the past. If this is correct, then black economic development under laissez-faire will indeed turn out to be an impossible dream.

NOTES

[1]See *Plessy* v. *Ferguson*, 163 U.S. 537 (1896).

[2]White-collar workers include owners, proprietors and tradesmen in the trade sector as well as those workers classified as "Other." In 1890, trade was included in the transportation and communication category. Given the 7 to 8 percent estimate for this category in 1910 and 1930, a rough guess would indicate a maximum of about 8 to 9 percent of the white work force to be in the trade sector in 1890, leaving an estimated 5 to 14 percent in the white-collar category.

[3]Gunnar Myrdal, *An American Dilemma: The Negro Problem and Modern Democracy*, 3d ed. (New York: Harper and Row, 1962), Vol. I, p. 236, Table 1.

[4]Ibid.

[5]The calculations in this and the next few paragraphs are based on the data in Tables 5 and 6. Only the nontraditional occupations have been included.

[6]This discussion is based on data from the 1950, 1960 and 1970 decennial censuses. These data are not reported separately on the tables included in this chapter.

[7]Regional data not shown separately were derived from the same sources identified in Tables 5 and 6. See, for instance, the U.S. Bureau of the Census, *1980 Census of the Population: Detailed Population Characteristics*, U.S. Summary, Part B: Regions, Report No. PC 80-1-D1-B (Washington, D.C.: U.S. Government Printing Office, 1980), Table 323, pp. 385-424.

[8]See Table 7.

[9]John Cummings for the U.S. Bureau of the Census, *Negro Population 1790-1915* (Washington, D.C.: Government Printing Office, 1918), Table 2, p. 503.

[10]U.S. Bureau of Labor Statistics, *Handbook of Labor Statistics*, Bulletin No. 2217 (1985), Table 25, p. 64; *Geographic Profile of Employment and Unemployment: 1984*, Bulletin No. 2234 (May 1985), Table 1, pp. 3-7; and *Geographic Profile of Employment and Unemployment: 1985*, Bulletin No. 2266 (September 1986), Table 1, pp. 3-7. Swinton has discussed recent trends in black economic status in several articles. See David Swinton, "The Economic Status of the Black Population" and similarly titled articles in National Urban League, *The State of Black America: 1983, 1986, 1987*, and *1988* (New York: National Urban League, 1983, 1986, 1987, and 1988), pp. 45-114 (1983), 1-21 (1986), 49-73 (1987), and 129-152 (1988).

[11]U.S. Bureau of the Census, *Statistical Abstract of the United States: 1984*, 104th ed. (Washington, D.C.: U.S. Government Printing Office, 1983), Table 699, p. 422; U.S. Bureau of Labor Statistics, *Geographic Profile of Employment and Unemployment: 1983*, Bulletin No. 2216 (October 1984), Table 1, pp. 3-7; and *Geographic Profile: 1984* and *1985*, op. cit., note 10.

[12]See references cited in note 10.

[13]James P. Smith and Finis R. Welch, *Closing the Gap: Forty Years of Economic Progress for Blacks* (Santa Monica, CA: Rand Corporation, 1986), p. vii.

[14]For a discussion on this issue, see William Darity and Samuel L. Myers, Jr., "Changes in Black-White Income Inequality, 1968-1978: A Decade of Progress?" *Review of Black Political Economy* 10: 4 (Summer 1980): 355-379; Richard B. Freeman, "Changes in the Labor Market for Black Americans, 1948-72," *Brookings Papers on Economic Activity* 4: 1 (1973): 67-137; Richard Butler and James Heckman, "The Government's Impact on the Labor Market Status of Black Americans: A Critical Review," in Leonard Hausman, et al., eds., *Equal Rights and Industrial Relations* (Madison, WI: Industrial Relations Research Association, 1977), pp. 235-281; and Charles Brown, "Black-White Earnings Ratios Since the Civil Rights Act of 1964: The Importance of Labor Market Dropouts," *Quarterly Journal of Economics* 99: 1 (February 1984): 31-44.

[15]See discussions in Andrew F. Brimmer, "The Negro in the National Economy," in John P. Davis, ed., *The American Negro Reference Book* (Englewood Cliffs, NJ: Prentice-Hall Inc., 1966), pp. 251-336; Myrdal, op. cit. note 3, chapter 14; and E. Franklin Frazier, *Black Bourgeoisie* (New York: The Free Press, 1957), pp. 53-59.

[16]U.S. Bureau of the Census, *Statistical Abstract of the United States: 1989*, 109th ed. (Washington, D.C.: U.S. Government Printing Office, 1989), Table 622, p. 377.

[17]Data for the top one hundred black businesses were taken from *Black Enterprise* 15: 11 (June 1985): 97-105; data regarding the Fortune 500 were taken from *Fortune* 111: 9 (April 1985): 266-284. (Editor's note: In 1987, Reginald F. Lewis' TLC Group purchased Beatrice International Food Company for $985 million and formed the TLC Beatrice International Holdings Incorporated, which in 1988 had sales of $1.958 billion. This is the largest black-owned company. Indeed, the only other black-owned companies to have sales in excess of $200 million in 1988, which were insufficient to make the Fortune 500 list, were Johnson Publishing Co., Inc., and the Philadelphia Coca-Cola Bottling Co., Inc., with sales of $216.5 and $210 million, respectively. See *Black Enterprise* 19: 11 (June 1989): 199.

[18]U.S. Bureau of the Census, *1982 Survey of Minority-Owned Businesses: Black*, Report No. MB 82-1 (Washington, D.C.: U.S. Government Printing Office, 1985), p. v.

[19]David H. Swinton and Julian Ellison, *Aggregate Personal Income of the Black Population in the U.S.A.: 1947-1980* (New York: Black Economic Research Center, 1973), Table 11, p. 32.

[20]Brimmer, op. cit. note 15, Table II, p. 259.

[21]See Table 20 in the text.

[22]U.S. Bureau of the Census, *Current Population Reports: Population Characteristics*, Report P-20, No. 99 (Washington, D.C.: U.S. Government Printing Office, 1960), Table A, p. 2; and U.S. Bureau of the Census, *Statistical Abstract of the United States: 1982-83*, 103d ed. (Washington, D.C.: U.S. Government Printing Office, 1982), Table 229, p. 145.

[23]U.S. Bureau of the Census, *Statistical Abstract of the United States: 1989*, 109th ed. (Washington, D.C.: U.S. Government Printing Office, 1989), Table 213, p. 131.

BLACK POLITICS: MOBILIZATION FOR EMPOWERMENT

Ronald W. Walters

Howard University

Introduction

Any serious study of the future impels one to grapple not only with objective trends, but also with the past and present subjective structure of social relations out of which such trends emerge, persist and change. This insight is not new in relation to race relations, as Morris Janowitz has suggested:

> Attitudes toward minority groups, especially concerning their human dignity and political rights, constitute key indicators of social change and social control. . . . Indicators of sociopolitical change must do more than measure income, education and well-being; they must be used to assess the trends in mutual respect, which is an essential element of effective social control.[1]

Problems of objectively different social status have bred a lack of mutual respect that has caused conflict between blacks and whites in the United States. A racial cleavage has existed in the society which reflects this social distance, and it continues to impede the achievement of societal harmony. This has prevented the society not only from having peace and internal stability, but also from achieving other generally valued objectives that are necessary to the fulfillment of the promise of democracy.

The rigid institutionalization of a system of white social control attendant to the system of slavery has slowly given way to more benign forms of black subordination which have been described as "internal colonialism."[2] Pierre van den Berghe, for example, has said that the paternalistic form of social control has resulted in a political and economic powerlessness that has consistently inhibited black social mobility.[3] Thus, the accuracy of any description of the nature of the racial cleavage would appear to depend upon the degree to which paternalism as a contributory factor to racial subordination manifests itself in any given period of the society's history.

Racial subordination in the United States in its various forms has produced what Martin Kilson has called the "politicization" of ethnicity, a term meant to indicate that racial conflict (or the politicization process) caused a movement toward "Black ethnocentric revitalization," especially in the 1960s.[4] This view, shared by others, is that the process occurred "within a framework not of rigid socio-political constraints upon Negroes but of steady modification of the social parameters dividing blacks and whites in American society."[5] Kilson's position appears to conflict with that of Lewis Coser, who posits that the intensity of social conflict is associated with the elasticity of the social system.[6] Moreover, subjective data do not support Kilson. Attitude surveys in the period from 1968 to 1971, taken at the height of the urban rebellions, indicated that blacks were skeptical of harmonious social possibilities based on their strongly negative evaluation of the severity of social constraints.[7] The evidence appears to suggest that what matters most profoundly is perception. Indeed, even if the material and legal aspects of the condition of blacks did improve throughout the 1960s, there remained a strong perception of continued oppression, which reinforced the will to oppose its future manifestations.

The existence of racial subordination has caused some scholars to suggest that the response of black politics to paternalistic social control has been an orientation toward change in the social status of blacks, and that this function has distinguished it from "the status-quo-oriented politics of the white society."[8] In attempting to use politics to achieve change in the status of blacks, another scholar has suggested that modern efforts may be distinguished from older ones by the fact that in the various theaters of activity, blacks are not only attempting to achieve the *right* of political participation, but also addressing the *reasons* for doing so as a sign of the refinement of their strategies of political participation.[9] These two thoughts give one indications of both the content and strategy of modern black politics.

There are two major theaters of black political activity: the internal system of patterns of interaction and participation within institutions controlled by blacks; and the external system of formal, white-dominated decisionmaking institutions. While internal black politics is often related to mobilization activity addressed to the major political institutions, there are areas of internal autonomy where decisions are made that have important consequences. One such area is the selection and organization of various kinds of leadership and initiatives addressed to specific issues. An intriguing aspect of this process is that blacks must put the tactics of autonomous mobilization into operation in order to participate at the community level and in systemic relations at the national level simultaneously, in order to maximize the achievement of their goals.

This chapter will discuss these two key attributes of what might be regarded as the comprehensive "black political system," in an effort to describe and explain its dynamic elements. It will discuss the "community mobilization" problem in its historical and contemporary dimensions, and suggest the pattern of resource mobilization which makes participation possible in the "external system" of formal political institutions. The characterization that emerges will establish the baseline of the forms of politics against which the conditioning factors (such as the nature of the racial cleavage and the quality of the black response) might be balanced in order to make some estimates of the future course of black politics.

The Internal System: Community-Based Mobilization

Matthew Holden, Jr., provides a very useful description of community-level black politics which characterizes the regularized processes and institutions through which community-level decisions are mediated.[10] He observes that this kind of politics is evidence of the existence of a "nation within a nation," where the "Black nation" is led by a black "quasi-government," defined as a system of influence, and where "the constant interplay between the elites of these various institutions produces a central tendency which becomes the judgment of 'the black community.' "[11] Holden further claims that the leadership function of this "government" is determined by the social characteristics of the group:

> Advocacy and practice have also been influenced by some other variables, notably the culture and class structure of the black "nation"; the degree to which black leadership is constrained by the approval and disapproval of a recognized "mass" constituency; the scale and subtlety (or simplicity) of the problems being addressed; and, perhaps above all, the North-South differential.[12]

In effect, Holden reaffirms the fact that the source of black political mobilization is still to be found within the fertile milieu described above. Black political mobilization has always been directed towards organizing the resources of the black community to cope offensively with community objectives, and defensively with the tensions introduced from the external environment. This might be illustrated by a brief summary of some key political events in the life of the black community in the nineteenth and twentieth centuries.

The politics of the black community after slavery was devoted to securing an adequate legal, economic and educational base that would make it possible for the community to grow and prosper. Yet, when the 1876 election of Rutherford B. Hayes to the presidency was decided by a "compromise" which, among other things, resulted in the removal of Union troops from the South, white southerners reclaimed their property with a vengeance. Unprotected blacks were shunned by both political parties and left exposed to the violence of such groups as the Ku Klux Klan. John Hope Franklin notes, for example, that in the last sixteen years of the nineteenth century, all but a few of the victims of some 2500 lynchings in the United States were black, and that by the outbreak of World War I another 1100 blacks had been lynched.[13] Symptomatic of the ferociousness with which blacks were subordinated during this period is the fact that they were driven from the land, excluded from the polls, resegregated in the use of public facilities, excluded from jobs, and deprived of their civil rights by southern legislatures.

In reaction to this turn-of-the-century repression, blacks began a great migration from the South to the burgeoning industrial centers of the North. They initiated a cultural movement that came to be known as the "Harlem Renaissance," defining their identities in the more aggressive terms of the "New Negro." The development of nonpartisan electoral organizations such as the National Independent Political League in 1913, and earlier ones such as the National Association for the Advancement of Colored People (NAACP) and the National Urban League, prefigured the cultural consciousness of the "New Negro." These organizations worked to oppose atrocities like lynching, and to acquire jobs, integrated education and civil rights through social work, protest agitation and the use of the courts.[14]

But while one stream of political action was devoted to the acquisition of a better status within the United States, another refused to relinquish the fundamental ties to Africa. In fact, the intensity of the violence against blacks in the period after 1880 simply confirmed to some that migration to Africa was their eventual destiny and only rational alternative. The Jamaican, Malcus Mosiah ("Marcus") Garvey, Jr., believed that the redemption of Africa through a migratory movement that eventually established a black, all-African government was the key to racial pride, and the propagation of his ideas generated a worldwide political movement among people of African descent. Garvey's movement, at its height from 1918 to 1924, attracted large numbers of poor urban blacks and mobilized them into the movement's various institutions and activities, providing them with psychological and ideological means to combat the contempt in which both whites and the black bourgeoisie held them. The power arrayed against Garvey by the federal government, however, aborted his specific plans for a return to Africa, but not his movement.[15]

Middle-class blacks also participated in a Pan-African movement, founded in 1900 in London by the Trinidadian lawyer, H. Sylvester Williams, and led by the distinguished black scholar, W.E.B. DuBois, from 1919 to 1928. Although Garvey and DuBois were bitter antagonists, the political implications of both types of Pan-African movements were important in helping to lay the foundations of the African independence movement and retaining a cultural link to an African identity.[16]

The racial mobilization of blacks, a key purpose of the movements just mentioned, was advanced by the work of a well-known progressive black leader, A. Philip Randolph. Troubled deeply by the persistent pattern of discrimination in employment, Randolph challenged President Franklin D. Roosevelt to end segregation in the war industries, while laying the groundwork for a massive march on Washington. Although Roosevelt capitulated and signed an executive order integrating the war industries in 1941 before the march could occur, Randolph had further lit the fires of national black political mobilization in an ongoing organization which would complement subsequent advances in the labor movement. The National Negro Congress, of which Randolph was first elected president in 1936, was to become for a brief period in the 1940s an effective instrument for community organization, as well as for grassroots activities among workers in the South.[17]

It would not be until the late 1950s that blacks would again begin large-scale national mobilization to achieve changes in racially discriminatory laws and social practices. The 1954 Supreme Court school integration decision, the fruit of the legalistic political strategy of the NAACP, became the touchstone of conflict between blacks and whites, especially in the South where segregated education was an ingrained attribute of the social system. White southern political leaders responded to the decision with massive resistance, and blacks retaliated with a broad movement that encompassed not only education but other areas of civil rights as well. Yet the civil rights movement that the decision spawned was not just restriced to the South. As Aldon Morris points out, it began in isolated communities in the Midwest and West, filtering into the South with the dramatic action of Martin Luther King, Jr., in the Montgomery bus boycott, and later blossoming in the freedom rides and sit-ins of the Student Nonviolent Coordinating Committee (SNCC).[18]

After 1960, SNCC and the Southern Christian Leadership Conference (SCLC), an organization of southern black ministers, initiated a dramatic confrontation with the southern system of white power. The civil rights movement was personified in the personality and philosophy of Martin Luther King, Jr., president of SCLC, but was actually led by the "big five" coalition of the NAACP, the SCLC, SNCC, the Congress of Racial Equality (CORE) and the National Urban League, all instruments for massive, national multiracial mobilization. The political objectives of the mobilization focused initially on citizenship rights and political participation in such activities as registration, voting and holding political office, but also encompassed such other issues as integrated education, access to public accommodations, and equal opportunity employment. Although it took over a decade, from 1957 to 1968, laws which attest to the success of this movement, such as the Civil Rights Act of 1964, the Voting Rights Act of 1965 and the Civil Rights Act of 1968, were enacted.[19]

Beginning in 1966, a more militant phase of the mobilization of the black community—termed the "black power" movement—began through the leadership of SNCC's young activists, most notably Stokely Carmichael. A host of new organizations then burst upon the scene to give additional confirmation to the basic change in the movement's direction, as the revolutionary Black Panther Party and a number of new Pan-African organizations were born. The extent to which links to African culture were retained and emphasized became of major importance in redefining black identity, and the Pan-African movement claimed a functional relationship to the political dynamics occurring on the African continent.

As this movement gathered steam, it fueled the activities of the unorganized youths involved in open revolt against white society, who violently attacked white-owned retail establishments with Molotov cocktails and engaged police with rocks and firearms. Although there was much social scientific debate concerning the political genesis, form, content and objectives of these rebellions, they were regarded as significant aspects of social protest.

> Yet collective violence, including ghetto riots, inevitably involves at least two sides, two formations of antagonists; one the dispossessed, and the other the agents of the state, fronting as it were for the powerholding group in the society.[20]

The rebellions, which began in earnest in 1964, lasted until the early 1970s; their scope moved from the plundering of 112 commercial establishments in the 1964 Harlem riot to over 2,700 incidents in Detroit in 1967.[21] In 1969, more than five hundred serious incidents of such violence occurred. At their height in the late 1960s, these protests came to be the most profound manifestation of the cleavage between the races.

As such, the strategies and tactics utilized by blacks in this conflict took on the appearance of the most extreme forms of dissent against colonial treatment by white institutions, a method of revolutionary change resembling that which was until then the province of Third World countries.

The Consolidation of Local Power Bases

The utilization of various forms of political action in order to improve the socioeconomic status of the black community has historically made possible the consolidation of a local power base in some measure. Such consolidation has encouraged both increased participation in local political systems, reflecting the electoral power of blacks, and more effective participation in the external political system. The success of these resource mobilization movements, as well as national economic and social trends, have, however, affected the state of blacks' historical urban base. Current trends in the distribution of the black population are shown in Table 1:

TABLE 1

DISTRIBUTION OF THE BLACK AND WHITE POPULATION: 1960, 1970, 1980

	Central Cities	Suburbs	Nonmetropolitan
1960			
Black	51.4%	13.3%	35.3%
White	30.0	32.9	37.2
1970			
Black	58.2	16.1	25.7
White	27.8	40.0	32.1
1980			
Black	57.7	23.3	18.9
White	25.0	48.4	26.7

Source: Adapted from the Joint Center for Political Studies, "Blacks on the Move: A Decade of Demographic Change," *JCPS Report* (Washington, D.C.: Joint Center for Political Studies, 1982), p. 42, table 6.3.

These data suggest that blacks progressively have comprised a larger share of the metropolitan area (central city and suburban) population and that, as the Joint Economic Committee of the Congress has put it, "large cities in 1990 will have populations that, relative to the population as a whole or the situation today, [will be] older, blacker, poorer, and more heavily composed of persons needing government services."[22] This is significant, since one-third of black inner-city residents live in one of five major cities: New York, Chicago, Detroit, Philadelphia or Los Angeles/Long Beach. The absence of southern cities from this list means that metropolitan areas in the South are generally of lower population density than their counterparts elsewhere, and that many blacks still live in older rural areas, although the number of blacks residing in large Southern cities should not be minimized.

Thus, despite some out-migration of blacks from the central city to the suburbs, blacks are maintaining their numerical dominance in the central city and increasing their proportional representation in the metropolitan area population as whites move to nonmetropolitan areas. In addition, higher birth rates will continue to augment the increase in the black population in central city areas. This means that blacks are not only consolidating their political control over central cities, but are capturing control of some suburban cities as well, since the predominant pattern is for blacks to move into suburban areas which already have a concentrated black population. For example, major cities such as Washington, D.C., Baltimore, Cleveland and St. Louis have all experienced considerable loss of black population. However, the adjacent suburbs have benefited, as 64 percent of the 79,000 blacks who went to Prince Georges County, Maryland, came from Washington, D.C.; 75 percent of the 32,600 who went into St. Louis County, Missouri, came from the city of St. Louis; 78 percent of the 25,700 who went to Baltimore County, Maryland, came from the city of Baltimore; and 55 percent of blacks who moved to DeKalb County, Georgia, came from Atlanta.[23]

Although it might be expected that the next migration trend would be for blacks to follow whites into nonmetropolitan areas beyond the suburbs, such factors as economics, racial prejudice, and both subtle and more overt forms of discrimination may severely limit such a development for some time. Still, blacks may well have an opportunity to increase their number of elected officials in suburban political jurisdictions and in the corresponding state legislative and congressional districts. In addition, because of both the increased influence of blacks in central cities and some artful "horse-trading" within state legislatures, blacks have been able to retain some congressional seats they might otherwise have lost due to population attrition. However, the gains that have been made in the various political jurisdictions should not deflect the attention of black leaders from the persistent systemic imperatives of the politics of apportionment.

As a result of demographic changes, the content of community-level politics will be influenced by the conflicting needs of affluent whites and poor blacks, majority blacks and minority whites, and young blacks,

Hispanics and the elderly. Although this pattern does not hold in every instance, it is sufficiently generalized to suggest that class tensions will become more pronounced, economic disparities more acute, and crime will continue to be a major concern, especially to an increasingly older population.

Politics at the Base

The consolidation of local black political power through winning elected office has been instrumental in the emergence of a stable leadership class that has helped to legitimate black participation. This has also helped to facilitate mobilization and achieve objectives outside of the black community.

The efficaciousness of stable black leadership has been undergirded, in part, by the emergence of groupings such as the National Black Leadership Forum, where thirteen of the top black leaders are from the NAACP, the National Urban League, the National Black Coalition of Trade Unions, the Joint Center for Political Studies, the Southern Christian Leadership Conference, the Fraternal Order of Masons, the National Council of Negro Women, the Martin Luther King, Jr., Center for Nonviolent Social Change, the Congressional Black Caucus, the National Urban Coalition and leading collegiate sororities and fraternities. Representatives of about fifty national black organizations, including some of the ones just mentioned, are members of the National Black Leadership Roundtable, which intends to grow to about five hundred members. There is some overlap of membership between the two organizations, but very little formal interaction, due not to differences in ideology but rather to differences in presumed status.[24]

Both groups provide convenient vehicles for coordinating positions on critical issues within the black community. For example, when the question of mounting a black presidential candidacy arose in the spring of 1983, the Forum was convened; similarly, when support is desired for the policy agenda of the Congressional Black Caucus, the Roundtable's "Action Alert Network" is put into operation. In addition, events such as the annual dinner of the Congressional Black Caucus, which attracts thousands of organizational representatives, and the annual conferences of individual organizations allow the leadership to meet and exchange ideas, information and program initiatives.

This organizational framework facilitates such participation in the public policy arena as the successful national effort in 1985 to deny confirmation of Assistant Attorney General W. Bradford Reynolds—a foe of affirmative action—to the third highest office in the Justice De-

partment, and the support of the Free South Africa Movement's mobilization against South Africa that resulted in the Comprehensive
Anti-Apartheid Act of 1986. The same organizational framework also
undergirded such political successes as the extraordinary mobilization
of national organizations by the National Black Leadership Roundtable to assist in the election of Michael Espy to the Second Congressional District of Mississippi. He thus became the first black representative from the Deep South since Reconstruction.[25]

Finally, although there are many conflicts inherent in an organizational milieu, the fact that there is a generally shared ideological orientation across the organizations minimizes the intensity of conflict. The
strongly supportive reaction of the leadership to Andrew Young's 1979
resignation from the Carter administration is evidence of this cohesion.
It is also illustrated by the lack of conflict when bona fide individual
members are seized by controversial issues, such as Mayor Wilson
Goode's handling of the MOVE bombing in Philadelphia.[26]

Politics and Protest

It is one of the presumptions of the late 1970s and 1980s that protest
politics has run its course, partly because of the institutionalization of
black leadership. James Q. Wilson observed in the late 1960s that "Negroes . . . will increasingly be able to play marginalist politics."[27]
Yet, in the task of protecting and expanding gains, it has been axiomatic that since the marginalist gains of institutional politics are rarely
large-scale, blacks have often turned to protest. The strategy of protest
demonstrations can be both offensive and defensive, and such tactics
are generally utilized in an effort to heighten the visibility and urgency
of an issue so that decisionmakers or other authoritative parties come
to consider it a priority. Both practitioners and analysts alike, however, misunderstand this strategy by thinking that it can effectively
bring important problems into view as well as *solve* them.

Many of the urban protests today, as in earlier periods, began as the
result of a "triggering" incident such as an allegation of police brutality; the trigger, however, was often not as important as the fact that
the incident occurred within the environment of a widespread oppositional social movement. Another similarity is that, except for the earlier spontaneous rebellions, planned protest demonstrations where
targets are carefully selected in accordance with a goal designed to advance racial self-determination have survived as a viable strategy of
social change. As one observes a range of protest demonstrations by
blacks from 1977 to 1985, all serious enough to have provoked high

levels of racial tensions in communities where they occurred, it is striking that they are only slightly different in character from those of the
1960s and early 1970s.[28]

The more recent cases of protest demonstrations, described in the
annual reports of the Community Relations Service (CRS), an agency
of the U.S. Department of Justice, illustrate that the trend toward re-
taliatory protest against police brutality continues. Other reactive (or
defensive) protests against a variety of perceptions of racist treatment
are also observed, as is shown in Table 2:

TABLE 2

ISSUES PRECIPITATING PROTEST DEMONSTRATIONS:
1977-1984

Issue	Percent
Administration of Justice	40
Education	20
Ku Klux Klan	10
General Community Relations	30

Source: Figures compiled from the U.S. Department of Justice, Community
Relations Service, *Annual Reports, 1979-1986* (Washington, D.C.:
Community Relations Service, 1979-1986).

The data above, and the *Annual Reports* from which they were compiled, suggest that the most common reason for protest demonstrations
in this period has been the reaction of the black community to the use
of deadly force, police brutality, and unjust sentencing. Issues surrounding the quality of life in schools for black children—substantially
the issue of how racial desegregation has been administered by school
authorities—follow. There have also been a series of confrontations
with the Ku Klux Klan and other hate groups, usually in the form of
counterdemonstrations at the Klan's planned appearances. Although
only a few sensational incidents provoked demonstrations by whites
and counterdemonstrations by blacks in 1985 and 1986, when blacks
attempted to move into areas such as Forsyth County, Georgia, and
southwest Philadelphia, the Klanwatch Project of the Southern Poverty Law Center has identified at least forty-five incidents of such
"move-in violence" in this period.[29] Discrimination in the use of city
funds and employment has also fostered protest, as well as nontraditional reasons such as the disproportionate placement of toxic waste
sites in black neighborhoods, corporate racism, racial violence by white
youths, and South African apartheid.

Protest demonstrations are also a continuing part of the national strategy of interest group politics and have been used with some success, as, for example, by the Free South Africa Movement in mobilizing national opposition to U.S. government policy concerning South Africa. These demonstrations grew out of a sit-in at the South African embassy on November 21, 1984, and continued daily for more than a year. Although the demonstrations differed from past protests by culminating in symbolic arrests for trespass on South African embassy property, the notoriety of those involved created the press attention that substituted for the nonsymbolic protest which would have provoked real conflict at the embassy site. The success of the demonstrations helped to create a national sentiment against the then existing policy of "constructive engagement" (or close association with the South African regime), and resulted in the creation of national pressure on Congress leading to the passage of the Comprehensive Anti-Apartheid Act of 1986.[30]

Even though it could be expected that the use of demonstrations which resulted in a solid legislative victory might be replicated in the domestic arena, this, for the most part, has failed to occur. In spite of their national scope, the demonstrations have revealed a strongly negative attitude on the part of some black and white analysts toward protest demonstrations, both when used against acts of racist violence and especially as a strategy for effecting social change.[31]

In a period when there is no widespread social movement to buttress the dynamism of protest demonstrations, thereby lending additional power to the issues the demonstrations seek to highlight, it seems reasonable to suggest that they have lost their overall utility to the process of social change. Moreover, there is a search for strategies that do not rely upon the episodic mobilizational cycle of demonstrations, but which are more routinized and exhibit closer links to the decision-making process.[32] At the same time, some evidence appears to confirm Michael Lipsky's earlier work, *Protest as a Political Resource*, which suggests that social action—including protest demonstrations—is effective in preventing a range of negative consequences of inequality.[33] Still, there are strong advocates who believe that the expression of a collective will through organized demonstrations may be the *only* effective strategy open to relatively powerless groups in order to make inroads at the policy level.[34]

What, then, is the most appropriate political strategy for groups situated in the American social order such as blacks? The answer would appear to rest in the juxtaposition of the nature of the leading issues and their origins, in both the reality and the perception of the status of blacks, and in the black community's ability to achieve various kinds of ameliorative objectives. Given the political tenor of the 1980s, a period in which the political system seemed opposed to the interests of blacks, with blacks possessing neither effective bureaucratic strength nor maximal political organization, *no proven* strategies and tactics of social change should be discarded for the foreseeable future.

The External System: Elections

Free, open and regular elections are the means by which representatives who make authoritative decisions, binding upon all, are chosen in a constitutional democracy. Thus, the struggle of blacks to participate equally in elections has been directed towards achieving a just share in the distribution of the public goods which derive from such representation, and which makes it possible for blacks to develop as individuals and as a community within the social order. That is why the acquisition of electoral rights and their strategic use have consumed the interest of black leaders since at least the early part of the nineteenth century, becoming an explicit common concern just before the Civil War. Voting by blacks begun during Reconstruction contributed greatly to the relative success of the Republican governing coalition until near the end of that century, and where they could still vote, blacks remained loyal to the Republican party until the era of Franklin Roosevelt.

Between 1870 and 1901, there were twenty blacks in the House of Representatives, three in the Senate, and numerous others at the state and local levels in the South, as a result of their enfranchisement.[35] By 1901 few blacks remained in these positions, just as concomitantly blacks were denied electoral participation in most of the southern states. This picture did not change until 1928, when the election of Oscar De Priest from Illinois' First District began the return to Congress by blacks. By 1936, blacks had begun to vote overwhelmingly for Democratic candidates at the presidential and local levels, essentially because Roosevelt's recovery program had given them access to greater employment and social opportunities. [36] In addition, under the Democrats blacks began to obtain valued appointments within the urban political machines of the North to match their growing numbers, as well as significant appointments within the Roosevelt administration. By the election of 1944, there was a consensus that blacks held the balance of power in the Democratic party with the potential to eclipse the southern vote.[37] The period from 1944 to 1964 was one of an expanding franchise for blacks. The Supreme Court decision outlawing the white primary in 1944[38] caused what Henry Lee Moon has called a "revival

of Negro participation in politics" that resulted in thousands register-
ing and voting.[39] While blacks had nearly been eliminated from the
electoral process, with the election of 1948 they returned to the polls in
increasing numbers.

The years from 1965 to 1984 might be described as the stage where
blacks institutionalized the turnout strategy as part of their participation in the Democratic party. As Table 3 shows, both white and black
registration and turnout slid downward in this period, until the rebound in 1980, as a response to the alienation fostered by the Vietnam
War and the black protest movements then occurring.

TABLE 3

REGISTRATION AND VOTING IN PRESIDENTIAL ELECTIONS
FOR BLACKS AND WHITES, 1968-1984

Registration	1968	1972	1976	1980	1984
Blacks	66.2%	65.5%	58.5%	60.0%	66.3%
Whites	75.4	73.4	68.3	68.4	69.6
Voting					
Blacks	57.6	52.1	48.7	50.5	55.8
Whites	69.1	64.5	60.9	60.9	61.4

Source: U.S. Bureau of the Census, "Voting and Registration in the Election
of 1984," Advance Report, Population Characteristics Series P-20,
No. 397 (January 1985), Table A, p. 1, and Table C, p. 3.

There are three interesting features of this information about the
black vote. First, although registration and turnout had been going
down since 1964, when turnout was 58.5 percent, the black vote did
play a role in helping to decide the outcome of some close presidential
elections. Although this critical role is well known in relation to the
election of both John Kennedy in 1960 (who had 49.7 percent of the
vote compared to Richard Nixon's 49.5 percent) and Jimmy Carter in
1976 (who defeated Gerald Ford with 51 percent of the vote), the failure of blacks to turn out to elect Hubert Humphrey in a close 1968 race
(won by Richard Nixon with 43.4 percent of the vote to Humphrey's
43.3 percent) was a negative demonstration of voting power.[40]

Second, the upturn in black registration and voting in 1980 continued strongly into 1984 and 1986. The political rationale for this occurrence will be discussed later; it should be observed here, however, that
the 1984 voter registration and turnout levels increased over those of
1980 by about 6.3 percent and 5.3 percent respectively, reaching the
highest levels since 1964. Similarly, the off-year elections of 1982

showed an increase, when the black turnout for congressional elections went up by more than 2 percent over the 1978 level.[41]

Finally, with the recent improvement in the turnout of the black vote, the racial difference favoring whites over blacks in registration and voting behavior has been narrowing, as has the regional difference among blacks, which has historically shown blacks in the North and West with higher participation rates than those in the South.

TABLE 4

DIFFERENCES IN PERCENT REPORTED VOTING AND PERCENT REPORTED REGISTERED, BY REGION AND RACE: NOVEMBER 1964 TO 1984

Blacks in North and West vs. Blacks in South	1964	1968	1972	1976	1980	1984
Registration	16.0[a]	10.2	3.0	4.5	1.3	1.6
Voting	28.0	13.2	8.9	6.5	4.6	6.7
Blacks vs. Whites, Overall						
Registration	11.4[a]	9.2	7.9	9.8	8.4	3.3
Voting	12.2	11.5	12.4	12.2	10.4	5.6

Source: Figures compiled from the U.S. Bureau of the Census, "Voting and Registration in the Election of 1984," Advance Report, Population Characteristics Series P-20, No. 397 (January 1985), Table A, p. 1, and Table C, p. 3.

[a]Figures for 1964 registration are the 1966 congressional election figures.

One conclusion which may be drawn from Table 4 is that it will not be long before blacks reach proportional equality with whites in the exercise of the franchise. That blacks might, in fact, someday vote at a rate higher than whites shows the necessity of implementing certain types of strategy heavily dependent upon turnout. It is also apparent that blacks in the South are on the brink of reaching a similar pattern of electoral participation as those in the North, a fact which comports well with the extent to which the South as a region is achieving similar levels of participation with the rest of the nation. Again, given the special opportunities which might be present in the South because of the concentration of the black vote, it could well surpass the rest of the national black population in electoral behavior early in the next century.

One outcome of the raw increase in voting behavior by blacks is that in many localities they are increasingly being elected to office. The growth in the number of black elected officials at all levels correlates

strongly with the rise of voting after the passage of the Voting Rights
Act of 1965, as indicated in Figure 1:

FIGURE 1

**RATE OF INCREASE IN NUMBER OF BLACK ELECTED
OFFICIALS, 1971-1986, ANNUAL AND CUMULATIVE**

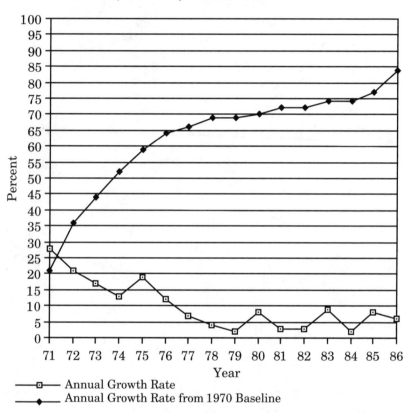

Source: Joint Center for Political Studies, *Black Elected Officials: A
         National Roster, 1987* (New York: UNIPUB, 1987), Figure 1, p. 9.

What may be surmised from the illustration above is that while the
actual number of elected officials is growing, the *rate* at which that
number is increasing is falling. This may be because many of the seats
in majority black areas are now filled by blacks, thus any additional
increases must come either from majority white political jurisdictions
in the North or in the more heavily black South where there are still
formidable barriers to the exercise of the franchise.

For example, of the existing cities with populations over fifty thousand with black mayors, only 40.7 percent are ones with black majorities. There are an additional fifteen cities with populations over fifty thousand and with black populations in the 40 percent range which do not have black mayors, although some are undoubtedly poised to elect one.[42] And since there are black mayors in cities with low black populations, the field of potential growth would appear to be expansive. Blacks, for example, hold elective offices other than mayor in such cities as Anchorage, Cheyenne, Montpelier, Vermont, Mitchell, South Dakota, and Portland, Maine.[43]

The same point might be made concerning black members of Congress; while 80 percent of these representatives serve majority black districts, seven come from districts with black populations in the 40 percent range. They are: Louisiana's Second District, south New Orleans, 45 percent; Louisiana's Eighth District, Alexandria, 40 percent; Mississippi's Fourth District, Jackson, 45 percent; New York's Eighteenth District, the South Bronx, 44 percent; North Carolina's Second District, Rocky Mount-Durham, 41 percent; South Carolina's Sixth District, Florence, 41 percent; and Virginia's Fourth District, Portsmouth, 41 percent.[44]

In a careful analysis, Robert Smith concluded that the factors which caused white incumbents to hold black majority congressional seats were largely nonsystemic.[45] Thus, it is impossible to predict with much accuracy those factors which make it possible for black candidates in black majority congressional districts to win seats which are held by white incumbents. That is why one cannot necessarily attribute any greater political skill and sophistication to black candidates winning seats in minority black districts than to those winning in majority black districts. Only one majority black district with white representation in Congress remains as of this writing (Louisiana's Second). Expanding the membership of the Congressional Black Caucus would appear to be possible due to the fact that there are members who represent minority black districts, including Ronald Dellums (Dem-CA), Alan Wheat (Dem-MO) and Clarence Towns (Dem-NY), whose districts are, respectively, 24, 31 and 32 percent black.

A fact that is evident from the listing above is that most opportunities for the acquisition of congressional seats are at present in the South. In any case, 64 percent of all black elected officials were located in this region in 1986, and it is in the South that the pool of such officials grew the fastest between 1970 and 1982, as seen in Table 5.

TABLE 5

NUMBER OF BLACK ELECTED OFFICIALS,
BY REGION, 1970 AND 1982

Region	1970	1982	Percent Increase
Northeast	238	577	142.4
North Central	396	1090	175.3
South	703	3140	346.7
West	130	308	136.9

Source: Adapted from Thomas Cavanagh and Denise Stockton, *Black Elected Officials and Their Constituencies* (Washington, D.C.: Joint Center for Political Studies, 1983), p. 7.

Yet, it is also true that the South remains a most volatile battle-ground in the effort by blacks to reflect fairly the political power sug-gested by their concentrated numbers. Whether the goal is winning a congressional seat or an elected position below this level, it presupposes continued success in eliminating the remaining barriers to voting and to the impact of the vote. These barriers, discussed briefly below, still include such practices as inaccessible and discriminatory registration, at-large elections, dual primaries, gerrymandering, exclusionary slat-ing, annexations, and so on.[46]

The Voting Rights Struggle

The 1982 congressional amendments to the 1965 Voting Rights Act, in effect, repaired whatever damage that might have been occasioned by the *City of Mobile* v. *Bolden* decision[47] in 1980, under which the *intent* of a political jurisdiction to discriminate by a change in a voting prac-tice would have had to have been proven by a complainant.[48] The amendments specify that it is unlawful to dilute the impact of the vote of minorities by discriminatory electoral procedures. This change was advocated by voting rights organizations which recognized that state election officials in the South had eschewed easily detectable discrimi-natory practices that denied blacks the vote in favor of more subtle ones which nullified the impact of a unified black vote.

The record indicates that due, in part, to vigorous intervention by the Justice Department during the Carter administration, the level of such blatantly discriminatory changes submitted by states for preclearance under Section 5 of the act has been lowered noticeably. Until 1970, registration and voting barriers made up approximately 33 percent of the relatively few changes to which the Department of Jus-tice objected. From 1970 to 1980, however, such barriers to individual voting constituted fewer than 15 percent of the changes found to be discriminatory.[49] Registration and voting barriers have since been replaced by other practices. As one analyst has observed: "In recent years, vote dilution schemes have constituted between 85 percent and 98 percent of the changes found to be in violation of the Act. Vote dilution has thus become a highly significant issue and will no doubt represent a growing proportion of voting rights cases in the years to come."[50] This has thrown tremendous weight upon the process of securing and protecting majority black electoral districts, necessitating increased attention to the process of legislative reapportionment after each decennial census.

The creation of single-member districts as an antidote to at-large systems was enhanced by the Supreme Court decision in *Thornburg* v. *Gingles* of 1986, which upheld a North Carolina court decision that a multi-member district system was unconstitutional.[51] Speaking for the majority, Justice William Brennan developed a standard for measuring the discriminatory impact of such schemes. He posited that they violated minority voters' rights when "the minority group is sufficiently large and geographically compact"; the minority group is "politically cohesive"; and the minority group competes with white racial bloc voting.[52] For the foreseeable future, the strict application of Brennan's standard will no doubt be vital to the maximization of black electoral power.

The Jesse Jackson Campaign

Perhaps the next stage in the development of electoral politics will be marked by strategies to maximize the use of the ballot, where increasingly the black community will expect a sufficient return in the accrual of public goods for its political support. Undoubtedly, this period will become one of concentration on the end product(s) of political participation, and those strategies—beyond voter turnout—necessary to ensure returns. Although blacks will soon achieve parity with whites in electoral behavior, proportionate returns nevertheless remain distant. Accordingly, there must be greater attention paid to achieving political and public policy goals by strategic methods.

The beginning of such a stage was represented by Rev. Jesse Jackson's campaign for the Democratic presidential nomination in 1984. In a broader sense, since it would be absurd to suggest that questions of new strategies were only of concern to Jackson, perhaps the diminishing returns from *client politics* have focused black leaders and their followers upon the value of wielding *autonomous politics*. Matthew

Holden, Jr., has articulated an invaluable critique of clientage. He observed:

> The rule of thumb which the practitioners of clientage seemed to follow, as far as one may be able to extract a rule from what they said and did, might be stated as follows: *Find a basis for coexistence by choosing objectives which the more influential outsider* (in this case whites) *will support, and by their support offer protection against those outsiders who are your irreconcilable enemies.*[53]

Discerning that clientage historically has not been an effective strategy, Holden describes two others, opposition and withdrawal, which have served the interests of blacks at one time or another. The alternative to clientage, though, need not necessarily be opposition or withdrawal in the strictest sense, but rather the autonomy of position which makes it possible either to cooperate or to oppose from a position of relative equality as the strategic situation demands.

The Jackson campaign was, then, an exercise in political autonomy within the Democratic party's process of presidential selection, although as a dedicated strategy for winning the presidency, it has been discredited by both political decisionmakers and participants in the process alike. The problem, of course, was skepticism about the presumption that a black person could run successfully for the presidential nomination of his party, or that he could eventually be elected were he nominated. This was true despite the fact that public attitudes on this question had moved from a low of 38 percent positive support for a "Negro for president" in 1958 to 70 percent support for a "qualified black" as early as 1971, reaching a 77 percent favorable rating in 1978.[54] One test of this proposition occurred in 1972 with the candidacy of Congresswoman Shirley Chisolm of New York which, although it did not attract significant support either in the black community or among whites, set an acknowledged precedent for Jackson's efforts in 1984 and 1988.

Evidence accumulated rather early in 1983 that the question among blacks was whether, in view of the actions which suggested that they would be ignored by the Democratic party, a presidential candidacy would attract the desired attention to black interests. For whites, however, it was probably the more racially sensitive question of whether a black person *should* become president, because in a public opinion poll of the "ideal type" of person desired for president, only one in twenty mentioned Jackson, even though he was rated second only to John Glenn as an interesting person with whom to "have breakfast" in another poll.[55] That there were strongly conflicting racial sentiments on this issue in 1984 is obvious from polls which theoretically pitted Jackson against Ronald Reagan:

TABLE 6

GALLUP POLL: REAGAN VS. JACKSON

	Jackson	Reagan
National	22%	61%
Blacks	75	5
Whites	15	69

Source: *The Gallup Report* (Princeton, NJ: The Gallup Poll), No. 215 (August 1983), p. 27.

This survey of registered voters in the summer of 1983 showed strong racially polarized attitudes in relation to Jackson's fitness for the presidency. Such attitudes were still found to be typical in the spring of 1987, as one observes in the response to a qualitative survey of an interviewee who, in considering Jackson among other potential presidential candidates, noted that he was "[n]ot ready for that . . . "[56]

The strategy of having a black person run for president was not a purely personal decision by Jackson, but a collective one developed by over twenty-five black leaders who met several times in the spring of 1983; by June they had decided that it should be done by someone. It was then left to Jackson to project the idea, and to the black community to respond with choruses of "Run, Jesse, run."[57]

The mobilization which became the Jackson campaign had a surprising degree of mass support, finding its origin in grassroots challenges to the politics of Reagan as early as 1982.[58] The importance of this fact is that the content of the grassroots politics became oppositional and autonomous in tone as it implicated Republicans and, in some cases, Democrats as well (such as Mayors Jane Byrne of Chicago and Frank Rizzo of Philadelphia) for the deterioration of the quality of urban life. There is some evidence supporting this observation in a survey, performed in 1984 by researchers at the University of Michigan, about the differences between the black supporters of Jackson and black supporters of Walter Mondale.

TABLE 7

SELECTED BELIEFS AND CHARACTERISTICS
OF BLACK SUPPORTERS OF JACKSON AND MONDALE

	Jackson	Mondale
Member of an organization working to help black people	27%	21%
A belief in the common fate of blacks	80	68
Blacks (to have power) should be more active in black organizations	43	37
Whites have too much influence (over black politics)	70	57

Source: Adapted from the Institute for Social Research, *National Black Election Study, Post-Election Survey* (Ann Arbor, MI: Institute for Social Research, University of Michigan, 1985).

What emerges from the data is a profile of Jackson's black supporters which marks them as more grounded in the beliefs that black political power is a prime resource, and that whites have inordinate power over black affairs.

Of course, in our review of the sources of Jackson's bid for autonomy, it has been recognized that the political mobilization of black organizations provided him with the necessary resources for the campaign to continue. The resources of the fraternal, political, religious, youth and other organizations were mobilized in this regard, as is indicated by Ronald E. Brown, who observes that:

> Overall, these findings demonstrate that a group-based process of political mobilization impacts upon levels of campaign participation. Group-based resources and individual resources are both essential for high levels of campaign activity. Nonetheless, the fact that membership in a black organization plays such a critical role suggests that involvement in interest group politics is vital for Black American activism.[59]

Brown goes on to indicate that black churches, party activism, and black women were all dynamic ingredients in the pattern of support for the 1984 Jackson campaign. These were replicated and expanded in his campaign of 1988.

A critical secondary function of Jackson's 1984 campaign strategy was unsuccessful: the extent to which the candidate was able to utilize the political resources that were accumulated (such as a network of campaign organizations in over forty states) to bargain effectively with

Walter Mondale to support a political agenda favored by the "Rainbow Coalition."[60] The bargaining function of the campaign was always presumed to be one of its greatest promises, and it did not require Jackson to win the nomination in order to be successful. However, even with an effort that surpassed every expectation, Jackson was unable to convert campaign political capital into commitments from Mondale that would facilitate the acquisition of public goods by his constituents had Mondale become president. This was, for the most part, also true in 1988, as Jackson found Michael Dukakis, to whom he was the runner-up for the Democratic party's presidential nomination, no less reticent than Mondale to make the sorts of commitments implied here.

In a very real sense, the 1984 campaign may be regarded as a "dry run" in this regard. At the very least, Jackson's efforts revealed the possibilities that the black vote, in coalition with Hispanics, whites and other "rainbow" constituencies, could have upon Democratic party presidential primary elections, as his campaign of 1988 also demonstrated ever so compellingly. In the 1984 primaries, Mondale attracted 6.7 million votes, Hart 6.4 million and Jackson 3.2 million.[61] Jackson did markedly better in 1988, more than doubling his total of 1984 with 6.6 million votes, but Dukakis received roughly one-third more with 9.7 million votes.[62] In the general election of 1984, 10.3 million of 12.2 million registered blacks voted, while in 1988 the corresponding figures were 9 million of 10.5 million.[63] There is, then, a substantial residual black vote which, if it voted in the primaries, might greatly affect the process of presidential selection. (The major problem with taking raw votes into account, however, is that the rules of the Democratic party presidential primary process say that votes are counted in electoral districts—a threshold of 15 percent obtained for the 1988 elections. Thus, many blacks could vote whose votes essentially would not "count" because they are concentrated in urban congressional districts, while white voters are distributed more evenly throughout a state.)

And so, future primary election turnout strategies must encompass a significant black vote in a coalition with others, and where possible, attract suburban and rural progressive voters. In any case, since the black vote alone amounts to 12 percent of the electorate in the general election and 24 percent in the Democratic primaries, it would be prudent to attempt to maximize an obvious advantage. It will be even more so in the future, as the black voting-age population is projected to increase by five million by the year 2000.[64]

Conditioning Variables

This discussion began with the observation that central to defining the content of black politics is the existence and nature of a racial cleavage in the United States. There is, therefore, an implicit understanding that the form, substance and persistence of this cleavage in the future will have a profound conditioning effect on the shape of black politics in the main internal and external theaters of action. A second dominant conditioning variable appears to be the nature of the black response to the racial cleavage. This presentation has been influenced heavily by the assumption that the choice of group strategies, whether proactive or reactive, is shaped by the need to achieve objectives in spite of the prevailing influence of racial subordination. One thus observes an interactive relationship between black political mobilization and white racial domination—an interaction that produces important secondary variables. Among these are the future character of the national leadership, and the strength of economic and class factors which influence social control. The presentation will now turn to the origins of some of the forces which contribute to the current racial cleavage, describing their implications for both electoral politics and community mobilization strategies.

The Persistence of Racial Cleavage

Racial polarization is a structural feature of American society which, although it appears to be decreasing in studies measuring racial attitudes, is increasing in actual behavior. Concerning attitudes, the Gallup Poll surveys done for the Joint Center for Political Studies (JCPS) in 1984 and 1986 suggest that there is, between blacks and whites, a roughly similar profile of issues considered to be "most important." In 1984, whites agreed with four out of five issues identified by blacks as most important: unemployment, government programs to help the poor, inflation, and protecting American jobs. Whites did not agree with the level of importance which blacks ascribed to civil rights.[65] The 1986 survey results were noticeably similar, except for the emergence of the related issues of drugs and crime.[66] What is even more striking beyond the agreement in the profile of issues considered most important is the consistently wide difference in importance on many key issues such as civil rights and government programs for the poor, and the difference in the intensity of support for an issue even where there is agreement that it is important.

The roots of the increasingly conflicting behavior emanate from a highly conservative ideological social temper which has facilitated the development of a white political consensus on the resubordination of the interests of blacks and other minorities. Michael Omi and Howard Winant have suggested that the effort by the Reagan administration to question the definition and utility of race within society amounts to the "rearticulation of race" in a way which attempts to reduce its profile as a major social problem.[67] Also, the concept of "status inconsistency" has been used to explain how a conservative white populist social movement was spawned by the reaction of some whites to the civil rights and anti-Vietnam War movements of the 1960s, and by the national economic decline of the 1970s.

In the 1970s, the political efficacy of white liberals began to become unstable, resulting in its eventual decline as the conservative ideological transition, which acquired momentum in the late 1960s, was consolidated in the 1980s. The conservatives' regained status manifested itself in national elections and within neighborhoods. For example, there was a sharp increase in racial/ethnic conflict and in incidents of racially motivated violence, the critical period appearing to be 1977-1978 when there was a 30 percent increase in such cases handled by the Community Relations Service of the U.S. Department of Justice.[68] This growing and more volatile racial cleavage influenced blacks in electoral politics and in other aspects of community mobilization.

The proof of the regained status of white conservatives was the election of Ronald Reagan in 1980. He promptly began to rearticulate the racial frame of reference on the symbolic level by fomenting negative relations with established black leaders. On the policy level, Reagan sponsored measures redirecting federal budget resources from community social services, crippled civil rights enforcement, attempted to scuttle small business funding, and developed close relations with the racist South African regime. This performance earned Reagan a cumulatively negative reaction in the black community to the extent that in the 1984 JCPS survey, 72 percent of the respondents said that he was "prejudiced."[69] By 1986 the cleavage was further reflected in the difference in the approval rating of Reagan's job performance; the survey found 25 percent of blacks approving as contrasted to 66 percent of whites.[70] This basic perception of Reagan contributed significantly to the content of black politics over the decade of the 1980s, and so a powerful conditioning variable in the future would appear to be whether the racial framework that accompanied the Reagan administration persists into the next century.

The Democratic Party Response

The data clearly indicate that racial cleavage in voting patterns and party identification has been in effect at least since 1948, and that it has persisted through the 1988 elections. They show that the cleavage was smallest in the elections of 1956 and 1960, and greatest in the elections from 1968 to 1988. In 1966, Philip Converse suggested that this gap could be accounted for in part by the reaction of whites to the civil rights movement and the increased level of support for Democratic party candidates among both southern and non-southern blacks.[71] His data on "status polarization" showed that a dynamic tension existed between strong black Democratic party identification and weakening white Democratic party identification, especially in the South. Republican dominance in presidential elections since the end of the 1960s, particularly in the white South, surely buttresses this analysis.

Politics within the Democratic party suggest that since 1984 the party's leadership has been prepared to participate in this racial rearticulation process. This is evidenced by the lessening of the structural relationship of minority caucuses to the party, the reduction in the degree of black autonomy through the kinds of choices of blacks for leadership roles,[72] the party's resistance to pressures for basic rules changes prompted by the proposals of Jesse Jackson, and the open courtship of the white Southern vote. Whether such measures alienate black voters from identification with the party is an obvious risk for the future of the Democratic party coalition.

In fact, blacks have distributed their party loyalty since 1964 in the following manner:

TABLE 8
BLACK PARTY IDENTIFICATION, 1964 AND 1984-1988
(IN PERCENT)

	1964[a]	1984[b]	1986[c]	1988[d]
Strong Democrat	54.4	44.4	49.0	49.9
Weak Democrat	22.8	23.6	29.0	22.4
Independent Democrat		14.6	6.0	10.2
Independent	15.4	5.6	2.0	2.5
Independent		24.0	10.0	15.1
Republican		3.8	2.0	2.4
Weak Republican	5.4	2.9	4.0	3.8
Strong Republican	2.0	1.4	3.0	2.7

Sources: [a]Gerald Pomper, *Voters Choice: Varieties of American Electoral Be-*

havior (New York: Dodd, Mead and Co., 1975), Table 2.3, p. 28. (1964 data are from the national surveys conducted by the Survey Research Center, University of Michigan.)

*b*Katherine Tate, Ronald E. Brown, Shirley Hatchett and James S. Jackson, *The 1984 National Black Election Sourcebook*, Program for Research on Black Americans (Ann Arbor, MI: Institute for Social Research, University of Michigan, 1988), Table 2.1.

c"Declining Loyalty to the Democratic Party," *Focus*, Joint Center for Political Studies, 14: 10 (October 1986), p. 5.

*d*Joint Center for Political Studies, "The 1988 Poll of the Black Electorate" (Washington, D.C.: Gallup-Joint Center for Political Studies, 1988).

These data indicate that the identification of blacks with the Democratic party has remained relatively stable over the past two decades. This is supported by the results of a NBES survey, which found that nearly 75 percent of blacks think that the Democratic party works either "very hard" or "fairly hard" for people like them.[73] Still, it would be difficult to conclude that black Democratic party identification is unshakable, since in the JCPS survey of 1984 there were indications of a significant correlation between those who supported Jesse Jackson and those who thought that blacks should have a "separate party."[74] The findings in a 1986 JCPS survey that demonstrate a reduction in "strong Democrat" party identification by blacks should be taken with a note of caution, though, given the tendency of such measures to fluctuate between presidential election years.[75] Nevertheless, if the factors which have worked to undergird the ideological predisposition of blacks towards the Democratic party were to weaken markedly, strong Democratic party identification among blacks would weaken as well.

Any prognosis regarding the prospects for black adherence to Democratic party registration and voting must take the following factors into account: (1) If blacks remain strongly involved in the Democratic party, whites will continue to manifest the countertendency of Republican support, unless the Democrats field an acceptably conservative candidate for president; (2) Attempts by the Democratic party leadership to reintegrate the white South and Northern white males into the party might result in the alienation of blacks; and (3) If blacks are alienated, there exists the capacity, as has been demonstrated, to develop some form of autonomous political behavior—whether through an independent movement within the party coalition or through leaving the party altogether and forming an independent, black-led party. An estimated 25 percent of black voters support the latter option.[76]

The Black Community Reaction

The most lasting effect of the persistence of cleavage is at the community level, where dominant political trends in the nation condition the political behavior of blacks. Racial polarization is not a new phenomenon, yet it could become worse if present trends persist. The impact of both the racial and economic elements of such trends, compounded during the Reagan era, could well intensify racial and class cleavages.

One possible counterfactual to the continuation of a largely unified negative reaction within the black community towards such trends may exist among the groups with the highest (10 percent) Republican party identification. At present, these groups include small segments of the 18-to-29-year-old age cohort and some suburban residents.[77] In each case, the increasing social and economic distance of these groups from the rest of the black community could stimulate intragroup tensions over priority issues and political strategies. This gap, however, is not expected to become as great as that which now obtains between the races as a whole, from which the present—and perhaps continuing— threat to social harmony emanates.

From the vantage point of the late 1980s, one observes a "new class," in the sense meant by Robert Bartley and B. Bruce-Briggs, which has profited most from Reagan-era policies. On the whole, it is not blacks, but educated and affluent whites, who constitute this class.[78] Inasmuch as a highly respected research organization, the Center on Budget and Policy Priorities, has indicated that even middle-class, two-parent, two-income black families have suffered under the Reagan policies, this would seem to confirm the observation of those such as Frances Fox Piven and Richard Cloward that there is, indeed, a "new class war," based substantially on differences in wealth and racial minority status.[79]

If there is indeed a "new class war," the disproportionate amount of blacks within the nation's lower classes signals that they will bear the brunt of its privations. They will not only be its victims in a narrow political and economic sense, but will also be symbolic victims of the increasingly uneven closure of the social order to the processes of democracy. The nature of black politics under such conditions could only become more volatile, even as it became more bureaucratized. Intriguingly, black politics is becoming more bureaucratized, yet at the community level, bureaucratic solutions cannot provide adequate defensive or offensive strategies for development. This leads blacks clearly in the direction of increasing concern with the mobilization of community resources, rather than with casual forms of unfocused "participationism," both in the electoral arena and in other theaters of politics.

NOTES

[1] Morris Janowitz, *The Last Half-Century: Societal Change and Politics in America* (Chicago: University of Chicago Press, 1978), p. 114.

[2] Robert Blauner, *Racial Oppression in America* (New York: Harper and Row, 1972). See, especially, ch. 3, "Internal Colonialism and Ghetto Revolt," pp. 82-110.

[3] Pierre L. van den Berghe, "Paternalistic versus Competitive Race Relations: An Ideal-Type Approach," in Norman Yetman and C. Hoy Steele, eds., *Majority and Minority: The Dynamics of Racial and Ethnic Relations* (Boston: Allyn and Bacon, 1971), pp. 64-79.

[4] Martin Kilson, "Blacks and Neo-ethnicity in America," in Nathan Glazer and Daniel P. Moynihan, eds., *Ethnicity* (Cambridge, MA: Harvard University Press, 1975), pp. 236-266 at 252.

[5] Ibid., p. 255.

[6] Lewis A. Coser, *Continuities in the Study of Social Conflict* (New York: The Free Press/Macmillan, 1962), p. 29.

[7] Howard Shuman and Shirley Hatchett, *Black Racial Attitudes: Trends and Complexities* (Ann Arbor, MI: Institute for Social Research, University of Michigan, 1974), pp. 13-15.

[8] Milton D. Morris, *The Politics of Black America* (New York: Harper and Row, 1975), p. 8.

[9] Charles Hamilton, Forward to Michael Preston, Lenneal Henderson, Jr., and Paul Puryear, eds., *The New Black Politics: The Search for Political Power* (New York: Longman, 1982), p. xx.

[10] Matthew Holden, Jr., *The Politics of the Black "Nation"* (New York: Chandler Publishing, 1973), pp. 1-41.

[11] Ibid., p. 4.

[12] Ibid., p. 43.

[13] John Hope Franklin, *From Slavery to Freedom: A History of Negro Americans*, 3d ed. (New York: Alfred A. Knopf, 1967), p. 439.

[14] William Toll, *The Resurgence of Race: Black Social Theory from Reconstruction to the Pan-African Conferences* (Philadelphia: Temple University Press, 1979), pp. 174-212.

[15] See Tony Martin, *Race First: The Ideological and Organizational Struggles of Marcus Garvey and the Universal Negro Improvement Association* (Westport, CT: Greenwood Press, 1976).

[16] P. Olisanwuche Esedebe, *Pan-Africanism: The Idea and Movement, 1776-1963* (Washington, D.C.: Howard University Press, 1982). (Editor's note: Professor Jan Carew told a small group at the University of Wisconsin-Milwaukee in February 1987 that when he served as an adviser to Kwame Nkrumah, the

former president of Ghana, DuBois (who passed his last days as Nkrumah's guest) told him that he had erred in his earlier judgment of Garvey.)

[17]Robert H. Brisbane, *The Black Vanguard: Origins of the Negro Social Revolution, 1900-1960* (Valley Forge, PA: Judson Press, 1970), pp. 150-158.

[18]See Aldon Morris, *The Origins of the Civil Rights Movement: Black Communities Organizing for Change* (New York: Free Press; London: Collier Macmillan, 1984).

[19]See Harvard Sitkoff, *The Struggle for Black Equality, 1954-1980* (New York: Hill and Wang, 1981).

[20]Joe Feagin and Harlan Hahn, *Ghetto Revolts: The Politics of Violence in American Cities* (New York: Macmillan, 1973), p. 16.

[21]Ibid., p. 173.

[22]U.S. Congress, Joint Economic Committee, "The Impact of Demographic Changes on Social Programs" (Washington, D.C.: U.S. Government Printing Office, 1982), p. 40.

[23]U.S. Bureau of the Census, "Summary Characteristics of the Black Population for States and Selected Counties and Places: 1980," Supplementary Report No. PC80-S1-21 (Washington, D.C.: U.S. Government Printing Office, 1987), p. 11.

[24]Ronald W. Walters, "Imperatives of Black Leadership: Policy Mobilization and Community Development," in Ronald W. Walters and Robert Smith, guest eds., "Reflections on Black Leadership: Styles and Strategies," *The Urban League Review* 9: 1 (Summer 1985): 20-41 at 29-40.

[25]See National Black Leadership Roundtable, "Final Report on Implementation of the 1985-1987 Two-year Goals for Collective Black Family Action" (Washington, D.C.: National Black Leadership Roundtable, 1987).

[26]Margot Henry, *Attention MOVE! This is America* (Chicago: Banner Press, 1987), pp. 173, 175-215.

[27]James Q. Wilson, "The Negro in Politics," in Lawrence H. Fuchs, ed., *American Ethnic Politics* (New York: Harper and Row, 1968), pp. 217-246 at 242.

[28]See U.S. Department of Justice, Community Relations Service, *Annual Reports, 1979-1986* (Washington, D.C.: Community Relations Service, 1979-1986); and Feagin and Hahn, op. cit. note 20, p. 145.

[29]"Move-In Violence: White Resistance to Neighborhood Integration in the 1980s," *KLANWATCH Project*, Southern Poverty Law Center (Montgomery, AL: February 5, 1987), p. 8.

[30]See my discussion in Ronald W. Walters, "African-American Influence on U.S. Foreign Policy Toward South Africa," in Mohammed E. Ahrari, ed., *Ethnic Groups and U.S. Foreign Policy* (Westport, CT: Greenwood Press, 1987). The Comprehensive Anti-Apartheid Act of 1986 was P.L. 99-440, 99th Congress, 2d Session.

[31]Dorothy Gilliam, remarks on "Racism" at the national conference of the National Association for Equal Opportunity in Higher Education (Washington, D.C.: April 10, 1987).

[32]See Rufus P. Browning, Dale Rogers Marshall and David H. Tabb, *Protest Is Not Enough: The Struggle of Blacks and Hispanics for Equality in Urban Politics* (Berkeley and Los Angeles, CA: University of California Press, 1984).

[33]See Michael Lipsky, *Protest as a Political Resource* (Madison, WI: Institute for Research on Poverty, University of Wisconsin, 1967); see also Justin M. Joffe and George Albee, eds., *Prevention Through Political Action and Social Change* (Hanover, NH: published for the Vermont Conference on the Primary Prevention of Psychopathology, University Press of New England, 1981).

[34]See, for example, Frances Fox Piven and Richard A. Cloward, *Poor People's Movements: Why They Succeed, How They Fail* (New York: Pantheon Books, 1977).

[35]Lucius J. Barker and Jesse McCorry, Jr., *Black Americans and the Political System*, 2d ed. (Cambridge, MA: Winthrop Publishers, 1980), pp. 239-240.

[36]Ralph J. Bunche, edited by Dewey Grantham, *The Political Status of the Negro in the Age of FDR*, ch. 19, "Negroes and New Deal Agencies" (Chicago: University of Chicago Press, 1973), pp. 608-631.

[37]See discussion in ibid., ch. 18, "Negro Political Activity in the North," pp. 572-606. See also Henry Lee Moon, *Balance of Power: The Negro Vote* (Garden City, NY: Doubleday, 1948).

[38]*Smith* v. *Allwright*, 321 U.S. 649 (1944).

[39]Moon, op. cit. note 37, p. 190.

[40]More than a negative demonstration of black voting power, Hubert Humphrey's defeat was a demonstration of the absence of the southern white vote, which in large part was captured by George Wallace, former governor of Alabama and presidential candidate of the American Independence Party.

[41]In 1978, 47.3 percent of voting-age blacks voted; in 1982, 49.9 percent voted. U.S. Bureau of the Census, "Voting and Registration in the Election of November 1984," Advance Report, Population Characteristics Series P-20, No. 397 (January 1985), Table A, p. 1.

[42]U.S. Bureau of the Census, "Summary Characteristics of the Black Population for States and Selected Counties and Places: 1980," op. cit. note 23, Table 9, pp. 35-36.

[43]Joint Center for Political Studies, *Black Elected Officials: A National Roster, 1987* (New York: UNIPUB, 1987).

[44]U.S. Bureau of the Census, *1980 Census of Population and Housing*, Supplementary Report No. PC80-S1-11, Congressional District Profiles, 98th Congress (Washington, D.C.: U.S. Government Printing Office, 1983), Table I, pp. 9-18.

[45]Robert Smith, "When Majority Black Districts Elect White Representatives" (Unpublished manuscript, Department of Political Science, Howard University, Washington, D.C., 1987.)

[46]Chandler Davidson, "Minority Vote Dilution: An Overview," in Chandler Davidson, ed., *Minority Vote Dilution* (Washington, D.C.: Howard University Press, 1984), pp. 1-23.

[47]*City of Mobile* v. *Bolden*, 446 U.S. 55 (1980).

[48]Howard Ball, "Racial Vote Dilution: Impact of the Reagan DOJ and the Burger Court on the Voting Rights Act," *Publius* 16: 4 (Fall 1986): 29-48 at 43.

[49]Kenneth H. Thompson, *The Voting Rights Act and Black Electoral Participation* (Washington, D.C.: Joint Center for Political Studies, 1982), pp. 22-24.

[50]Ibid.

[51]*Thornburg* v. *Gingles*, 478 U.S. 30 (1986).

[52]478 U.S. at 50-51.

[53]Holden, op. cit. note 10, p. 43. (Author's italics.)

[54]*The Gallup Report* (Princeton, NJ: The Gallup Poll), No. 212 (May 1983), p. 18, and No. 216 (September 1983), p. 9.

[55]Phil Gailey, "Poll Cites Qualities of Ideal President," *New York Times* (October 9, 1983), Sec. A, p. 32; CBS Morning News Poll (February 5, 1984).

[56]David Broder, Paul Taylor and Haynes Johnson, "A Grassroots Report: Voters Grow Increasingly Disillusioned," *The Washington Post* (April 22, 1987), pp. 1, 14-15 at 14.

[57]Ronald W. Walters, "The Emergent Mobilization of the Black Community in the Jackson Campaign for President," in Lucius J. Barker and Ronald W. Walters, *Jesse Jackson's 1984 Presidential Campaign: Challenge and Change in American Politics* (Urbana, IL: University of Illinois Press, 1989), pp. 35-54.

[58]One such challenge began in Chicago where a coalition of blacks, whites and Latinos formed to boycott Chicago Fest in 1982, and was able to guide a mass voter registration drive in September and October 1982, thus providing the underpinning for Harold Washington's election as Chicago's mayor in 1983. Abdul Alkalimat and Doug Gills, "Black Power vs. Racism: Harold Washington Becomes Mayor," in Red Bush, ed., *The New Black Vote: Politics and Power in Four American Cities* (San Francisco: Synthesis Publications, 1984), pp. 53-179 at 78-79.

[59]Ronald E. Brown, "Group-Based Determinants of Campaign Participation in the 1984 Presidential Election," in Institute for Social Research, *National Black Election Study, Post-Election Survey* (Ann Arbor, MI: Institute for Social Research, University of Michigan, 1985), p. 14.

[60]See the discussion in Ronald W. Walters, *Black Presidential Politics in America: A Strategic Approach* (Albany, NY: State University of New York Press, 1987), ch. 7, "Intra-Party Scenarios: The Jackson Campaign for the Democratic Party Presidential Nomination," pp. 159-183.

[61]See the *Congressional Quarterly* (June 16, 1984), p. 1443.

[62]Gerald M. Pomper, ed., *The Election of 1988: Reports and Interpretations* (Chatham, NJ: Chatham House Publications, Inc., 1989), Table 2.4, p. 47.

[63]"Portrait of the Electorate," *The New York Times* (November 10, 1988), p. B6.

[64]U.S. Congress, Congressional Black Caucus, "Forecast Population, Middle Series Census Projection, 1980-2000" (Washington, D.C.: U.S. Government Printing Office, 1987), Table 15, p. 81.

[65]Whites felt that the federal budget deficit was as equally important as the first four issues cited, and relegated civil rights—deemed highly important by blacks—to a position near the bottom of their priorities. Thomas Cavanagh, *Inside Black America: The Message of the Black Vote in the 1984 Elections* (Washington, D.C.: Joint Center for Political Studies, 1985), Table 1, p. 7.

[66]Frederick Harris and Linda Williams, "JCPS/Gallup Poll Reflects Changing Views on Political Issues," *Focus*, Joint Center for Political Studies, 14: 10 (October 1986): 4.

[67]Michael Omi and Howard Winant, *Racial Formation in the United States: From the 1960s to the 1980s* (New York: Routledge and Kegan Paul, 1986), p. 84.

[68]Community Relations Service, U.S. Department of Justice, *Annual Report, 1977 and 1978* (Washington, D.C.: U.S. Government Printing Office, 1978 and 1979), p. 15 (1979) and p. 14 (1978).

[69]Cavanagh, op. cit. note 65, Table 12, p. 33.

[70]"Higher Approval Ratings for President Reagan," *Focus*, Joint Center for Political Studies, 14: 10 (October 1986): 5.

[71]Philip Converse, "Social Cleavage in the 1964 Election," in William J. Crotty, Donald M. Freeman and Douglas S. Gatlin, *Political Parties and Political Behavior* (Boston: Allyn and Bacon, 1971, © 1966), p. 426.

[72]Editor's note: Since this writing, Ronald Brown, an African-American, was chosen (1989) as the chair of the national Democratic party.

[73]Institute for Social Research, University of Michigan, *National Black Election Study, Pre-Election Survey* (Ann Arbor, MI: Institute for Social Research, University of Michigan, 1984).

[74]Cavanagh, op. cit. note 65, Table 11, p. 32.

[75]"Declining Loyalty to the Democratic Party," *Focus*, Joint Center for Political Studies, 14: 10 (October 1986): 5.

[76]Institute for Social Research, op. cit. note 73.

[77]Cavanagh, op. cit. note 65, Table 13, p. 41.

[78]See Robert L. Bartley, B. Bruce-Briggs, et al., eds., *The New Class?* (New Brunswick, NJ: Transaction Books, 1979).

[79]See Frances Fox Piven and Richard A. Cloward, *The New Class War: Reagan's Attack on the Welfare State and Its Consequences* (New York: Pantheon Books, 1982).

INTEGRATION OR SEPARATION: BEYOND THE PHILOSOPHICAL WILDERNESS THEREOF *

Winston A. Van Horne

University of Wisconsin-Milwaukee

Between the grandeur of the day before yesterday, and the glory of the day after tomorrow, lies the anguish of yesterday, today and tomorrow for peoples of primary African origin and their descent. In the very last sentence of his introduction to this volume, Bernard Boxill lays down a task of unenviable difficulty, but nonetheless of inescapable necessity, in relation to the well-being of the generations of black people in the twenty-first century and beyond.

For more than a century now, the ceaseless struggle of blacks for justice, freedom and equality has occurred within the bounds of the possibilities and limits either of integration into, or separation from, the political society of the United States. Both integration and separation are means to the the realization of three ultimate ends—justice, freedom and equality. Integration is enlivened by the idea that by striving continually to become full members of "the political community formed and brought into existence by the Constitution of the United States, and as such become entitled to all the rights, and privileges, and immunities, guaranteed by that instrument to the citizen,"[1] blacks will be made whole from their historical infirmities by becoming constituent members of the "sovereign people." Separation is quickened by the idea that the defining attributes of the "sovereign people,"[2] most notably racism, preclude black people from enjoying true justice, freedom and equality within "the political community formed

*I should like to thank my colleagues James Barnes and Doreatha Mbalia, who suffered me for endless hours of discourse on the subject matter of this chapter; Bernard Boxill, who read the manuscript and made very valuable comments; the chair of my department, Patrick Bellegarde-Smith, for arranging a departmental seminar at which I was able to have my ideas subjected to close critical scrutiny; Mensah Aborampah and Cheryl Johnson, for their very perceptive observations at the departmental seminar; and Thomas Tonnesen, who has worked closely with me since the inception of the *Ethnicity and Public Policy* series.

and brought into existence by the Constitution of the United States,"[3] thus they can never be made whole from their historical infirmities by striving to become constituent members of the sovereign people. There is, then, a hard line of demarcation in countervailing ideas that sets apart integration and separation. Yet, intriguingly, both are trapped by the philosophic foundation that undergirds the liberal democratic politics and capitalist economics of the political community. What is the nature and significance of this trap? What are its costs? Can it be broken? If so, how?

I

The autonomy of the will of the individual and the efficaciousness of the market are the twin pillars upon which the entire edifice of liberal democratic politics and capitalist economics rests.[4] The political principle that the will of the individual should be unfettered by public authority, except insofar as its fettering is essential to civil peace and societal harmony, and the economic principle that free, open and competitive markets are essential to the maximization of individual initiative and societal prosperity, conflate to form the animating transgenerational spirit of American political society. This spirit sanctifies the individual *qua* individual, who is imbued with an intrinsic dignity, value and worth. Here, the humanity of man is consummated in the integrity and inviolability of the individual, whose will is free to will whatsoever it wills, constrained only by the limits of its own power and the fetters it has consented to place on itself in the form of the authoritative decisions of those to whom it has given authority to act in its behalf. All of liberal democratic political theory and capitalist economic theory emanate from this most fundamental of all the axioms that ground them. How has this axiom played out transgenerationally in relation to individuals of primary African origin and their descent in the political society of the United States?

It is well to begin by observing that Africans who were transported to the New World to be slaves came from societies whose cultures grounded the dignity, value and worth of the individual not in the individual *qua* individual but in the individual *qua* collective. The African realized the possibilities of his life in the context of his participation in the collective oneness of himself, his ancestors, his unborn progeny, and those with whom he shared the land. He actualized his capacities, potentialities, interests and good by sharing selflessly his spirit, work and material possesions with those who gave meaning and purpose to his life. Outside the collective, the African was a lonely, solitary and wretched creature. Within the collective, the African was a social, productive and caring human being. It is vital that one understands well this grounding of the African's psyche and social life prior to his involuntary relocation and twelve-generation bondage in colonial America/the United States.

Searing was the individualism that confronted the African in the United States. The communal will—whereby individual consciousness and collective consciousness, as well as individual purpose and collective purpose, dissolved one into the other to yield patterns of authority that assured the dignity, worth and value of the individual—gave way to the autonomous will, which cut the individual loose from the transgenerational authority of the nurturing collective and left him to fend for himself. But there is a contradiction of grave historical record here. Against his own will, as well as the will of the collective of which he was a part, the African was forced from cultures that nurtured the communal will into one(s) that held sacred the autonomous will, yet he was forbidden either to develop or to exercise the autonomy of his will as an individual. No intrinsic dignity, worth and value were discerned in his person by those who enslaved him. Such value and worth that he did have emanated, for the most part, from efficacious market considerations, and not ethical and moral imperatives pertaining to (wo)man *qua* (wo)man. Put differently, the ethical and moral principles that sustain the dignity, worth and value of the individual through the autonomy of the will were denied to the African, even though the culture that now determined the contours of his life made an ultimate virtue of the autonomy of the will. And herein lay the tug-and-pull of the generations of blacks since the Fourteenth Amendment to the Constitution in 1868 made them citizens of the United States. Martin Luther King, Jr., like Frederick Douglass before him, exhorts and admonishes the political society to honor, defend and protect the autonomy of the wills of black individuals, in consonance with the standing of the autonomy of the will of the individual *qua* individual as an ultimate virtue of the culture that grounds it persistence. El-Hajj Malik El-Shabazz (Malcolm X), like Martin Delany before him, exhorts and admonishes black people to become conscious of the fact that the structure of the political society in which they live precludes it from really honoring, defending and protecting the autonomy of their wills as individuals. Hence, it is only by securing for themselves alternative arrangements to those provided by the political society that blacks will ever fully regain dignity, worth and value in their persons, which have been violated unremittingly ever since the collectives to which they once belonged were sundered by the trading of them as "ordinary article[s] of merchandise and traffic, whenever a profit could be made by it,"[5] as Roger Taney put it ever so aptly in the *Dred Scott* decision.

Now, for nigh seven generations since the Emancipation Proclamation of January 1, 1863, black people have wandered hither and yon in the philosophical wilderness bounded by integration and separation. If it is to be understood well, this wandering must be observed in a larger historical context. No africologist—who spends his/her life in reflection on the cosmological, ontological, ethical, moral and social-psychological ideas, concepts, principles and states into which the discipline of africology inquires transmillennially and transgenerationally—can fail to be touched deeply by the profound significance of Cheikh Anta Diop's observation that " [i]n 661 B.C. Ashurbanipal attacked Egypt and pillaged the city of Thebes. . . . The fall of the most venerable city of all Antiquity aroused deep emotion in the world of that time and marked the end of the Nubian Sudanese or Twenty-fifth Ethiopian Dynasty. That date also *marked the decline of [b]lack political supremacy in Antiquity and in history.*"[6] The black (wo)man's political decline in the world has been accompanied inexorably by a corresponding decline in the power and dominance of his/her ideas in organizing human societies and in determining and guiding behavior throughout the world. With the political emergence of Greece around 600 B.C., and the dominance of Euro-Mediterranean/Euro-American ideas on the world stage since then, the Afroworld has been largely in a state of continuous penetration by ideas and concepts which peoples of primary African origin and their descent did not originate.

Innumerable have been such ideas that have penetrated deep into the psyches and souls of peoples of primary African origin and their descent, and the psyche and soul of this author stand as no exception. One does not wish to imply here that all such ideas have been/are wholly lacking in human value in relation to the nurture and development of the dignity, worth and value of peoples of primary African origin and their descent. One does, however, wish to call out with the greatest possible resonance that since 600 B.C., Euro-Mediterranean ideas have, for the most part, bestrided the Afroworld like a colossus. The cost of this has been incalculable as one reflects upon the twenty-seven centuries of black political decline. How is this transmillennial and transgenerational political decline to be halted and reversed? In one form or another, this question imposes itself upon the work of every africologist, and in point of fact on everyone who questions the claim that "it all started with Greece," as this author was once informed by a senior university administrator at a conference. And so, one is drawn back to the immediate task of this chapter: Is there any way out of the philosophical wilderness of integration and separation in the United States?

There is no way out of the wilderness if one's moral compass is set in the autonomy of the will of the individual. It must be said here and now that having been guided by the moral principle of the autonomy of the will of the individual from one's youth, it is a hard thing in middle age for this author to observe that it has been a principle of entrapment for peoples of primary African origin and their descent in the United States. On what grounds does one make this personally painful observation? The autonomous will is grounded in the rationality of man and the reasonableness, nay, right, of the individual to govern himself according to his own reason. The idea of the rational individual and rational conduct stands at the very core of the principle of the autonomy of the will. If the dictates of reason are amenable to intersubjective corroboration, should not rational individuals be free to act individually in conformity with the reason's dictates? Most assuredly, observe the theorists of liberal politics and capitalist economics. The rational activity of autonomous wills expands the freedom of individuals individually, and by extension collectively. Collective freedom is thus an extension of the rational activity of the autonomous wills of individuals, and has no moral standing apart from the reason-guided activity of the autonomous will of the individual. Collective freedom, then, is a rational derivative of the autonomy of the will. But how does this square with the denial of collective freedom to the twelve generations of black people whose lives were circumscribed by the captivity of slavery, given the universality of the construction of the autonomy of the will?

The denial lay quite simply in the disavowal of the activity of reason-guided wills in those who were of primary African origin and their descent, and in the corruption of the communal will, which had heretofore guided the conduct of those who were transported into bondage, into the heteronomous will. The original principle of the communal will presupposed an essential equality between intuition, reason, passion and appetite. There was nothing inherently suspect about the will being directed by passion or appetite or intuition. Behavior emanating from any or some combination of these inclining, impelling and guiding the will was no less honorable, noble, praiseworthy and virtuous than conduct which emanated from the will directed by reason. Intuition, reason, passion and appetite conflated to occasion in the African and his community what might be called a simultaneity of individual and collective consciousness. The European either never understood or, if he did, intentionally and deliberately elected to debase this archetypal principle of African individual and community life.

By elevating reason to a position of rule over intuition, passion and appetite in determining honorable, noble, praiseworthy and virtuous conduct, and in grounding the autonomy of the will in the primacy of the rule of reason, the European put in place a structure of ideas that made easy the corruption of the African's communal will. The original conception and construction of the communal will were degraded and debased by the radical downgrading of the standing of passion and appetite, as well as of intuition, in relation to that of reason. By conjoining virtue with the rule of reason, and grounding the autonomy of the will in the rule of reason, Euro-Americans who enslaved Africans subordinated the communal will to the autonomous will, and by extension afforded themselves a ready justification for the subjection of the wills of Africans to their wills.

If the African was largely devoid of reason, and if reason was the efficient cause of the activity of the autonomous will, surely the African was not free to act individually in conformity with the dictates of reason. And surely, if he were not a reason-guided creature, he "might *justly and lawfully be reduced to slavery* for [the white man's] benefit,"[7] without any abridgment of his freedom either individually or collectively. Frederick Douglass' denunciation[8] and the revisionism of later historians pertaining to the language of the *Dred Scott* decision notwithstanding, Roger Taney was absolutely correct when he noted that this sentiment "prevailed in the *civilized* and *enlightened* portions of the world at the time of the Declaration of Independence, and when the Constitution of the United States was framed and adopted. . . . [Moreover, it] was . . . fixed and universal in the civilized portion of the white race."[9] The correctness of Taney's observation dissolves any doubt that for twelve generations the principle of the autonomy of the will in relation to the nurture and development of the dignity, worth and value of the individual, which was so fundamental to the liberal politics and capitalist economics whereby whites pursued their interests and good, was irrelevant for the 90 percent of black people who were enslaved, and only of nominal relevance for the 10 percent of blacks who were free, given the severe constraints that distorted and disfigured their lives. But what of the generations of blacks who have been guaranteed since the Thirteenth Amendment to the Constitution that they would never again be subjected to "slavery nor involuntary servitude, except as a punishment for crime whereof the party shall have been duly convicted . . . [?]"[10] Have they not been the beneficiaries of the principle of the autonomous will insofar as they have prospered individually?

This is an exceedingly troublesome question. It is founded in the singling out from the masses of black people this or that individual who has ostensibly prospered—by whatever criteria prospered happens to be judged at a given point in time — as symbols both of individual and collective progress. But there is no one-to-one correspondence between symbol and substance, either conceptually or empirically. Were there not black individuals who "prospered" during slavery? Ostensible symbols of progress often mask societal decay and rot. None has made this point more compellingly than Christopher Dawson in his *Progress and Religion*.[11] The critical point which is being made here is that the ostensible prosperity of this or that black individual entails neither the true autonomy of that particular individual's will nor progress for the masses of black people. The soundness and resonance of this point were very lively in the mind of the twentieth century's most venerated integrationist, Martin Luther King, Jr. Recognizing that black individuals could "prosper" even amidst the oppressive injustices of the system of Jim Crow, King called out with unmistakable clarity that "[a]ll segregation statutes are unjust because segregation distorts the soul and damages the personality. It gives the segregator a false sense of superiority, and the segregated a false sense of inferiority."[12] Regardless of ostensible prosperity, a nagging and persistent sense of inferiority no doubt haunted the recesses of the unconscious mind, even if blocked out by the conscious mind, of every black individual who suffered the indignities of constitutionally sanctioned segregation statutes. There is no autonomy of the will where a false sense of inferiority "distorts the soul and damages the personality."[13] And so, one can safely say of the generations of black people from the Emancipation Proclamation through the passage of the Civil Rights Act of 1964, the Voting Rights Act of 1965 and the Supreme Court's decision in *Loving* v. *Virginia* (1967),[14] which together mark the end of constitutionally and statutorily sanctioned Jim Crow, that though they may have benefited from the efficaciousness of markets in ways that were impossible during slavery, the political community continued to constrain them unduly in their exercise of autonomous wills as individuals.

If integration in the context of liberal democratic politics and capitalist economics entails the nurture, defense and protection of the autonomy of the will of the individual, without which there can be no true justice, freedom or equality, one can say without fear of successful contradiction that from the time that the first of their numbers was enslaved through the mid-1960s, peoples of primary African origin and their descent were never integrated into the political community of the United States. Material considerations aside, this is indubitably true insofar as the political community never recognized in them the capacity to use reason to incline, guide and impel their wills to will autonomously. What are the efficient cause and sufficient reason for the lack of such recognition?

For the antebellum period, the historian Eugene Genovese provides as compelling an answer as this author has observed anywhere. He writes: "Any attempt, no matter how well-meaning, indirect, or harmless, to question the slave system appeared not only as an attack on [the slavemaster's] material interest but as an attack on his self-esteem at its most vulnerable point. To question either the morality or the practicality of slavery meant to expose the root of the slaveholder's dependence in independence."[15] For the slavemaster, the corruption of the African's conception of the communal will, and the sanctity of the autonomous will within the framework of liberal politics and capitalist economics, were essential to his own self-esteem. Put differently, the material and psychological independence of the slaveholder was grounded in his direct dependence on his domination of both the African's labor and will. Those whites who were not slaveholders did not have this sort of direct dependence on the African. Still, for the most part, they did not believe that persons of primary African origin and their descent were capable of having truly autonomous wills—at least not in any foreseeable future. No less a foe of slavery than Harriet Beecher Stowe subscribed to this belief. In this cross section of historical time, integration was obviously impossible.

For the postbellum period through the mid-1960s, legalized and constitutionalized Jim Crow was engrafted onto the dominant social-psychology of whites, regardless of region. They believed that peoples of primary African origin and their descent passed their lives animated largely by the heteronomy of the will, and as such, could not be the social equals of those whose lives were quickened by the autonomy of the will. Put more bluntly, the philosophic principle of the autonomy of the will of the individual provided a luxuriant host for the social-psychological parasitism of white racism, and worked to the economic, political and social advantage of whites individually and collectively, even as blacks were disadvantaged simultaneously. Accordingly, in the objective reality of the political society, integration was at best an epiphenomenon and at worst a downright delusion in this period. But what of the period since the mid-1960s?

Legalized and constitutionalized Jim Crow has been banished from the political society. A range of new forms of economic, political and social interaction between whites and blacks has emerged over the generation since the passage of the Civil Rights Act of 1964. (It is truly of the most profound historical significance to observe that of all the generations of blacks in colonial America/the United States, the only one that has not had its life chances constrained severely by the law is the one born since 1964.) Have blacks not availed themselves of the removal of the law's constraints to position themselves in the political society/political community in ways that were unheard of heretofore? In 1989, did not General Colin Powell, a black man, become chairman of the Joint Chiefs of Staff—third, behind the president and the secretary of defense, in the chain of command for the armed forces of the United States? In that same year, did not the Democratic majority in the House of Representatives elect William Gray, a black man, to be the party's whip—the third highest ranking member of the party's leadership in that house of Congress? Did not Reginald F. Lewis, a black man, acquire Beatrice International Food Company in 1987 for nearly one billion dollars? Was Clifton Wharton, a black man, not still serving in 1989 as the chairman and chief executive officer of the Teachers Insurance and Annuity Association-College Retirement Equities Fund (TIAA/CREF), the country's largest private pension system, with some $70 billion in assets—having served previously as the president of Michigan State University, one of the largest universities in the country, and as chancellor of the State University System of New York, the largest university system in the country? Were not five black individuals among the top ten entertainers in 1988-1989 earnings—Michael Jackson, $125 million; Bill Cosby, $95 million; Mike Tyson, $71 million; Eddie Murphy, $57 million; and Oprah Winfrey, $55 million? Was Tom Bradley, a black man, not in his fifth consecutive term as the mayor of Los Angeles, the second largest city in the country, in 1989? In September of 1989, did David Dinkins not become the first black man to win the mayoral primary of the Democratic party in New York City, the country's largest city, by defeating three-term mayor Edward Koch, a white man, which virtually assured his victory in the November general election as the city's first black mayor? Was 1989 not also the year in which Bill White, a black man, became the president of baseball's National League, and Ronald Brown, also a black man, the chair of the Democratic party's national committee? Finally, was L. Douglas Wilder not elected governor of Virginia in 1989, the first black person ever elected as the governor of a state?

Assuredly, the preceding examples—spanning politics, economics, business, education, the military and entertainment—evince more than symbolic progress. They represent fundamental structural change in the society since the mid-1960s, and constitute incontrovertible evidence that in tangible increments King's dream of a fully integrated society is coming to pass. Such is the position of those who claim that race/racism has largely ceased to constitute a hard color line of demarcation in the society. The objective reality of integration is at hand, they assert. Integration does not entail the use of public policy to redistribute societal resources, nor some skewed notion of freedom and equality that manifests itself in blacks and whites living next door to one another. Rather, it entails the removal of undue barriers to the nurturing and development of autonomous wills in individuals, so that they might govern their lives rationally in conformity with their particular tastes, preferences, wants, needs and desires. Only in this context can the dignity, worth and value of the individual blossom, as true justice, freedom and equality flourish. Undue barriers emanating solely from race have been largely removed now, thus the prospect of a fully integrated society is wide open and is limited only by individual initiative, industry, skill and the willingness to work hard and make sacrifices. The examples just called out corroborate this observation, or so those who believe in the objective reality of integration at the end of the 1980s maintain. But do they?

Yes—at the end of the 1980s the United States is an integrated society. Is this meant to be ironic, given what appears to be an exponentially expanding black underclass? No. The black underclass is but one product of our integrated society, just as the set of examples cited earlier is another, in which the autonomy of the will of the individual is the conceptual anchor that moors integration. It is of the greatest doubt whether integrationists from Douglass to King ever thought out clearly the range of consequences in objective reality of integration grounded in the autonomy of the will of the individual, which wills within the framework of the efficaciousness of the market— especially where the social-psychological parasitism of racism upon the philosophic principle of the autonomous will has obtained as a transgenerational societal norm. Put differently, a black chairman of the Joint Chiefs of Staff and distressingly high numbers of black teenage mothers are both quite consistent with the philosophic mooring of integration. Little wonder that since the late 1960s a sort of social schizophrenia has really taken hold in the black community, as the social-psychological, not to mention material and status, distance between the ones "taking off" due to the demise of undue barriers to the exercise of the autonomy of the will and those who have not done so widens ever more and more. This, of course, is harmonious with the dominance of the idea of the autonomy of the will of the individual. Happy are the blacks who, having taken off, "make it." Unhappy are those blacks who do not take off, and fail to make it. Individuals are free either to succeed or to fail, contingent only on their own wills unfettered by undue societal constraints. Such constraints are presumed to emerge in the context of the denial of negative rights, which many claim have been undone by civil rights legislation since the mid-1960s. However, the limits of this position become excruciatingly obvious to even the most casual reader of this volume who spends any time whatsoever on Boxill's discussion of negative rights and positive rights.

There is no need here to recapitulate Boxill's sound and perceptive observations pertaining to negative rights and positive rights. The crucial point to be made is that the idea of negative rights emanates from the idea of the autonomy of the will of the individual. Constructed differently, the autonomy of the will is conceptually prior to negative rights. Indeed, negative rights have as their axiomatic purpose the preservation of the autonomy of the will. The will of the individual should be left alone to will as it wills, constrained only by its own intrinsic limitations. This means that it should be free of all undue interference from other wills to will, and it itself should not interfere unduly with other wills to will. This is precisely the purpose of negative rights that liberal politics and capitalist economics assure. But what of positive rights? Surely it is silly, one might say inane, for anyone to claim at the end of the twentieth century that liberal politics and capitalist economics assure only negative rights. Boxill makes plain that this is not so. That positive rights have been engrafted onto liberal politics and capitalist economics is not at issue; what is important for our purpose is the ethical and moral standing of positive rights in relation to the autonomy of the will.

The autonomy of the will entails negative rights; it does not entail positive rights. This point is critically important in relation to integration. Conceptually and empirically, integration grounded in the autonomy of the will of the individual necessitates negative rights; it does not necessitate positive rights. From Douglass to King to the present, integrationists have evinced a conceptual and empirical blind spot to this truth. Many have been the lamentations and putative explanations concerning the end of the civil rights movement and the failure of integration to deliver what all too many black people expected of it. None, of whom this author is aware, have heretofore isolated the first cause and the efficient cause of the disjunction between the subjective reality and the objective reality of integration. Subjectively, black people expected integration to provide and assure both negative rights and positive rights. Objectively, integration has largely assured only negative rights. It could hardly have been otherwise, the disappointments of black and other integrationists notwithstanding. The conceptual mooring of integration in the autonomy of the will of the individual meant empirically that once a range of negative rights had been secured by blacks, ones deemed essential to the autonomy of the will in the liberal-capitalist political economy of the United States, the defining purpose of integration was satisfied. The problem, then, that bedevils integrationists who are unhappy with the outcome(s) of integration since the mid-1960s is to find a way to transcend the limits of the autonomy of the will of the individual in relation to the nurture of the dignity, worth and value of blacks, and by extension the justice, freedom and equality that they should enjoy.

How is this to obtain? By conceptually engrafting onto the principle of the autonomous will the idea of positive rights, which are assured by authoritative decisions binding upon all. This has already obtained apart from integration. There is a rub, however. Engraftments pertaining to integration must necessarily contend with the objective reality of the social-psychological parasitism of racism on the autonomy of the will of the individual, and those that have taken hold and developed to date have been ones which fit within this reality. Put differently, positive rights that have been deemed, within a determinate cross section of time, to be consistent with the autonomy of the will of the individual, and not ruinous to the social-psychological parasitism of racism—while serving the interests and good of whites, whether long-term or short-term or both—have generally taken hold. The obverse has not been true. Daunting, then, is the task of integrationists who seek to engraft positive rights onto the autonomous will where doing so would be destructive of racism, or is perceived, rightly or wrongly, to be outside the bounds of the interests and good of whites. I dare say that though such engraftment might be conceptually possible, it most assuredly will not take hold empirically within the extant framework of liberal democratic politics and capitalist economics. (Moreover, I shall venture to observe that even if the political society were to be reorganized according to some version of Marxism-Leninism, the subjective and objective intractability of racism would persist. Nothing that this author either has observed or read through the middle years of his life undoes the piercing agony of Richard Wright's soul, or confutes his observations pertaining to Marxism-Leninism, in *The God That Failed*.[16])

The conceptual and empirical limits of integration that have been called out make plain that integration affords the masses of black people no way out of the philosophical wilderness in which integrationists have been wandering since the Fourteenth Amendment to the Constitution. For even if, by some fortuitous stroke of good luck, class-drawn distinctions that the autonomy of the will also sustains were to wither away, the race-drawn ones would persist. Does Thomas Sowell not remind us that "only about one percent of blacks who are currently being married have brides or grooms of a different race, and even outside the South the intermarriage rate of blacks is only about 4 percent."[17] One surely does not wish to corrupt the idea of integration by inferring that it necessitates intermarriage between blacks and whites. Still, it cannot pass unnoticed that within the bounds of integration a hard color line of racial demarcation persists, as individuals in the exercise of their autonomous wills replicate patterns of behavior that set them apart on the basis of race. Martin Luther King, Jr., exhorted and admonished the political society to live out the true meaning of its creed, without perhaps ever fully perceiving the conceptual and empirical limits of that creed in relation to the life chances of the masses of black people. People of primary African origin and their descent owe King a debt for leading them out of the legal backwater of Jim Crowism that can only be repaid through their generational and transgenerational work both in halting and reversing the millennia-long decline of which Diop speaks. But in leading black people out of the legal backwater of Jim Crowism, he left them in the philosophical wilderness of integration. Is separation the way out of this wilderness?

II

If integration is animated by a steadfast belief in the possibility that in objective reality peoples of primary African origin and their descent in the United States will, in time, secure true justice, freedom and equality, separation is quickened by an oscillation between the physical departure of black people from the country and their remaining in the political society—though relying on what Martin Delany termed "self-efforts" to assure their well-being both individually and collectively. Over the generations, separation has been marked by two clear and distinct impulses, if one may so speak. These have been captured well by Delany, who writes:

> Our common country is the United States. Here were we born, here raised and educated; here are the scenes of childhood; the pleasant associations of our school going days; the loved enjoyments of our domestic and fireside relations, and the sacred graves of our departed fathers and mothers, and from here we will not be driven by any policy that may be schemed against us.

> *We are Americans*, having a birthright citizenship—natural claims upon the country—claims common to all others of our fellow citizens—natural rights, which may, by virtue of unjust laws, be obstructed, but never can be annulled. Upon these do we place ourselves, as immovably fixed as the decrees of the living God.[18]

> Central and South America, are evidently the ultimate destination and future home of the colored race on this continent; . . . The advantages to the colored people of the United States, to be derived from emigration to Central, South America, and the

West Indies, are incomparably greater than that of any other parts of the world at present. . . . There is nothing under heaven in our way—the people stand with open arms ready to receive us. . . . [T]he voice of the people say come—and God our Father bids us go.—Will we go? Go we must, and go we will, *as there is no alternative.* To remain here in North America, and be crushed to the earth in vassalage and degradation, we never will. . . . Our race is to be *redeemed*; it is a great and glorious work, and we are the instrumentalities by which it is to be done. But we must go from among our oppressors; it never can be done by staying among them.[19]

These two impulses may be termed the "stay-but-rely-on-self-help" impulse and the "leave-out-of-necessity" impulse. For some separatists, being in the United States is a birthright which can neither be annulled nor destroyed (the *Dred Scott* decision notwithstanding); for others, the idea of birthright is vacuous insofar as the substance it implies can never be brought to fruition. Both impulses of separatism aim at the same end, namely, the dignity, worth and value of black people individually and collectively. And both spin off the same conceptual axis, that is, the autonomy of the will of the individual. The leave-out-of-necessity impulse does, however, evince a measure of sensitivity to the original construction of the communal will that is not true of the stay-but-rely-on-self-help impulse, which may well be a product of the former's groping for a transcendent, African-grounded cosmogonic reality to moor the redemption of peoples of primary African origin and their descent. Still, paradoxical as it may seem at first blush, in the context of the political society of the United States, both separation and integration tap deeply into the autonomous will. How can this be so?

Integration constructs the autonomy of the will as impelling individuals over time towards a political society in which social intercourse is consistent with the dignity, worth and value of the individual *qua* individual, in conformity with the dictates of reason. Separation constructs the autonomy of the will either as rationally impelling black individuals to leave the political society in order to actualize their dignity, worth and value individually and collectively, or guiding blacks to stay by birthright in the society, with the rational knowledge that as individuals their race sets them apart in a way that necessitates their own self-help activities in order to give empirical substance to their ethical and moral claims to dignity, worth and value individually and collectively. If integration looks outward from the black community but within the bounds of the civil order of the society, separation looks either inward to the black community bounded by the society's civil order or outward beyond the civil order of the United States. But whether separation looks inward or outward, it is still trapped by the limits of the autonomous will. (At what cost to peoples of primary African origin and their descent did European colonialism beyond the shores of the United States propagate the principle of the autonomous will?)

Separatists subscribe to a range of politics from liberal-democratic to other-than-liberal-democratic, and a range of economics from capitalist to other-than-capitalist. Regardless of where they fit on the range, and whether they act in conformity with the imperatives of the leave-out-of-necessity impulse or the stay-but-rely-on-self-help impulse, separatists (absent the ones who are nihilists and anarchists) never break free of the dominance of the idea of the reason-ruled will. Once this critical point is grasped clearly, it becomes ever so easy for one to observe why separation affords peoples of primary African origin and their descent in the United States no exit from the philosophical wilderness in which they have been wandering ever so long.

When one observes the period from the early 1630s, when Virginia sanctioned slavery statutorily, through the mid-1860s, when the Constitution prohibited slavery and involuntary servitude, it is clear that both impulses of separation were irrelevant to 90 percent of those of primary African origin and their descent living in the United States. For the 10 percent of black people for whom they may have had some relevance, two points are abundantly clear. First, most of these persons did not wish to leave the United States, which, of course, continues to be the sentiment of all but the barest few of the black population as the end of the twentieth century approaches. Second, whether they desired to leave—as is evidenced by the founding of Liberia and Sierra Leone on Africa's West Coast—or to stay, their psyches and souls drank heavily of the draughts of liberal politics and capitalist economics, and correspondingly of the autonomy of the will of the individual. Recognizing the severe constraints on their exercise of autonomous wills as individuals in the United States, some opted to leave, not because of any quarrel with the principle of the autonomy of the will of the individual itself, but because as individuals they were constrained unduly in the exercise of their autonomous wills. For those who elected to stay in spite of the perceived/perceivable barriers to the autonomy of their wills as individuals, there was always the hope that by subscribing to the fundamental values on which the society was founded and making use of them, a path to separate development within the bounds of the extant civil order could be charted. The dreadful limitations of this position were demonstrated all too vividly over the generations until the end of slavery.

The stay-but-rely-on-self-help separatists have fared better since the black (Thirteenth, Fourteenth and Fifteenth) Amendments were added to the Constitution in the 1860s. Still, they have failed to realize within the bounds of civil order the sort of development that generations of them have hoped for, namely, a state of affairs in which the autonomy of their wills as individuals becomes readily manifest in a free, equal and self-assertive (wo)manhood. There is no mystery to this. A hard line of demarcation has obtained between what reason-ruled wills inform black separatists and what reason-ruled wills, upon which racism is parasitic, inform whites, who have dominated and continue to dominate the political society.

The leave-out-of-necessity separatists have been trapped by a cruel reality; there is just no place for them to go. One may wish to forgive Delany's naive romanticizing of the open arms with which the peoples of Central America, South America and the Caribbean stood to receive hordes of black people from the United States. Delany's romance was of the 1850s. The world at the end of the twentieth century permits no such romance. There is no place on the face of the earth for tens of millions of blacks in the United States to go. The leave-out-of-necessity separatists are thus faced with a stark truth of the objective reality of their position: Absent the dissolution of the republic, the masses of peoples of primary African origin and their descent cannot leave the United States. And were the republic to dissolve, they would still remain within some portion of what is now called the United States. (It need not be said that a civil war was fought to save the republic.) The crucial point here is that having no place for large numbers of blacks to go physically—Malcus "Marcus" Garvey's dream of mass migration to Africa was, perhaps, even less realistic than King's dream concerning future relations between blacks and whites—the leave-out-of-necessity separatists are, at best, reduced to romanticize the possibilities of the autonomous will in black people free of oppression, and at worst, wholly irrelevant to the construction of the foundation of ideas and activities for which Boxill calls.

How, then, shall peoples of primary African origin and their descent find their way out of the philosophical wilderness that excites in them diverse illusions and delusions which skew their sensibilities to their true transhistorical state as a people — especially in the context of the twenty-seven centuries of political decline of the black (wo)man of which Diop speaks ever so hauntingly? One is tempted to ask, how shall black people be redeemed?—as did Delany. But I shall not, and shall no more speak of redemption, since all too many have believed that the full fruits of redemption lie beyond the temporality of the earth. Rather, I shall ask, is there not some sweet, oblivious antidote to the generations-long lures of integration and separation? There is, and it is to be found in the reconstitution of the will.

III

Let us resolve here and now to speak no more either of the autonomous will or of the heteronomous will (expect for antiquarian or reconstitutive purposes) but of the *conjunctive will*.[20] What does this mean? The attributes of both the autonomous will and the heteronomous will are well-known. By what attributes is the conjunctive will known, and who knows of them? To make known more widely the attributes of the conjunctive will and their significance, not only in relation to the transgenerational well-being of black people in the United States but the transcenturial climb of peoples of primary African origin and their descent to the glory of the day after tomorrow, is the task at hand.

The conjunctive will consists of four discrete but interrelated faculties—intuition, reason, appetite and passion. Intuition perceives, recognizes, knows and understands in fleeting moments of time what is not yet perceived, recognized, known nor understood by reason. It also senses that which is not yet sensible either to passion or appetite.[21] Its activity thus affords the will clear directives pertaining to what has come to be known as leaps of faith. It provides a bridge between the known and the not known, the understood and the not understood, and the sensible and what is not yet sensed. Intuition expands the horizon of what is sensed, known and understood in ways that reason neither knows nor understands. It could well be on account of this that Plato, who no doubt knew of the standing of intuition among peoples of African antiquity but sought to establish the primacy of the rule of reason over the soul (no distinction is made here between will and soul[22]), drew intuition within the bounds of reason and ended thereby its independence from reason. Though he was wrong in bonding intuition to reason, Plato had the good and timeless sense to recognize its indispensability in animating the activity of the soul/will. Both his liberal and socialist successors have not only jettisoned intuition from the bounds of reason, but they also have largely expunged it from the will. The conjunctive will restores intuition to its proper standing, and opens to the individual and his/her community all the possibilities of sensing, knowing and understanding intuitively. (It should be added parenthetically that had the standing of intuition been wholly debased in the wills of peoples of primary African origin and their descent in bondage, it is unlikely that they would have survived their captivity nearly as well as they did. For example, was it not absolutely imperative that a slave sense, know and understand—intuit correctly—the many moods of one's master/mistress in order stave off, as much as possible, the brutal physical and psychological effects of the master's/mistress' whims?[23] It is indeed a truth that black people in the United States know and understand white people much better than the latter either know or understand the former. I dare say that sound intuition has played no little role in this.)

Much too much has been written about and made of reason in the Euroworld. Reason is but one of the faculties of the will, and it was given no right by nature to rule over the other faculties. Its natural function is to facilitate the activities of its companion faculties. It generates and manipulates ideas; it contemplates and deliberates alternatives; it computes costs and benefits; it makes judgments about self-interest and other-regarding interest; it clarifies choices; it connects ideas and activities; it constructs conceptions of value; and it corrects the judgments/conclusions of intuition where these are in error. Reason does not feel. It is indifferent to feelings of compassion, sympathy, pity and mercy, as well as to ones of kindness, tenderness, affection and attachment. Hope and despair, love and hate, magnanimity and vengeance do not emanate from it itself, and nature gave it no power of its own to compel the will to do anything. In the conjunctive will, reason does not rule; it cooperates equally with the other faculties in setting the best course of action for the will as a whole. (It should always be remembered that it is the will as a whole that wills/acts, although what is willed at a given point in time may be influenced more heavily by one particular faculty than by others.) There are no dictates of reason in the conjunctive will, only representations and inferences of reason.

For all too long, appetite has been maligned in relation to the activity of the will. One observes this in Christian fathers of the Church such as Saint Augustine, Christian slave masters, Christian integrationists and Christian separatists, as well as in pre-Christian Plato. But they all have been wrong in their judgment of appetite. Appetite is but nature's instrument to assure the preservation of the species. It feels, it desires, it craves, it has needs; its sensations of pleasure and pain radiate beyond the will and throughout the whole (wo)man; it alerts the will to the need for action pertaining to the health and well-being of the individual; and, most important, it provides the energy for the activity of the whole will. As appetite waxes and wanes, so too does the activity of the will. Many, such as Thomas Hobbes and John Locke, have constructed the appetite as insatiable. This is false. An insatiable appetite is an unnatural appetite. Nature implanted in the appetite itself the capacity to sense its own limits, thus the appetite does not require reason to inform it of these. Insofar as reason does this, it is simply a manifestation of nature's sound redundancy. Thus whenever and wherever, always and without exception, appetite is observed to be dependent on reason to inform it of its limits, one can say with certainty that it is not in its naturally healthy state. Nature designed reason to provide appetite with ways of satisfying its needs, desires and wants, even as the costs and benefits, good and evil, of these ways are made known to the whole will. Should reason's guide and appetite's drive be at odds, how the will wills cannot be separated from the relation that has obtained between reason and appetite, and the relation of both to intuition and passion. If reason's representations and inferences have been convincing to appetite over time — as well as to intuition and passion — appetite is pushed to make the adjustment necessary to confirm with reason's stance. The critical point here is that in the conjunctive will, appetite is not the wild, many-headed beast that Plato believes must be tamed;[24] rather, it is the natural, life-sustaining faculty of the will.

While appetite has been maligned, passion has been both praised and damned. It has been praised for impelling individuals to make noble sacrifices; it has been damned for propelling individuals into ignoble excesses. Praise and blame aside, passion is the faculty from which the resoluteness of the will emanates. It fortifies the will, enabling the will to stand its ground once it has willed. Regardless of intuition's insights, reason's representations and inferences, and appetite's sensations, the will is but vanity without the resolution of passion. Resolution does not entail inflexibility, rigidity, self-righteousness, false pride and mindless constancy; it does entail clarity and steadfastness of purpose, as well as the flexibility to yield without vitiating purpose. In a very real sense, passion draws and preserves the identity of the conjunctive will. What, then, is the conjunctive will?

The conjunctive will unites intuition, reason, appetite and passion in equality, and values equally the insights, representations and inferences, sensations and resoluteness of each respectively. And of what significance is the conjunctive will to the movement of peoples of primary African origin and their descent out of the philosophical wilderness in which they have been wandering since the fall of Thebes, and more particularly to the well-being of black people in the United States?

It is well to begin by observing that the conjunctive will is a liberating will. It frees peoples of primary African origin and their descent, indeed it frees all, from the undue influence of reason, the belief that evil abodes in appetite and passion, and the tendency to ridicule intuition. Evil, and there is evil in the world, neither abodes in nor emanates from appetite and passion. Rather, it is the product of the will willing when the balance of equality among its four faculties is skewed disproportionately towards one or more. Such imbalance may arise from deformities in nature's work, such as natural impairments of the body and/or mind, or from improper nurture, development and sustenance of the body and/or mind. Increasingly, (wo)man is able to correct deformities in nature's work, and this will become ever more so as the United States and other countries pass into the posttechnologic age. (In 1989, for the first time in recorded human history, nonhuman genes were implanted successfully into humans in the United States.) In freeing peoples of primary African origin and their descent from a range of improper influences, beliefs and tendencies pertaining to the will, the conjunctive will opens up a new world of possibilities in relation to the proper activity of the will. And what are some of the possibilities opened up by the conjunctive will?

Reason's dominion over the autonomous will has occasioned a constant rebellion by appetite and passion, which forces reason to exhaust itself trying to keep them in check. In the heteronomous will, appetite and passion have free rein over the will, but are constantly checked by the activity of reason outside the will itself, that is, by reason of the autonomous will. Thus, wherever the autonomous will and the heteronomous will animate behavior, there is a constant and ever-trying struggle, sometimes implacably hostile and at other times tolerably civil, for control both over the self and others. Rational self-control, the archetype of the autonomous will, fosters not calm but storm within the will whose faculties are neither of equal value nor valued equally, and no will wishes to will only that which some other will, save perhaps that of God, admonishes it to will as right and proper. The conjunctive will sets all of this aside. Self-control emanates not from reason's dominion over the will, but from the balance of equality among the faculties of the will. The tension between the control of the self and the control of others that accompanies the autonomous will and the heteronomous will disappears where the conjunctivity of the will of the individual obtains, for the balance of the will of the individual extends to the balance of the will of his/her community and vice versa. Plato attempted to do this, but he failed in large measure because of the primacy of reason's rule over the soul which he mandated. The conjunctive will thus opens up here on earth the possibility of a genuine harmony between the interests and good of the individual and the interests and good of the community, the very thing that Plato sought so desperately in the commonwealth that he set in the heavens, and for which Christians hope ever so much in the New Jerusalem.

There are other exciting possibilities that flow from the conjunctivity of the will. It is a well-known tenet of the political economy of liberalism that the individual may be as selfish as he/she pleases in the accumulation of material goods, but none should be allowed to starve. The foundations of this tenet are easily discerned in John Locke's *On the Reasonableness of Christianity*.[25] Unencumbered acquisitiveness is consistent with the autonomy of the will; reason-ruled will and unfettered appropriation of material goods are not at odds with one another. Still, none should starve to death. Rational appropriators should pay some heed to the needs of appetite and the dangers of passion of those whom reason does not instruct in the art of unlimited appropriation. True, all sorts of limitations have been placed on appropriation since Locke's day, yet a material and social-psychological gulf of immense proportions persists between those who struggle to stave of starving (both literally and metaphorically) and those who prosper from rational appropriation. Though this author had heard it untold times before, he was still struck when Thomas Brophy, the director of the Department of Social Services of Milwaukee County, Wisconsin, stated at a meeting of the Community Brainstorming Conference — a large cross section of Milwaukee's black community that has met monthly since June 1986 — on September 23, 1989, that he hated the welfare system, for at best it fostered the bare survival of the ones who used its services, and at worst it robbed individuals of their dignity. But is this not quite consistent with rational appropriation in the context both of the autonomy and the heteronomy of the will? It is precisely this state of affairs that the conjunctive will reconstitutes.

By repositioning the standing of reason in the activity of the will, and willing from the balance of equality among its faculties, the conjunctive will constitutes a foundation for dignity that nurtures equality both individually and collectively. There is no homogenization of individuals into bland arithmetic equality here; rather, individual preferences, tastes, desires, wants and needs fit within a collective framework that emerges out of the activities of diverse wills in which the balance of equality among their faculties obtains. Unlimited appropriation by any, and the survival of any just above the level of starvation, is unthinkable here; the activity of the conjunctive will rules this out. The conjunctive will undergirds an order of relations in which none has too much, none has too little, and all have enough. The possibility of a new order of relations among individuals, and between individuals and the collective of which they are a part, in which the balance of equality among the faculties of the will enables everyone to look within one's own will to know, understand and accept willingly all consistent outcomes of the will, is thus opened up by the conjunctive will.

But what about inconsistent outcomes? These emanate from wills in which the proper balance of the equality of faculties has been unhinged either by the work of nature, or (wo)man, or both. The inconsistencies

are thus acted upon in the context of what properly balanced wills
would have willed had they done the willing. There is something all too
troubling here, though. Is this not the very homogenization of individuals that was just proclaimed to be contrary to the conjunctivity of the
will of the individual? And is it not dreadfully coercive? Should everyone not be warned by Isaiah Berlin's perspicacious observation that

> [i]t is one thing to say that I may be coerced for my own good
> which I am too blind to see: this may, on occasion, be for my bene-
> fit; indeed it may enlarge the scope of my liberty. It is another to
> say that if it is my good, then I am not being coerced, for I have
> willed it, whether I know this or not, and am free (or "truly" free)
> even while my poor earthly body and foolish mind bitterly reject
> it, and struggle against those who seek however benevolently to
> impose it, with the greatest desperation.[26]

Berlin's fear is perfectly justified in the context both of the autonomous will and the heteronomous will; but it finds no justification in the
conjunctive will. Murder, starvation, excesses of wealth and poverty,
and survival that corrodes human dignity are inconsistent with the
conjunctive will; differences in artistic expression, tastes in food,
choices of careers, and the use of one's legitimate resources are not.
Indeed, the conjunctive will renders Berlin's anxiety wholly irrelevant.
How, then, shall the possibilities of the new order of individual and
collective relations that flow from the conjunctive will be transformed
into objective realities for the masses of peoples of primary African origin and their descent in the United States?

It may be well to begin by reflecting upon the early Christians under
Roman rule. Christianity emerged out of a perceived need to liberate
the will/soul, and by extension the whole person, from the yoke of Roman domination. The idea of the reconstituted will and the truly free
individual was made manifest in the person of the Christ Jesus, who
laid the foundation upon which a body of doctrine was built. At that
time, the barest few subscribed to this body of doctrine. This was of
marginal relevance to Rome. But the Christians took Rome, and by
the 390s the Emperor Theodosus was able to declare *tempora christiana*
throughout the length and breath of his dominion. How was this possible? Surely, the Christians had no armies to fight the mighty legions of
Rome. It happened in consequence of the resoluteness of Christian be-
lievers, conjoined with their ability to alter Roman culture by persuading large numbers of persons from generation to generation that their
doctrine posed no threat to Roman hegemony in the world and actually
enhanced it by making individuals better persons. Thus, by the time
Christians came to hold the power of the institutions of the political
economy of Rome, they had already altered radically the culture of

Rome. Peoples of primary African origin and their descent in the United States can glean much here as they strive to answer Diop's call for ideas and actions designed to reverse the twenty-seven century-long decline of the black (wo)man on the earth.

What has just been said seems to call peoples of primary African origin and their descent to a struggle covering untold numbers of generations. Let one simply say to this that twenty-seven centuries of decline will not be undone in one generation or even in one century, but the work of undoing it must be energized by a new resoluteness in the twenty-first century. For such to happen, a clear, coherent, compelling and potentially transcenturial body of doctrine (does prudence require that one say theory, a term of endearment to this age?) must be developed to guide the activities of peoples of primary African origin and their descent, just as the doctrine of the New Testament guided the activities of the early Christians, the doctrine of liberalism guided the early capitalists, and the doctrine of socialism/communism guided the early socialists/communists. Just as the grace-purified will provided the foundation for a body of doctrine that in time transformed the culture and political society of Rome, the conjunctive will, which merely has been sketched here, has within it the potential for a body of doctrine that could in time transform the culture and political society of the United States, and by extension the standing of peoples of primary African origin and their descent both within the country and elsewhere around the earth.

The preceding observation concerning the conjunctive will sounds very much like religious conversion. Is it? How, for example, does it relate to Christianity, since most black people in the United States are, at least nominally, Christians? The transformation implied by the conjunctive will does pertain to what may be called spirit, but it is basically cultural, political, economic and social. It has no definitive relation to organized, denominational religion. The conjunctive will does not, for example, countenance original sin, and does not subscribe to the proposition that man is a fallen creature. It does, however, recognize, as was noted earlier, that there is evil in the earth. From whence cometh evil, and what can be done about it? Was this not one of the two questions (the other pertained to truth) that so harassed Saint Augustine, the preeminent father of the Church? Evil emanates from the activity of the conjunctive will when there is a gross imbalance in the equality of its faculties. And how does such imbalance arise?—from deformities in the work of nature and/or from the dissimilitude of the individuality of interacting human beings. Since the balance of equality among the faculties of the conjunctive will does not entail a perfect will—the balance can never be attuned perfectly—the matter of the perfection of (wo)man does not arise in relation to the presence of evil in human society. The critical point here is that whatever abridges unduly the dignity, worth and value of the individual by distorting the balance of equality among the faculties of the conjunctive will is evil. Judaism, Christianity and Islam sought to undo the evils of paganism, liberalism the ones of feudalism, and socialism/communism those of capitalism through transformations of both culture and political society. In spite of these transformations, the decline of the broad masses of peoples of primary African origin and their descent has persisted. The need for some other archetypal anchor for behavior designed to occasion fundamental transformations of culture and political economy in the societies of the Afroworld to the end of the coming into being of the day after tomorrow is distressingly obvious. The conjunctive will provides such an archetypal anchor. And so, let the work of doctrinal (theoretical) formulation begin.

A stone has been laid upon which an edifice that reconstitutes the ancient glory of peoples of primary African origin and their descent might be built. Should it prove to be of insufficient strength to withstand the weight of the edifice, let it be removed and replaced with another; should it be of sufficient strength but of incorrect location, let it be removed to the correct location. But let the work begin.

NOTES

[1] *Dred Scott* v. *Sandford*, 60 U.S. (19 How.) 393 (1857), in Derrick A. Bell, Jr., *Civil Rights: Leading Cases* (Boston and Toronto: Little, Brown and Company, 1980), p. 1.

[2] Ibid., p. 3.

[3] Ibid., p. 1.

[4] Whenever the term liberal politics is used, I am always sensitive to the evolution of liberal politics into liberal democratic politics.

[5] Bell, op. cit. note 1, p. 6.

[6] Cheikh Anta Diop, *The African Origin of Civilization: Myth or Reality*, trans. Mercer Cook (Westport, CT: Lawrence Hill & Company, 1974), p. 221. (Author's italics.)

[7] Bell, op. cit. note 1, p. 6. (Author's italics.)

[8] See Frederick Douglass, "Speech on the Dred Scott Decision," in Howard Brotz, ed., *Negro Social and Political Thought: 1850-1920* (New York and London: Basic Books, Inc., 1966), pp. 247-262.

[9] Bell, op. cit. note 1, p. 6. (Author's italics.)